MASTERPLOTS
1976 ANNUAL

1976 ANNUAL

MAGILL'S LITERARY ANNUAL
Essay-Reviews of 100 Outstanding Books
Published in the United States During 1975

Edited by
FRANK N. MAGILL

SALEM PRESS
INCORPORATED
NEW JERSEY

PRINTED IN THE UNITED STATES OF AMERICA

LIST OF TITLES

CONTRIBUTING REVIEWERS FOR 1976 ANNUAL

KENNETH JOHN ATCHITY

WILLIAM BOSWELL

RENNIE W. BRANTZ

PETER A. BRIER

GORDON W. CLARKE

JOHN CLEMAN

ROBERT M. COLLINS

JAMES C. CRISP

PAUL M. DEBLINGER

LEON DRISKELL

JOHN W. EVANS

NANCY B. FERRIS

JAN KENNEDY FOSTER

BONNIE FRASER

FAITH GABELNICK

WILLIAM E. GRANT

MAX HALPEREN

HARRY A. HARGRAVE

DAN JOHNSON

WILLIS KNAPP JONES

EDWARD P. KELEHER

HENDERSON KINCHELOE

JOSEPH MAIOLO

HARRY A. MAXSON

MARGARET MCFADDEN-GERBER

WALTER E. MEYERS

LESLIE B. MITTLEMAN

CATHERINE E. MOORE

PATRICK MORROW

KEITH NEILSON

BRUCE D. REEVES

ANN E. REYNOLDS

MICHAEL S. REYNOLDS

STEVEN C. SCHABER

L. WALTER SEEGERS

HENRY TAYLOR

J. R. VAN LAAN

JOHN N. WALL, JR.

THOMAS N. WALTERS

BERNARD WELT

MARY C. WILLIAMS

PREFACE

THIS IS the twenty-second volume in the series of literary annuals designed to provide a brief survey of the literary year and, in so doing, update MASTERPLOTS. As for the books of 1975, the year seemed to be better than average. In this volume we find essay-reviews of 31 novels, 6 collections of short stories, 12 biographies and autobiographical works, 8 volumes of poetry, 3 dramas, 13 works dealing with history, 5 books of essays, 4 collections of letters, 6 studies of literary criticism, and 12 works categorized as miscellaneous.

As noted above, fiction accounts for more than a third of the space in this year's Annual. Perhaps no finer example of the novelist's art appeared in the United States in 1975 than the late Yasunari Kawabata's BEAUTY AND SADNESS, a work sensitively interpreted by Thomas N. Walters on Page 21. Another minor masterpiece of style and content—a moving experience to read—is Peter Matthiessen's FAR TORTUGA. Those familiar with some of Matthiessen's other work,, especially his unique nature study entitled THE CLOUD FOREST, will appreciate the experimental aspects of his latest novel. THE DEAD FATHER, a highly imaginative satire by Donald Barthelme, provides, amidst its rollicking comedy, some serious commentaries concerning fathers as a breed. Another satire, William Gaddis' J R, is by no means a nonsense novel of a child-prodigy business tycoon; the author provides much more substance than that as he attacks the absurdities of the phony modern world. The almost enigmatic style of Iris Murdoch lends a special dimension to all her work, and A WORD CHILD is no exception. Other novels of the year that deserve special mention include Saul Bellow's HUMBOLDT'S GIFT, Jerzy Kosinski's COCKPIT, James Clavell's SHOGUN, Larry McMurtry's TERMS OF ENDEARMENT, and THE ASSASSINS, by Joyce Carol Oates.

Short fiction of note is well represented by such fine collections as Patrick White's THE COCKATOOS, Vladimir Nabokov's TYRANTS DESTROYED AND OTHER STORIES, and a brilliant collection by Anna Kavan called JULIA AND THE BAZOOKA, a volume whose stories are filled with despair and marked by a style as haunting as a lonesome train whistle in the night.

Who's Afraid of a Sea Lizard? Not Edward Albee. He has again stretched his dramatic imagination to produce a play called SEASCAPE that touches on matters cosmic and eternal as it teaches the oneness of life in the universe. David Râbe's IN THE BOOM BOOM ROOM is less positive about the goodness of life. Chrissy, the go-go dancer, finds her state sordid and depressing, her future the nadir of despair.

Several excellent volumes of poetry appeared in 1975, including John Ashbery's SELF-PORTRAIT IN A CONVEX MIRROR, David R. Slavitt's VITAL SIGNS, Henry Taylor's AN AFTERNOON OF POCKET BILLIARDS, Howard Nemerov's THE WESTERN APPROACHES, and a fine collection by Adrienne Rich.

Those readers who favor history will find some admirable works reviewed this year. Parts III and IV of THE GULAG ARCHIPELAGO continue Aleksandr I. Solzhenitsyn's report of the infamous Russian "Corrective Labor Camps," this time from the inside. In AMERICAN SLAVERY, AMERICAN FREEDOM, Edmund S. Morgan treats an enigmatic condition in Colonial America with sound reason, and he provides an acceptable answer. Fernand Braudel, in THE MEDITERRANEAN, deals with the time of Philip II and offers an imaginative treatment of a fascinating period of Western civilization. More contemporary in theme is TUBE OF PLENTY, in which Erik Barnouw presents a scholarly history of radio and television, especially the latter medium, about which the author finds little good to say. In A WORLD DESTROYED, Martin J. Sherwin continues the pro and con arguments covering our use of the atomic bomb in World War II, and he handles this volatile subject in a thoughtful and knowledgeable manner.

Biographical studies were plentiful in 1975. In DYLAN THOMAS, Andrew Sinclair offers an intimate revelation of a genius with plenty of faults and human frailties. EDITH WHARTON is an excellent work, one that may spark a revival of interest in the novels of this neglected artist. For a superior study of a frustrated woman who found herself in the expression of her art, one should see Ruby V. Redinger's GEORGE ELIOT: THE EMERGENT SELF on Page 98. JOURNEY is a beautiful story of parental devotion; LAMY OF SANTA FE, a brilliant recounting of another kind of devotion—Willa Cather's "Archbishop" in real life. Professor Willis Knapp Jones brings Paul Horgan's biography alive beginning on Page 157. Other worthy studies include John Wain's SAMUEL JOHNSON, Virginia Spencer Carr's sympathetic portrait of Carson McCullers in THE LONELY HUNTER, and Brendan Gill's nostalgic romp through the sophisticated playland that was the NEW YORKER milieu.

Several volumes of letters enlivened the year. The first of the proposed six volumes of Virginia Woolf's letters covers the period up to her thirtieth year and reveals some interesting aspects of her early life, including her social insecurity. Letters of Sylvia Plath, Bernard DeVoto, and James Joyce were also published, the latter volume containing some of the material deleted from letters published in Joyce's earlier three-volume collection. Also published were excerpts from the notebooks and diaries of Edmund Wilson, under the title THE TWENTIES, an intimate volume about an interesting period.

Among the noteworthy collections of essays published in 1975 are Allen Tate's MEMOIRS AND OPINIONS, Geoffrey H. Hartman's THE FATE OF READING AND OTHER ESSAYS, Nora Ephron's CRAZY SALAD—which she subtitles "Some Things About Women"—and AFTER BABEL, George Steiner's perceptive view of the importance of empathy and specificity in the complex field of translation.

Some excellent studies in literary criticism are dealt with in this year's Annual. Patricia Meyer Spacks's THE FEMALE IMAGINATION is an acute and thorough analysis of the forces at work in female creative writers. Hugh Kenner's A HOMEMADE WORLD advances an interesting thesis about American literary values. Another study of interest is Robert Coles's examination of the fiction of poet William Carlos Williams.

Outstanding works in miscellaneous categories include Susan Brownmiller's AGAINST OUR WILL, an in-depth historical study of rape; MINAMATA, a journalistic account by W. Eugene and Aileen M. Smith of a Japanese town poisoned by industrial pollution; Studs Terkel's WORKING, a documentary about workers' jobs that only a confirmed extrovert could have dreamed up; and GLOBAL REACH by Richard J. Barnet and Ronald E. Müller, a study of multinational corporations and their economic and social impact. The authors seem to find the whole concept bad for nations and bad for individual citizens. Defenders of the idea, however, might claim that what the diplomats haven't been able to accomplish in hundreds of years (peace among nations) may be achieved through the greed of the "business community." (What board chairman would want to see war destroy his corporate property *anywhere*—at home or halfway around the world?)

It is always a pleasure to review the literary year in this way. If we have slighted some of your favorites, lack of space is likely the reason. We regret the many necessary omissions.

FRANK N. MAGILL

AFTER BABEL
Aspects of Language and Translation

Author: George Steiner (1912-   )
Publisher: Oxford University Press (New York). 507 pp. $17.50
Type of work: Essay

The process of translation is important to the understanding of, and intimately related to, all linguistic processes, even the transmission of culture itself

George Steiner's *After Babel* is one of those works of Tamburlainian scope that are the despair of reviewers, dealing as it does with masses of evidence in a variety of fields, and cutting against the grain of present scholarly and academic notions in those fields. The author's aim is ostensibly to make some observations toward a theory of translation, but the book mushrooms beyond that modest purpose. His approach compels him to place the process of translation in a broader context. He notes that it is not different from the process involved in any linguistic activity; hence he deals with the seeds of a theory of language. Since language is the medium of transmission of culture, we end up with a theory of culture itself.

In order to provide a theory of translation, Steiner must first clear the ground of competitors. The most prestigious rival is Chomsky's transformational-generative grammar (TG), tending as it does towards an explanation of speech-acts that will encompass a theory of translation. Briefly and baldly put, one form of TG argues that speech begins as a structure closely related to meaning. This structure is changed (transformed) in specifiable ways by an ordered set of rules, and the resulting form is the sentence as it is spoken or written. The underlying structure is sometimes called the "deep structure," and the form that actually occurs, the "surface structure." Some, but by no means all, transformationalists argue that the original deep structures are composed of elements that are universal—that is, they are common to all humans by virtue of our common neurobiological equipment—and that it is different sets of transformation that produce the different languages we encounter. Some putative universals would be notions of causation, change of state, inception-completion, and the like.

According to this variety of TG, in translating a sentence from language A to language B, the polyglot in some way runs back through the transformations of language A to the deep structure, then processes it forward through the transformations of language B, producing the counterpart sentence in B.

Steiner's objections to TG are surprisingly scanty, both in view of the length of this work and the many substantive arguments leveled against the theory. Because there exists no working model of the grammar, he argues, the theory is therefore unworkable. But time alone is a sufficient defense here; TG has been around now for

1

less than twenty-five years. Since the aim of such a grammar is to duplicate the ability of a native speaker in predicting the grammaticality of sentences, we should not be surprised to find only partially complete, partially successful formulations.

Steiner agrees with Robert A. Hall that "no set of rules will describe the utterances possible in any living language." Perhaps the difficulty here is one of terminology: the phrase "set of rules" may be what causes the disagreement. We recognize that each speaker of a language can judge whether a given sentence, any sentence, is partially or fully grammatical in his language. But this ability on the part of the native speaker must be embodied in some finite schema, since the mind is finite in capacity. And we have no reason to assume, *a priori,* that this schema cannot be extracted from the data of speech, since that is in fact what each child does in the process of acquiring a language. If the schema is finite and derivable from speech, it should also be statable. It would be surprising indeed if the schema did not turn out to be statable in the form of rules, since to assume the contrary we would have to assume that all grammarians of every age and language were mistaken in a profound way.

To be sure, many sentences cannot be judged as either flatly grammatical or ungrammatical, but TG is not in principle restricted to two-way judgments either.

In many cases, Steiner seems to misunderstand the purpose and procedure of all grammars, not just transformational ones. He argues that "metamathematical models of language," unlike true mathematical systems, are not verifiable. In their results, grammars are verifiable in the strongest sense: their predictions can be submitted to the judgments of native speakers. In their details, TG grammars are obviously not verifiable: no one has discovered deep structures or transformations when dissecting brains. However, if this is a defect, it is one not restricted to a particular form of grammar: all theories of grammar are similarly lacking in direct evidence, and grammarians have thought it sufficient to account for the results of the linguistic process without waiting for evidence of mechanisms that may never come.

The title of the book derives from Steiner's unique view of the Babel myth; it is his contention that the story of the tower of Babel records the triumph, not the frustration, of mankind, showing the method by which humans succeeded in finding a private psychic space—through the creation of mutually unintelligible languages. As evidence, he points to the large number of languages now existing and known to have existed. It is his contention that the ordinary explanation of language variation—the piling up through time of small differences between groups isolated from one another—is insufficient. His chief, indeed his only, support for this claim is that there are a great many languages, some of which are spoken by very few people.

The argument by itself lacks conviction, since there would seem, since the invention of language, to have been more than enough time for the variety we find. The thousand years following the fall of Rome was enough time for Latin to fragment into a dozen or so languages and a host of dialects, despite three factors that we would presume would retard change: first, travel and trade continued more or less without interruption throughout that millennium; second, the parent language continued to be written that whole time; and third, Latin even continued as a spoken language for hieratic, scholarly, and diplomatic use the whole time over the whole region.

Moreover, the fact that languages change is not, as Steiner seems to imply, an argument against the possibility of grammars. It means only that grammars need to be revised from time to time, and simply provides job insurance for grammarians.

The book is singular in another way, one that derives from the idea of language as a means for privacy. Steiner suggests that the purpose of language is not primarily communication, but withdrawal into oneself, and that the development of different languages is an aid to that isolation. But here the means seem all out of proportion to the end sought. We do not need to invent four or five thousand languages to be set apart from others—silence will do just as well. As Steiner correctly observes, the complexity of language is out of proportion to the evolutionary advantage it confers upon man. A far simpler speech would have served just as well to give us the edge over the beasts. But what pressure leads to the level of complexity we now have if not communication? Privacy is maintained just as well by avoiding communication as by masking communication, and if we admit this, then Steiner's argument from evolution collapses.

A second argument for the privacy thesis runs like this: "Only a small portion of human discourse is nakedly veracious or informative in any monovalent, unqualified sense." If only a small part of speech communicates, we are wrong in looking exclusively at the communicative function to understand language. Although the statement seems clear enough on the surface, it dissolves under closer inspection: exactly who has measured how much speech is used for its various purposes?

In fact, in pushing the notion of private language and the difficulty of translation, Steiner comes close to painting himself into a corner, for the obvious existence of translations all around us at every time and in every language furnishes counterexamples in abundance. To rescue himself from this dilemma, Steiner proposes a notion of translation that would be a partly intuitive and partly empirical model of language. To this end he devises a set of terms, *penetration, alternity, transmutation,* and the like, that may or may not be useful in future discussions of translation. But what is important to note is that Steiner does not furnish that model. He gives us a highly personalized metaphor for talking about translation, nothing more. What details he provides come in the chapter where he discusses particular examples of the process.

After Babel is a book that would surprise if it accomplished even a little of its aim. To be sure, Steiner does not pretend that the book is a complete formulation of a theory in the rigorous sense. He hopes that it points the way in an area, translation, where there are few paths. He does provide an insider's view, so to speak, of the process, as one who has four languages as native tongues, and he gives some enlightening examples of failures and successes of individual translations. In his final chapter, "Topologies of Culture," he comes perhaps closest to realizing his aim. He discusses various versions of tragedy translated through several languages, and a single genre in its various forms in one language—the elegy in English—and shows something interesting and important about the transmission of culture.

One has the feeling that Steiner starts too far from his subject, that the lengthy discussions of formal grammar and the history of languages are poorly done, and hardly necessary to the job he wants to do. The book deals too much with language and not enough with translation.

Walter E. Meyers

AN AFTERNOON OF POCKET BILLIARDS

Author: Henry Taylor (1942-   )
Publisher: The University of Utah Press (Salt Lake City). 78 pp. $6.00
Type of work: Poetry
   A large and varied collection of recent poetry which reflects the author's rural background

An Afternoon of Pocket Billiards is Henry Taylor's third book of poems. His first, *The Horse Show at Midnight,* was published by the LSU Press, and appeared in 1966; *Breakings,* a limited edition of seven poems produced by The Solo Press, came out in 1971. The new book combines the poems from *Breakings* with more recent work. It is arranged in four sections: "Breakings," "Learning to Face Extinction," "From Porlock," and "Harvest." Poems in the first and last sections deal mainly with the poet's rural experience; political poems, funny pieces, and poems on literary subjects are concentrated in the middle. It is a substantial collection, full of variety.

In a recent interview Henry Taylor said this about his work: "If you write most of your best poems, as I do, out of one basic kind of subject matter, which is my rural background, you run the risk of writing the same poem over and over again." A quick study of *An Afternoon of Pocket Billiards* confirms that these new poems are indeed rurally based. Yet this book outruns the risk of easy repetition; the poems are different. Rural aspects, particularly those involving the poet's awareness of family history, are among his ongoing concerns, and are an energy source important to his work. Yet the flow of this experience is firmly controlled from poem to poem by various formal devices, including turnabouts in

tone from whimsical to serious, and by several unusual postures in which the past and present blend.

Formal considerations are evident and well-handled throughout the book. There are two sestinas, a poem with identical end-words, not rhyme, patterned in terza rima, and a dozen other works employing various rhyme schemes. The best of these are inventive. In "The Hughesville Scythe," for example, the middle stanza pivots, providing a way for the poem to shift formally without losing any structural integrity; the rhyme scheme is regular yet innovative. Here is the third, pivotal stanza, describing the reaction of a shopkeeper who has been robbed by a burglar who got in through the chimney:

The old man took a scythe-blade from
   his store
and fixed it in the chimney, across
   the fine-
edged dark, where it would split a man
   who tried
to come that way again and steal his
   gold.

These lines anchor the poem narratively by relating key action. The scythe blade fixed in the dark remains for years, untested by another burglar. The image is more memorable because the poem fulfills its formal task without straining; the expectations created by form are satisfied.

The title poem, "An Afternoon of Pocket Billiards," is at once complicated and engaging. It consists of eleven ten-line stanzas, all rhymed; and the last stanza is composed of the first lines of all the preceding stanzas. The speaker of the poem is playing pocket billiards, reaching in his confused way for elements of order and predictability in the game, through which he hopes to escape the effects of a recent loss of love. It is hopeless, of course, yet he clings tenaciously to the game as though he could rescue himself. But memory is stronger:

High and low, striped and solid balls
    rotate
in endless formations as time grows late.
    My concentration breaks
just at the dead-reckoned instant before
each shot: testing stroke and angle,
    I ease
down on the felt and line it up once
    more;
too late, I feel that slight vibration seize
my arm—too late to stand. My knocking
    heart
shatters skill and chance, and takes the
    game apart.
    I make my own mistakes.

The speaker exists in limbo between two songs. One melody brings his loss to mind; it is like an undeniable disease, and it is always there, at his elbow, vibrating, destroying his prospects for escape in the game. The other song is a bizarre creation of his beleaguered mind. It is the conviction that if only he plays the game enough, he can overcome his sorrow. This scene, suspended as it is within the constraints of a most demanding formal situation, floats for 110 lines. Its language matches the character's internal state: the situation, the past, the game, the loss all are turned over and over again. With the possible ex-

ception of "Things Not Solved Though Tomorrow Came," published in his first book, this poem stands as Taylor's best long work.

There is fortunate good humor in some of these poems. It emerges head-on at times in short pieces where the action is quickly developed; often a character steps up to conclude a poem with a punch line. In "Riding Lesson," an expert teacher is thrown during a demonstration of horsemanship. He gets up, dusts himself off, and says:

"See, that's the way
to do it. When you see
they're gonna throw you, get off."

Other poems are funny because of their unusual premises. "Snapshot" is one of these, another quick-hitting anecdote about a circus fat man whose great size requires special attention: he keeps a boy around to help him execute one of his bodily functions. This sort of thing is pleasantly unforgettable, and it might be argued that the "weird premise" poem reaches a kind of zenith in such short pieces. Yet, in "Buildings and Grounds," Taylor manages to sustain the same technique in a longer poem, in which aspects of the speaker's Southern home, complete with a hound and junked car, are imported to suburbia to combat an insufferable landscaping code. The volume benefits from such light poems, which balance the mood.

Much of the work in this volume relates to home life and the family. The pressures of close relationships are explored in the poem "Breakings." Here the poet speaks directly about leaving the farm, its work, his father, and then of being driven back by unexpected events, things he was not prepared for. A similar theme recurs in the two sestinas, "Goodbye to the Old Friends" and "Return to the Old Friends." The clash of new and old ways culminates in the second poem, the poem of return, when at his grandfather's funeral the poet reaches back into his Quaker heritage to examine "this silent music in my blood." These poems of the family are among the most straightforward in the book.

Family history is explored in another poem, "My Grandfather Works in His Garden." The grandfather is seen first in the present, an old man working in the sun. Then a shift occurs: the speaker is suddenly a boy again, the grandfather a vigorous man engaged in a struggle of the past, subduing a bull that has escaped. It is entirely possible, as the action progresses, that the man who goes to face the bull is neither the grandfather, nor the grown-up speaker who is remembering and telling it, nor the boy who watched it all, but some combination of these people. It is an intensely personal kind of statement, and an interesting blend of time and character, that can lead to a line such as "I feel my grandfather's breath/go slowly out of me."

Time shifts occur elsewhere in *An Afternoon of Pocket Billiards*. Sometimes a figure simply breaks from one time and enters another, as in "An Old Rhodes Scholar," when an elderly professor, gazing out the window, recalls his past as a pole-vaulter: suddenly he is there, sprinting down the runway in a tweed suit, then is frozen in an arc above the bar. In "Smoking in Bed in the Fire Chief's House," the speaker has dreams within dreams about drowsing on the beach above Nantucket, riding the ferry, riding a horse on the beach, and of a persistent, painful memory. The various scenes of this poem are interwoven, united yet fluctuating.

An Afternoon of Pocket Billiards is a book that reflects its author's mature outlook toward the writing of poetry. The poems here were composed throughout a ten-year period, during which Taylor improved as a writer and evolved, significantly, into a poet capable of criticizing his own work with some accuracy. This kind of self-awareness has helped him produce a group of poems unencumbered by easy indulgence or the triviality that often accompanies haste.

Despite their traditional appearance on the page, many of these new poems are essentially experimental in nature. They grow out of a working philosophy that welcomes the stimulation of a formal obstacle or other risk. The attitude is one of readiness. The poet's skill is marked by discipline and a delightful sense of play.

Dan Johnson

AGAINST OUR WILL
Men, Women and Rape

Author: Susan Brownmiller
Publisher: Simon and Schuster (New York). 472 pp. $10.95
Type of work: Sociological treatise

A comprehensive, in-depth historical analysis of how, from prehistoric times to the present day, rape has been used to intimidate women and keep them in subjection to men

It was inevitable that the present climate of women's liberation and the concurrent reexamination of the historical relationship of the sexes would produce a serious study of the phenomenon of rape. Susan Brownmiller's book does a thorough job and, for all of its excesses and prejudices, presents an important and undeniably provocative picture of the never-ending battle between men and women. Rape, according to the author, is a conscious process of intimidation by which *"all* men" keep *"all* women" in a state of fear. This political definition of rape forms the basis of her long and scholarly book, and from it arise both the strengths and weaknesses of her study.

To write this work, Brownmiller became a scholar of the history, literature, and law of rape, and consequently produced an intelligent and ambitious book. But it is also an unbalanced book, and one which makes several unwarranted assumptions. By forming her study and maintaining her point of view on ideological lines, she has warped what would have been an extraordinary study. It is a credit to her industry and intelligence that the work remains, despite its lopsided approach, an important book which all future explorations of the roles of men and women in society must acknowledge.

Brownmiller offers interesting and provocative arguments concerning the methods used by men—intentionally and unintentionally—to oppress women, and she uses masses of documentation to support her claims. But, in the end, the dogma behind her writing and the very relentlessness of her documentation combine to overwhelm the study's more thoughtful, less excessive passages. At times, the reader feels bludgeoned by Brownmiller's prose. This is a book obviously inspired by anger, which gives the narrative a force which it very likely would not otherwise possess. No reader will be quite the same after having read it. From that standpoint, it is a successful piece of writing.

The book is well-organized, beginning with a psychological picture of rapists and rape victims and moving into a historical perspective. Brownmiller points out that the laws against rape tended to be laws more to protect the upper classes than to protect women. Throughout history, it was lower-class women who suffered most from the threat, as well as actual experience, of rape. And, during wars and invasions, it was the lower-class women, the peasants and unprotected common women, who were victimized by armies.

Rape also has been used as a propaganda device, Brownmiller explains, and has been used to stir up public opinion against the enemy. She cites the example of the German invasion of Belgium during World War I. The great outcry against the German invaders had little to do with the rights of women, but was very effective in arousing the rest of the world against the "brutal" and "barbaric" Hun. Thus, rape became a symbol, a simplistic tool of governments to manipulate the masses.

Brownmiller examines the language that societies have employed to describe the act of rape, the laws connected with it, and the testimony of its victims throughout history. She explores the often ignored fact that even in time of war the men in charge of society (the generals, diplomats, soldiers, and historians) have considered rape a peripheral event, an "inevitable" by-product of civilization's conflicts. The violence of war, the stresses of urban living, the psychological strain of existing with the bomb or the cold war—any number of excuses are found, by men, to excuse the prevalence of rape. The author argues convincingly that acts of violation and sexual mutilation, whether they occurred during the American Revolution, in Germany during World War II, in Bangladesh, or in Vietnam, whether they were acts of white mob violence against Southern black women or black mob violence against white women in the Congo, were not only purposeful but revelatory of a basically masculine concept of women. In other words, *because* men feel as they do about women, rape and violent mutilation of women are inevitable. Men tend to feel that *all* women exist for their use, and find it all too convenient to override any laws that interfere with their sexual prerogatives. Men simply

do not feel that rape is wrong. The "stronger" of the sexes has been psychologically conditioned to believe that might is right.

The testimony of scores of rape victims—children, mothers, grandmothers—that the author has unearthed is as troubling as it is impressive. Many of the women later were ostracized (as was the case in Bangladesh) by their own societies. The author suggests that many people still do not want the truth about rape, its victims, and its perpetrators, to be known. It is a subject that many people feel should be left alone. The rape victim should suffer in silence, rather than call attention to the crime which has been committed against her body and mind.

Brownmiller quotes Nietzsche to the effect that "Man should be trained for war and woman for the recreation of the warrior." This point of view of woman as the plaything of the man has contributed, through the centuries, to the violent crimes against females of all ages, nationalities, and races. Along with this, we have the common attitude of masculine prowess as a form of "conquering." Men show their masculinity in two ways, by physical possession of a woman and by violent conquest. The masses are seen as weak and feminine, the all-powerful armies as strong and brutal and *male,* the ramrods of history. During World War II, for example, the Nazis conceived of themselves as Supermen, and, naturally, Supermen would be super-virile, possessing violently everyone who lay in their path. Rape for the Germans, and to a similar extent for the Japanese, played a serious and logical role in the achievement of what they saw as their ultimate objective: the total humiliation and destruction of "inferior peoples" and the establishment of their own master race. It was no coincidence that Hitler was said to elicit an almost masochistic surrender and submission from his audiences, to commit a form of "psychic rape" upon them. He did not convince his audiences, he conquered them. And conquest is the natural role of the male, according to the point of view that has been prevalent through history and which probably reached its peak during World War II.

However, this attitude, as Brownmiller makes clear, is still with us in many ways, and is still resulting in the suffering of countless women and a surprising number of men. The myth of the "heroic rapist" has been with us from the time of the ancient Greeks (when the masculine gods swept down to earth to take their pleasure with mortal females) to the exploits of such groups as the Hell's Angels and such archetypal heroes as James Bond. Even maniacs such as Jack the Ripper and the Boston Strangler become objects of hero worship for their brutal sexual murders. Such figures are seen as sexual Supermen and are admired and envied, Brownmiller claims, by other men.

Rape, the author contends, seeps into our consciousness from infancy, through fairy tales such as Little Red Riding Hood and through legends and myths, literature and art. It is suggested time and again, in many ways, that rape is a natural occurrence, an action even welcomed by most women. This accounts, Brownmiller says, for the well-known clichés such as: "All women want to be raped" and "No woman can be raped against her will" and "She was asking for it" and, perhaps most offensive of all, "If you're going to be raped, you might as well relax and enjoy it." Many people have come to believe, their attitudes reinforced by Freudian explanations, that women really do long for domination by men as exemplified in physical rape. The conditioning of women by society has, through story and song and subtle suggestion, perhaps created this fantasy of fulfillment through violence. But, Brownmiller points out, men have always controlled the definitions of sex; it is men who have created this illusion that women secretly desire to be raped, and then eagerly endeavored to provide the service.

For all of its faults, this book is an overwhelming indictment of sexual prejudice and its consequences. It very likely will force many men, and women, to reassess their attitudes with regard to sex and violence and the roles of men and women in society. It is a book which already has assumed a place beside its predecessors: de Beauvoir's *The Second Sex,* Friedan's *The Feminine Mystique,* and Millett's *Sexual Politics.*

Bruce D. Reeves

AMERICAN SLAVERY, AMERICAN FREEDOM
The Ordeal of Colonial Virginia

Author: Edmund S. Morgan (1916-   )
Publisher: W. W. Norton and Company (New York). 454 pp. $11.95
Type of work: History
Time: Seventeenth and eighteenth centuries
Locale: Virginia

A history of slavery in Colonial Virginia which analyzes the paradox of "the marriage of slavery and freedom" in America's past

The distinguished American historian, Edmund S. Morgan, whose first study, *The Stamp Act Crisis,* was followed by a series of works dealing with the New England Puritans, here turns his attention to an analysis of the economy, social structure, and politics of Colonial Virginia. Professor Morgan posits the hypothesis that two seemingly contradictory developments taking place simultaneously over a long period of time—the rise of liberty and equality, or freedom, in America accompanied by the rise of slavery—constitute the central paradox of American history. He contends that Americans should understand this paradox if they would understand themselves, and that the paradox poses a challenge to the historian to explain the dedication to human liberty and dignity of the founding fathers who at the same time maintained the system of slave labor which continuously denied human liberty and dignity. He maintains that the key to the puzzle, historically, lies in Virginia, since at the time of the American Revolution and the nation's founding, Virginia was the largest and the most influential of the states, furnished the most eloquent spokesmen for freedom and equality, produced the presidents of the new republic for thirty-two of its first thirty-six years, and yet repre-

sented the largest slaveholding state in the union. Hence, he asserts, if it is possible to understand the American paradox, Virginia is surely the place to begin a study of "the marriage of slavery and freedom."

After a brief discussion of the forces in the late sixteenth and early seventeenth centuries which prompted the beginning of English colonizing in North America, the author develops his thesis by describing in detail the nature of economic life in Virginia during the seventeenth century, the interrelationship of that economy with the kind of society which developed, and the ways in which both economy and social structure interacted with politics and government. He next analyzes the reasons for the conversion from the free labor system characterizing the plantation system of seventeenth century tobacco production, to the slave labor system of the eighteenth century, and describes its impact on agriculture, the social order, and the political affairs of Virginia. Finally, he attempts to explain how Virginia's economic, social, and political leaders could simultaneously be supporters of slave labor and devotees of the concepts and institutions of human liberty. In attempting such an explantion, the author must rely more on inference and supposition than on solid historical evidence. Morgan's treatment of seventeenth century nonslavery Virginia, on the other hand, is well-documented; it is more thorough than that of the eighteenth century slave labor colony, and constitutes approximately three-fourths of the work.

In his opening treatment of American colonization, Morgan points out that there was considerable anti-slavery sentiment among English colonizers, but that it was not so much a reflection of abolitionism or repugnance to slavery *per se,* as it was an outgrowth of anti-Spanish feeling and the belief that slavery in the Spanish colonial empire constituted an element of strength and therefore a threat to England. The author then describes the years under the aegis of the Virginia Company, 1607-1624, years of almost uninterrupted hardship and threat of failure for the colony. However, just when the Company's existence was ended by action of the monarch in 1624, the basis for the success of the colony appeared: the profitable production of tobacco. In fact, the decade of the 1620's was one of the most profitable for the Virginia tobacco growers and created conditions favorable for the establishment of a system of slave labor. Virginia tobacco planters at this time were primarily using the free labor of dependent whites, chiefly the indentured servants imported under the headright system of land distribution, supplemented by other types of servants and some tenants. Only an insignificant number of Negro slaves was evident in Virginia for most of the seventeenth century.

The tobacco culture under the plantation system was responsible for most of the chief features of Virginia life in the first century of its existence. In economic affairs these took the form of concentration of wealth, chiefly in the form of land monopoly in the hands of large planters and merchant-planters; a constant demand for dependent labor to work tobacco fields; a growing number of small landowning tobacco planters made up largely of freed servants; and a growing dependence on the profits of tobacco culture for the economic well-being of the colony. There were social and political concomitants of these economic characteristics. A social order with marked class distinctions arose, made up of wealthy planters with a sense of social superiority and a poor class inculcated with a sense of inferiority and strict limits. These social distinctions bred feelings of antagonism. The upper economic and social class held the reins of political power, which they used to establish English-type constitutional rights and freedoms for themselves, while oppressing the lower order of small farmers. This oppression took the form of deprivation of participation in colony government, as well as of financial exploitation for the benefit of the rulers. The growing social and political tension between the upper and lower classes erupted in the 1670's into armed conflict in Bacon's Rebellion, which was precipitated by a crisis in economic affairs stemming from the depressed state of tobacco farming.

It is Morgan's contention that the resolution of the conflict between the large landowners and the small farmers ultimately was the consequence of the conversion from free to slave labor. The Virginians turned from white servants to Negro slaves as the main type of labor in tobacco farming as the supply of indentured servants decreased and slaves simultaneously became more plentiful in supply and more profitable to use. The larger number of slaves available and the increased profitableness of their use, stemmed largely from lowered prices, which in turn were due to English slave traders' recently gained access to Spanish slave market sources. Furthermore, the monopoly in English slave trading, previously granted by the monarch to the Royal African Company, was taken from the Company in 1698.

The transition to a slave economy produced fundamental social and political changes. Whereas previously the large planters and small farmers had faced one another in economic, social, and political conflict, a feeling of community of interest now developed, with the small farmer, who was generally also a small slaveholder, perceiving his economic interests to be more closely identified with those of the large planter. Socially they were drawn closer together by the growing feeling of racism that stemmed from the color and race distinction between the black slaves on the one hand and the white masters on the other. Morgan maintains that this shift in social alignment explains the phenomenon that by the end of the colonial period the elite ruling class of Colonial Virginia could espouse the republican concepts of liberty while retaining a slave-labor system with its lack of freedom. The position of the lower class of white farmers was sufficiently raised so that their extended rights no longer constituted a threat to the upper classes, while the legal foundations of the slave system guaranteed that the same liberty and equality would not apply to the blacks.

American Slavery, American Freedom is based primarily on the use of contemporary sources, both published and unpublished, drawing on the official English and colonial records as well as private materials; but the author also incorporates the results of the best and most recent monographic studies. An appendix contains an analysis of the growth, sources, and distribution of the population of the colony in the seventeenth century which is drawn from county tax records, records of headrights, and reports of colonial officials to their English superiors.

L. Walter Seegers

ANNIVERSARIES
From the Life of Gesine Cresspahl: August 1967 - February 1968

Author: Uwe Johnson (1934-   )
Translated from the German by Leila Vennewitz
Publisher: Harcourt Brace Jovanovich (New York). 504 pp. $10.00
Type of work: Novel
Time: August 21, 1976 to February 24, 1968; retrospectively, 1933 to 1967
Locale: New York City; Jerichow and Gness, Germany (now East Germany); Richmond, London, England

In this complex "memory novel," the first volume of a projected two-volume work, a woman of determination who was a former inmate of an East German refugee camp, together with her ten-year-old daughter, tries to make the necessary social adjustments and compromises to the moral patterns of her new life in New York City

Principal characters:
> GESINE CRESSPAHL, a thirty-four-year-old German woman now living in New York City
> MARIE, her daughter
> LISBETH PAPENBROCK, her mother
> HEINRICH CRESSPAHL, her father, a cabinetmaker
> LOUISE PAPENBROCK, her grandmother
> FRANCINE, a young black girl, schoolmate of Marie
> ANNIE KILLAINEN, a friend of Gesine, a radical and antiwar activist
> UWE JOHNSON, the author, also a character in a scene of the novel
> JACOB, now deceased, the father of Marie

A "memory novel" in the same sense that Tennessee Williams describes *The Glass Menagerie* as a "memory play," Uwe Johnson's complex, richly detailed *Anniversaries From the Life of Gesine Cresspahl: August 1967-February 1968* is not limited in chronology to the dates of the title, but moves backward and forward in remembered time. For Gesine Cresspahl, every day of her journal is an "anniversary," fixing a a point in time both from the present and the past, recording the processes of memory and moral education. On Monday, August 21, 1967, Gesine begins the first entry in her journal, which she writes as much to inform her ten-year-old daughter Marie about her former life in Europe as to sort out her own ambiguous impressions about America and herself. Since they arrived in New York on April 28, 1961, they have sublet a three-room apartment on Riverside Drive, a crowded, ethnically diverse neighborhood by the Hudson River. At thirty-four, Gesine has managed to structure for both of them a fairly comfortable, somewhat detached life. She has worked with quiet efficiency at a Lexington Avenue bank since 1964; she has acquaintances but few close friends, except for her perpetual suitor, D. E., a well-educated but tedious scientist whom she first met at the Marienfeld refugee camp in East Germany. To learn about the realities of America, each morning she reads avidly her copy of the *New York Times*. Like a "moralistic auntie," the newspaper reports with cool, rational objectivity information about the madness of the world—about the war in Vietnam; the political absurdities of the Johnson administration; the senseless street brutalities, rapes, and murders that are everyday items of curiosity. Although the newspaper confirms her sense of social isolation, her memory spurs her into painful self-analysis. She cannot free herself from oppressive thoughts of the past.

The background of Gesine's story parallels, at least in part, some experiences in Uwe Johnson's life. For two and a half years, from 1966 to 1968, Johnson lived in the United States, working as an editor of Harcourt Brace Jovanovich. Like his fictional character, who is a native of what is now East Germany, he was born in 1934 in Pomerania, the province furthest east on the Baltic; Gesine, a year older, was born in 1933 at Jerichow in Mecklenburg-Schwerin, a province also on the Baltic and adjoining Pomerania. Moreover, Johnson, like Gesine, has lived in England and West Germany. Apart from their similar philosophical outlooks, author and subject actually converge in the novel. In one of the most effective scenes, the journal entry for November 3, 1967, Johnson appears as a "character"—or at least a historical figure—in Gesine's life. She recalls that, on January 16 of the same year, Johnson was invited by the Jewish American Congress to speak on a subject concerning the election results in West Germany. His message was that the

neo-Nazis appeared not to be a powerful force in contemporary West German politics. The audience received his speech with grim, even hostile skepticism, many of the Jews there having suffered from Nazi persecution in concentration camps during the war. Although Rabbi Joachim Prinz defended Johnson as a friend, some people in attendance considered the author an enemy, seemingly complacent in the face of a Nazi resurgence of strength. With irony, Johnson reminds the reader that his vision of reality, like that of Gesine, may be influenced by his own comfortable experiences. "Who's telling this story, Gesine?" he asks. "We both are. Surely that's obvious, Johnson," she replies. Thus author and character are exposed for their moral frailties—all too human, but reprehensible nevertheless.

As a moralist, Johnson explores the sources of corruption, whether in pre-Nazi Germany or in America during the late 1960's. He shows how the East German persecution of liberals parallels the Nazi brutality toward dissidents, especially Jews; furthermore, he shows how these totalitarian injustices resemble the American mistreatment of its racial and ethnic minorities. Throughout the novel, two characters—Annie Killainen, a radical and antiwar protester, and Francine, a "token" black student in Marie's Catholic school—remind the reader that America has not yet resolved its own moral problems. Pursued by the police for her violent activism, Annie appeals to Gesine for shelter. Reluctantly, Gesine accepts the burden, one that threatens her family with police reprisal. Yet she responds to the sum-

mons with moral courage. Similarly
for Marie, Francine provides a test
of character. Product of the black
ghetto, Francine is nearly dehumanized because of the terrible conditions of her bleak existence. Slow to
accept her as a friend, Marie finally
comes to understand the finer qualities in the girl. Although she cannot
help Francine overcome the circumstances of her social degradation,
Marie at least empathizes with her.
Unlike Sister Magdalena, who treats
the child with the empty platitudes of
benign concern, Marie respects Francine as a person. Nevertheless, Johnson underscores the irony of Gesine's
prejudiced attitude toward blacks. A
refugee and former victim of persecution, Gesine enrolls her daughter in
a parochial school with a very low
number of blacks and Puerto Ricans.
Through her actions the mother is
guilty of perpetuating class and social
discrimination.

Of course, contrasted with the
horrors of pre-World War II Germany, contemporary American social
injustices appear, on the scale of relative standards, to be less repugnant.
By slow degrees, most of the decent,
God-fearing German townspeople of
Jerichow accept the poisonous Nazi
doctrines. From the maternal side of
Gesine's family, her cousin Horst
Papenbrock joins the Party. A de-
generate neighbor, Friedrich Jansen,
persecutes the few remaining Jewish
families who have not committed suicide or fled. Dr. Arthur Semig, the
Jewish veterinarian surgeon, is pub-
lically humiliated in court, then driven
from Jerichow in disgrace. Once
awarded the highest commendations
for bravery in World War I, he is an
innocent victim of tyranny. When

Lisbeth Cresspahl, Gesine's mother,
speaks out in his defense, she too is
marked out as an enemy of the State.
Later, with even greater courage, she
slaps the Nazi Jansen in the face after
he and a gang of ruffians have murdered Marie Sara, a "Jewish brat."
For her defiance, her house is burned
and she dies, under ambiguous but
suspicious circumstances, in the con-
flagration. In a powerful scene,
counterpointed with another scene
many years later, on February 23,
1968, when Francine returns to the
ghetto to take her mother's place,
Heinrich Cresspahl is interrogated by
the police, who try to learn about his
political sympathies. Before his wife's
funeral, he flees to catch the Gneez
train. But others, including Pastor
Brünschaver, remain, each person in
Jerichow—either through fear or
acquiescence—sharing responsibility
for the Nazi crimes against humanity.

Removed from Jerichow in time
and space, Gesine also wrestles with
the problem of her individual responsibility for the crimes. She pays Frau
Creutz, wife of the cemetery gardener
in her native town, to maintain the
graves of her mother and of Jacob,
her lover—Marie's father—about
whom she rarely speaks. In her mind
she measures the defiance of Eartha
Kitt, who insulted Lady Bird Johnson
at a Washington social gathering,
with that of her mother. She contrasts the petulant rebelliousness of
Svetlana, Stalin's daughter, with
Annie Killainen's antiwar protest.
Through the staid columns of the
New York Times she tries to learn
the appropriate responses that satisfy
her essentially conservative nature.
Yet she is a divided soul, half German and half American, living partly

in the present and partly in the past, inwardly unsettled though others see her as composed and complacent.

For his English-speaking audience Johnson has not yet completed Gesine's story. *Anniversaries* (in German *Jahrestage* One and Two) comprises only Volume One and part of Volume Two of the original work. The second book of *Anniversaries* will probably treat in greater detail Gesine's life under the Communist authorities in East Germany, her privations at the Marienfeld refugee camp, the full story of her affair with the mysterious Jacob, and perhaps more information about her present suitor, D. E. Although the first volume, ably translated by Leila Vennewitz, fails to answer all the reader's questions about the fate of the characters, some preliminary judgments about Johnson's artistic accomplishments may be offered. The novel, complex and rewarding, is a major study of the moral collapse of Nazi Germany. Less successful is Johnson's attempt to draw parallels to the American scene. In the New York episodes he simply fails to provide the same rich background of realistic detail that makes Jerichow come to life. Moreover, in reporting news stories, some verbatim and others paraphrased, from the *New York Times* as a gloss to the actions of Gesine and Marie, the author burdens his reader with an unnecessary freight of historical anecdotes. A few news items would surely have added an ironical dimension to the narrative; but taken *en masse,* the items nearly overwhelm the story. In *U.S.A.,* John Dos Passos had skillfully collected news reports in the sections of his book titled "Newsreels," a running account of actual events. Johnson, however, interlaces the reports throughout the novel. The effect of such massive irony (for the history of the recent past always strikes a contemporary as ironical) is only to weaken the author's force. Nevertheless, *Anniversaries* is a novel of rare integrity, moral insight, and intellectual breadth. When the second volume is translated into English, the whole work will represent a significant literary achievement.

Leslie B. Mittleman

THE ASSASSINS

Author: Joyce Carol Oates (1938-   )
Publisher: The Vanguard Press (New York). 568 pp. $8.95
Type of work: Novel
Time: The present
Locale: New York, Albany, Brandywine, West Virginia

An exploration of varying points of view as they are dramatized in the story of how the family of an assassinated influential political scientist reacts to the aftermath of his death

Principal characters:
ANDREW PETRIE, an assassinated political figure
YVONNE PETRIE, his widow
HUGH PETRIE and
STEPHEN PETRIE, his brothers

The wave of assassinations touching the American public so deeply beginning in the 1960's was not only shocking, it was also a series of touchstones for a plethora of literary and speculative endeavors. More important, people in general, Americans in particular, were prodded into asking themselves serious questions: Who are the assassins? Are we, in a sense, the assassins? Extending the implications of these questions, one is forced to ask of himself, who are the actual targets of assassination? In *The Assassins,* Joyce Carol Oates attunes herself keenly to such issues, drawing a finely detailed picture of society polarizing itself, feeding off itself, eventually destroying itself to the extent that the act of destruction is a necessity. And as a result, each individual is his own assassin, blindly fulfilling a grotesque death wish in which individuals are reduced to abstractions and only the concepts of the society survive, laying low everything within their scope to ensure their survival.

Andrew Petrie, a willful, undauntable, and influential conservative political scientist, is found murdered under unclear circumstances before the action of the novel begins. The reactions of three remaining family members—the deceased's brother, Hugh; his widow, Yvonne; and his younger brother, Stephen—comprise the body of the novel's exploration of varying points of view. Each survivor is left in a state of madness, ranging from Yvonne's subtle madness to Hugh's destructive schizophrenia.

Hugh Petrie's running dialogue in the novel's first section is by far the most powerful statement of the paranoia our society not only causes but also nurtures. The individual has become accustomed to living with such paranoia in quite an accommodating fashion. Through others, we learn that Hugh has always been considered slightly eccentric, but because his eccentricities are fairly well accepted in contemporary society, his pleas for help, his threats of destruction, go unheeded. It is his brother's assassination that thrusts his sickness from the realm of the latent to the overt, that "precipitating factor" that seems to release him from his fear of being discovered as mad into a state where he both recognizes and accepts the contorted machinations of his brain and relishes his sickness and self-deception for their pure intensity.

Hugh's intensity of feeling is underscored by the very language of his monologue: it is precise and so immediate that he fails to see the moment-to-moment changes in his psyche that are brought about by his frenzy. Hugh spirals from a relatively cognizant, relatively productive and successful human being to one who is capable of living only within those moments through which his mind writhes. Eventually he consciously focuses on the experience of such moments, beginning early when he reflects on the instant his sister informs him of Andrew's death. "The day's death," he pronounces, "the day's murder. . . ." These segments of life have become unrelated for Hugh. And so have they become arbitrary, as arbitrary as death itself. Finally, Hugh's obsession with his society's disjointedness and arbitrariness culminates in the at-once ludicrous and pathetic double attempted assassination of himself and the brook trout *meunier*.

Hugh's mental ramblings raise many issues that remain constant throughout the novel. Among them is the question of who Andrew's real assassins are. Aside from raising the question of who actually pulled the trigger, Hugh comes to recognize the widow Yvonne as one who sapped his brother mentally with an unidentifiable coldness that stays with her long after her husband's death. Yet eventually, in believing that Yvonne is somehow slowly murdering him as well by her rejection of his advances, Hugh expands the idea that we are all being murdered by our society into a larger concept: as his contorted association of himself with Yvonne grows, he sees himself as an assassin, too. Consequently, we are all being murdered, we are all murdering; we are all killing ourselves. The sense of Us versus Them raised early in Hugh's discourse fades away; we are all Us, we are all Them.

Part Two of the novel, Yvonne's section, uses the theme of meshing identities initiated in Hugh's section and carries it a step further into the quasi-normal world of the widow. The young woman does not suffer from the strain of blatant madness as does Hugh; hers is a more subtle madness, and as such it is potentially even more dangerous. Unlike Hugh, Yvonne does not indicate that her husband's death has been that touchstone to a life governed by a mental sickness. Rather, Yvonne's loss only sharpens a distinct pattern of egocentric obsession that was always latent in her life. It is this form of madness that is potentially more dangerous than overt forms because it often goes unrecognized until it has totally manipulated the person or object against which it is directed.

And in Yvonne's case, the object of the obsession is not the late political figure, not even his memory. Instead, Yvonne is dedicated to her own image, to the denial of all else. When her husband is gone, she fuses his image, from which she found such support, with her own and dedicates all her energies to perpetuating the synthesis of the two. Once one has a full grasp of the range of Yvonne's drive, one learns that Yvonne's power to dupe is extensive and, even more significant, virtually unconscious. She performs according to a conceptualized image, and once that image is accepted, regardless of its origins, she adopts it as her own.

Again, as with Hugh, Oates employs literary devices to emphasize the dominating feature of Yvonne's character. We want to understand her and are given potential clues into understanding her, but they are misleading. Oates's use of false imagery is most successful in her description of the ring Hugh first notices Yvonne wearing at the funeral. The author describes the two snakes on the ring elaborately from multiple points of view. But, there is no real substantial symbolism to the ring and we are left without a clue again. Not only the symbolism but also the origin of the ring is vague and arbitrary (Yvonne found it somewhere on the floor of a bus station restroom). Only the vagueness of Yvonne's own origin can match the nebulous quality of this perplexing symbol. She is without past, present, or future, and her husband's death or absence is the only reality through which she can affirm her existence or presence.

Of the three survivors focused on in the novel, only Stephen, the central figure of Part Three, seems to have been generally recognized as mad during Andrew's life. And whereas the murder of Andrew served to drive Hugh and Yvonne closer to their own sicknesses, Stephen brings something positive away from his encounter with death through the loss of his brother.

There is another important difference between Stephen and the others: he is the only one of the three to emerge intact (Hugh fails in his suicide attempt but remains in a vege-table state, kept alive by machines; Yvonne courts danger and is murdered). For, although Stephen is equally guilty of obsession, and equally guilty of ignoring himself as a social being in order to support his obsession, he is the only one to focus his mental processes on something outside himself. His religious preoccupations do keep him from merging himself with society, but they also keep him from destroying himself in frenzy. Consequently, Stephen's successful emergence from the trauma seems to indicate two alternatives open to the individual for survival: a merging with society with a concomitant denial of self, shown by negative example in the first two sections of the novel; or, a losing of oneself in a higher concept to the denial of any subjective or objective personality. This second alternative is emphasized by Stephen's reactions to his vague travels once he realizes that he can no longer find comfort or explanations in either his fellow human beings or in God. "Thank you," he explains to nameless, descriptionless acquaintances, "I can accommodate myself to anything."

Despite the contemporary subject matter of *The Assassins,* the novel treats very classic concepts and elevates them to undeniable truths. This is a book of mistaken identity; individuals are assigned functions by one another which they are incapable of performing, and similarly, are given responsibilities over which they have no control. Oates presents fine portraits of individuals obsessed and limited by their own egos and fragmented personalities."

Bonnie Fraser

BEAUTY AND SADNESS

Author: Yasunari Kawabata (1899-1972)
Translated from the Japanese by Howard Hibbett
Publisher: Alfred A. Knopf (New York). 206 pp. $7.95
Type of work: Novel
Time: The 1960's
Locale: Tokyo and Kyoto, Japan

A realistic, yet mystical, psychologically probing depiction of the passions of love, hatred, and revenge told with disturbingly cool dispassion

> *Principal characters:*
> OKI TOSHIO, a successful, middle-aged novelist restlessly attempting to recapture something of his youth
> FUMIKO, his wife
> UENO OTOKO, his former mistress, whom he has not seen for twenty-four years
> KEIKO, Ueno's protégée and lover
> TAICHIRO, the novelist's son

Like a traditional Japanese ink-brush drawing, Yasunari Kawabata's *Beauty and Sadness* is haunting in its ability to say much in what is actually depicted while showing perhaps as much again through what is suggested. As in those paintings, Kawabata's images alternate between starkness of statement and partial, peculiar emergence. Like *Haiku,* this novel is compressed and rich in suggestion, and demands reading between the lines. It consummates the author's— and that tradition's—craft of exquisite ellipsis and concision. It is Kawabata's final statement, and it is polished like a water stone. The effect is, as it was in the author's earlier *Snow Country, Thousand Cranes,* and *The Master of Go,* to draw, even to force, the reader into a consideration of love—that ultimate theme—within a world of deceptive quietude and dignity beneath which lurks breathtaking complexity and nuance. Kawabata so immerses the reader in his characters, scenes, themes, and plot that the reader becomes, literally, a participant in the story. This is a masterful feat for an Oriental, intuitive intelligence to perpetrate on an Occidental, more linear, mind. It is psychological art, careful and calculated. In one concentrated, crystallized sentence, Kawabata can depict and suggest more than most Western writers do in a paragraph. The dialogues he creates between his characters are terse, alternating between harsh, even painful, clarity, and "floating world" allusiveness, elusiveness. The silences between his people during these conversations scream with implications of thoughts, insights, of conclusions drawn—yet unspoken. The reader is *made* to know these things.

Kawabata disconcerts the reader's complacency, refuses to let him merely read, makes him a participant in the mystery of strange, real lives and thoughts for which there are no easy utterances. Typical of this enigmatic effect is the manner in which Kawabata ends this novel—suggesting death, possibly deaths, and further, hopeless alienation—all through the voices of three characters talking disjointedly, cryptically on multiple levels separate from one another, and themselves, while in the same small room. Finally, as with traditional Japanese paintings, a *pattern* of feeling, realization, is perceived more than communicated. In reading *Beauty and Sadness,* the reader, even if unwilling, must provide the links— if they indeed exist. Kawabata enthralls, but he refuses deliverance of solutions. His vision is too harshly honest for that.

Kawabata writes with lean beauty, baring both the beautiful and the hideous in life. An obvious inspiration for the *Nouvelle Vague* school of writers, his plots are bizarrely real, his prose is crisp and coldly dispassionate—exact—and those elements disturb because he deals with emotional, violent, and erotic subjects all equally as though the narrator spoke from behind a stylized *Noh* mask frozen into inscrutability. His story is told. The reader must perceive, must judge in a cell of aloneness that is horrifically existential. To read Kawabata is to be shaken, made to wonder. But he makes his tale so tantalizingly elusive that it captivates. Kawabata's Japan is painfully alive, torn between old and new —his temple gardens are the most silent, his snows the coldest, his rains the wettest, his hearts the most mysterious, his people the most real, their problems the most poignant, his plots the most compelling drawn in recent memory. And he achieves it all with an astonishing economy—through, again, an exactness that is masterful. His Nobel Prize, awarded in 1968, a surprise at that time to most West-

terners, was, it is now apparent, profoundly deserved. His craft was his life. It is surprising in some ways that the Western world recognized and rewarded his supreme absorption, his Zen-like fusion of self with art. One cannot escape the thought that *Beauty and Sadness,* in all its seeking and despair, is spiritually autobiographical. If so, what an effort of the heart and mind went into its writing, for it is, finally, merciless in its depiction of the writer himself.

Beauty and Sadness is the story of Oki Toshio, a successful, middle-aged novelist who, much earlier in his career, betrayed his wife, Fumiko, by having an affair with Ueno Otoko, a young woman—actually just a girl of sixteen. The girl loved him. Infatuated with her, he called his emotion love, yet when she became pregnant by him, and lost the premature baby, he failed her by taking no supportive action.

The novel opens with the novelist, melancholy and empty in the midst of his material success, deciding to visit Kyoto ostensibly to hear the temple bells ring in the new year. His real motive, however, is to see again, after a passage of twenty-four years, his mistress, now a well-known artist living in the guest house of a temple in the old city. Strangely, for an artist, insensitive to the effect his visit may have on the woman, he goes selfishly in a blind attempt to rejuvenate his flagging spirits.

When Oki sees Ueno, he discovers her to be even more beautiful, more sadly seasoned in her emotions, and, though unalterably convinced of its futility, still in love with him—and with the memory of their love affair. His egotistical opening up of the past thus sets in motion a train of events destructive and agonizing to all the characters involved. Having caused loss, Oki will now experience it.

Ueno lives in a mild lesbian relationship with her beautiful young protégée, a girl of eerily brilliant talent, fierce loyalty, and eccentric passions so unorthodox as to be slightly mad. Impatient with her older lover's passive acceptance of what she sees clearly as a wrong, this girl, Keiko, embarks upon revenge. She shakes Oki's gravity, nearly seduces him, and ultimately does seduce and cause the death of his son, Taichiro.

In the physical sense, those are the events of *Beauty and Sadness*. They are profoundly motivated and powerfully treated. But it is in its psycholological and aesthetic nuances that the novel most deeply impresses.

The problem of diversity in human definitions and perceptions of basic emotions of illusion and reality is a major theme in Kawabata's work. In *Beauty and Sadness* he explores the problems of love and lovelessness, of right and wrong, of passivity and action, of youth and age, of past and present, by showing each character's need to be the way they are. Oki seems incapable of real passion. His depiction in words on paper of that experience is more real to him than the experience itself. In pursuit of self and craft, he callously hurts his wife and mistress. Saved from the sorts of hurt they suffer by his innate ability of remaining aloof, Oki is simultaneously cut off from any real joy by it. This coldness makes him a stranger to his wife, whose discovery of his infidelity so traumatizes her that she becomes a nonentity. In further contrast to Oki's selfish, im-

penetrable stance, the uncomplicated natural passion which his mistress, Ueno, had felt for him causes her such anguish that she attempts suicide and later spends her life withdrawn into unnaturalness, trying to quell, to sublimate her real passions through painting extremely controlled, tradiitional images. In a sense, both Oki's and Ueno's lives appear successful to the outer world only through their being unnatural—stunted and contained like bonsai because, like those small trees, they repress and twist their inner worlds. And they both are spiritually discomfited by that truth. Oki resents the continuing success of his first novel, *A Girl of Sixteen*. It is an undisguised account of his and Ueno's affair which, after his horrified wife has typed the manuscript, becomes a critical and popular success. It makes his reputation but loses for him his wife and causes additional pain to his mistress. Significantly, he hates the book not for these reasons, but because it draws attention from his recent and, he feels, more artistic works. He hates it because it reminds him not of passion uncontrolled—not of possible joy denied—but of art too naïve. Dissimilarly, but equally devastatingly, Ueno distrusts her talent because it is popularly commercial, not really of her self.

In their many conversations about abstract as opposed to realistic art, Kawabata's characters are, on the surface, speaking of art. But they are also speaking of—searching for—symbolically, the properly protective lense or aesthetic veil to superimpose between them and their experiences. In every case it insulates them from human warmth. Older, more traditional, caught in modes of conduct out of the past, Ueno and Oki have their stances shattered, their worlds destroyed by the unfettered impetuosity of the more contemporary and heartless Keiko, who lives and moves in a world too frighteningly real for either of them any longer to grasp. While they bide their times and discuss proper forms of illusion, a reality beyond their understanding emerges through Keiko and has its disastrous effect. The title "Beauty and Sadness" functions to reveal the uncontrollably multilayered consciousness of such concepts as "beauty and sadness." For Ueno and Oki and Fumiko, beauty *is* sadness, deliberate, controlled and contained—they think. For young Keiko and Taichiro, beauty is to be defended because it can be joyous; sadness is to be attacked, revenged. And these disparate views, the traditional and the modern, both fail equally, inevitably leading to destruction and despair. Neither youth nor age, love nor hate has an answer. Kawabata's world shows that events rule; people and their principles are doomed to a beautiful futility.

It is interesting and disturbing to observe this thought about despair developing into fruition throughout Kawabata's canon, beginning its culmination in his earlier novel, *The Master of Go*. Published in 1972, that novel was a touching and symbolic story of the defeat of a traditional grand master of Japanese chess at the hands of a younger, more modern-minded challenger. In April of that year, Kawabata took his own life, and having made his fusion of life to craft his testimonial to an unremittingly honest vision of existence, he left no further note or explanation for his suicide. In that sense, *Beauty and Sadness* is the last entry in a lifelong suicide note. The dream gone bitter, the act of dreaming become repugnant, it is the disillusioned dreamer's outcry: "If this is the all of beauty and sadness, if love is impossible—then why go on?"

From his lonely, Olympian position as a man and an artist, Kawabata came as close as any writer may to seeing through the veil. When he had finally said what he saw, as he brilliantly does in *Beauty and Sadness*, he stopped—completely. For those who admired his gifts, there is both sadness and transcendent beauty in that.

Thomas N. Walters

BEFORE MY TIME

Author: Maureen Howard (1930-   )
Publisher: Little, Brown and Company (Boston). 241 pp. $6.95
Type of work: Novel
Time: The present
Locale: Boston, Long Island, and New York City

A story about two related families, their problems, experiences, and search for meaning and security in the modern world

Principal characters:
> LAURA QUINN, a forty-year-old housewife and journalist unsatisfied with her life
> HARRY QUINN, her husband, a Boston lawyer
> JIM COGAN, their seventeen-year-old second cousin who faces drug possession and conspiracy charges
> MILLICENT (MILLIE) MURRAY COGAN, his mother
> JACK COGAN, his father
> SIOBHAN AND CORMAC COGAN, his pre-teen twin brother and sister
> SHELLEY WALTZ, Jim's girl friend
> P. J. CLAUSON (KRISHNA NURU), a phony religious "guru"
> HAROLD (HOSHIE) FEINMARK, a rich, aged Jewish client of Jack

In her third novel, *Before My Time,* Maureen Howard explores the complex relationships in and between two families, the Quinns, a "successful" and apparently stable Boston clan, and their cousins, the Cogans, a Long Island family that treads perpetually on the brink of financial and emotional disaster. The catalyst that brings them together is the arrest and pending trial of seventeen-year-old Jim Cogan, accused of drug possession and involvement in a conspiracy to blow up a New York public library. Since Harry Quinn is a moderately prominent Boston attorney with political connections, young Cogan is sent to the Quinn household for a few weeks prior to trial. But Jim Cogan's plight is little more than an excuse to set the narrative in motion; there is never a danger that he will suffer any punishment more severe than a stern judicial lecture. The importance of his visit lies in the effect it has on Harry's wife, Laura Quinn.

Jim arrives at a time when Laura is especially vulnerable. Having recently turned forty, she is feeling the discontents of early middle age, is unsatisfied with her role as wife and mother, and is not getting the expected satisfactions out of her foray into free-lance journalism (she is completing a series of taped interviews with feminists for an article/book). Although sophisticated and aware, she realizes that her contact with the environment around her is shallow, and further, that her writing is like her life. Her prolonged encounter with the young Cogan stimulates a defense of herself and her life style to him and, more importantly, a crucial self-examination of her past experiences, relationships, and frustrations. She feels an urgent need to justify herself to him or, perhaps, only to herself: "I must have been ready for a stranger to ask me questions and he, with all his promise and the years ahead, would just as soon ask and not listen. . . ."

Jim Cogan provokes her into the confrontation for several reasons: he represents a new start, a chance vicariously to experience both the great moments that happened and those that did not ("I never did tap dance along the pavements in the rain," Laura muses. "I've drunk too little and now the good wine's gone to vinegar"); he reminds her of her deceased brother Robert, a symbol to her of lost potential; and he comes from that "other family," the Cogans, who, in their perpetual defeat, remain to Laura a threatening, distorted mirror image of the Quinns.

But it is unfair to abstract Laura's dilemma from the work in this manner. At worst it makes the book sound like a subjective, melodramatic "frustrated housewife" lament, one of the more popular and trivial of current literary clichés, and it suggests that her relationship with Jim resembles the tritest of generation gap clichés (Guilty-Middle-Aged-Liberal-Matron versus Mixed-Up-Young-Counterculture-Rebel). Nothing could be further from the truth; in fact, the strategy of the novel is almost the opposite.

Laura Quinn's self-probing search for identity and justification is simply the most important of several such explorations in the novel. Because she is the most sensitive and self-conscious of the characters, and because her personal sense of failure, especially as provoked by young Cogan's visit, has brought her discontents to the surface, the author uses her as the focal point for an ex-

amination of the nature, causes, and meaning of failure in modern American society and particularly in the context of the family. Most of the other characters in the book, both major and minor, are either failures or potential failures, some objectively, according to the usual social and economic criteria, others only in their own eyes.

Thus, the novel is organized on a carefully controlled theme and variation pattern in which a number of separate characters and situations are juxtaposed to reinforce and illuminate the total meaning of the book—a "meaning" that is not so much a set of intellectual conclusions as a sensitive montage of human beings groping existentially with the frustrations and ambiguities of their own lives and, perhaps, occasionally coping with them meaningfully.

"Memories are draining," Harry Quinn tells his wife early in the novel. "They are false." The truth of Quinn's remark becomes evident as the book progresses: memory can be a dangerous trap. The pervading sense of failure that plagues the characters is largely the product of unrealistic expectations and faulty self-images based on misperceptions about the past.

Laura's "trap" is her obsessive romanticization of her brother Robert. Shaken by his early, meaningless death in the Korean War, she has exaggerated his personal sensitivity and modest promise as a poet-actor into an impossible ideal which probably bears little resemblance to what, in fact, he could have become. And if Laura has made Robert into the hero of her past, she has cast her father as the villain, primarily because of his disdain for Robert's sensitivities. The practical result of these false visions is that they have frustrated her present life, destroyed communication with her husband, whom she unfairly identifies with the hated parent, and damaged her sense of personal identity. "Look at my work," she tells Jim, "I skim over the top of things. There's no place to get at me. I'm just not there."

Millie Cogan's "trap" is the belief that she gave up an exciting career for a marriage that has gone sour. Once personal secretary to Darwin Spears, the president of Minotaur Press, she quit to marry the robust, amusing, apparently ambitious Jack Cogan, only to discover, too late, that he was a compulsive gambler and a mediocre salesman. Millie's vision of herself as a career woman, when it is unlikely that she could have ever become more than a good secretary, is another romantic vision, less complex than Laura's, but probably more stultifying. "What's gone is gone," she says over and over. "Here we are now. There's no point in dwelling on the past," and then she dwells on it relentlessly, drinks continuously, and lets the bitterness poison all of her personal relationships.

Harry Quinn's distorted image is that he might have won an important public office. Jack Cogan dreams of the "quick kill" as a gambler and spectacular success as a salesman. His son, Jim, is equally trapped by the past, although his mistake lies in the belief that it has no effect on him at all. Superficially disillusioned by his family situation, young Jim is vulnerable to the most obviously shallow counterculture clichés, especially the studied nonconformity of his girl-friend, Shelley Waltz, and the religious fakery of P. J. Clauson's "Church of Creative Resignation and Love" which have led him into his legal tangle.

This thematic coherence not only gives the apparently fragmentary structure of the novel its unity, but it also allows Howard the flexibility to move from character to character and scene to scene without losing the central focus. It further grants her the opportunity to digress into some marvelous set pieces—Jim's clipping poodles at the *Chateau du Chien,* Millie Cogan's conning money from her aged, irascible father and later returning a "Prayer Book" to her ex-boss's embittered widow, the Cogan twins setting up housekeeping in the model apartments of a suburban Condominium development, Jack Cogan's comical philosophical exchanges with Hoshie Feinmark, an aged Jewish millionaire—which probably represent the best writing in the book.

Before My Time is, finally, a mosaic or patchwork in which the author manipulates her materials, arranging the squares with apparent randomness, until all of a sudden it is in front of us, complete and fully integrated. This wholeness is achieved in the final segment of the book, "Scenario: Before My Time":

From this point on—to the end let us say—I would like to picture for you quick-moving scenes . . . these images sometimes fill my mind at once or follow one upon another with an insistence like motion. . . . Running time: undetermined . . . for there are places where I like to stop and look . . . . To satisfy myself with that vision and then refreshed, move on. My projection of the waking dream

. . . . Like an ending, a completion
for me . . . not quite. And in the dark
his voice.—Stay here. Speak of familiar things awhile.

It is appropriate that Howard shifts
to the present tense in this section,
since the point of the novel is the
present and how to deal with it.
There are no sudden dramatic epiphanies for any of the characters or
lengthy articulations to resolve their
problems. But there is a definite
sense that the characters, especially
Laura, are coming to terms with
themselves, and this is suggested not
so much in statements as in their
actions.

Harry comes to accept himself as
as a backstage politician, incapable
of direct action, who is willing to pay
the price needed to achieve limited,
worthwhile ends. Jim Cogan realizes
the thinness of his rebellion and admits that "I want to go back. My
mother and father are pitiful, but I
miss them. . . . I want to see them
all. It's an idea you gave me, that it's
my life, my real life." And Laura
takes her own advice. She puts the
past in its place by erasing the tapes,
which have become false to her, and
saying goodbye to Robert's memory.

Later, coming back from a political
dinner, she and Harry break through
their communication barrier. Like
teen-agers, they make love on the
back seat of the car. That night the
whole family sleeps together on the
roof, a final sign of communion:

He turns to her in his sleep.—
Come out, he says. It's fun out here.
That's all he says, and she steps
through the window and stands above
him looking out over the cultivated
gardens, as though she were on a ship
looking out to the wild sea.

"Family life is like the classics
played in modern dress by an amateur group," says the narrator at one
point in the book, "Vulgarized versions of the old tales." But despite
the amateurishness of their gropings
and the vulgarity in their understandings, the characters in *Before
My Time* do make real contact and
do manage to find a core of meaning
in their relationships. The final mood
of the novel is a mixture of honest
resignation and muted hope; there are
no climactic resolutions, only the
kind of glimpsed accommodations
that echo the problematical, ambiguous nature of life as it is lived.

Keith Neilson

BEING WITH CHILDREN

Author: Phillip Lopate (1943-   )
Publisher: Doubleday and Company (New York). 392 pp. $7.95
Type of work: Reminiscence
Time: 1968-1972
Locale: New York

A warmly receptive account of learning experiences, told by a poet who teaches creative writing to children

Principal personages:
PHILLIP LOPATE, poet and teacher
EDOUARDO JIMENEZ, elementary school principal
TED GLASS, assistant principal
DENISE LOFTIN,
LEO GELBERT,
STANLEY RIEGELHAUPT, and
MARGARET TRABULSKI, classroom teachers
MAUREEN McGUIRE, pianist
BRITT, CLIFFORD, DOLORES, GENE, GREGORY, JAMIE, KAREN, LUIS, MARIA, MARVIN, RICKY, ROBERTO, SCOTT, STEFAN, VICKY, VIRGINIA, WILLIE, AND XIOMARA, the author's sixth-grade students

The decade of the 1960's will be remembered primarily as a period in which all established institutions were under concerted intellectual and political attack, with liberal elements leading the assault and demanding radical change. Not quite a revolution, the movement nonetheless created a state of upheaval in which, as might be expected, many innocent persons were injured or made to suffer; but at the same time basic tenets were probed in depth and a great deal of chronic injustice was subjected to public scrutiny.

One major target of this insistence upon reform was the American public school system, the indictment of which led to much soul-searching on the part of those who worked in and with it. A period of experimentation has followed, characterized by alternative approaches and new concepts. The most significant of these, in some respects, is the change agent. This designation, originated by a Ford Foundation executive, is applied to the person who is placed in a deteriorating educational situation to act as a catalyst and point it in a new direction. Originally limited to cultural and intellectual stimulation, the concept has since been expanded to administrative areas and now includes innovative public school superintendents and college presidents who have been brought into static or moribund institutions to revitalize them. The process is always traumatic for everyone concerned, and it is essential that the agent depart as soon as sweeping changes are consolidated and reorientation well-established—provided he lasts that long, since the task is usually far more painful and disruptive than his employers anticipate. The temporary nature of the assignment maintains his role as outsider, and promotes a return to stability after he is gone; at the same time he is effectively prevented from digging new intellectual or bureaucratic ruts of his own.

Phillip Lopate is a poet who became a change agent in the original sense of the term. As he wryly observes, it was inevitable that the schools would eventually turn to entertainers for inspiration. The Teachers and Writers Collaborative is an organization that was established to meet this need, and Lopate joined it in 1968. During the next two years he moved through a succession of school assignments and rapidly became disenchanted with the change agent concept. A product of the intellectual climate of the 1960's, Lopate took his role as young reformer very seriously and soon found himself repeating a monotonous and discouraging cycle: he was making waves for their own sake, getting himself fired, and accomplishing nothing constructive in the process. He eventually realized that his greatest challenge lay in working creatively with students, and that he could meet it only by surviving in one institution long enough to be effective as a teacher. Assigned to an elementary school in New York City's Upper West Side as part-time instructor in creative writing, Lopate set about fitting himself into the life of the school. *Being with Children* is an account of his first two years there.

Lopate is able to view himself with greater honesty than many writers can muster, and one important aspect of the book is its delightful chronicle of his own professional growth. As he becomes acquainted with them, the teachers cease to be establish-

ment stereotypes and gradually become complex individuals, hard working and harassed, with "a shared sense of being overwhelmed." The principal, first seen as an arbitrary and inscrutable authoritarian figure, emerges as a compassionate person under tremendous pressure; the building gradually evolves from a dreary, run-down structure into an acceptable environment with connotations of home; the children cease to be a screaming mob and become instead a multitude of diverse and challenging personalities. Lopate establishes meaningful two-way communication with his share of them. The relationship between teacher and child, as Lopate has discovered and experienced it, is what *Being with Children* is all about.

Maturity is in part the process of forgetting. Physical, mental, and emotional changes that occur during the metamorphosis from child to adult are such that our life as a child, once we have left it behind, is an alien and imperfectly remembered world that we can never quite recapture. Our own immaturity, seen in retrospect, is incomprehensible to us, and we find it embarrassing. Thus the child becomes something of a mystery to the adult, by turns fascinating and frustrating—so much so that children are currently referred to as a repressed minority and courted politically as a separate race might be. They are also studied scientifically as though they were a different species altogether.

The ability to understand children and to relate to them effectively is largely intuitive; comparatively few adults possess it in large measure, even in the teaching profession.

Phillip Lopate is one of this fortunate number, and his discovery of the fact is also his real discovery of himself.

The elementary school that Lopate calls P.S. 90 is a progressive institution, employing an informal and loosely structured approach to education that is known as Open Corridor. It is a cosmopolitan place in which many racial, ethnic, and class backgrounds are represented, and it forms an environment into which assignments such as Lopate's can fit with comparatively little disruption. He is one of a team of writers funded with grant money, but the team members function individually; this book is almost entirely an account of his own effort. He provides a wonderfully perceptive evocation of the school as a living organism. It is a place incredibly busy, bustling, filled with continuous uproar; at the same time, there is the constant uneasy feeling that it is also an incipient disaster area, with some sections already total chaos and the rest a reasonably happy, semi-orchestrated bedlam.

Many of the projects Lopate and the children undertake have the same manic quality. They are at times irreverent and zany, even surrealistic. They are also very entertaining. The necessary rapport did not come immediately, but once Lopate and the sixth-graders he worked with got together they accomplished a great deal. By the end of the first year they were writing poetry, short stories, and plays; they were writing scripts and producing videotapes and films; they were producing and directing their own stage works. Lopate describes and analyzes a number of these projects, successful and otherwise, in

some detail. Among the best are a videotape interview and report on the school lunchroom; a class play entitled *The Substitute Teacher,* which contains, in addition to some really good lines, a final scene in which one of the students takes wing; and the high point of the book, a blow-by-blow chronicle of *West Side Story* as produced and performed by the children.

In addition to the project analyses, an appendix is provided which forms a comprehensive, and broadly representative, body of the children's written work. Much of it is astonishingly high in quality. More significant is the fact that each composition is distinctly an individual expression by an individual human being. Too many anthologies of work by students in the various art forms are obvious reflections of the teacher's own stylistic or socio-political orientation. There is no such undue influence apparent in the output of Lopate's sixth-graders —only a very impressive result of his commitment to helping them achieve genuine self-expression.

Lopate dispels a number of myths fostered by idealistic adults whose link with childhood has become the tenuous memory of a Golden Age— among them the notion that all children have transcendent imagination and a rich poetic gift. He finds that the distribution of talent among children is much the same as it is among adults: some are fluent, some inarticulate; some are unexpectedly frank and incisive, others subtle; some express their innermost feelings, others maintain privacy; no two viewpoints are quite the same.

Being with Children abounds in arresting, if necessarily incomplete, portraits of the children themselves. All are memorable, a few unforgettable: Britt, the talented mime and dramatic actor; Xiomara, the brooding cynic who is wise beyond her years; Roberto, a seething cauldron of barely repressed violence. Lopate deplores the sterility of mass approaches to sensitivity, and his book is an eloquent testimonial to the uniqueness and integrity of the individual.

People enter the teaching profession for a variety of reasons. Some do so through a genuine love of children and of the vocation itself. Some fall back on teaching as a second choice when faced with an unfavorable employment situation in their major subject area; others, particularly within the past decade, have become teachers for ideological reasons and work within the system, through indoctrination, for social change. A few become successful and dedicated teachers, as Lopate did, more or less by accident. Many members of his generation assumed the essentially negative role of chronic protester, or adopted the premise that all human activity must be politically motivated and guided: Lopate, whose social conscience is obviously as well-developed as theirs, has channeled his talents into a path far more meaningful.

Being with Children is an exciting and beautifully written account of learning experiences; it should be required reading for anyone involved in the creative process.

John W. Evans

BEYOND THE BEDROOM WALL
A Family Album

Author: Larry Woiwode (1942-   )
Publisher: Farrar, Straus and Giroux (New York). 619 pp. $12.50
Type of work: Novel
Time: 1935-1975
Locale: North Dakota, Illinois, Minnesota, New York City

A large, experimental novel covering three generations of a Midwestern Catholic family

Principal characters:
CHARLES NEUMILLER, a carpenter and builder
MARTIN NEUMILLER, one of his sons
ALPHA JONES NEUMILLER, Martin's wife
JEROME,
CHARLES,
TIMOTHY,
MARIE, and
SUSAN, their children
ED AND ELECTA JONES, Alpha's father and mother
LIONELL JONES, Alpha's brother
LAURA, Martin Neumiller's second wife

Larry Woiwode's second novel, *Beyond the Bedroom Wall: A Family Album,* is a long, complex, and many-charactered family novel which was ten years in the making. Fourteen of its forty-four chapters first appeared as stories in the *New Yorker,* and other chapters were published as stories in several magazines, including *Mademoiselle* and *McCalls.* Such publication by accretion is not new in American long fiction. Thomas Wolfe, William Faulkner, and John Updike are only three among many who have published as magazine stories material which appeared later, usually in somewhat different form, as parts of novels. Bringing out a large novel bit-by-bit over the course of a decade is most unusual, however, and as a result, *Beyond the Bedroom Wall* has developed through a variety of styles, devices, and techniques. There are many shifts in time, in narrators, in point of view, and in tone. The narration is sometimes in the present tense, sometimes in the past; characters are now adult and then children again, either through their own memories or through the memories of others. Generally, there is a progression in time from Part I, which opens with the burial by Charles Neumiller of his German immigrant father in 1935, to the close of the last chapter of Part V, a generation later in the 1970's when all of Martin Neumiller's five children have grown up, three are married, and Martin has become a grandfather and has been widowed a second time. Within the individual chapters, though, time often moves backward as well as forward.

The title *Beyond the Bedroom Wall: A Family Album* partly suggests both the novel's content and its form. The scene of "The Street," the single story in the section entitled "Prelude," is both a bedroom in the present and the main street of a small town in North Dakota in 1950. Tim, the narrator (not until more than a hundred pages later do we learn that he is Timothy, the third son of Martin and Alpha Neumiller), lies sleepless by his sleeping wife and recalls in sharp detail the unpaved main street of Hyatt, North Dakota, the small town in which he lived until he was six. By the time his memory has taken him beyond the bedroom wall and back in time to the Fourth of July when he won a foot race against his older brother Charles and several other boys, he has fallen asleep. Later chapters or stories (the second term often seems more appropriate) take us to bedrooms or to other rooms in houses in Hyatt and elsewhere, and to many outdoor scenes. Gradually we learn through one character or another, and sometimes through the author, the inner nature or the outward actions and talk of three generations of the Neumiller family over a period of about forty years. It is as though we are being shown pictures in a Neumiller album by one member of the family or another, or by the author, who is attempting to recapture, like Marcel Proust, but here with a modern American flavor, his own past and that of his family and friends.

One very brief chapter, entitled "A Family Album," describes a much-used book filled with mounted and neatly captioned photographs and other memorabilia of past events as well as numerous photographs that were slipped into the book for some later mounting which never occurred. Photos from the album become parts of later chapters as scenes or times or actions which they commemorate are recalled. Other mementos appear in many chapters of the novel. Charles Neumiller, preparing to bury his father on the site of Otto's little homesteading hut on a North Dakota farm, finds in Otto's bedroom a three-year-old letter—written in German and nearly fallen to pieces from folding and unfolding—from Charles's son Martin sending from college his love and best wishes on the old man's seventy-fifth birthday. Charles silently wishes he himself had been able to express so well his affection for the parent for whom he has now so meticulously and lovingly constructed a wooden coffin and dug a grave. Chapter Three contains Martin's detailed two-page application for a teaching job. Chapter Four comprises selections from Alpha Jones's five-year diary which she began to keep in 1936 before her marriage to Martin. An editor's note in brackets describes the diary and the eccentricities of certain long entries which ingeniously fill the limited space with writing which moves up and down as well as across the page. Some of the diary entries are so intimately revealing that one feels Alpha would not have wanted anyone except herself and perhaps her husband to see them. Later diary entries, which make up Chapter Six, were written before her marriage and during her first year as Alpha Neumiller. An editor's note at the end of the chapter states that "at this juncture in her writing, she is twenty-two and Martin twenty-six" and that the diary was kept daily until late in 1940. In Chapter Twenty-three, when Martin Neumiller is preparing to burn the clothes and other belongings of his young and deeply loved wife who died at thirty-four in convulsions as a result of the stillbirth of her sixth child and of uremic poisoning, he finds the diary, flips through its pages "to see her handwriting and see it move," closes it, and sits on Alpha's vanity bench lost in grief.

Of the numerous Neumillers and Joneses in Woiwode's novel, many are only sketchily presented so that one recalls them rather dimly at the end. Charles Neumiller is so vividly portrayed in the beautifully written opening chapter, "Burial," that one regrets his later dropping into the background, until his death in Part V stirs the memories of his children and grandchildren who recall him with love and admiration. Most of the novel is concerned with Charles's son Martin (one of nine children), Alpha Jones (one of seven children), and their three sons and two daughters: Jerome, Charles, Timothy, Marie, and Susan. Martin, one supposes, was modeled after the author's father (to whom the novel is principally dedicated); and Tim, the family poet, is perhaps the fictional character closest to Woiwode himself.

Martin and Alpha's love for each other and for the children enables them to survive somehow in the face of an economic struggle that causes Martin to resign as a poorly paid smalltown teacher and principal in order to sell insurance, drive a farm tractor, and work as a plumber. The possibility of getting a principalship of a new consolidated school in a small Illinois town near where his parents live prompts Martin to make what evolves as a disastrous move from North Dakota, since he is de-nied the position after the move, possibly because of anti-Catholic prejudice in a largely Methodist town. Alpha dies not long after the move, and Martin finds that being for the five children "Father, mother, nurse, teacher, arbiter, guardian, judge— all the roles were too much." Martin eventually marries again, but Laura remains for the reader not much more than a name, so that when she too dies, one feels little sense of loss. Even Martin seems so little touched by the death of his second wife that his son Charles (named for his grandfather) repeatedly wonders, "Who is this man?" It is as though the death of Alpha years earlier had dried Martin into a mere shell of his former self.

The fifth and largely unsatisfactory section of *Beyond the Bedroom Wall* opens with two stories that seem almost to have been forced into the novel simply because Charles Neumiller is in them. The scene of both is New York City, where Charles hopes to become an actor. In "Five at the Table" Charles and four friends —two girls and two young men—all get stoned and engage in aimless, foul-mouthed chatter. "The Village Poet" introduces an eccentric Greenwich Village poet who talks lengthily about himself and reads some of his poetry to Charles. The most significant part of this long story is Charles's vision of a book, a journal written by his mother that develops into the kind of book that Woiwode has actually put together, "a series of multicolored pieces about North Dakota and Illinois, . . . each piece complete in itself, . . . bearing no outward relationship to any other piece . . . ," and so on. One feels that the author has attempted to explain and justify his unusual assemblage of the parts of his novel. Yet in "The End," the long chapter which concludes *Beyond the Bedroom Wall,* the author drops his structural unorthodoxy and writes like a nineteenth century novelist letting us know what happened to his characters after the major action had ended. "Charles was the first of the children to marry . . . ." "Tim was married a year and a half later. . . ." "Jerome was doing an additional internship. . . ."

"Marie was majoring in Special Education. . . ." "Martin had been attending night school. . . ."

As a novel, *Beyond the Bedroom Wall* is so broken into pieces, small and large, that one wishes for a greater unifying or smoother connecting of the parts. Perhaps this could have been attained without too much wrenching of the "reality" that Woiwode has tried to present. As they are, however, the book's best parts—such as "Burial" and "Snowfall Along the Illinois"—are excellent.

Henderson Kincheloe

CELEBRATION

Author: Harvey Swados (1920-1972)
Publisher: Simon and Schuster (New York). 348 pp. $8.95
Type of work: Novel
Time: The present, combined with memoirs dating back to the beginning of the century
Locale: Twelvetrees, country home of Samuel Lumen in the Berkshire hills

A novel about a famous eighty-nine-year-old radical, told in diary form, which confronts issues of personal, social, and political morality

> Principal characters:
> SAMUEL LUMEN, the protagonist and narrator, an aged pioneer of progressive education and child-welfare reform
> JENNIFER LUMEN, Sam's young, third wife, a photographer
> LARRY BRODIE, Sam's protégé, an ambitious White House aide
> ROGER GIRARD, Sam's right-hand man and secretary
> SETH FOX, Sam's illegitimate son
> WALTER HONIG, Sam's friend, adviser, lawyer
> LILY HONIG, Walter's wife, Sam's abiding friend

Samuel Lumen, the hero and first-person narrator of Harvey Swados' fifth and last novel, is an aged radical, a survivor of the social activists of the 1930's who had to carve a new American Dream out of the Depression wreck of the old one. Sam has an old coon hound named Lincoln Steffens, a sentimental reminder of his first career as a muckraking journalist. He went on to become a leader in progressive education and child welfare reform as the headmaster of an experimental school, and was an antiwar crusader.

Now, as he approaches his ninetieth birthday, Sam is facing a long television interview with a celebrity reporter in conjunction with his forthcoming birthday celebration; the central event is to be the dedication of the Samuel Lumen Children's Center in Washington, the culmination of his life's work, and it is to be presided over by the President. Sam's long, eventful life has come full circle. He has lived long enough to become a venerable rebel courted by the Establishment.

Sam is disconcerted under inner pressure because he knows that there is a vast difference between the public figure and the private person, that he is as much human sinner as saintly humanist. He is guilt ridden by failures in his personal life: by the death of his first child and the failure of his first marriage, brought about, in part, by his neglect while he pursued political idealism, and by his middle-aged sexual promiscuity, which may have resulted in an illegitimate child by his son's fiancée, and certainly helped precipitate her suicide.

Sam had met his first wife, Luba Lefkowitz, on a picket line during the textile strike of 1912. After the birth of their daughter, Sophia, he had gone to prison, convicted of sedition for resisting American entry into World War I. Returning from jail in 1919, he found that the asthmatic child had died and that Luba had left him. Dismayed, he felt that he

had betrayed his personal commit-
ments for self-indulgent political
idealism.

Sam's next wife was the rich Hester Boatwright, who bore him a son,
Philip, but also turned out to be
psychotic. He made a deal with the
proud Boatwrights not to commit
Hester to a mental hospital in return
for their financial underwriting of his
famous but financially insecure
Sophia School, named for his dead
daughter.

The main burden on Sam's heart,
however, was the memory of Philip
and Philip's fiancée, Louise Fox.
Sam's one sexual escapade with
Louise, shortly before Philip was
killed in the Pacific during World
War II, may have resulted in the
birth of her son, Seth, and led her, in
guilt and sorrow, to fly her plane into
the side of a mountain. Seth was sent
to live with the parents of Louise,
who had, for twenty-one years, been
receiving a monthly check from Sam
through his longtime lawyer and adviser, Walter Honig.

But Sam Lumen is not simply an
egotistical cad. He is a truly great
man, an authentic hero who has
fought all his life for the oppressed
(especially the exploited or mis-
treated young), a man of conscience,
as his guilt feelings demonstrate,
committed to his social ideals. As
are many great men and women, he
is a complex figure, larger than ordinary life in both his vices and virtues,
and Swados drew his portrait surely
and powerfully. It might be argued
with some justification that Lumen's
surfeit of guilt is overdone; that
Swados relied too much on a tyrannical libido in order to humanize a
man with the credentials of a legend;

or that Lumen's memoir of his encounter with Louise is a melodramatic flaw in an otherwise controlled,
convincing novel. Nevertheless, Samuel Lumen is the finest characterization of Swados' fiction output.

Outer pressure on Sam Lumen has
become even more intense than his
inner torment. His young, third wife,
a photographer named Jennifer, and
Larry Brodie, a former student and
protégé of Sam who is now a presidential assistant, are determined that
he not rock the political boat and
thus lose the President's endorse-
ment of the Children's Center that
they want as the climax of his career.
The fact that Jennifer and Larry are
having an affair does not affect their
deep love for Sam. Sam's secretary
and right-hand-man, Roger Girard,
is also solicitous of Sam, but Rog is
a traditional anti-Establishment liberal, and is suspicious that Larry and
the President want to use Sam and
defuse his reputation as a defender
of the outsider.

One day Sam has a sudden visitor.
Seth Fox has learned of the payments
Sam has been sending to his maternal
grandparents, and has begun to question his real relationship to this great
man who is supposedly his grandfather. Seth subtly threatens scandal,
applying leverage for a group of
young rebels, the "Children of Liberty," who want Sam to disavow the
Center and the President, to turn
aside from what they regard as capitalist hypocrisy.

So Samuel Lumen, determined to
leave an honest record of his life,
and to protect his sense of self against
the demands upon him, writes a diary
of the last half of his eighty-ninth
year. The result is this *Celebration*

of many of the causes that occupied Harvey Swados most of his life and throughout his writing career, and one of the finest American novels in years. It is a joyous novel, despite the elements of strife and pain, because Swados believed in life, had tremendous concern for people as individuals and society in general, and never wavered in his belief that life and society were worth the constant struggle for improvement. Swados was unapologetic about being idealistic. "How ashamed we are of our desire to do good!" he has Lumen lament. "It has become a term of derogation, as if it were worse than doing evil."

This is a novel that balances two major themes: the difference between public image and private life, and, more importantly, the middle line that the real radical must walk between bowing to the Establishment and supporting anarchy. For the real radical throws ideas, not bombs, and strives to create change and challenge, not chaos. Such a man was Harvey Swados, and such a man is his creation, Samuel Lumen.

Yet there are two big differences between the novelist and his creation which also help to make this a remarkable book. In his early fifties, Swados wrote a novel about a man nearing ninety, and made him believable. He also created, in Sam Lumen, a hero who, for all his greatness, is a grand rascal. Judging from the written record of those who knew Swados best, this makes Lumen the opposite of his creator.

Celebration also has its sad aspect, since Harvey Swados died in December of 1972, shortly after completing the novel. This book marks his death

with a special sense of loss because it is evidence that Swados was just reaching the height of his power as a novelist. His last previous novel, *Standing Fast* (1970), the book he possibly considered his major statement, is an impressive, wide-ranging, political novel, stretching from the late 1930's and the end of the Depression to the early 1960's and the beginnings of the Civil Rights movement. Through the stories of eight men and their families, it outlines the social idealism and personal integrity for which Swados never ceased to strive; but it is somewhat marred by clichéd characters and obvious plot maneuverings. With *Celebration,* Swados seemed to have found a subtlety of style and complexity of character portrayal to both counterbalance and increase his passionate voice of concern. His fiction reached that plateau of conviction that is conveyed in his better essays.

Swados was an important American writer, but never a popular one. Often he had to work at other jobs, first as a blue-collar worker, later as a college teacher. As a writer who concentrated on theme and content, he was out of step with the current vogue for stylistic posturing and black humor.

None of this stopped Swados, who simply went his own way, fighting the good fight in the honorable tradition of socially concerned American individualism. His essay, "Why Resign from the Human Race?," first written as a challenge to his class at Sarah Lawrence College, may have been the seed which germinated the Peace Corps. Out of his work on a Ford assembly line came a fine collection of nine short stories, *On the Line*

(1957), about the American worker, probably the most neglected subject in our literature. Out of his social and political concerns came the brilliant collection of essays *A Radical's America* (1962).

Among his thirteen books, he left two other story collections and five novels, of which this last is probably the best; hopefully, its publication will bring his work to the attention of the much larger body of readers that he deserves.

William Boswell

CHARLES IVES AND HIS AMERICA

Author: Frank R. Rossiter (1937-   )
Publisher: Liveright (New York). 420 pp. $12.50
Type of work: Biography
Time: 1874 to the present
Locale: The United States

A biography of Charles Ives which analyzes the composer and his music in terms of his relative isolation from the social and artistic milieu of his day

This work has generally been recognized as the most important book on Ives yet published, and in view of Ives's importance in American music it may be considered one of the most significant works on musical life in America to have appeared in recent years. It is noteworthy that the author is not, however, a musician. Frank Rossiter has his Ph.D. in American history from Princeton University, and has taught in that field at the Universities of Michigan (Ann Arbor) and Texas (Dallas). While the work centers around the life and work of Ives and the development of American music since the later nineteenth century, it is never a study of music *per se;* one will not find here an analysis of Ives's compositions or much in the way of technical information. Rather, the work, as its title suggests, is more of a social history of attitudes and traditions, as well as what might be termed a psycho-history of Ives, investigating the ways in which his development was influenced by the cultural pressures of the world in which he lived. The book is divided into two main sections, "Development" and "Recognition," with the first section primarily focused on Ives himself, and the second on a discussion of Ives's relationship to the musical world since 1921 and the work of his admirers in achieving recognition for his music.

Apart from his stature as a composer, Ives is a fascinating and complex figure, having stood outside the mainstream of American musical life during his period of greatest productivity, virtually isolated from contact with other artists, and in fact devoting his primary energies to his career as an insurance executive. It was only in the 1920's and later that his music became known, largely through the efforts of younger, *avant-garde* composers and conductors. The "Ives Legend" grew up in those years, the image of Ives as an example of the integrated artist-businessman, typically American, creating his individual style without dependence on Europe, a cantankerous Yankee, a native American genius. Rossiter sets out to cut through this legend and to come to a clear picture of the actual forces which determined Ives's relationship to his society, to musical tradition, and to the musical life of his time.

Charles Ives grew up in the small town of Danbury, Connecticut, and his family came from old colonial stock, having arrived in 1635. Although his father was a musician of somewhat *avant-garde* spirit himself, Charles grew up surrounded by a society in which classical music, as opposed to popular or folk music, was looked upon as foreign, effeminate, aristocratic, and therefore undemocratic. Rossiter cites both contemporary and modern examples of this prejudice, according to which young boys are supposed to be interested in baseball rather than ballet, and are manfully to resist having to learn to play the piano. The musical life of the nineteenth century, especially in small towns, was in fact dominated by women, and was regarded as an especially feminine province. European musicians, and artists in general, were looked upon as Bohemians, parasites, and effeminates. Ives, who accepted the cultural values of his community, was thus raised with an internal conflict, one which, contrary to the legend, he never resolved. Externally, he pursued a thoroughly respectable, genteel career, cultivating the attributes of masculinity. He mocked any music that fell agreeably upon the ears, and regarded dissonance more with a moral approbation, as a masculine sound, than with an aesthetic judgment. He marked one satirically lyrical passage in his work "andante emasculata" and jokingly referred to Rachmaninoff as "Rachnotmanenough." Rossiter makes much of the intersection of moral and aesthetic judgments in Ives's pronouncements and work, and thus approaches the question of the reasons behind his peculiarly dichotomous life from a basically psychosocial point of view. Ives is seen as caught between these accepted social values and his creative impulses, confronted with a choice, as Rossiter puts it, "between being an artist and being a good American. Ives chose to be a good

American." Thus, one may account for the inability of Ives to relate to the musical life of his time—he simply scorned most of the men who should have been his associates and supporters—and his inflexible adherence to conservative middle-class values, gentility, and Puritanism. His radicalism found expression solely in his music, but it was experimental and individualistic rather than systematic. It was only in later years, when America experienced its first generation of *avant-garde* composers, that Ives was discovered and hailed as a man before his time, the anticipator of what was to come. But these men were all committed artists, and there could be little communication between them and Ives, who for years had composed only in his free hours, and virtually in secret, never really accepting himself as an artist, or placing art first in his values.

Rossiter draws a comparison between Ives and such Russian composers as Dmitri Shostakovich and Sergei Prokofiev, both of whom were attacked by Soviet authorities as decadent, subjective, and Western in their music. Both were forced under pressure to redirect their thinking and return to a socially acceptable style. In their cases, the pressure was directed at their artistic creations specifically, rather than their life style, and was crudely, if nonetheless effectively, external. In Ives's case the pressure of society was no less forceful, although it came not from a centralized source but from an entire social system. It was inculcated from an early age and thus functioned internally. Furthermore, its object was not artistic conformity, of which Ives was never guilty, but social conformity, which in fact did characterize his whole life. But this commitment to conservative American social values as they touched upon the arts, did in fact have its effect upon his art, not only in molding his aesthetic values, but in preventing him from establishing relationships with the *avant-garde* either in Europe or in America, and enforcing an isolation which, for better or worse (and Rossiter never makes a decisive judgment in this respect) made it inevitable that the majority of Ives's work would be composed in a kind of vacuum. While this condition operated to the benefit of originality and independence, one can only guess as to the results had Ives's music been known, performed, appreciated, and criticized, and had a more active interchange with the musical world been possible.

Even when Ives's work was made known from the 1920's on, it was through a group of younger *avant-garde* composers—Nicolas Slonimsky, Henry Cowell, and John Kirkpatrick among others—who undertook the massive job of editing and in some cases deciphering scores, arranging for performance, and conducting the works. The great Fourth Symphony, composed in 1916, was not performed until 1965, when it was given its premiere by Leopold Stokowski.

In the second section of the book Rossiter traces this development in detail, and in the course of his discussion develops a virtual history of American attitudes toward the arts in the period. It is heavily ironic that one of the men most active on Ives's behalf, Henry Cowell, proved to embody Ives's worst suspicions about Bohemian artists, and the gulf that separated Ives's attitude from those of his younger supporters is evident. In 1936, Cowell, one of the most innovative American composers, theorist and founding editor of the *New Music Quarterly,* was arrested for a homosexual offense involving a minor and sentenced to fifteen years in prison. Ives, to whom even talk about sex was offensive, felt himself personally betrayed; in fact, the event struck squarely at his whole system of values. Whereas the other composers in the group sought to help Cowell, Ives broke off communication and vowed never to speak to the man again. It even appears that Ives withdrew in the late 1930's from all musicians, losing interest in promoting his own work and moving deeper into isolation. When Cowell was released from prison in 1940, his colleagues, regardless of their private opinion of his acts, accepted him warmly and helpfully as an artist, and his rehabilitation was almost instant. In 1941 he was piano soloist at the inaugural concert of the New York Philharmonic's centennial season. Ives, however, continued to refuse to see him, and it was only after Cowell announced his impending marriage, thus restoring himself to bourgeois respectability, that Ives relented.

The final pages of this section trace the subsequent rise of Ives to acclaim and renown, all dimmed by the fact that he was growing too old and handicapped to take full enjoyment of them. One is left, however, with an awareness of the severe and deep-rooted inner conflicts that lay beneath the unbending rigor of the composer's personality, and in spite of the dry tone of Rossiter's account, one cannot help but be touched by the isolation, rigidity, and loneliness of this divided man. The biographer reveals the complexity of his subject's internal life, the subterranean pressures which were the motive power behind his intense creativity— the products of which now belong to the landmarks of musical art.

Steven C. Schaber

THE COCKATOOS

Author: Patrick White (1912-   )
Publisher: The Viking Press (New York). 307 pp. $8.95
Type of work: Short novels and stories
Time: World War II to the present
Locale: Australia, Greece, and Italy

An impressive, if uneven, collection of shorter works by Australia's most important novelist

Patrick White, Australia's most impressive author, is a writer of epics —long, complicated, sprawling narratives that chronicle such things as the opening up of the Australian interior (*The Tree of Man, Voss*) or the working out of family dynasties (*The Eye of the Storm*), and feature larger-than-life characters of great force, complexity, and moral ambiguity such as Johan Voss and Hurtle Duffield (*The Vivisector*), and Elizabeth Hunter (*The Eye of the Storm*). To realize such large visions demands the full range and scope of the long novel, and few moderns have succeeded so well in realizing their intentions on such a scale.

But the short story, even the novelette, depends on focus, precision, and economy; it is a form of fictional synecdoche. When a writer of epic talents attempts to "reduce" or "concentrate" his vision into the shorter forms, his admirers must approach the products with trepidation. Must such a writer abandon his large conceptions and settle for "slick" short stories (as, for the most part, White did in his earlier collection of short pieces, *The Burnt Ones*)? Or can he make up for his loss of scale through greater selectivity and dramatic intensity?

In the case of White's *The Cockatoos,* the answer lies somewhere in between these extremes; the stories are uneven, but the best of them is extraordinary and even the weakest is interesting. In all but one narrative, White shows some awkwardness in handling these shorter forms, but the stories are sharp and provocative and the characters are memorable—if generally weak, petty, and depressing.

Four of the stories are structured around the same basic situation. An aging married couple, childless and either retired or economically settled, stagnate in dull, pointless routines. They realize, with varying degrees of insight, that their relationship is dead and their lives largely wasted. They muse about lost potentials—real and fancied—and wait for something to happen to break the monotony of their last years. In each story that something does happen—a meeting with an old friend, a flock of wild cockatoos, a husband's toothache, a stranger asking for help—allowing one or more of the characters to act out the implications of those past fantasies and present yearnings.

The most thorough exploration of the situation is "A Woman's Hand," the first and longest story in the collection. Harold and Evelyn Fazackerley are an old pair who have been forced into a premature, economically insecure retirement by the Suez crisis. Among other time-killing activities, they walk the shore and survey the beach houses with a mixture of disdain and envy. One day they meet an old friend, aging bachelor Clem Dowson, who lives in a small house well-separated from the expensive beach property. The meeting with Dowson triggers memories in the old couple—nostalgic reveries in Harold and bitter recollections of lost opportunities in Evelyn. Harold openly admires Clem's self-sufficiency: "Clem has come out of it with so much more than most of us . . . he has learnt to sit still. He has learnt to think"—but Evelyn is resentful in her silence.

This resentment is not only deep, but also long-standing, going back at least to the time, years before in Egypt, when Dowson had lived with them and rejected Evelyn's advances; she has hated him ever since. " 'Why don't I know you?' she asked him. 'If we are meant to know a person, then we do,' he replied." The meeting on the beach provides Evelyn with a chance to even things up and impose her will on her old antagonist.

But Evelyn is, of course, completely unaware of these hidden motivations. On the conscious level her machinations against Clem are done in the honest conviction that she is improving his lot by giving him the "woman's hand" he needs. So she arranges a meeting between Dowson and Nesta Pine, an apparently self-sufficient woman whose life suggests a feminine mirror image of Dowson's. Once brought together, the eccentric pair are attracted to each other and do eventually marry.

The result is disastrous, an outcome that Evelyn had instinctively expected. Nesta, used to being the strong, independent member of a female twosome, has no talent for subordination to a male ego. Dowson is too solitary and rigid to accept female companionship, and, more important, dependence upon a woman. The saddest aspect of the relationship is that both parties are deeply sensitive people who understand themselves and each other; unlike the Fazackerleys, they communicate all too well. These new contradictions, understandings, and tensions overwhelm them. Nesta has a nervous breakdown and Clem commits suicide.

Thus, Evelyn Fazackerley wins her undeclared war against the two eccentrics whose self-sufficient deviance has so deeply irritated her. But her feelings are too suppressed to allow her consciously to enjoy her triumph. Evelyn is basically not an evil or vengeful woman; she is a mediocre person trying to assert a sense of self in a world that she feels has ignored her. The story demonstrates the latent cruelty and destructive potential of mediocrity, and that is what gives it so much sinister force.

"A Woman's Hand" is provocative, almost profound fiction, and yet it does not come fully alive. The treatment of the Fazackerleys is too attenuated, that of Clem and Nesta too sketchy—and they are the more interesting characters. The action of the narrative is insufficient to support its length; the thematic implications of the story and potential complexity of the characters, on the other hand, offers more than enough material for a very long novel.

The title story in the volume is the best of the shorter pieces. Its central defect is the opposite of that seen in "A Woman's Hand"; "The Cockatoos" is too crowded with characters and incidents, and the plot manipulations are too deliberately contrived to be fully convincing. But even if somewhat forced, "The Cockatoos" is a short story of considerable power and immediacy.

Again the main couple live in a state of stagnant noncommunication. Olive and Mick Davoren are perhaps the oddest of the odd couples in the book. They have not spoken to each other ever since, as Olive reports it, "I went down to Kiama for Essie's funeral—he let my boodgie [her pet bird] die!" For seven years they have communicated to each other by written notes. Olive sits alone in her wing of the house contemplating her music (which she gave up playing a long time ago) and the memory of her Dadda; after losing his job as a bus driver, Mick wanders aimlessly about trying to sell "Miracle Openers," a gadget invented by one of his fellow drivers. Their lives are sharply altered by the arrival of a flock of wild cockatoos which take up residence in the Davoren's back yard.

Others in the neighborhood are likewise affected by the wild birds. Busby Le Cornu, a shy, inhibited spinster, begins an affair with Mick about the same time that the birds appear, and her romance, which leads to an awakening of her sensuality, is associated with the flock. To Tim Goodenough, a sensitive young boy undergoing early adolescent traumas, the birds are magical creatures, and he feels the need somehow to partake of their magic. To Mr. Figgis, the neighborhood grouch, they are "dirty, screeching, destructive brutes!"

The climax comes with sudden ferocity. At almost the same moment that the Davorens finally make physical contact with the birds and verbal contact with each other, Figgis appears with a shotgun and begins to shoot at the flock; but he kills Mick instead. This forges a bond between the two strange women, Olive and Busby, and leads to Tim Goodenough's magical connection with the birds; he keeps the body of one as a talisman.

The other two stories that utilize the "old couple" plot are somewhat less successful. "Sicilian Vespers" follows another aging, vaguely discontented female, Ivy Simpson, through a course of self-understanding via adultery. The tone is light and amusing, and White's social observations are acute, but the substance of this longish narrative is not worth the pages devoted to it. "Five-Twenty" is a shorter, more grotesque treatment of the situation. An old, semi-infirm couple sit watching rush-hour traffic, pondering their pasts and the identity of a driver who regularly appears at 5:20 in a pink car. The husband dies, and his wife, in fact or fantasy, has an affair with the mysterious driver. Although entertaining, it is hard to take this short, slick, quasi-surrealistic story very seriously.

Only two of the stories, "The Full Belly" and "The Night the Prowler," deviate significantly from the situations and themes described above— and they represent the worst and the best stories in the collection. "A Full Belly" is a bitter short tale about the ways in which a formerly aristocratic Greek family is reduced to bestiality in their attempts to survive the Nazi occupation during World War II. The peculiar environment of occupied Greece is never quite believable, and the characters are unreal; the situation is simply too extreme and complex to be rendered in twenty-five pages.

"The Night the Prowler," on the other hand, is a powerful, disturbing, deeply provocative story of disintegration and restoration. It is the one story in the volume in which White has masterfully compressed his vision into the form of the short novel and realized its potential for character intimacy and dramatic intensity.

If the other stories in the collection are about old age, paralysis, emotional deadness, and self-deception, "The Night the Prowler" is about youth, vitality, passion, and self-awareness—even at the risk of self-destruction. And if the other fictions leave one with a depressed, hopeless feeling about the possibilities of man, "The Night the Prowler," for all of its delving into psychological misery and degradation, is a powerful affirmation of the human will and spirit.

Felicity Bannister, a plain-looking young woman soon to be married to a very proper young man, is raped one night in her own bed. The experience shakes her to the core, but not in the way one would expect. It crystallizes doubts and fears that have been simmering for some time about her own identity, her relationship to her society and parents, and her feelings about the meaning and worth of life itself.

Felicity's doubts about her parents are confirmed by their reactions to the event. They care little about her state of body or mind and only worry about how it will affect their own lives and social postures. Her mother, another of White's horrendous manipulating matrons, is torn between a

fear of what it will do to their status, especially as regards the engagement, and a positive glee toward the event as gossip—she can hardly wait to phone her best friend with the news. Her father, Humphrey Bannister, is obsessed by Felicity's loss of purity ("Oh, dear Humphrey—virginity isn't a sheet of iron!" "In my day it was") and takes it as almost a personal insult. Felicity's doubts about the neighbors are likewise confirmed by their attitudes ("you could only treat the matter as though the family had gone through a serious illness"). Her doubts about her fiancé are justified by his willingness, after enough formal protest to demonstrate "understanding," to break off the engagement.

But the social rebellion is superficial. Felicity's real doubts are much deeper and more dangerous. A simple change in style from neo-Victorian to swinging modern gives her no satisfaction ("all the young men and girls . . . had similar names and interchangeable bodies"). Her new friends are irrelevant to her real needs. "She herself couldn't at first accept that frightening, still partly dormant, cone of her own will."

So she becomes a prowler herself and sets out to destroy the symbols and images that have heretofore bound her. She secretly breaks into houses much like her own and defaces and destroys, in a kind of sensuous rage, their artificial signs of material opulence, social power, and sexual indulgence. Then she wanders the park at night, encountering society's outcasts, and challenges them on their own turf: talking with drunks, mocking singers, defying leatherjackets, interrupting sex acts.

Accused by one angry lover of being "a menace to the community," she retorts fiercely: "Like hell I am! All of us here at night are on the wrong side of the railings. The difference is only in purpose." But her defiant rage is not really aimed at society or even her family; it is at herself for having absorbed so much of their weakness and for being nothing herself: "to destroy in one violent burst the nothing she was, to live, to know."

White underscores the psychological relationship between Felicity and her father and how his weakness is central to her defiance and confusion. As she slashes a picture of a successful man in the first house she ravages, she thinks "all men are soft." The rapist, it is revealed in a powerful flashback scene, was also a weakling who cowered before her dominance. Felicity finally projects this hatred of her father and herself to a cosmic level. But her regeneration also comes through a man, a man so degraded that he forces her to assert meaning and compassion in the face of his misery and despair. After her most vociferous rage against man, self, and God, Felicity wanders into an abandoned house where she finds a naked, sick, old man. Shocked, she feels a need to help him, but "the most she could do was attempt to comfort the fetid skin, with its crust and semi-cancerous moles."

When the man awakens, his words cut to the center of her being:

> 'I never believed in or expected anything of anyone. I never loved, not even myself. . . . I always saw myself as a shit. I am nothing. I believe in nothing. So you've no reason for being afraid.'
> 'I am afraid,' she admitted.

She is afraid because this old man represents the logical extension of her own ideas. Realizing this, Felicity recoils into compassion and a new sense of personal worth; in ministering to him she finds herself.

"The Night the Prowler," alone would make *The Cockatoos* a memorable collection. "A Woman's Hand" and "The Cockatoos," despite defects, are strong, stimulating narratives. And even the three lesser efforts reveal Patrick White's skill and perceptiveness. The best introduction to White's work remains his epic novels, but *The Cockatoos* deserves the attention of every serious reader of contemporary fiction.

Keith Neilson

COCKPIT

Author: Jerzy Kosinski (1933-   )
Publisher: Houghton Mifflin Company (New York). 248 pp. $8.95
Type of work: Novel
Time: The present
Locale: International

A picaresque novel whose black humor is centered on the diabolical and disinterested cleverness of its sinister anti-hero

Principal characters:
TARDEN, a refugee from Ruthenia and ex-spy
THEODORA, a widowed ex-intelligence agent who bears his child
VERONIKA, a prostitute he liberates, enriches, and murders

Critical reaction to Kosinski's *Cockpit* ranges from high aesthetic praise to sweeping moral censure. Eric Korn views the novel as a sign of Kosinki's artistic maturity:

> . . . after so many novels where the occurrence of nothing-very-much-thank-you is subjected to the most rigorous analysis, it is a relief, an entrancement, to sit open-mouthed gulping the stream of episodes—comic, hateful, compassionate even, but always astounding, the narrative cascade uncontaminated by overt metaphysic, of an artesian inventiveness like Chaucer's.

Stefan Kanfer agrees with this assessment, concluding that "Kosinski's terse, unstructured style has always created images of power and authenticity. . . . Not since Conrad has an Eastern European found so profound a voice in the English tongue." A. H. Studenmund sees *Cockpit* as a turning point for the much-publicized author (president of American P.E.N.), "successfully combining the narrative style of *The Painted Bird* and *Being There* with the epigrammatic-anecdotal style of *Steps.*"

Certainly there is continuity of style and content in this new book whose protagonist, Tarden, reminds us of the ruined boy of *The Painted Bird* (1965), "dehumanized by the brutalities of war" (Korn) as Tarden has been dehumanized by the realities of postwar repression, "peaceful coexistence," and universal espionage. Korn points out that in *Steps,* the boy has become a "man perpetually vigilant, ready for any violent or manipulative exercise of power, a survivor." It is because *Cockpit* carries the evolutionary process a step further—in the creation of Tarden as an anti-hero "beyond good and evil" and the very opposite of Dostoevski's underground man because he lives in the secure luxury of high-rises from which he swoops down, like one of Tolkien's Nazgûl, to prey upon the innocent—that other critics have considered the book an irresponsible moral outrage. Peter S. Prescott calls it "the least tolerable of Kosinski's novels," while Jonathan Baumbach dismisses it as a "mix of poetic justice and whimsical viciousness." Christopher Ricks, writing in the *New York Review of Books,* questions the morality of "retailing such sick fantasizing," as ministering

> to wholesale sickness. . . . A writer has a duty—as even Kipling at his most

cruel realized—to help human beings, not to thrill to cruel imaginings. . . . Tarden . . . is the diseased fashionable novelistic imagination . . . licensed to commit the cruelest irresponsibilities in the name of administering salutary shocks to the complacent liberal imagination.

What Ricks fails to recognize is that Kosinski's brand of satire is a departure from the kind of humanism expressed by Byron's Don Juan when that hero said, "And if I laugh at any mortal thing, 'tis that I may not weep." There is no redeeming social value in a mirror that simply reflects the possible moralities of the times; that is what *Cockpit* does, dramatizing the moral Vonnegut attached to his *Mother Night*: "We are what we pretend to be." Vonnegut, however, went on to add, "so we should be very careful about what we pretend to be." The difference between the visions of the two men— both satirists, both masters of the terse reportorial style, both manipulators of episodic structures that fall into the reader's lap like a house of cards which he must reassemble thematically for himself—is an all-important matter of emphasis and perspective. Where Vonnegut still believes in humanity, and therefore continues to consolidate an increasingly necessary, increasingly desperate, sense of humor, Kosinski has no such faith, no hope, no humor, and, most importantly, no love. Tarden is Skinnerian man, whose only identity is that of a data processor, an image projector, a machine self-trained to perform whatever function it needs to maintain its vital energies in self-stimulating channels. This is the hero totally liberated from society, taking

with him as he escapes, no social conscience, but instead only all the tools society has sharpened through the centuries to destroy itself. The scene from which the novel draws its title is essentially horrible because it points out the horror within us: a pilot who under orders from the air force computer that guides his plane, has killed thousands of unknown people in Vietnam, is unwilling to kill one woman by switching on the radar button even when Tarden offers to pay him more than his entire combat pay. Tarden is amazed that assassination bothers a mass murderer, when it seems much less momentous to him than destroying entire villages. And we realize how much easier it is for us to conspire in wars than in murders.

Tarden is the ultimate anti-hero with a thousand faces, none of which, we finally understand, is his own. Kosinski destroys the very concept of the self upon which we have confidently relied so long. Tarden is only the accumulation of his acts, made possible through inherent and learned abilities, applied by pure serendipity: it is the same to him if he causes a city to suffer from an imaginary epidemic, surreptitiously urinates in his wine glass at a banquet, presides over the gang rape of an old girl friend, helps recover a socialite's missing diamonds, or performs superhuman acrobatics on skis at the risk of his life.

The archetypal model for Kosinski's amoral protagonist (for whom all other human beings are automatically antagonists) is Homer's Odysseus. In that story, so different from the heroic war epic in which Achilles finds his glorious identity in death, we meet a very opposite kind of man. Odysseus is not part god— he is the first fully human character in Western literature. During the course of the epic named after him, Odysseus learns from the goddess Athena what it takes to be fully human. From that education he derives his epithet, "many-turning," and the mythological figure to whom he corresponds—Proteus, the old man of the sea who is constantly assuming different shapes. And so Odysseus is the first professional liar, fabricating a new story on each new occasion until his defensive fear of speaking the truth becomes habitual. The truth, Homer perceives, is, after all, relative to the situation; it is not absolute, in human experience. Through the history of Western thought since the *Odyssey* this view of the relativity, and essential inaccessibility, of truth has provided a contrapuntal tension underlying the great products of the human mind—the plays of Shakespeare, *Don Quixote,* the novels of Proust, Joyce, and Mann, the stories of Kafka and Borges. Kosinski follows in this tradition, as does his Polish near-contemporary Wittold Gombrowicz, whose *Ferdydurke* was banned in Poland because of its anarchical implications.

Reading *Cockpit* is indeed a frightening experience to anyone who maintains a vestige of traditional morality and social idealism. The world in which Tarden operates with such disastrous repercussions is the world predicted by Huxley and Orwell. The simple difference between the reality of *1984* and the reality of *Cockpit* is that the individual, not the State, triumphs—if "triumph" is the right word to describe the bellicose

coexistence Tarden enjoys with the system that has taught him its own paranoid and deadly methods. His apartments, identical fortresses of gadgetry he has outfitted in cities around the world, are locked with three-digit combinations from the inside so that his lovers become his victims more effectively; the rooms are equipped with concealed viewing places from which advanced photographic equipment records the sordid acts he stage-manages, admittedly for no purpose. Tarden is the thorough technician who realizes that technique by itself, though it rules the world, implies no responsibility, no relationship to truth. He sees a woman hit by a car and immediately begins snapping pictures. Later, "I selected shots for the cab driver that could best prove his innocence. . . . The woman's set of photos, which I mailed to her relatives, suggested she had been hit by a careless driver who hadn't noticed her crossing." Those who consider Tarden's behavior and attitude cynical fail to comprehend the scathing depth of Kosinski's vision; Tarden is only being realistic. We live today with images that are more powerful, more meaningful to us, than their supposedly corresponding realities. "People notice only what they want to," Tarden remarks, to explain a particularly petty and bizarre trick. At a uniform-maker's in Florence, he has himself fitted in a uniform of his own design—once the tailor accepts an enormous sum of money in lieu of a simple explanation.

"Exactly what mood do you want your uniform to convey?" He stressed the word "mood."

"Power, but restrained power. Importance, but subdued importance."

Tarden recognizes in the Italian tailor's question a confirmation of his own observations. And no one questions his uniform, just as in Vonnegut's *The Sirens of Titan,* no one asks *which* government is sending them to Mars for $9 an hour. We live in a world of surfaces, moving too fast and in too many directions to be aware of what may lie beneath. We can pretend to be anything and succeed, as long as we move fast enough, with convincing camouflage, "moving horizontally through space, invading other people's spheres,"

and destroying them if they themselves are not moving with equal speed. Kosinski's world is a cockpit from which only the pilot with quickest reflexes can hope to control, or even see, the life through which he rushes faster than time has ever flown for man before. Socrates is said to have remarked that "the mask an actor wears is apt to become his face." Kosinski has recognized that the necessity for rapid change of masks lies in modern man's terrifying discovery that he has no face.

Kenneth John Atchity

THE COLLECTED STORIES OF HORTENSE CALISHER

Author: Hortense Calisher (1911-   )
Publisher: Arbor House (New York). 502 pp. $15.00
Type of work: Short stories

A collection of three volumes of previously published stories, together with one long story not published before in book form, "The Summer Rebellion," by a modern master of the genre

"A story is an apocalypse," says Hortense Calisher, "served in a very small cup." The particular reason why the cup must be small is that each story wants to be considered discreetly, "in its own company only." Other stories change it, even when they are all by the same hand. Notice that Calisher does not intend to describe the proverbial tempests in teacups, great events reduced in scale to a small fable, so that their importance seems diminished. Her stories are truly apocalyptic. They deal with terrible moments of discovery, of illumination. In the sense of James Joyce's "epiphanies," these moments are insights that make whole and sacramental the fragmented pieces of everyday life.

In her most recent collection of thirty-six stories, Calisher includes complete *In the Absence of Angels,* and all the stories, but not the title novelettes, from two later volumes— *Tale for the Mirror* and *Extreme Magic.* Because the three prior collections are "only weakly chronological," she arranges the stories according to a different "natural rhythm," by contrasting themes. Yet it is unfortunate that Calisher neglects to date the time of completion or of initial magazine publication for each story, because the reader might care to know how her art has matured, how her subjects have evolved or

changed. Certainly, many of the stories relate to her longer fiction, either to adumbrate their final expression or to serve as alternative patterns of a single idea. For example, in "One of the Chosen," Spanner—as Calisher mentions— "faintly anticipates" the Judge in *The New Yorker* (1969); the young, sexually ambiguous Peter Birge of "In Greenwich There Are Many Gravelled Walks" is "very close, in the writer's sympathies," to the hero of *Eagle Eye* (1973); Eleanor and her baby in "The Rabbi's Daughter" are "kin" to the young mother and child in *Textures of Life* (1963); and the bored aristocratic women in "Songs My Mother Taught Me," who, to startle their smugly vapid male companions, pull off their blouses in a pantomime half-modest, half-insulting strip tease, foreshadow the heroine in *Queenie* (1971).

Other stories, especially those of the Elkin family, first published in *The New Yorker,* are quasi-autobiographical, inasmuch as they concern, in disguised form, the author's "relations." Kinny Elkins of "The Gulf Between," says Calisher, "is my real brother, as a sibling seen." And the sensitive Hester, one of the most skillfully observed of her characters, is a portrait drawn, it is reasonable to say, from her own life. Just as the stories provide insight into Calisher's personal vision, so they offer to her readers valuable clues about the direction that her later fiction will take. Like the Salinger-watchers of the late 1950's and early 1960's who followed with eager attention the adventures of the Glass family, many Calisher-watchers of our time read the partly autobiographical Hester stories to discover more information in disguised form, the author's "rela- about the Elkins family. Yet, unlike J. D. Salinger, who seems to have abandoned his Glass family perma- nently, Calisher promises her readers that she "might at any time return" to Hester and her family.

One hopes that she will keep her promise, for the Elkins stories, among her finest, sharply etch her major con- cerns. Typically, she contrasts the themes of freedom and restraint, capriciousness and prudence, romance and disillusionment. In "The Gulf Between," for example, twelve-year- old Hester and her younger brother enjoy the brief excitement of an ad- venturous day. They skate toward Broadway, race down the top of a hill to explore a new sidewalk, win- dow-shop the stores of their delight, then dawdle homeward. In the back of their minds is apprehension. Their parents have been quarreling. In bed that evening, Hester cannot sleep, fitfully alert to the sounds of a men- acing argument. From a child's view- point, her parents' antagonism seems to tear her into two selves. With a maturity beyond her years, she weeps "sparse grudging tears," sensing how she is "flawed with their difference." She recognizes, as in a shattered dream, the disenchantment of her daytime hopes for joy.

Often in Calisher, a character's

awareness of defeat is the beginning, not the end, of consciousness. Her protagonists do not collapse in self- pity when their dreams fail. The fail- ure is to be expected, a circum- stance of reality. So disenchantment strengthens the heart, restraint dis- ciplines the spirit. In "The Rabbi's Daughter," a young mother—sensi- tive, intelligent, and capable—is burdened with the unromantic re- sponsibilities of caring for her house- hold. She is forced to renounce, to compromise. Even a rabbi's daughter, after all, must wash dishes. In the "erosive, gradual . . . chip-chipping of circumstance," she foresees her life settling into a routine of tedium. People count on her: her relatives, her husband, her baby. To live more expansively, freely, as she had wished, she must deny others. For the time being, she acquiesces to the demands of duty. Yet she is by no means con- tent, nor is she defeated by circum- stances. She perceives that "this will have to stop," for she will not allow the denied half of her to "persist, venomously arranging for the ruin" of her fullest capabilities. Although Calisher is not an activist, she shares with more conventionally feminist writers a belief that a woman's chief duty is to develop her special abilities with independence and integrity.

Nevertheless, Calisher understands that one's independence must be earned, often at the risk of injuring loved ones. She deplores easy choices, for they are mostly selfish. In "Songs My Mother Taught Me," the well- bred, respectable narrator describes a "semi-diplomatic" dinner party at which the guests, stuffy fatuous peo- ple, react at first with shock and then capriciousness as Lady Catherine strips off her blouse. With near-hysterical abandon, the other women follow Lady Catherine's example. Only Frau Ewig, a plump, corseted matron, and the narrator prudently remain suited. Though tempted by the delirium of the moment to join the strippers, the narrator is restrained by the notion of her mother's disapproval. Granted that "moral instruction by moral illustration has long since disappeared from the training of the young," some measure of discipline remains. And Calisher suggests that self-discipline, no matter whether it deprives us of our fullest joys, shapes our characters.

"In Greenwich There Are Many Gravelled Walks," an early story, also shows the risks of total freedom. Susan, Robert Vielum's twenty-year-old daughter, visits her father, who is now living openly as a homosexual with his lovers. Their meeting is strained. The relationship between father and daughter, each pretending to accept without moral censure the presence of the other, is outwardly casual but at the roots poisoned. Susan is contemptuous not only of her father and his companions—including the neurotic homosexual who commits suicide in Robert's apartment—but also of her mother, who practices a corrupt form of serial monogamy, experimenting with a succession of husbands. Still vulnerable,

Susan longs for the capacity "to care." Calisher makes clear to the reader that the girl's life, disoriented from her experiences with her promiscuous parents, is fated to destruction. Mrs. Grundy, the Victorian symbol of prudery, "wasn't around much," Susan says, when she grew up. The reader understands that Mrs. Grundy's departure from the scene has not been wholly without loss. Some discipline, some sense of decorum and responsibility is necessary to create civilization.

Within the "apocalyptic" small cups of her stories, Calisher ranges widely. Her characters, for the most part middle-class urbanites, are brilliantly realized, not simply from the exterior but also from inside. A master stylist, she captures an entire scene in the brush stroke of a few words, distills a poignant emotion in a gesture. In "The Hollow Boy," the closing of a window reveals tragedy; in "A Wreath for Miss Totten," a classroom recitation fixes itself in memory; in "The Scream of Fifty-seventh Street," a stifled cry symbolizes mankind's terrible pity, terrible guilt. "I go to the short-story world," Calisher writes, "most perhaps for the multiplicity of its voices. . . ." These voices, like seared memory, remain in the consciousness of her readers.

Leslie B. Mittleman

THE CONSERVATIONIST

Author: Nadine Gordimer (1923-   )
Publisher: The Viking Press (New York). 252 pp. $7.95
Type of work: Novel
Time: The present
Locale: South Africa

The story of a wealthy industrialist who will go to any lengths to conserve his privileged way of life

Principal characters:
MEHRING, a wealthy white South African industrialist and land-owner
TERRY, his son
JACOBUS, one of Mehring's black workers

The twentieth century has witnessed a tremendous change in the concept of the novelistic "hero," a change which is continued with the character of Mehring in Nadine Gordimer's *The Conservationist.* Although Mehring does not have a total realization of the mediocrity of his life and the common, undemanding goals he sets for himself, he does catch a glimpse of his transience and replaceability, and demonstrates an unnamed urge to belong to something higher than himself or his social circle. His subliminal longing brings him to a desire for a sense of roots, of belonging, but he attempts to fulfill this desire by acquiring land and wealth in a country where the white man, as only a newcomer, has at best a questionable right to pursue self-aggrandizement. Consequently, his actions and reactions express the unconscious fact that in order to "conserve" his land and way of life, molding it to a sense of his own self, he must destroy much of what is indigenous to the land: the people, their societal organization, and their culture. Mehring is a wealthy industrialist who realizes that his financial stability no longer depends on his

maintenance of a slaveholding system. Rather than pull out of the situation, however, he continues to order his life in the conventional ways. He has a mistress who disdains his money, and a farm in the country which serves both as a tax shelter and as a stand-by bucolic rendezvous setting.

Although it cannot be said that Mehring actually identifies himself with his farm, he does grow into a certain reserved fondness for its elementary life. Mehring realizes that his weekly visits to the farm are more than mere token gestures. The land is *his,* substantiated by the sense of responsibility he begins to feel toward it. The differences between the city and the country become as vivid as his ideas about the feelings one has in paying for a woman as opposed to paying for land; in the case of the woman, he enjoys a negative sense of freedom stemming from lack of reciprocity and responsibility, whereas from his land he gains the positive sense of freedom that is inherent in ownership. Similarly, the city offers Mehring the opportunity to work and earn profits, but also allows him to close himself off from it at any time.

The rural areas, by contrast, bring him face to face with the basic aspects of himself, and with a feeling of life and death that alludes to those roots for which he longs. It is this aspect of the land that he tries to conserve.

Consequently, what Gordimer accomplishes in Mehring is a picture of the dichotomies to which man is reduced; yet she avoids making value judgments. Although city life consists of a harried montage of parties, social invitations, and dinner engagements, Mehring does not disdain it. And although the country brings him as close as he ever comes to experiencing a communion with something beyond the immediate, he does not prefer it. As he intimates to the daughter of a business associate, he knows that if his work becomes abhorrent or disgusting he can leave it by simply walking away. He chooses not to, however, and in fact makes no choices whatsoever.

What Mehring is most interested in conserving is his way of life, one that is substantially undefined so that it can accommodate dichotomies that demand no choice, just as the vast social differences between himself and the blacks is one he chooses neither to question nor resolve. Relatively late, Mehring comes to realize that what he sincerely wants to preserve is a sense of himself within his own pattern of life.

To perpetuate this pattern, Mehring plans to prepare his son Terry to carry on the tradition. His farm, begun as a calculated tax shelter and rendezvous place, thus becomes a legacy which he attempts to hand down to an estranged son seen seldom and briefly. Mehring's dream of an idyllic family estate peopled by his son and grandchildren is foiled for several reasons. First of all, Terry shares little, if any, of his father's values, and opts to leave the country and live with his mother in New York rather than spend a year in conscription with the Republic of South Africa. Second, Mehring works himself into believing that Terry is homosexual, and consequently will not reproduce heirs for his dynasty. Even more significant are the sociological effects of the blacks' lives on the farm and surrounding area. There is white alarmist talk, half in jest, of not being able to maintain land for more than another generation, for by then black rule will have taken place. The fear has a dampening effect on all the plans of the whites. Gordimer creates a mood of fear and tension through her descriptions of the blacks' meetings with their drum music, and through her technique of filtering events through Mehring's biased point of view.

One symbol in particular ties the different themes of *The Conservationist* together: that of the egg. The egg symbol appears in three prominent scenes, at each time fulfilling a different function. The pale freckled eggs mentioned in the opening line of the novel are a brilliant, delicate commodity, both to the black children who play with them in awe, and to Mehring, who wants to preserve them to prevent the rapid decrease of guinea fowl on his farm. The children's involvement is one of innocent fascination with one of life's secrets, but Mehring's interest provides symbolic groundwork for Gordimer's complex exploration of what it is to be a conservationist.

The egg emerges again in a more threatening and immediate way during Mehring's visit with his son. The boy casually displays a gift he has bought for his mother, "a semi-precious stone in the shape of an egg." Although the father says nothing to the boy about it, the egg is an annoyance to him. Again, he sees it in terms of a commodity. It will serve no purpose; he envisions it will sit neglected on a table in the mother's New York apartment, gathering dust. And, it is threatening because it tells of the boy's affection for his mother —an affection he has never felt for his father.

The final appearance of the egg symbol does not involve Mehring. The black worker Izak sees an odd, egg-shaped insignia being painted on the side of a water tank. He has seen people wearing the sign, and feels a tremendous urge to participate, because, as he tells the Indian shop-keeper who is painting it, it gives him a sense of belonging. The Indian, however, refuses to stock the egg-shaped symbols in his store. Thus, the symbolism in this section helps to create an atmosphere of need and unfulfilled longing; Izak, ironically, never realizes that the emblem is a peace sign.

The novel concludes as powerfully as it began. Death opens the action of the novel, with the appearance of an anonymous black man's body on the farm—an incident which gives Mehring his first notion of mortality. Death moves closer with the suicide of a business associate at a time when Mehring is increasingly questioning the meaning of his life. When death finally catches up with him, it comes in an arbitrary and unexpected fashion. Despite all the economic and social differences between races that have been underscored throughout the course of the novel, Mehring's death is just as solitary and anonymous as that of the murdered black man. The novel comes full circle, then, when Mehring attains the only communion he is able to have with the land—when it consumes him in his grave.

Bonnie Fraser

CRAZY SALAD
Some Things About Women

Author: Nora Ephron
Publisher: Alfred A. Knopf (New York). 201 pp. $7.95
Type of work: Essays
Time: The present
Locale: The United States

Twenty-five informal, sensible, often witty glimpses behind the feminist curtain in America today, exposing with pointed prose what it is like to be a woman in the 1970's

In one of the pieces in this collection, Nora Ephron discusses what may be the chief difficulty a female writer faces today: honesty. Using several personal examples, Ephron explains that as a writer she feels an obligation to be objective and honest, but as a woman she feels an equally strong need to support the Movement, or, at least, not to damage it. The conflict arises in a number of ways, such as when she is called upon to review a book by a woman writer, a book dealing with an important topic and making some points with which Ephron personally agrees, but, at the same time, a badly written, self-indulgent, and poorly researched book. What is she to do? Some women tell her to gloss over the faults, to avoid criticizing a book which might help the Movement; she is counseled to be a good Sister. Such an approach may be good politics, Ephron agrees, but it is bad criticism and bad writing.

To her credit, in this collection of articles written for several different magazines, Nora Ephron is never guilty of even slight equivocation. She is sharp and honest, exposing herself when necessary and others when she feels obliged to do so. She does not attack for the sake of the attack, and often, because of her fairness, she is able to provide refreshing insights on old subjects and familiar personalities. Ephron's political orientation has not limited her vision as a writer. Instead, she uses it as one more tool among many to produce her vivid pictures of women in America.

As an intelligent woman and a feminist, Nora Ephron has no patience with sexual stereotypes. Many of her essays deal in varying degrees with the role-stereotyping which still is prevalent in America today. In "A Few Words About Breasts" she writes with humor and sensitivity about the often traumatic experience of a young girl's early development (or lack of development). Because of social pressures, women themselves often feel compelled to make competitive remarks about breast size, about sexual roles, and about the clichés that label a person feminine or masculine. These clichés limit the options open to individuals, and the Women's Movement is, in the fundamental sense, about options. Even today, as Ephron points out in "On Never Having Been a Prom Queen," beauty or the lack of it can limit one's options. Sexual behavior and the relations between the sexes cannot change unless our sexual fantasies change. Many of the conscious and unconscious ways men and women treat one another have to do with romantic and sexual fantasies that are deeply ingrained in society and literature. Perhaps the present generation of men and women will never be entirely free of these stereotypes, but the next generations hopefully will be truly liberated.

Ephron is perhaps at her best when writing about the desperation which fills the lives of many women today. In "The Girls in the Office," she points out that society makes women believe that to be with a man, any man, on whatever terms, is better than being alone. One senses that this desperation lurks beneath the lives of the people in her consciousness-raising group, a weekly meeting of women that offered the fun of being both exhibitionist and voyeur. But the confessions turned into a weekly soap opera, she explains, and no one really cared about anybody else. Each woman waited for her own opportunity to speak, to reveal her own misery. Consciousness-raising groups, Ephron implies, are tied in with the current term "rapping"— which is a process in which people in groups pretend that they are not simply self-absorbed because they are talking *at* one another. Ephron admits that her own life has not been untouched by its moments of desperation, and she is both poignant and funny about it, and always, one feels, honest.

But basically Nora Ephron is a reporter, and a good one. Her accounts of events ranging from the Women's Caucus at the 1972 Democratic National Convention in Miami to the Pillsbury Bake Off to the strug-

gles of some of the women involved in the Watergate scandal are objective, clear-sighted, and sensitive as well as touched with a levelheaded humor that is often missing in partisan reporting about causes and struggles. Ephron is clear about her own position, but she never lets it cloud her vision. As a result, this volume gives the reader an unusual, and quite valuable, picture of society.

The spectacle of Betty Friedan, Gloria Steinem, Bella Abzug, Shirley Chisholm, and other women leaders battling it out at the 1972 Democratic Convention is awe-inspiring. While individuals such as Shirley MacLaine and Marlo Thomas maneuvered on one level and Germaine Greer took notes, the feminist wheelers and dealers fought for their lives, for their beliefs, for their political futures. Nora Ephron candidly reports the infighting among the Movement's leaders, the misunderstandings, the antagonisms, the mistakes and petty jealousies, and the small triumphs. At the same time, one part of her consciousness holds back, in order to maintain personal perspective. There is about some of these women, she implies, a quality which she does not understand. When Gloria Steinem weeps over a political slight, she thinks: "*I* have never cried over anything remotely political in my life." Yet, Ephron *cares* about what these women are doing, and this gives her reporting an additional edge. Her writing combines the personal perspective with the objective technique of traditional reporting; the result is less flashy than the "New Journalism" of Tom Wolfe, yet is related to it.

A number of essays explore the

personalities of individual women, including Dorothy Parker, Julie Nixon Eisenhower, and Linda Lovelace. When her preconceptions about an individual are altered, Nora Ephron admits it and then explains how the change of attitude came about and why. In articles about persons such as Rose Mary Woods and Martha Mitchell, it is clear that Ephron has done her homework. She uncovers unexpected facets in these women, and presents the story as well as she is able, from their point of view. One almost feels that she admires certain personality traits in Woods and Mitchell; at least, she never stoops to mockery or easy witticisms at the expense of her subjects. Any humor that arises from her writing is inherent in the subject and caught by her shrewd eye. Above all, she does not indulge in condescension either to achieve laughs or to show her own superiority.

The longest as well as the most controversial article in this book is the one titled "Dealing with the, uh, Problem," about the marketing of feminine hygiene sprays. This is a piece of genuine reportorial research and is fascinating simply because of the facts that the author has amassed. At the same time, Ephron sees this entire phenomenon as perhaps the ultimate absurdity of the free-enterprise system, capitalism, and advertising. Millions of dollars have been spent on creating a product and building an imaginary "need" for a product that is considered demeaning by women's liberationists, unnecessary by consumerists, and dangerous by doctors. Yet, "in spite of the widely shared belief among these groups that the product is perhaps *the* classic example of a bad idea whose time has come," the feminine hygiene spray appears to be here to stay. In the long essay, Ephron traces the history of this product, from its origins in Europe, its development by American companies, the search for inoffensive but suggestive names, and the all-out efforts to sell the product to the American woman. The essay is a classic because it reveals so vividly the extremes to which merchandising can and often does reach. By quoting the men at the cosmetic companies, the people at the advertising agencies, psychologists, doctors, and others involved in the history of the product, Ephron exposes a dramatic and amazing segment of the American economic world, and shows how it dictates human needs and wants by appealing to fears, insecurities, and social prejudices. This one essay will inevitably be quoted and reprinted for years to come.

Crazy Salad is a collection, and like many collections suffers from being dragged together from different sources. However, the themes of the different pieces are united by Nora Ephron's consistent integrity and her continuing interest not only in women's rights but also in human rights. The author is a feminist, but she is also a humanist, and a prose stylist of grace and wit.

Bruce D. Reeves

CRUCIAL CONVERSATIONS

Author: May Sarton (1912-   )
Publisher: W. W. Norton and Company (New York). 156 pp. $5.95
Type of work: Novel
Time: The present
Locale: Upper-class suburbia of a large northeastern city

The story of a middle-aged woman's search for an identity independent of her husband and children

Principal characters:
> REED WHITELAW, a middle-aged businessman
> POPPY WHITELAW, his wife
> HARRY, SUSIE, AND EMERSON, their children
> EVELYN STODDARD, Poppy's mother
> CECELIA WHITELAW, Reed's mother
> PHILIP SOMERSWORTH, the Whitelaws' best friend
> KATHY FLANAGAN, a policewoman, Philip's mistress

The media charts the divorce between husband and wife, between parent and child, between citizen and republic, between member and churches. Divorce seems to have become a way of life for most Americans. May Sarton's *Crucial Conversations* analyzes the divorce syndrome at its roots, in the interdependence of the family and society. In this work the disintegration of the family mirrors that of the society; the disintegration of America's moral values is observed in the family. The novel is a *post facto* account of why one particular divorce took place, a detective story which takes on universal significance.

True to Stephen Dedalus' requirements for great art, May Sarton's craftsmanlike, objective control gives *Crucial Conversations* wholeness, harmony, and radiance. As Philip Somersworth struggles to understand the sudden decision of Poppy Whitelaw to divorce her husband of twenty-seven years, the reader discovers several complexly interwoven themes in the novel. First, Poppy, herself an artist, is in search of a personal wholeness, harmony, and *claritas*— her moment of personal discovery. It is such a moment, when she understands the relationship of herself, her husband, and their best friend, that makes her decide to leave. What the other individuals concerned and what the American society at large has to do with her decision is yet to be learned. Poppy condemns not only those who compromise their "essential self, the conscience" by lying to themselves, but those who hide their corruption through hypocrisy. Yet, such compromises and lies are what link Poppy's life with the lives of others, even of such people as corrupt government officials. Thus, the novel is not simply an exploration of the development of one woman stifled and suffocated by marriage, but an exploration of the numerous layers of relationships between all ages and sexes of society, seen in microcosm within one family. In addition, it shares certain features with the long-established genre of novels about growing up, although in *Crucial Con-*

versations, the pains of growing up are not limited to the young—Philip and Poppy are in their fifties. It becomes increasingly clear that the suffering and self-testing associated with youth is experienced by people of every age; those who cease to search and suffer, who wall themselves off from painful growth (as does Reed), become walking fossils.

The novel begins with the shock and anger felt by Reed Whitelaw and his friend, Philip (Pip) Somersworth over a letter left behind by Poppy Whitelaw, announcing her intent to divorce Reed and seek a new life for herself before it is too late. After twenty-seven years as a housekeeper/mother/wife/amateur artist, Poppy at fifty feels that she has only a few years left to live and grow as an individual and as an artist. Surprisingly to them, she links her own decision to the discoveries of the deep inner corruption of Watergate, which managed, at least for a while, to preserve the surface of the government as good and decent. In each of the main trio of characters, Poppy's decision touches off moments of self-revelation, of anger and violence, of cruelty and fear of the unknown. Each becomes more aware of the other's and his own self-centeredness, lack of true compassion, and, finally, lack of completion as an individual.

This journey to awareness is most obvious in Philip, whose sensitive reactions and education process distinguish the novel. While speaking as a friend to the couple's mothers and children, he comes to realize that he, like Poppy and Reed, has failed to realize his own potential. He has borrowed off their home and security, and as a result is being used as a buffer, and finally as a garbage can for their refuse. At the beginning of the novel, he muses on how little we know our neighbors; by the middle, he realizes how little he knew of himself; by the end, he, like Poppy, has decided to fight for his own self-survival, even if it means abandoning the complacent happiness of the past.

Although she is actually present in the novel for only a short time, Poppy dominates the conversations from which the title is taken. The root of Poppy's decision, the desire for an honest, authentic existence, for an integrity uncompromised by lies to herself or to society, by guilt, by false fronts, or by a compartmentalized life, is questioned by Reed and Philip's contention that in real life, compromise is a necessity—one which Poppy has never had to face. Sarton also makes clear that Reed is as little understood by Poppy as she is by him. Even her mother, Evelyn, states that Poppy is like a child, a case of arrested development because of her marriage, unaware of what she wants. Poppy, however, in contrast to the two men, recognizes her own need to mature; she accurately analyzes the last ten years of all their lives as empty habit, and bravely reaches out, although aware of the risk, to become the complete, whole kind of person that her mother already is.

Reed Whitelaw, although occasionally over-simplified as an insensitive, chauvinistic, amoral, capitalistic male, develops as a more empathetic figure than the reader might at first expect. A self-made business man, he has tried valiantly, if insensitively, to provide a happy life for his wife and children. He really cannot understand why his wife would leave him —which is probably the strongest evidence for his wife's argument that he has become hardened and cut off from reality by his success. He has become accustomed to making decisions that hurt others, not just to make a profit, but in order to survive.

One such decision (which Poppy later cites as a turning point in their marriage) occurs when Reed, totally ignoring her objections, fires half of his employees. Philip, sympathizing with Reed, points out that if Reed had not taken this action, the total workers of the plant would have been dismissed when it went bankrupt. However, not all of Reed's decisions, such as his appropriation of another man's invention (which resulted in legal action), are so easy to explain or excuse. Eventually, one of Reed's callous, amoral actions leads to a serious break in his family, when he insists that his son serve in Vietnam rather than following his own morals and becoming a Conscientious Objector. Reed's insensitivity to others is further revealed when he insists to Philip

that he, of course, could never be expected to both work and run the house, although his wife's talent should be easily satisfied by an expensive hobby house, where she can work when not preoccupied by more important affairs relating to him or to the children. Yet this basic assumption that his work is true work and that his wife's "vocation" is secondary, while totally false, nevertheless cuts in two directions. Reed has indeed made the living for the family, and it is easy for Poppy and the children, who have lived comfortably off him, to condemn his morals.

There are no totally right or wrong, pure or corrupt characters in *Crucial Conversations*. Instead, the author treats us to the diversity and fickleness of humanity as writers have found it in every age, amazingly abundant but inconsistent and wayward. Sarton's depiction of characters, symbolic setting, and concise yet comprehensive structure and style, successfully combine to illuminate problems experienced by mankind in this and every other age.

Ann E. Reynolds

THE DEAD FATHER

Author: Donald Barthelme (1931-   )
Publisher: Farrar, Straus and Giroux (New York). 177 pp. $6.95
Type of work: Novel

A tale of high farce and sophisticated satire based on the classic myth of a hero's need to survive and surpass his father

Principal characters:
THE FATHER, a prototypal father of epic stature
THOMAS, his son
JULIE, Thomas' wife

Donald Barthelme, the *New Yorker's* madman in residence, has previously published several collections of short stories (*Come Back, Dr. Caligari; Unspeakable Practices, Unnatural Acts; City Life; Sadness*) and one novel (*Snow White*). Each has been experimental, provoking, and slightly insane. Each has employed bits and pieces of myth and folklore. Each has paid its dues to Kafka, Beckett, Ionesco, Robbe-Grillet, and Borges. Each has had parts that were not readily accessible to most readers. In *The Dead Father* he has created his most sustained work and his most mature, if the Absurd can ever be mature. In it he deals with the universal experience that all sons must endure: the burial of the dead father. Here is a theme that in other writers might be at best tragedy and at worst melodrama. With Barthelme, it becomes high farce and sociopsychological satire, if such a genre exists, at the epic and mythic levels. As always with Barthelme, the critical vocabulary one develops for standard genres fails, for he is not interested in plot, nor is he precisely interested in character. His interest is in the total cultural response to this universal experience, including all past myths, legends, and tragedies.

Other literary fathers have died and children have buried them in their time: one thinks of *Hamlet, King Lear, Oedipus Rex,* and *Finnegan's Wake.* Barthelme weaves them all into his tale, and draws on all of the familiar epics as well: *Beowulf, The Odyssey,* the *Old Testament. The Dead Father* is wrought on epic proportions; the Father himself is a giant of a man, literally and figuratively. It requires an entire team of men hauling on cables to pull him cross-country to his grave. Bulldozers are needed to fill the pit. Barthelme's treatment of his material is always surreal in the manner of Samuel Beckett and Eugene Ionesco. The structure of the work is episodic and picaresque; one chapter does not lead logically to the next, except that they take place in a chronological sequence. There is no suspense; the reader knows from the beginning that the story ends with the grave. The Dead Father may think that he is on a quest for the golden fleece that will restore his life, but his son Thomas, knowing where they are going, humors him as best he can. When Thomas is cajoling the Father into the enormous grave, the Father asks if there is no fleece. Julie, Thomas' wife, lifts her skirt. "Quite golden, said the Dead Father. Quite ample."

There are no tears, there is no sentimentality; Thomas never grieves the old man's passing. Instead there is a series of object lessons in the problems of living with an epic father and of getting rid of him figuratively and psychologically when he is dead. There is no tragedy here, only catharsis from start to finish. In the prologue, where the Dead Father is described as of a size comparable to the sleeping giant figure in William Carlos Williams' *Paterson,* we are told that he "controls what Thomas is thinking, what Thomas has always thought, what Thomas will ever think, with exceptions." There's the universal rub: the interminable influence of the past on the present— Ibsen called it *Ghosts.* The son can never be apart; he always has his Dead Father in his blood and mind.

The novel is divided into twenty-three chapters. Following Chapter Seventeen the action is interrupted by *A Manual for Sons*—the play within the play. *A Manual for Sons* also has twenty-three divisions, containing apothegms for recognizing and dealing with various sorts of tyrannical fathers. In its closing divisions, the manual assures Thomas that "memory is more potent than the living presence of a father." Thomas can never become absolutely himself. The son should refrain from parricide only because "It is not necessary to slay your father, time will slay him." The true task of a son is not to kill his father but to become his father, to "reproduce every one of the enormities" found in the manual. Thus the sword is double-edged. Not only can the son never be rid of his father, but in time will only become more like him, but "a paler version." Thus he will always know that he is never the man that his father was. As Julie comments, "Seems a little harsh."

In the course of the cross-country hauling, Thomas slowly strips his Dead Father of the symbols of power. First he takes the beautiful jeweled buckle. Next he takes the enormous sword and then the passport. Finally, on the edge of the grave, Thomas forces his father to surrender his keys. Thus the Dead Father gives up his identity, his power, his control, and the buckle which guards his sexual prowess. A good deal of the conflict in the novel centers on sexual activity. The Dead Father is sexual on a mythic level. He has fathered nations, with more "begatting" than one finds in the Book of Genesis. He is a Father of godlike stature. Like Zeus, he can become whatever and whoever he wants in order to enjoy whichever female catches his eye, and many females have caught his eye. Once he became a haircut in order to take over the body of a young man seducing a woman. His sexual drive is slowly diminished in its effect through the course of the action. He is no less desirous, but he is unable to perform, for no woman will let him. Early in the action he tries to supplant his son Thomas with his daughter-in-law, Julie, but she turns him down. Later he attempts to seduce Emma, but she tells him he's too old.

When his sexual drive is misdirected, he "slips his cable" literally and wreaks havoc of epic proportions. All the mythic destructive father figures are woven into his character. He is the Giant that Jack must kill, a Giant that devours his children; he is the dead king in the Sacred Grove from *The Golden Bough.* If all of this sounds Oedipal in the Freudian sense, Barthelme means it to. Thomas relates to his Dead Father a bedtime story, a Kafkaesque nightmare he had in which he is faced with the Great Father Serpent (Jungian), who asks a riddle. Those who cannot solve it are devoured. The riddle is: "What do you really feel?" Thomas gives the right answer: "Murderinging." The Dead Father is not reassured.

There is also a playing out of the sexual fears that supposedly exist at the unconscious level in all men. The fear of castration, for example, is acted out when the traveling band is refused lodging in a small town until the Dead Father is deballocked. Thomas refuses, but the threat is there. When the Dead Father surrenders his sword to Thomas, the son feels he has won without offending the Old Man. But the Dead Father immediately gives Thomas a present of a knife, and tells him to "cut something off." "I spoke too soon," Thomas said. "He is not reconciled." Thomas knows exactly which "something" he had in mind.

In one of the novel's more succinct phrases, Julie, speaking of the Dead Father, says: "They have this way of making you feel tiny and small." This is the point, or one of the points. The giant father figure so dominates Thomas that it requires a narrative at the epic level to bury him psychologically. As Thomas is told: "A son can never, in the fullest sense, become a father." Which is to say, a son by definition has a father, and as long as the father lives, the son will remain a son. It is only with the death of his Father that Thomas can himself be a father.

On their trek, the party comes across the City of the Wends, where all men are fatherless because they are their own fathers. They have become what all men have always wished to be. "The mechanics of the thing eludes me," says Thomas, who has to prove his Father is truly dead before the Wends will let them pass. There is a great deal that eludes Thomas. At the edge of the grave, Thomas is awed by the resonant tone of his Father's voice. "Intolerable. Grand. I wonder how he does it." This tale is male from beginning to end. Julie and Emma are necessary for their sexuality; they are pragmatic and bitchy; but they have no important role to play in the journey and burial. Nor does the Mother have anything to do with it; her one appearance is brief, and Thomas and the Dead Father immediately dispatch her to fill an endless shopping list. Mother, once she has mothered, is indistinct and not particularly useful except as cook. The Dead Father says: "I don't remember her very well." He may be Zeus, but she is never Hera.

What begins like Faulkner's *As I Lay Dying* ends with neither a bang nor a whimper. There are simply the bulldozers. What the reader experiences is a zany kind of catharsis without the preceding tears; the tears he supplies from his own memory, or from his imagination. The reader wonders, when he is through, exactly what he has participated in. The question is valid, for it is raised by the cable-hauling troops midway in the journey. They ask for an explanation, "no matter how far fetched or improbable." Thomas tells them in a stroke of brilliance: "It is, you might say, a rehearsal." And it is.

Michael S. Reynolds

DYLAN THOMAS
No Man More Magical

Author: Andrew Sinclair (1935-   )
Publisher: Holt, Rinehart and Winston (New York). Illustrated. 240 pp. $15.95
Type of work: Biography
Time: 1914-1953
Locale: Wales, England, United States

The life of a man of contradictory passions in his personal life, of pure lyric genius in his poetry

Principal personages:
DYLAN THOMAS, Welsh poet, playwright, and fiction writer
CAITLIN THOMAS, his wife

This is a picture book as well as a narrative biography in words—a handsome book that reinforces what is said about the man who is its subject with, at times, a sadly revealing photo-album-like quality. It is a book of sixteen chapters, whose epigraphs are from the writings of Thomas or his wife. There is an epilogue, "Dylan on Dylan." And there is the crisp, evocative prose of Andrew Sinclair, the biographer of the man whom he not only knew much about, but knew personally. Sinclair is himself the author of several novels and works on American social history and, above all, the writer and director of the film version of Thomas' *Under Milk Wood.* Thus, the writer of this book comes eminently qualified to the task of re-creating parts of the man he calls "the finest lyric poet of his age."

Thomas' great loves and influences and crutches—sometimes they were indistinguishable from each other— were Wales and the sea, the pub, words, and Caitlin, his wife. His hometown of Swansea is familiar to anyone who has read his stories; although he loved it with great biting criticism and sometimes unabashed emotion, it was to Laugharne and

London he went, alternately, in his mature days as a poet. Except for few trips to Europe's mainland and the evidently ill-omened and ill-fated tours to America, he spent his life on the British Isles—living near the sea, drinking in the pubs, writing in a tool shed study, fighting with and loving Caitlin.

It has become familiar by now, although it apparently never ceases to fascinate those interested in a life such as Thomas': raw genius mixed with madness or volatility, moistened with tankards of liquor, at times softened and then fueled by at least one love, but more often by many. The reason, of course, that people are so interested in such a story is that the individual talent, the genius, is unique, and that out of a life lived much as any other came something of lasting value.

Thomas' first fascination in life was with words. As he described it in his "Poetic Manifesto," "I tumbled for words at once. And, when I began to read the nursery rhymes for myself, and, later, to read other verses and ballads, I knew that I had discovered the most important things, to me, that could be ever."

Moving through the chapter headings, one can easily see the level-headedness with which the biographer approaches his subject. In the first part of the volume, Sinclair examines the poetic myths and Welsh milieu from which Thomas evolved. Storytelling lives in the land like another folk, and always there is the Welsh sense of sin and evil and the spirit of Thomas' great-uncle Gwilym —a bard, a preacher, and a radical. It is a land of family—mother, father, cousins, sister—to which the poet would return again and again, to worry, to heal, to bother, to help. Sinclair makes the interesting assertion that it was because Thomas was steeped in the Puritan heritage that he would never forsake his father and mother when they were old, and insisted on caring for them—or having Caitlin do so.

Having shown the familial bonds that kept the poet a son to the end, Sinclair curiously omits a reckoning with Thomas-the-father. One does learn that three children were born to Dylan and Caitlin: Llewelyn, Colm, and Aeronwy. The fierce battles between the parents are everywhere displayed: in the pub, in America, in the home where, as Caitlin has written, "the house rattled, and banged, and thudded, and groaned with our murder of each other." The question that arises is not so much *where* was Father Dylan (he was reading or broadcasting, writing or drinking), but what was the relationship that existed between father and children? The pictures show Caitlin dutifully domestic (when she was not pubbing herself), coming out of the river at Laugharne, her skirts hiked, the dog in the boat, Aeronwy tugging at the bowline.

Many such pictures speak with a conspicuous absence: there are few that show the family, the Caitlin-Dylan family, together. There is none that shows Dylan alone with his children.

The truly lyrical parts of this book, which evoke the very essence of Thomas' own source of inspiration, are those that deal with the same concerns as the poems and stories: death, youth, greenness, the sea, guilt, fear, and the love of language. Sinclair seems to have drawn inspiration and knowledge of his own from the very same wellsprings that washed the poet. He knows the lines to quote, not merely to illustrate, but to evoke, to suggest, to cause one to want to read *more* (perhaps even to want to write a poem). Whatever popularity or appreciation Thomas enjoys today can only be enhanced by this book.

It is disappointing to learn that Dylan Thomas spoke no Welsh. This is one of the first important illustrations of a theme laced throughout: that contradiction was the core of the poet's life and heritage, and that out of this pervasive contradiction came his art. For instance, Thomas was certainly no snob. He would as soon have worked in his tool shed study (and did) as have a private library studio. He would as soon have drunk common beer at the working-man's pub (and did) as clink brandy goblets with royalty. (In fact, beer was his favorite drink.) Yet, his father refused to teach him Welsh and, in fact, held those in contempt who did speak it in his village since it betrayed, to his way of thinking, the lot of the commoner. In later years, critics would deride Thomas for not being "true" Welsh while taking from the lore of the land.

Thomas' early flirtation and letter swapping with the poet Pamela Hansford Johnson, when she had sought him out at Swansea after having read one of his poems, is strikingly reminiscent, except for the humor of the letters, of the Fanny Brawne letters of Keats. In fact, Sinclair says that it was Keats who was Thomas' spiritual, if not poetic, forebear. Dylan seems to have wanted a romantic life and to have wished for, if subconsciously, an even more Keatsian death. Many of the photographs and portraits strike the pose of a Byron, the lips full and sensual, the neckdress oddly Elizabethan.

Thomas seems to have courted briefly, then disavowed completely, a sketchy surrealism. His taste for politics was virtually absent, although he did make a trip to Prague to help the Communist Writers' Union. But his heart was not in it, and after declaring that he was a Welsh poet and wanted only to write, he returned home. He did, however, sign the Stockholm Peace Petition and the Rosenberg Petition when others would not touch them. He was sympathetic to the goals of Communism because it declared itself an opponent of industrialism and capitalism. Sinclair concludes that if Thomas could be labeled in any way with a political tag it would be as a "romantic Socialist." All Thomas wanted was to write, to not have to work at other jobs (although he was finally *compelled* to work); the state, he claimed, should take care of the other business so that his writing time would be possible.

Throughout it all, as one chapter declares, he was getting "older and deeper in debt." Money and housing problems plagued him; he had five mouths to feed. Evidently the Thomases lived a kind of peripatetic hand-to-mouth existence. Friends gave them quarters and care. And finally, when the lecture-reading tours in America offered the opportunity for a way out of the financial stranglehold, Thomas took it. Each time, however, he returned with less money than before, and still further in debt.

The blame which Sinclair and Caitlin place on the American, John Malcolm Brinnin, who was responsible for promoting the tours, and on the Americans of the time who courted and lionized the poet from Wales, may be well-founded. It is difficult from the details given to judge. But there does seem to be almost total blame laid on others while excusing Thomas' own penchant for receiving adulation and drinks. He toured of his own free will, and in fact sought an American university position. He enjoyed a new audience, many of whom undoubtedly idolized him for all the wrong reasons. While the Americans who followed him, wined him, and catered to him were undoubtedly guilty of philistinism and star gazing, to place all the culpability on them is, finally, unfair. Such a stance portrays Thomas as a victim, when in reality he was already bloated with drink and his own excesses. The contradictions, the veritable death wish that formed him, had been ingrained since childhood.

Thomas, interestingly, with his satiric wit, saw his own guilt in the matter, and could laugh at himself. In his "A Visit to America" he has tremendous fun inventing situations that must be thinly veiled equivalents of his own: "See the garrulous others, also, gabbing and garlanded from one nest of culture-vultures to another: people selling the English way of life and condemning the American way as they swig and guzzle through it; . . . myself among them booming with the worst." So Thomas not only found fault with the Americans; he ridiculed the Europeans, himself included, for going where the new money was.

This book is an obvious effort of love and admiration. The prose is often poignantly eloquent. The pictures are haunting: a subtly moving, impressionistic portrait of Thomas by Rupert Shephard; Richard Burton in mackinaw with the setting of *Under Milk Wood* in the background; Augustus John, the painter, and his fine portrait of Caitlin; an ink wash drawing by Michael Ayrton of the poet in caricature, his belly bulging, his clothes a shambles, his perpetual cigarette dangling like a snowman's; and, above all, the deathly Thomas in the cemetery where his father was just buried.

Joseph Maiolo

EDITH WHARTON: A BIOGRAPHY

Author: R. W. B. Lewis
Publisher: Harper & Row Publishers (New York). 592 pp. $15.00
Type of work: Biography
Time: 1862-1937
Locale: New York City; Newport, Rhode Island; Lenox, Massachusetts; London; Paris

The definitive biography of one of America's undervalued major authors; winner of the Bancroft Prize, the National Book Critics Circle Award, and the Pulitzer Prize

Principal personages:
> EDITH WHARTON (NEE EDITH NEWBOLD JONES), daughter of a socially prominent New York family who became one of America's most successful writers during the first three decades of this century
> EDWARD (TEDDY) WHARTON, her husband
> WILLIAM CRARY BROWNELL, fiction editor at *Scribner's*, friend and literary adviser to Edith
> MORTON FULLERTON, journalist and writer with whom Edith probably had an affair
> WALTER VAN RENSSELAER BERRY, Edith's closest male friend for many years
> SARA NORTON, friend and confidante of Edith
> HENRY JAMES, American novelist who, as friend and mentor, influenced Edith
> BERNARD BERENSON, art critic, close friend of Edith
> PERCY LUBBOCK, literary critic and friend

One of the salutary effects of the growing interest in women in our history and culture is the movement toward reevaluating women writers whose reputations have been overshadowed by those of their male contemporaries. An excellent candidate for such a reevaluation, Edith Wharton has for too long been regarded as a pale moon to Henry James's sun—her work dismissed with faint praise while her reputation languished. In this fine biography, R. W. B. Lewis convincingly argues that Edith Wharton is in her own right an important, if not major, author who deserves a place in the national literary canon not as an imitator of James, but as a writer whose work bears comparison with the best fiction of her time.

Nothing at Edith Newbold Jones's birth in January 1862 seemed to portend her future as a serious novelist. As a daughter of New York's aristocratic upper class, the young girl was neither educated to seek a place in the world outside her circle nor to value the artistic life she would later lead. "It was not a world that encouraged literary leanings. Edith retained the impression that the intellectuals and artists who might be encountered . . . were on the whole a boring lot." Wharton's own characterization of this period as an "age of innocence" is as much a description of her youth, when choices seemed so simple, as of the period itself, during which an era faded away.

Left independent means at her father's death, Edith might never have drifted into writing had financial need been her major motivation. Rather, what had been a private diversion deepened into a vocation following her marriage to Teddy Wharton, a weak and selfish socialite. Henry James would later characterize this marriage as "an almost—or rather an utterly—inconceivable thing," and there seems little doubt that the relationship was destined to be an emotional disaster for both partners from the start. According to Lewis, "the marriage was not consummated for three weeks. Whatever happened on those first occasions, it had the effect of sealing off Edith's vibrant but untutored erotic nature for an indefinite period, with far-reaching consequences for her psychological makeup and the very practice of life." In spite of her emotional frustrations, however, the early years of Edith Wharton's marriage were a time of growth for her through the influences of travel, reading, and association with some of the brilliant men of her society. Her ambivalent attitude toward her life was reflected in her first published fictional sketch, which appeared in 1890. Though Wharton's reputation in later years would rest on her brilliant characterization of her period and class, this early sketch, "like several others . . . has no obvious bearing on the life she was actually leading; it was, rather, an imaginative escape from that life."

The crucial year in Wharton's development was 1895, when several conflicting pressures drove her to a

serious nervous breakdown. The burden of her marriage weighed increasingly upon her, and this failure seems to have been complicated by her growing literary success. She had achieved some distinction as a writer, which led to an invitation to bring out a book of short stories—a commitment which amounted to electing a professional career in letters.

These factors came together in the challenging question that could no longer be postponed. What, at the age of thirty-two, was her fundamental role in life: wife, social hostess, observer of foreign parts—or, drawing on all these, a writer of fiction? There is evidence that she had absorbed into a guilt-ridden corner of her being her society's and her mother's distrust of a person of good family who took seriously to writing. One can only employ the phrase "severe identity crisis" to describe the terrible and long-drawn-out period of paralyzing melancholy, extreme exhaustion, constant fits of nausea, and no capacity whatever to make choices or decisions.

Recovery was slow, and it was not until 1898 that Wharton finally began a sustained literary career—at an age (thirty-seven) when many writers have already done their best work.

The pressures which accounted for Wharton's breakdown never left her entirely, and in some important respects they came to be the dominant concerns of her best work. Significantly, the only work she produced in 1895, the year of her collapse, was a sonnet dramatizing a woman's lamentation for never having experienced sexual fulfillment. In *The House of Mirth,* her first successful novel, Wharton drew upon her own life to explore her alienation from the role American society would have had her play. *Ethan Frome,* Wharton's single masterpiece, treats marriage as an entrapment of the spirit, reflecting Edith's own feelings of being trapped by Teddy. Such themes, the most constant of which is a sensitive woman's disillusionment with the man to whom she is attached, pervade the works and suggest the extent to which Edith Wharton's fiction served as an outlet for the fears, frustrations, and hurts of her own inner life.

One of the most fortuitous influences on Wharton's development was that of Henry James, whose early advice and later friendship were instrumental in shaping her career. Though Wharton would come to resent—justifiably, as Lewis points out —those critics who insisted upon regarding her as a mere imitator of James, he nevertheless was of prime importance in her emergence. In particular, James, who had himself earned his reputation with the "International Theme," advised Wharton "in favour of the American subject." Urging her to profit by his own example of "exile and ignorance," he challenged her to *"Do New York!* The 1st hand account is precious." As Lewis puts it, this "was the most important and the wisest literary advice Edith Wharton ever received." As Wharton developed into the foremost novelist of manners in her generation, James's admonition proved a prophetic recognition of where her greatest powers lay.

Even while she elected for the American subject matter, Wharton shared James's love of Europe; increasingly she came to make Paris her primary residence. Convinced

that "all that charms life" was available only in Europe, as America was rapidly degenerating into a cultural wasteland, Wharton would eventually remove permanently to Paris. Yet, she remained American in her sensibilities and loyalties in a way James did not. She never seemed to share his real sense of exile, and when James became a British citizen on the eve of World War I, Wharton regretted his decision to renounce the land of his birth. "Unlike many of her fellow expatriates . . . Edith Wharton never took on the manners and speech habits, the critical posture, and . . . the pseudo-identity of the re-created European." Instead, she never at any time "was . . . anything *but* an American: which is to say . . . never anything but herself."

Wharton's exile from her native country may, in fact, be related to the general sense of restlessness which seems to have kept her almost constantly on the move. In love with travel and with the automobile as a symbol of freedom, Edith lived her life as a series of royal processions through continental Europe, England, North Africa, and elsewhere. The connection between her travels and her emotional life seems implicit in the fact that "during the fifteen months that followed the divorce [from Teddy Wharton] Edith Wharton traveled farther and more constantly than ever before in her life: traveled almost compulsively, in seven countries and on three continents, and even to scenes that lay quite outside the range of her previous experience and cultural traditions." As divorce represented for her an escape from the prison of an unhappy marriage, so travel represented what Henry James termed a "fantastic freedom" answering some deep need within her emotional nature.

Lewis' unwillingness to probe Wharton's emotional makeup is one of the very few complaints a reader might direct against this splendid biography. At the outset, he professes an unwillingness to wander "into far psychological fields, possibly fascinating but increasingly remote from the human reality—from the emotions and impulses, the sometimes irrational gestures, all the rich texture of behavior and response that constitutes the flesh and blood woman with whom we have to deal." Convinced that Wharton's "deepest life—that is, her deepest feelings—existed more in her writings than in the externals from which they had sprung," Lewis concentrates largely on the objective facts of Wharton's life and work. The result leaves the reader with a strong sense of some needed key to make the patterns of Wharton's life fit into a coherent whole. There is a sense of mystery about Lewis' subject that suggests he may well have bridged the usual gap between the novelist and the biographer in this work which creates as much mystery as it dispels.

Bernard Berenson characterized Edith Wharton, along with himself, Henry Adams, and Henry James, as one of the "most authentic Americans" of her generation. R. W. B. Lewis' biography has captured some sense of this complex person who, as writer and as individual, reflects so much of what it means to be an "authentic American." In so doing, he has added an important chapter to American literary and cultural history. Additionally, he has proven that the biography, in capable hands, is itself a beautiful literary form.

William E. Grant

ENCOUNTER WITH AN ANGRY GOD
Recollections of My Life with John Peabody Harrington

Author: Carobeth Laird (1895-   )
Publisher: Malki Museum Press (Banning, California). 190 pp. $8.95
Type of work: Biography
Time: 1915-1921
Locale: The American Southwest

A portrait of one of the first great American Indian anthropologists as viewed by his former wife

Principal personages:
> CAROBETH LAIRD, Harrington's wife and assistant for six years
> JOHN PEABODY HARRINGTON, the brilliant and eccentric Indian ethnologist
> GEORGE LAIRD, the Indian informant who became the author's second husband

The ancient Hebrew curse, "May thine enemy write a book," certainly backfires in Carobeth Laird's record of her short-lived marriage to John Peabody Harrington. Laird's anthropological-mythographical study *The Chemehuevis,* the first full-length book about that Indian group, is a substantial contribution to the field of American Indian ethnography. But *Encounter with an Angry God* is a sad demonstration of the "occupational hazard" of autobiographies: the author is herself the main character, and the impact of the book depends upon the reader's ability to trust her, or at least sympathize with her. Attempting to paint the darkest possible picture of the tormented, driven genius who was her husband for only six years, Laird simultaneously paints herself into a corner. We become most uncomfortable in such close proximity to her as we realize that vengeance is the most unworthy literary motivation—one that can only produce a book that is neither fish nor fowl. Her book fails as history because it is admittedly inaccurate, as autobiography because it is too narrow, as anthropology because that is only a peripheral interest, and as biography because it is excessively biased. It is nonetheless valuable for the little insight it does offer on the personality of a man whom all agree has remained an enigma.

John Peabody Harrington (1894-1961), a linguist-ethnographer by training, was field ethnologist for the Bureau of American Ethnology for forty years, beginning in 1915. As a member of the first generation of university-trained anthropologists, he was a contemporary of Robert H. Lowie, Alfred Kroeber, Edward Sapir, Elsie Clews Parsons, Paul Radin, and Leslie Spier. As Harry W. Lawton says in his foreword to Laird's book, "it is believed that no other anthropologist ever gathered such a staggering quantity of material in the field as did Harrington. His notes on the Chumash Indians alone filled sixty boxes." These field notes progressively inundated the Bureau of American Ethnology archives, the basement of the Freer Gallery, and two commercial warehouses in

Washington, D.C. Scholars are still discovering caches of Harrington's notes in forgotten hiding places around the country.

Harrington's linguistic studies with A. L. Kroeber and Pliny Earle Goddard at Stanford and Berkeley confirmed his interest in the California Indians; indeed, he became so impatient to begin field work that he never completed the doctoral studies he began at the Universities of Leipzig and Berlin. After initial work with the Chumash, Mohave, and Yuma Indians, he focused his research on the linguistics and ethnology of the Indians of the Southwest—especially the Shoshonean, Chumashan, and Yuman linguistic families. In 1917 he published his *Ethnobotany of the Tewa Indians,* which Lawton calls "a classic work far in advance of its times." M. W. Stirling remarked that "no linguist was ever acquainted with so many American Indian languages over so wide a territory. . . . An alphabetical list of those American languages on which he left at least several hundred pages of manuscript would include Abnaki, Achomawi, Apache, Arapaho, Aztec, and so on through Wintu, Yunka, and Zuni." Thomas C. Blackburn, whose *December's Child, A Book of Chumash Oral Narratives* (1975) is derived from Harrington's notes, concludes that Chumash was his major effort and interest and points to papers based on Harrington's research by Craig, Linda King, Heizer, and Chester King as indications of the seminal nature of Harrington's work. Laird does not even reveal the tip of this iceberg in her recollections. When she quotes one of Harrington's own poems, it is obvious that she does not understand it:

> Give not, give not the yawning graves
>   their plunder;
> Save, save the lore, for future ages' joy;
> The stories full of beauty and of wonder
> The songs more pristine than the
>   songs of Troy,
> The ancient speech forever to be
>   vanished—
> Lore that tomorrow to the grave
>   goes down!
> All other thought from our horizon
>   banished,
> Let any sacrifice our labor crown.

Harrington clearly saw himself as a martyr to scholarship, and a happy martyr at that, because he recognized the cultural significance of his research on languages on the brink of linguistic extinction. In Laird's book he is presented as a demented witch doctor who sacrifices his wife: " 'I called him an angry god,' I thought in amazement, 'and all the while he was just a dirty little boy having a tantrum.' " It may be true, as Lawton admits, that Harrington had no sense of perspective and allowed himself to be immersed in detail. But the more important truth is that "the wealth of information left by Harrington is already broadening or changing our knowledge about many Indian groups, and it has barely been tapped"—as Lawton also points out.

Against this scientific assessment Laird's book appears only as a vengeful tirade, a rationalization of her own unhappiness by exaggerating Harrington's defects, a retrospective self-justification and memorial to her beloved second husband. Perhaps she is right to have been initially intimidated by Theodora Kroeber's biography of her famous husband, "so gracious, so lacking in anything derogatory"—although an error on the positive side of the balance is no more objective than Laird's negative record. Yet Kroeber's own inspiration is the point of his wife's recollections, a point clearly expressed, and therefore inspiring to those who read her book. Lawton calls Laird's invective approach courageous. But it requires little courage to indict the dead, without witnesses.

The worst aspect of the book is its lack of methodology, as the author herself admits: "There is merely a jumble of impressions, of vignettes bright or lurid, a few of which happen to correspond with remembered dates, private or historical." Her armchair tribunal is presented in a self-serving, overly dramatic style that makes it all the more distasteful: "I was beyond fatigue, beyond pain, beyond fear." Equally distasteful to the contemporary reader is Laird's collusion in her own subjugation, which somehow tempers Harrington's obvious male chauvinism by her eagerness to nurture it. She does not mind that he made her learn to drive and to type, "but he never undertook the task of transforming me into an educated, let alone a cultured person; he merely molded me into a competent assistant." Her resentment forms the leitmotif of her angry catalog of Harrington's flaws: always wanting to "make a good impression"; never tipping in hotels or restaurants; regarding his established superiors "with a mixture of fear, envy, and self-protective scorn"; commending her taciturn deportment; forcing her into "unnatural" sex acts; being a "congenital worrier"; refusing to support even his own child; asking her to run over one of his legs, so

that he could avoid the draft; making her shield him from traffic in Washington, D.C.; and resenting her not scraping the white from egg shells. Their conversation about the draft is insightful, though Laird herself misses the insight:

"Because I don't want to die," he explained, "I can't afford to risk getting killed."

"Everybody has to die sometime," I argued tritely. "Lots of things are worse than dying."

"Nothing is worse than dying," he returned. Then added with a heartfelt emphasis that I had never heard in his voice before, "I would rather be sick, blind, in prison, and undergoing daily torture than be dead."

"I wouldn't," I shuddered. "What would there be to live for?"

"I could still *think*," he answered. "It would be terrible not to be able to think."

Laird's resentment, then, is also based on her inability to comprehend the obsession characteristic of truly productive human beings. She attempts to understand, but the results are superficial:

He deplored wasting time and tortured himself continually about not accomplishing more, yet I have never known a more proficient time-waster. This seems to be characteristic of persons who drive themselves without respite and eschew all forms of recreation.

It seems to be characteristic of persons who do not drive themselves that they cannot comprehend how those who waste so much time can also produce literally tons of observations. On the other hand, the productive time wasters, like Harrington, when they find time to think about them at all, cannot understand how the others can waste so much time without producing anything.

Some of Laird's negative memories can be used to construct an integral view of Harrington's personality. His worship of his mother may explain his indifference toward the wife who adored rather than loved him. His hatred of miscegenation is obviously related to his unique love for the individual languages he recorded. His "lack of fastidiousness" in personal hygiene, contrasted with the "paranoiac belief" that led him to ask Carobeth to draw straight lines "where he could write [his signature] with care," suggests a man whose driving ambition was consciously aggravated by a kind of native indolence and lack of self-discipline. That he was able, so amply, to overcome that tension in his own personality is admirable, even if he never managed to become the exemplary husband and lover Laird desired. In retrospect, the author says,

Now looking back . . . I begin to understand, I begin to have compassion for a very lonely man, a man whose self-imposed isolation was due as much to a deeply rooted sense of inferiority and alienation as it was to dedication to his work.

In light of the book she has written to darken Harrington's memory—written almost wholly without psychological perspective—her sympathy is hardly convincing, and not nearly enough to excuse the immense disservice she has done to a man who served his scholarly muse so prodigiously. Harrington deserves an objective biographer who is able to separate, then to synthesize, the man and the scholar. He may not have been a beauty of a man, though there was beauty in his single-minded labors; but he certainly could not have been the beast Laird, like Circe, turns him into.

Kenneth John Atchity

FAR TORTUGA

Author: Peter Matthiessen (1927-   )
Publisher: Random House (New York). 408 pp. $10.95
Type of work: Novel
Time: April, 1968
Locale: Aboard the sailing ship *Lillias Eden* in the Caribbean Sea between Jamaica and the Honduras and Nicaragua coasts

> *An impressionistic, highly experimental novel, almost poetic drama, concerning the ill-fated voyage of a crew of sailors hunting sea turtles*

Principal characters:
RAIB AVERS, the iron-willed captain of the Lillias Eden
WILLIAM PARCHMENT, the ship's mate
VEMON DILBERT EVERS, the angry, cowardly, yet ultimately heroic butt-of-all-jokes on board
JIM EDEN AVERS (BUDDY), the captain's son
JUNIOR BODDEN (SPEEDY), the new man aboard
MIGUEL MORENO SMITH (BROWNIE), a tattered refugee from guerrilla warfare under Che Guevara

A naturalist and explorer, Peter Matthiessen is a restless world-searching man, a restless writer of prodigious energies and talents. As evidenced by his considerable body of writings in seven nonfiction and five fiction books, he is measurably in love with the elemental, wilderness forces of this planet—its wildlife, rivers, seas, and jungles—and with those humans who attempt to live closest to, and who struggle with, those forces. These being his interests, it is noteworthy that he ranges as a writer from method to method, never repeating himself thematically or stylistically, always seeking a new way of approaching his task, and always surprising his readers with his construction and mastery of each new approach. He has always demonstrated skillful grasp of the unexpected. At the same time he renders each new work into a unified whole that is astonishing in its satisfying completeness within his innovative framework.

His massive earlier novel, *At Play in the Fields of the Lord,* a National Book Award nominee, was as densely textured and rich in character, theme, and action as are the South American rivers and jungles which comprised its setting. It was an exciting departure from the traditional form of the novel, Proustian in its exactness of recall and precision, Joycean in its word magic, its brainplay. It was a haunting work, whole sections of which demanded multiple readings because of its complexity of power and content combined with its elusive, imagistic style. That novel was, nevertheless, a more "novelistic" novel than is *Far Tortuga.* In this most recent work, Matthiessen has brilliantly designed a new framework beyond the usual novelistic restrictions for what might have been just another sea yarn. Typically, he breaks all the old rules which would hold him back, makes new ones, and contrives to make it all succeed.

As a stylistic craftsman, as a questioner of philosophical rules, and as a teller of stories, Matthiessen is a writer whom Melville would have surely described as "a deep diver"; in *Far Tortuga* with both story and form, with his deep questionings, the author takes enormous risks, but makes them pay off.

Far Tortuga is a deep dive into the hearts and minds of a group of men who are themselves "deep divers," not always consciously or by choice, but nonetheless heroically, as they navigate the elemental charts of their lives. As a tale of men who make their livings as sailors—more precisely as hunters of green turtles —who both love and fear the sea, Matthiessen's story is one which would have equally impressed such sea-writers as Joseph Conrad, Richard Hughes, and Rockwell Kent. Moreover, his startlingly unique style of telling this tale would have delighted their experimental spirit. Because of the manner in which *Far Tortuga* "emerges" to the reader (one does not so much *read* it as *hear* it, *feel* it, *know* it) Matthiessen also effects a deep probing into the heart and mind of the reader, testing all he has come to accept as truth.

The reader is impelled to participate in the creating of, the experiencing of, the story. The book is not easy reading. Like life, it comes together in fragments—*when* it comes together. Gradually, as the characters' voices reveal ignorances and wisdoms, pains and joys, fears and triumphs, the reader is able to recognize them as individuals even as he is forced to identify with all those traits as they reside in his own spirit. The reader becomes a part, truly, of the accumulation, the multilayering

of images and impressions. This is a powerfully evocative experience, archetypal, one not easily put aside. Indeed, reading this work is not unlike the feeling one sometimes has after swimming long in the surf, then coming up on land only still to have the carry-over sensation of oceanic lift, swell, and fall. The book, like the sea, stays with you. Matthiessen's triumph is in having the reader smell the sea after the book is closed, hear the cries of birds, the creaking of rigging, see the sun blaze, see the slow blinking of a dying turtle's eyelid.

More than a novel, *Far Tortuga* is a profound composition—a poem of the Caribbean. It is a collage of precisely caught images and sounds of a terrible tropical beauty. It is as stark and simple as the curved line of the horizon and the circle of the sun. It is as complex as the representative hearts aboard the ship. A tale of mythic proportions, it is prose music—an opera for sailors' voices soaring above the eternal sweep of the sea. The dialects, syntaxes, and rhythms of the Caribbean speech are caught faultlessly, as in this typical conversation; the speakers are Will Parchment and Byrum Watler, although their distinctive voices and attitudes are their only identification:

> I don't know, mon. As a coptin, he okay. Got to give de mon dat much; he know de sea. It only de way he treat de men—dat de back-time way.

> He a wind coptin, dass de trouble. He a sailin mon, and he used to de old-time way. All his life he been ziggin and zaggin, he don't know how to go straight.

The rhythms of those speeches have

the chop and swell of the sea, the laziness of long days in the sun.

The book is written as though Matthiessen invisibly accompanied the doomed crew of the tattered turtling ship, *Lillias Eden,* taking with him an omniscient camera and tape recorder with which he merely recorded everything. Thus, in a way, the tale is told in a strangely *cinéma verité* style, with the editing of sight and sound seeming to be effected by the hypnotic cycles of the sea, the sun, and the wind. The moods of sea and sky dictate the book's arrangement into patterned movements, pauses, crescendoes. Like the sea, they seem at times capricious, without plan.

A preliminary examination of the book reveals its poetic texture and collage-like structure. Most of the pages consist of fragments of speech, leanly suggestive abstract drawings which appear and re-appear in an almost seasonal sequence, different typefaces intermingled, and peculiar punctuation—all balanced or augmented by tersely impressionistic descriptions of the elements surrounding the various speakers. An interesting device Matthiessen employs has the ship's radio—which can only receive, not transmit—report weather conditions in clipped, standard English while at the same time the sailors are talking in their superstitious way about the same weather. They are strangely different weathers. Occasionally, only one word appears, or a name, or a single line or drawing. Occasionally, there are only a few sharply etched words strewn like sea spume, wind-driven across a page. Other pages are thickly packed, like muscle on a sailor's back, with conversations within conversations within thoughts within impressions. Like a painting heavy with layers of impasto, this style obviously does not make for simplicity of communication. The reader who remains aloof from the elemental will often not know who is speaking to whom or who does what—or even *what* has happened. Nevertheless, the style has an eerily realistic effect in the end, since the author is merely reproducing the confused, unorderly way in which we generally perceive events around us. Life in the happening is nonlinear, and we often realize only later what has happened, or who said what. Thus, once the reader becomes immersed in Matthiessen's process, becomes part of it, each of the voices becomes so distinctive that the characters' identities are obvious, and one comes to appreciate Matthiessen's shrewdly artistic seaman's economy in not wasting time identifying. Such traditional devices as "said the captain" or "they all looked" become, in *Far Tortuga,* superfluous clutter on a deck which must be clear and scrubbed clean as a bleached bone. Through it all, Matthiessen triumphs in creating the feeling that not he, but rather the sea, wrote this book.

Set in the Caribbean near Grand Cayman and the Misteriosa Reefs, the story, aparently based on actual incident, is of the schooner *Lillias Eden's* last voyage and about the nine men (and later a tenth) who were aboard. It is about what happens to them and between them as they sail, already too late in the season, in quest of sea turtles to sell. The quest is futile because the turtles are already in migration south. But these are stubborn, calloused men who know no other way of living, so they go, grumbling over hardships and failure, dreaming dreams while knowing in their cores that they are destined only for hardships and failure. Members of the crew come from different levels, different backgrounds. Some are learners, some teachers. Some are kind, others cruel; some happy, some sad; some vocal, even intellectual; others as mute as a sea conch. The captain seeks a commercial cargo; he finds his father. He tries to teach his son; he ends by learning from him. Some of the men we grow to like and trust turn treacherous and despicable under pressure. As real as life, these men are always surprising.

The voyage lasts only a few days. Tempers flare, violence emerges. Tenderness is revealed and wisdom is voiced. The elements and other desperate men threaten the crew from without while they threaten and comfort themselves and one another from within.

Finally, through a mixture of senseless violence, headstrong, Promethean bravado, and deep existential despair, the ship is lost, torn apart on a reef in the dark of night and storm. In the cat boats, the crew languish and die one by one, with the (possible) exception of one man, Speedy, whose dream all along has been to return to his acres and cows in Roatán. Strangely, this character has all along been sure, gentle, and patient. In the boats, his will to survive becomes so elemental as to make him a Nietzschean figure in his ruthlessly single motive of enduring. The novel ends in intentional, natural ambiguity about Speedy's survival. Only the sea knows.

It is significant that there are only a few passages actually having to do with turtling; the hunting of turtles is a vehicle of escape from the mundane for these men. It is all they know. It is their only real pride. It is merely the excuse, the "ground" for the "figure" Matthiessen paints in this play for voices. For the book is not *about* turtling. It is about men who blindly do what they must. *Far Tortuga* is a story about human nature and destiny. It happens to take place on the sea. But its theme is larger and older, wilder than even the sea.

To call such unlettered men as these sailors victims of "existential despair" requires explanation: certainly they never would use, or could use, those words to describe their condition. They fight hopelessness with the only weapons they have. They employ their human strengths (which fail), they sing songs (which are torn from their lips by the wind, smothered by salt water), they establish companionships and rely upon one another (only to see those concepts disappear under naturalistic conditions). Finally, they are like the turtles they hunt. They are born, they live, eat, work, procreate, have feelings, and die. They glimpse only the briefest flashes of possible meaning in their existences. They lose their lives sliding into the sea depths as they have fallen through life—with nothing to which to cling except the world itself, which is engaged in the inexorable process of killing them.

A recurrent phrase spoken by the men is indicative of their negative acceptance of their lot. They cap several conversations about how sad, how bad the world has become by saying "Dass de way do world go —modern time, mon!" And that is as close as they can come to voicing their sense of what is wrong. They are caught between the past and the future in a present devoid of any meaning. Naïvely, they blame the tourists or the big fishermen for ruining their world, their fishing grounds. And at the same time they are themselves thoughtless, wasteful despoilers and polluters in a world grown too small to absorb any longer their pollution—yet large enough to confuse and kill them. They are losers. They have nothing but their transient bodies. They are in search of the Far Tortuga, a storied paradise for turtlers, an island which may never have existed. The Far Tortuga they long for is not for them to find; they know only enough to experience loss, and to gain nothing. Matthiessen suggests in this work that all is temporary: philosophies, creeds, men, ac-

tions—but also suggests how beautiful and awesome these things are in their brevity.

Matthiessen loves these men, the fools and the hombres equally. They are men, and he is unrelenting and unsentimental in his admiration of them, of their fierce persistence, of their facing hardships with such nakedly meager defenses. They do what they must, and they do it with such portions of honor and dignity as they are allowed. The author suggests that what meaning there is to any life must be created. And we can only hope that as long as man lasts, some part of that which was us will remain to talk and sing about. That is what Matthiessen's novel is about: man's defiance of foreknown defeat. *Far Tortuga,* elementally honest, yet filled with human love, dreams, and respect for the human spirit—and all life on this globe—is a memorable and beautiful declaration.

Thomas N. Walters

THE FATE OF READING AND OTHER ESSAYS

Author: Geoffrey H. Hartman (1929-   )
Publisher: University of Chicago Press (Chicago). 352 pp. $15.00
Type of work: Literary criticism
Time: 1660 to the present
Locale: Europe, England, and America

A collection of essays on trends, applications, and contemporary concepts of literary criticism

There is a review of a work of literary criticism somewhere which begins, "This is a work for gentlemen and not for scholars; that is, the Greek quotations are translated and the Latin ones are not." Hartman's work, in this tradition of description, is clearly a work for scholars and not for gentlemen; that is, Hartman demands of his reader a close knowledge of a number of contemporary European languages, a variety of trends in recent literary criticism, and a wide range of literatures from the age of Milton to the present. Geoffrey Hartman is a controversial figure among many scholars and critics; his writings challenge accepted approaches to literature, while his methods and styles of writing criticism are often unorthodox; his conclusions, often radically different from received opinion. This collection of essays, many of which have already appeared in literary journals, is a generous selection demonstrating Hartman's approach both on the theoretical level and on the practical level of explication of specific literary texts. Since it contains seventeen essays, along with an introduction, it is also a difficult volume to review in a limited space. For this reason, it will be impossible to note every essay; instead, Hartman's overall purpose will be sketched and illustrated through reference to a number of the more important essays.

Hartman's range in this volume is both broad and deep; he brings within the scope of his consideration a large number of literary texts, from the works of Milton and the poems of Keats to the modern detective novel and the critical writings of Harold Bloom. His approach is comparative; he is as at home in the works of Valéry as he is in those of Wordsworth. Hartman's purpose in this collection is to extend the concerns of his previous book *Beyond Formalism* (1970); impelled by a sense of crisis in both language and literature, he sets out in these essays to broaden the scope of literary interpretation on the one hand, and to examine the discipline of literary study on the other. As literature proliferates, and criticism with it, Hartman fears that literary study becomes increasingly ineffectual. Yet his essays are an act of faith in the value of interpretation, especially that interpretation which is voluntarily dependent on the text. Hartman is wary of a number of trends in recent criticism, especially those which find masterpieces everywhere, or try to change our way of reading so that we find art to be "productive" in one sense or another. He is equally concerned about the psychoanalytic approach, although he does, in the early essays, try to prepare the way for an approach to literature which he calls "psychoesthetics." Another concern is the attempt to treat literature in isolation from its historical context, through seeing in it the expression of myth or ritual or the forms of non-historical structures. In each case, Hartman's analyses are sharp, precise, and to the point; his criticism, bracing and invigorating.

If Hartman has an overall thesis in this volume, it is to argue for the value of finding a newly enlivened method of historical analysis, a method intrinsic to literature rather than external to it. Such an approach, focusing on the historical consciousness of the poets themselves, Hartman believes reinvigorates the Aristotelian view of art as mimesis while it enriches our sense of the poetic voice. At the same time, it protects the concept of art from being captured by the ideologue or from being devalued by the formalist. The goal of the critic, in Hartman's view, is to find an "answerable style" appropriate to the work under study. As a model of such an approach, Hartman's work is an eloquent argument for its value. If, as he also admits, such an approach is demanding of the reader as well as the critic, his own examples of its application well repay the effort required to understand them.

As mentioned before, the first group of essays in *The Fate of Reading* explores the possibilities of an approach to literature Hartman calls psychoesthetics. This section of the book begins with an essay entitled "The Interpreter: A Self-Analysis" which reflects much of what is contro-versial about Hartman's work. Written in an allusive, epigrammatic, and highly personal style, this essay explores the image of the interpreter, or Hartman's self-image as interpreter, in a series of disjointed, playful, highly speculative sections the connections among which are often a challenge to the reader to detect. Filled with puns —"The interpreter, molded on me, is an overgoer with pen-envy strong enough to compel him into print"— and witty asides, the essay argues that the proliferation of criticism has produced a proliferation of critical opinions; as a result, the critic-to-be should shield himself from them and devote himself to the text, else he will be drowned in the flood of secondary work.

In a ramble among a variety of ideas and concepts ranging from Freud through the Bible to Hegel, Hartman defines the role of the critic as one who is called upon to evaluate and to discriminate among the claims of language. His work is often less than fiction, and sometimes more— a fantasia which combines a sense of reality with a sense of fiction so that the sense of reality is delighted and brought to cooperate with the spell of the fiction. Hartman's final image is of the critic as Hamlet, confronted with the question of whether he or the fiction he interprets is real, and which of the two is the ghost. With this as background, Hartman then moves on to a brilliant discussion of the work of I. A. Richards which locates Richards' thinking in the context of twentieth century ideas, especially those of Freud, and a review of Harold Bloom's *Anxiety of Influence* which discusses Bloom's debt to Freud and assesses both the strengths and weaknesses of Bloom's approach to post-Romantic poetry. Finally, he applies his own sense of the appropriate use of psychological categories in a brilliant pair of essays, the first of which explores the author's sense of self in Keats's "Hyperion," while the second discusses patterns of representation in Christopher Smart's "Magnificat."

The second section of Hartman's book considers the historical situation of art, and of writing about art. Hartman believes that art before the modern age served to sort out the past, to reject what was not useful to the present, and to revivify what was. Now, however, as a result of the explosion of knowledge, art is crowded by interpretation and can no longer serve the purpose of enriching the present with the useful forms of the past. As a result, role-models collapse and the present is impoverished; nihilism prevails as the revelry of creativity is lost. Hartman, however, looks with some hope to the history of art itself as a reserve of forms which can serve for the present even as social forms served the past. From this base, Hartman moves to a discussion of Hegel's concept of influence ("From the Sublime to the Hermeneutic") and to an inspired reading of Keats's ode "To Autumn." He then traces the image of the evening star in a variety of Romantic and post-Romantic writers, especially Wordsworth, and concludes the section with a review of the place of Wordsworth and Goethe in literary history.

The next section of *The Fate of Reading* is devoted to a consideration of changes in the canon of literary classics, as, in Hartman's view, we declare the death of the past and embrace the study of the contemporary. He begins with an insightful comparison of the popular mystery story with major works of contemporary fiction. What he discovers is that while the detective story is concerned to render the inexplicable, or mysterious, intelligible in rational terms, much modern fiction precisely lacks a moment of revealing mystery, because it refuses to admit that there is any mystery to be revealed. Then, after a detailed reading of Valéry's "L'Abeille" (Fable of the Bee), Hartman turns to the essay which gives its title to the collection. Another of Hartman's gatherings of speculations, asides, parables, and forays into vision, "The Fate of Reading" explores the possibility that our modern war with mystery will ultimately result in the death of reading, which depends so heavily on the experience, and enjoyment, of mystery. His outlook is pessimistic; nevertheless, he retains faith in the ultimate elusiveness of figurative speech. Along with this comes his faith in the role of the interpreter, whose proper function is not to take away the mystery of literature, but to reinvigorate it. Along the way of this discussion, Hartman attacks modern attempts to make criticism more scientific; such techniques as semiotics, linguistics, and textual structuralism all too often combine sophisticated technique with a distressing parochialism of culture which lead them to divorce reading and writing in destructive ways. Hartman's ultimate faith is in the simultaneous power and mystery of the tale, which he finds enriched and preserved through the responsive and sensitive reader-interpreter.

The final section of the book consists of occasional pieces—reflections on the theory of Romanticism, a review of the achievement of Lionel Trilling, and some short reviews. The impression which Hartman's work leaves is one of having been for a time in the presence of a mind and a spirit deeply responsive to literature, profoundly knowledgeable about it, and capable of communicating a rich and true vision of it. While we may take Hartman's sense of the threat to literature in our age as seriously as he does, we must also conclude that he sets a splendid example of the reader-interpreter who will enrich all the tales we have inherited and keep them alive for us even in our time.

John N. Wall, Jr.

FATHERS AND CHILDREN
Andrew Jackson and the Subjugation of the American Indian

Author: Michael Paul Rogin (1937-   )
Publisher: Alfred A. Knopf (New York). 373 pp. $13.95
Type of work: Biography
Time: 1767-1845
Locale: The United States of America

A psychohistorical interpretation of the central role of the "Indian question" in the life and times of Andrew Jackson

Principal personages:
ANDREW JACKSON, orphan, frontier politician, Indian fighter, war hero, and seventh President of the United States
ELIZABETH JACKSON, his mother
RACHEL JACKSON, his wife
THOMAS HART BENTON, an early Tennessee rival who later became an ardent Jacksonian
JOHN C. CALHOUN, Jackson's Secretary of War during most of the Indian campaigns
JOHN H. EATON, a close friend
MARTIN VAN BUREN, Jackson's Secretary of State
SAM HOUSTON, a Tennessee protégé of Jackson, and a leading figure in the Texas Revolution and the cause of Manifest Destiny

The Bible-reading American farmers of the early nineteenth century easily found Scriptural justification for their dispossession of the Indians. As agriculturalists, they followed the Lord's command to "subdue and replenish" the earth, while the red man clung to a more primitive relation to nature. They believed that in America as in the Book of Genesis, the more sophisticated tiller of the soil would seize the birthright of the simple hunter and warrior. "Jacob," proclaimed a congressman from Georgia, "will forever obtain the inheritance of Esau."

Just as the ancient tale of the patriarch Isaac and his two warring children "prefigured" the history of America, claims psychohistorian Michael Paul Rogin, the troubled early life of Andrew Jackson pre- figured the social tensions of the American age that bears his name. This argument by analogy is characteristic of Michael Rogin's *Fathers and Children: Andrew Jackson and the Subjugation of the American Indian.* His work is a fascinating and extremely literate theoretical interpretation of one man's inner conflicts and the historical consequences for America of his psychic struggles. History, however, neatly follows neither Scripture nor psychoanalytic theory, and while Rogin's complex study raises a host of interesting questions about Indian relations in Jacksonian America, it provides as few precise answers as does the Bible.

The object of Rogin's interest lies beyond the saga of Esau and Jacob in the larger and more powerful "cultural myth" through which paternalistic whites justified the destruction of their red "brothers" and "children." In *Fathers and Children,* Rogin pursues this myth in the form of a set of symbols consciously and unconsciously rooted in familial relations. He explores the myth's power to structure events, its psychological and socioeconomic origins, and its ironic consequences for whites and Indians alike.

Rogin's pursuit of the myth leads him inexorably toward two conclusions. The first is that the "Indian question," so often relegated to the periphery of American history, must instead be recognized as the central and decisive element in the development of American society in the first half of the nineteenth century. The second, virtually a corollary of the first, is that the prime mover, dominating figure, and "representative man" during this time was Jackson.

In the early 1800's, the United States was moving, in Rogin's view, along two related but distinct lines of development, with Jackson the protagonist in each. On one level was a national psychohistorical experience—a quest for national identity, analogous to the individual's striving for maturity, that may be described within the same Freudian theoretical framework that places family relationships at the center of personal experience. The pattern for maturity that America followed, argues Rogin, was Jackson's own. The country experienced drastic economic growth and change within a dialectical process that was largely initiated, though never controlled or even understood, by Andrew Jackson. The dispossession of the southern Indians by Jackson as soldier and President

stands at the intersection of the two lines of development. The conquest of the Indians and their lands was the culmination of Jackson's personal quest for a secure identity and a certification of the nation's maturity; it signaled at the same time the beginning of the territorial expansion and concomitant market revolution which disrupted, and eventually destroyed, the Jacksonian social system.

Fathers and Children is an ambitious attempt at historical synthesis on multiple planes of understanding. Rogin brings to bear on his subject the analytical insights of a half dozen disciplines, and pushes his analysis into virtually every hidden corner of the American psyche, sometimes pushing beyond the limits of credibility. His focus, however, is on the meaning of Jackson and Indian subjugation for American history.

The legacy of the American Revolution was ambiguous for both Jackson and the new nation. America emerged free of the parental domination of England; Jackson emerged an orphan. But for neither Jackson nor America was the Revolution the purifying experience proclaimed by its own rhetoric. The young country retained the vices of fraternal strife and acquisitive materialism for which the mother country had been blamed, and these vices were personified in the wild young Jackson. Dominated by a growing sense of their inferiority to the Founding Fathers, Americans of Jackson's generation sought a path to maturity by which they could assert their own paternal authority, overcome their weaknesses, and return to the values of their fathers not as children but as truly free men. What few men of this generation realized was that the source of most of the tensions and vices of their age was the free market revolution arising from the success of their fathers' revolution. The new freedoms were threatening the new order that had created them.

National social tensions were exaggerated for Jackson because of his unique personal history. The decline of familial support which all Americans experienced in some form under the atomizing pressures of *laissez-faire* capitalism was felt by Jackson as a searing personal loss. What was anxiety for others, suggests Rogin, was for Jackson primitive, infantile rage linked to the trauma of maternal separation. In Jackson's early adult years this rage often surfaced in the form of self-destructive violence.

It was to Indian warfare that Jackson eventually turned for therapy. By projecting his own primitive violence onto the Indians, externalizing his inner enemies and triumphing over them, he successfully sublimated his rage in socially acceptable and politically useful activity through which he achieved, in Rogin's words, "mature political authority." Rogin further demonstrates that it was through Jackson's experience in Indian relations that he forged the key elements of Jacksonian Democracy: egalitarian nationalism, personal charismatic leadership, the defense of agrarian values against imagined conspiratorial enemies, the patronage system, rampant capitalism, and a national destiny based on westward expansion. As President, it was through the program of Indian removal that Jackson achieved in its most striking form the Jacksonian state's peculiar synthesis of paternal authority and liberal egalitarianism: he *forced* the Indians to be "free"— to sell their lands and enter the free market system they had resisted in their traditional communal life.

Through this policy of enforced Indian dependence, Jackson was also redefining the Indian by the process of infantilization. As a "child" who must be guided by a "paternal" government, the Indian became a perfect target for the projection of the primitive fears and longings of the whites. The Indian represented for Americans the natural world they had left behind—that infantile, indulgent oral stage of development which was both attractive and forbidden. Here was that regressive fragment of the self which had to be destroyed in order to reach maturity. "By killing Indians," asserts Rogin, "whites grounded their growing up in a securely achieved manhood, and securely possessed their land."

The therapy which had worked so well for Jackson, however, was ultimately unsuccessful for the United States. The dispossession of the Indians was not only an assertion of American maturity, but an integral part of the market revolution which so disrupted American society. Jackson was "heroic" not only in terms of mortal combat with the primitive, but also in terms of primitive capitalist accumulation. The removal of the southern tribes cleared a major barrier to market expansion and to *laissez-faire* ideology, and the cotton kingdom which took their place was a prime factor in the rapid economic growth of the United States.

The agrarian whites had siezed the Indian lands only to be cursed with the Midas touch. The virgin land did not bring pastoral stability, but became instead just another commodity to be bought and sold in the impersonal world of the market which they found so disturbing. It is not surprising that Jacksonian reform has been called the politics of nostalgia.

Jacksonian Americans, notes Rogin, "were beginning to become the victims of the forces they embodied," and Andrew Jackson was, no less than his countrymen, a prisoner of the dialectic. His war on the Bank of the United States was a futile, counter-productive reaction to the market's disruption of American society. He could not stop with the government's removal of its deposits what he had started with the government's removal of Creeks and Choctaws, nor could the destruction of the Bank reverse the effects of the destruction of the Indians. The growing, invisible power over men's lives which Jackson mistakenly identified as the "Mother Bank" was actually the power of the free market itself, which grew even faster after the restraining Bank's demise.

Manifest Destiny, the final Jacksonian formula for averting fraternal strife and the evils of the market, proved equally self-destructive. Westward expansion entailed the sacrifice of Indians (or Mexicans) in order to unite white brothers; it was the answer of the Jacksonian Southern nationalist to the minority strategies of a Calhoun. But the Southern faith in agrarian expansion was ultimately doomed by the tensions of slavery and the strength of the free and aggressive market economy of the North. The fruits of Manifest Destiny finally turned brother against sectional brother in a fratricidal war, and "westward expansion, the linchpin of the Jacksonian system," declares Rogin, "shattered the politics which produced it."

Manifest Destiny was the ultimate extension of the original therapy of regeneration through frontier violence. It failed not only because it actually furthered economic disruption of society and led to a civil war, but also because the therapy was misdirected from the beginning. Unlike the symbolic return to childhood in psychoanalysis, the confrontation and conquest of primitive impulses in the form of Indians produced no self-awareness in whites, but turned them away from themselves in a tragic system in which "progress" was predicated upon destruction.

True to its genre, *Fathers and Children* is most stimulating when it is least reliable; its interpretive strengths rely on techniques that suggest methodological weakness to the traditional historian. Rogin's irrepressible imagination sometimes leads him into fascinating but distracting digressions, and his zeal to incorporate into his synthesis virtually every aspect of Jacksonian culture pushes him into at least one serious error (the confusion, in his discussion of Manifest Destiny, of the Neches and Nueces rivers of Texas in the boundary disputes of President Jackson and Polk). Yet the tragic and undeniable fact that the success and progress of the United States has depended upon a system of violence, fraud, and ultimate self-deception makes this study in historical psychopathology a valuable and unforgettable book.

James E. Crisp

THE FEMALE IMAGINATION

Author: Patricia Meyer Spacks (1929-   )
Publisher: Alfred A. Knopf (New York). 326 pp. $10.00
Type of work: Literary criticism

An exploration of recurrent themes in the prose of American and British women writers of the past three centuries which utilizes both traditional and creative methods of criticism

Patricia Meyer Spack's feminist criticism is neither heavily ideological nor particularly radical. She presents no appeals for abolishing the prevailing male-originated canons of critical judgment. Yet she does not simply pour old wine into new bottles, rehashing accepted critiques of Jane Austen or George Eliot. Rather, she presents a frankly feminist literary criticism which proceeds phenomenologically in trying to discover "the ways of female feeling, the modes of responding, that persist despite social change" and "the characteristic patterns of self-perception which shape the creative expression of women." Spack's book focuses on these concerns, as the various chapters delineate the characteristic modes of expression and the recurrent themes which the literature reveals.

Explicitly renouncing the historical approach and refusing as well that strategy which treats each author separately, Spacks traces a problem or theme in the works of several women writers. The result is a refreshing blend of criticism about well-known works (*The Mill on the Floss, Pride and Prejudice, To the Lighthouse*); about standard feminist "texts" (*The Bell Jar, The Awakening, The Diary of Anaïs Nin*); and about little-known works (*The Story of Mary MacLane,* Marie Bashkirtseff's *Journal,* Ellen Glasgow's *Vein of Iron*).

Spacks, a professor of English at Wellesley, intersperses student comment from her course, as well as occasional observations from her own experience. The effect of this technique, always used sparingly, is to give the reader the opportunity to draw on her or his own experience in ways not usually acceptable in responding to literature. Feminist literary criticism has been instrumental in questioning the received methods of critical analysis and in making reader response (sometimes called the "affective fallacy") an acceptable category of criticism; Spack's work strengthens this tendency.

After an opening chapter which critiques female theorists such as Virginia Woolf, Simone de Beauvoir, and Kate Millett, Spacks moves to her first theme, "Power and Passivity." This chapter explores the thesis that "the limitations imposed on women . . . may provide opportunity rather than impediment in the struggle for moral and emotional fulfillment." Nineteenth century women were powerful only *by means of* their passivity. Their one important choice in life—whom, and whether, to marry—could bring both the possibility of power and a threat to their independence. Various women novelists create a variety of heroines and situations. George Eliot's Gwendolen Harleth (*Daniel Deronda*) and Kate Chopin's Edna Pontellier (*The*

Awakening) understand only too late what matrimony costs them and are not able to survive within the institution of marriage. Charlotte Brontë's heroines manage happy marriages and gain power only because their men are either maimed or poor. All of these novelists implicitly question marriage as a happy fate, understanding the threat it poses to the woman's inner life.

"Taking Care" examines woman's traditional role—caring for child, husband, parent—and the women writers' image of marriage "as a state of moral possibility, the successful marriage both reward and arena for a woman's goodness." Here Spacks devotes much space to Jane Austen, whose novels are well concerned with the making of "good" marriages. But Spacks also studies Fanny Burney, Elizabeth Gaskell, Ellen Glasgow, Louisa May Alcott, and Virginia Woolf. The eighteenth and nineteenth century writers saw woman's vocation of service as a moral issue: although women must carefully balance their service to others against the demands of preserving selfhood, it is clearly "good" to help others and "bad" to be selfish. Virginia Woolf, in *To the Lighthouse,* portrays Mrs. Ramsay as an epitome of feminine altruism and Lily Briscoe as the artist who refuses to "take care" of others before herself. According to Spacks, Lily's final realization that she and Mrs. Ramsay *both* equally give form and meaning to life's small illuminations suggests that self-sacrifice may energize and fulfill—that the choice between family and profession "may be a choice between different versions of identical experience."

"The Adolescent as Heroine" analyzes such female *Bildüngsromane* as Austen's *Emma,* in which the young heroine grows up and obtains her moral education. But the chapter also explores more complex themes, such as female adolescence as the only genuine period of freedom for a woman (before the commitment to "taking care"), and the exploitation of female narcissism by men. Emily Brontë's *Wuthering Heights* and Sylvia Plath's *The Bell Jar* present heroines who value themselves *because* they cannot adjust to the adult world, although they refuse to be treated as children. Catherine Earnshaw Linton and Esther Greenwood are both alienated from themselves and irresponsible to society in their radical individualism. Martha Quest, in Doris Lessing's novel of the same name, is an anti-heroine, unable to rebel meaningfully, wallowing in self-pity and finally marrying in defeat. Spacks maintains that there are no serious works by women that "*celebrate* female adolescence."

The chapter on "The Artist as Woman" examines typical self-portrayals by women, some of whom were artists (like Isadora Duncan), others of whom created little art beyond their creation of themselves (like Margaret Anderson or Mary MacLane). Spacks analyzes Mary McCarthy's autobiography as art and artifice, showing how the image of the artist can transcend that of the adolescent.

"Finger Posts" chronicles those women whose lives are spent totally vicariously, directly channeling and nourishing others. The finger post is a sign, frequently shaped like a pointing finger or hand, which indicates a direction. The specific metaphor comes from the eighteenth century writer Hester Lynch Thrale, whose *Thraliana* both details the lives of Dr. Johnson and those of his circle and also offers insight into her own unhappy life. Women who see themselves as "finger posts" are actually expressing a negative or darker side of female altruism than that which emerges in the novels in the form of "taking care." In autobiographies the women writers often find inadequate outlet for their energy in "taking care" of family and turn outward to become "finger posts" for society. Spacks discusses the autobiography of Charlotte Perkins Gilman as paradigm here, brilliantly analyzing Gilman's breakdown, successful career, and final suicide.

The complex relationship between the inner reality of the self and the outer reality of "the world" in women's experience constitutes the subject of the chapter called "The World Outside." Among other works, Spacks explores George Eliot's *Middlemarch,* with its emphasis on female vocation; Edith Wharton's *The Buccaneers,* which suggests that the female imagination *creates* personal misery; and Virginia Woolf's *Mrs. Dalloway,* with its intense awareness of the ways that the outside world impinges on woman's possibilities. "The World Outside" may provide a screen behind which women can conduct their inner lives, or, at best, it may "supply a means for expressing the dimensions of inner reality" of a woman.

"How a woman is to find freedom for work and for love"—this is the conundrum that Spack discusses under the rubric of "Free Women." The

autobiographies of Beatrice Webb, Lady Mary Wortley Montague, Lillian Hellman, Isak Dinesen, and Anaïs Nin furnish evidence for her contention that female autobiography is concerned with freedom, freedom's limitations, and "defensive narcissism." The section also studies fictional "free women" such as Anna in Lessing's *The Golden Notebook* and Martha Quest in *The Four-Gated City.*

Spack's conclusions suggest that women's needs, finally, seem to be identical with men's: some kind of balance between work and love, independence and dependence, solitude and relationship, community and self. These polarities, however, seem often to become contradictions for women, because only the second element in each of these pairs is assumed to be a proper female goal. Those women, real or fictional, who seek the opposite experiences must pay a high price. And the response to that price is often a peculiar form of anger, a manner of rage which can issue in either growth or defensive reactions like self-pity, passivity, masochism, or narcissism. At the same time, such anger has often occasioned much of the great writing done by women: one thinks immediately of Charlotte Brontë or George Eliot, Virginia Woolf or Doris Lessing.

The strength of Spack's book lies in its profusion of illustrations (she presents more than eighty different titles from the obscure and scholarly to the more popular); in the clear exposition of some lesser known works; in the sensible commentary; and in the excellent index and useful bibliography. Hers is neither a brilliant synthesis nor an astonishing thesis, but it is one that needs to be presented. Spack's methodology is close textual analysis—hardly a new departure. Presenting her students' comments about various works and their relevance to their lives is a novel technique, but it does not really give support to her own critical views. Indeed, the full meaning of these views is not always clear; at times one feels that Spacks is using her thesis to force her subject matter, as if the analysis would be the same with a totally different thesis.

The book is sound literary criticism. One wishes, however, for more insights into the actual phenomenon of "the female imagination," more analyses of style, a discussion of the differences—if there are any—between male and female style, more comparisons with "the male imagination." In *A Room of One's Own,* Virginia Woolf worried about whether there is (or should be) a distinctive female style. She failed to reach a conclusion, saying at one point that "it is fatal for anyone who writes to think of their sex," while at another point suggesting that women may use characteristic sentence structures, forms, or images. The debate continues, and Spacks might have furthered the discussion greatly had she commented on style as well as theme. After all, "modes of responding" include not only *forms* of writing but also sentence structure, vocabulary, images, structure of work; that is, style.

The Female Imagination sustains and quickens that dramatic process of sexual reeducation which the past decade has witnessed. One feature of this powerful trend is the recovery and assessment of the legacy of female writing. The real value of Spacks's work becomes evident only if one places it in this historical context.

Margaret McFadden-Gerber

GEORGE ELIOT: THE EMERGENT SELF

Author: Ruby V. Redinger (1915-   )
Publisher: Alfred A. Knopf (New York). 515 pp. $15.00
Type of work: Biography
Time: 1819-1880
Locale: England, Scotland, Switzerland, Germany, France, Italy

An interpretive study of the opposing psychological forces which thwarted Mary Ann Evans but which also served the emergence of the mature woman and novelist George Eliot

Principal personages:
> MARY ANN EVANS (later GEORGE ELIOT), English novelist
> ROBERT AND CHRISTIANA EVANS, her parents
> ISAAC EVANS, her brother
> MARIA LEWIS, her childhood teacher and friend
> CHARLES AND CAROLINE BRAY, AND SARA HENNELL, friends in young womanhood who provided intellectual stimulation and entry into the world of letters
> JOHN CHAPMAN, a London publisher, editor of the *Westminster Review*, who gave Mary Ann Evans employment and friendship after her father's death
> HERBERT SPENCER, the philosopher who became her friend in London
> GEORGE HENRY LEWES, the philosopher and critic who became her common-law husband
> JOHN W. CROSS, the writer whom she married after the death of Lewes, who became her biographer

Ruby V. Redinger's biography is a study of the "emergence" of George Eliot both as a great woman and a great novelist. Redinger, a Professor of Literature at Baldwin-Wallace College in Berea, Ohio, has spent over fifteen years working on this biography. Acknowledging the work of modern scholars such as Gordon S. Haight, whose seven-volume edition of Eliot's letters is a primary resource, this biographer offers not new facts but a personal interpretation of the facts to discover how the "writing self" of the novelist grew out of the discordant selves of Mary Ann Evans.

George Eliot: The Emergent Self thus focuses not on the novelist but on the woman who could not be a novelist until she had come to terms with the forces which had thwarted her life. Redinger presents a fascinating chronicle of inner conflicts resolved painfully, almost one at a time over a great span of years, through a series of frustrating relationships and experiences. This history of the gradual emergence of the whole self culminates in the productive liaison with George Henry Lewes at the only period when George Eliot could have coped with such a relationship, an example of almost miraculous timing in the growth of the personality.

Redinger's premise is that George Eliot was a woman whose psyche was so severely damaged in childhood that nothing less than a long, painful process of self-discipline and self-discovery, as well as a compulsion—often repressed—to be a writer, could have created the woman who in 1857 became George Eliot. The biographer argues convincingly that during earliest childhood Mary Ann Evans suffered serious emotional deprivation, the absence of real parental love, and the subsequent failure to obtain any satisfactory substitute in the crucial early years. The chronic invalidism of Mrs. Evans—otherwise a strong, domineering woman—was a defense against motherhood, and her aversion to children was expressed by putting them in boarding school as soon as possible, Mary Ann having been sent away at the age of five. George Eliot's relative silence about the mother who lived until the daughter reached the age of sixteen is read as evidence of the mother's withdrawal. The mother simply never gave the kind of assured love necessary for normal emotional growth. It was a crucial loss to the child. The hardworking father, a man of conservative views with a habit of indecisiveness and a compensatory boastfulness and authoritarian willfulness, would not have been likely to supply the love lacking in the mother. Redinger persuasively suggests that George Eliot's boast of having been her father's favorite was mostly wishful thinking. Others who might have cherished the little girl, the older sister and the children of Mr. Evans's first marriage, were no longer living at home. Only the idyllic companionship of brother and sister, in the years between the ages of three and five when Mary Ann and her older brother Isaac were playmates, could have eased the loneliness. George Eliot remembered the relationship as the one perfection in her childhood. But Redinger finds evidence that it was instead the more common situation among children in which the older brother exploits his advantage over the younger sister, who must constantly court but seldom win his approval.

More interesting than the study of a loveless childhood is Redinger's interpretation of its lasting effects upon the future novelist. The negative forces are those one might anticipate, especially the obsessive desire to be "all in all" to one person, coupled with an expectation of failure in obtaining that desire. In her quest for approval, the child, and later the woman, was sometimes willful and demanding, but more often submissive and self-effacing. Desiring to identify with Isaac, Mary Ann consciously imitated him, developing the strongly masculine traits which were to trouble her as she sought her own identity as a woman. On the other hand, the results were not all negative. An independent, imaginative ego existed alongside the dependent spirit with its unfulfilled yearnings. Despite tradition that the child used her imagination as a defense against unhappiness, Redinger concludes that the imagination operated most strongly when Mary Ann was happy —when Isaac was kind, for example —so that the creative impulse was linked originally with positive forces. On the other hand, it was suppressed by Isaac, who regularly became angry with his sister's daydreaming. As a consequence the maturing woman always felt guilty about indulging herself and her creative gifts. She was caught up in a cycle of misery. Because she felt unloved, she was unworthy of love. Because her happiness and her daydreaming provoked anger, she must renounce those self-indulgences. To win love, she must in effect deny herself, and yet she succeeded so seldom that she expected to fail. Hers was a long journey towards respect for her ego and her creative powers.

Redinger traces throughout George Eliot's life, especially prior to 1857, a progression in which these various conflicts are gradually resolved. For example, the youthful experience with Evangelicalism was primarily a brief respite in which the young girl could assuage her guiltily assertive ego through self-renunciation and unselfish giving. But it also produced a positive increase in her capacity for sympathy. Both her work as translator and as editorial assistant for the *Westminster Review* eased the guilt associated with writing, for in working with the words of others she could not accuse herself of asserting her own ego. In these cases the relief was only partial, for her emotional life suffered. During the years of the translation of Strauss's *Das Leben Jesu,* she was afflicted by a depression which her friends called her "Strauss-sickness." She grew similarly weary of her work on the *Westminster Review,* telling her friends: "Here I am a poor never-having-time-to-clean-myself potter's vessel." But from her dissatisfaction she learned that she was better than a mere potter's vessel, and she gained confidence in her talents.

Her relationships, even after the liberating experience of finding a congenial intellectual circle among the Charles Brays of Coventry and later among her new friends in London,

continued her lifelong pattern of self-abnegation. George Eliot's various relationships before her union with Lewes are nearly all depicted as poignantly ludicrous, the spectacle of an insecure young woman clutching desperately at love, not only repeatedly disappointed but also repeatedly placing herself in situations that would bring disappointment. But again, George Eliot learned.

Redinger uses these crucial stages of learning to provide the main structure of this biography. For example, the chapter entitled "The Dire Years" deals with Mary Ann Evans' bondage to her aging father and to the difficult translation of Strauss. Her prevailing mood was one of low self-esteem. The most significant personal event of those years was an apparent defeat after a brief rebellion against her father and brother in the matter of church attendance. Yet, Redinger believes, it was ultimately an important personal triumph. The young woman chose defeat on her own terms. In submission, she discovered genuine self-restraint. As she realized that her open revolt was an act of destructive ego, she was enabled to empathize with her father's feelings, not judge them. She voluntarily submitted because she acknowledged a bond of love which for her was a sacred obligation. Out of this situation came a central point in her own philosophy, her belief that "sympathy, all-embracing love" is the basis of the moral nature. This belief saw her through those dire years and became the informing spirit of her fiction in later years. Paradoxically, through her sacrifice, she also gained some measure of independence, for, as Redinger notes, having submitted to her father, she never again allowed any external pressures to influence her decisions. The moral courage, the respect for the bond of love, the great powers of sympathy so characteristic of the novelist, were the forces evolving out of a situation which seemed merely repressive.

In her frustrated love for John Chapman as well as in her successful work as his editorial assistant, George Eliot came to terms finally with the most destructive forces she had inherited from childhood. She emerged from that experience for the first time relatively free of a craving for love, in possession of herself as both woman and writer. This was the turning point of her life, for it was during this period of emotional equilibrium that she met George Henry Lewes. Only then, at the age of thirty-two, had she matured sufficiently for a serious relationship with this particular man. Indeed, earlier she had considered him somewhat frivolous. Had she loved him earlier, she might have expected failure of her hopes in this irrevocably married man. Of course, some of the old forces were once more at work. George Eliot again sought a love that would be all in all, that would provide the long-lost comradeship of her happiest moments with her brother, and that would assure ego satisfaction through approval of her service as a helpmate. As in her previously unhappy relationships, she shored up her defenses through a bond of love which would test her moral courage. The difference was that Lewes gave what she required, and she had the strength to risk everything for him. In a lengthy analysis of their relationship and of Lewes's own personality, Redinger concludes that the "personal bond between them had been growing, unknown to either in their past lives," their union a fortuitous, or perhaps providential, meeting of like natures.

Lewes himself enabled George Eliot to resolve other conflicts. By fostering his sons' affection for her, he made her a surrogate mother, confirming her feminine role. She wrote an acquaintance that because the sons called her "Mother," it was not "mere egoism or personal dignity" that made her insist upon being addressed as "Mrs. Lewes" but her obligation to her place in Lewes's life. The liaison also opened the way to writing fiction. Although George Eliot had come to accept herself as intellectual, she still regarded fiction writing as self-indulgence. Financial need gave the necessary justification, while Lewes maintained the emotional support essential to her creativity. With remarkable insight he not only recognized her genius, but also perceived the destructive inner forces which blocked her creative powers and acted upon his discovery that her imagination could flourish only in happiness. He made it possible for the writing self, George Eliot, to emerge.

Lewes's share in the choice of the pseudonym is suggestive. "George" is obviously borrowed from him, although there is some evidence that it is partly a tribute to George Sand, in whose novels the young Mary Ann had first discovered the value of human passions. According to tradition, the second name also refers to Lewes, acknowledging plainly, "To L I owe it." More important is the value of the name to its possessor. It re-

solved the conflict of "double consciousness" which had developed out
of Mary Ann Evans' sense of un-
worthiness, the split between the self
which lived and acted and had its
being as Mary Ann Evans or Marian
Evans or Marian Lewes and a second
self which stood apart and dis-
approved. Once the second self was
christened George Eliot, it was transformed from destructive critic into
constructive analyst. Furthermore,
the masculine name served to reconcile the "opposing demands of her
androgynous nature." In addition,
although the masculine name George
Eliot and the feminine name Mrs.
Lewes were both fictions, they became realities—or, as the biographer
suggests—"highly operative symbols"
of her real life. As a result, "Her
inner self responded to her outward
life as signified by the two names, so
that the process of self control which
had begun [earlier] was carried on."

In the last chapters of the biography, Redinger provides useful insight into the novels of George Eliot,
reading them as explorations of the
hidden impulses which had rendered
life despairing to the young Mary
Ann Evans, and of the painfully
learned lessons which had effected
her mature triumph. The carefully

documented history of the novelist's
long journey into maturity gives cre-
dence to these interpretations, as does
the biographer's scrupulous efforts
not to claim too much. The final
chapter deals with the brief period
after Lewes's death, when George
Eliot shocked many by her marriage
to John Cross, and when she apparently lost her compulsion to write.
In these two facts Redinger finds evidence that all conflicts were resolved.
Marriage to Cross maintained the
emotional security essential to George
Eliot. More important, perhaps, the
legality of the union restored her
brother Isaac, who had never acknowledged either George Eliot or
Mrs. Lewes but who congratulated
Mrs. Cross. As a result the need to
write slackened, not because of the
loss of Lewes or because of ill health,
but simply because "the past had
been restored by a means other than
through writing, and she had come
home again."

This biography is of obvious interest to students of literature, but it is
even more significant as the history
of the emotional life of a woman
with every disadvantage, including
the stigma of genius, who emerges
after long struggle into wholeness
and creativity.

Catherine E. Moore

GLOBAL REACH
The Power of the Multinational Corporations

Authors: Richard J. Barnet and Ronald E. Müller
Publisher: Simon and Schuster (New York). 508 pp. $11.95
Type of work: Economics and current affairs
Time: The 1960's and 1970's
Locale: The world, particularly the United States and Latin America

An exposé of the revolutionary vision, power, and impact of large multi-national corporations whose recent phenomenal rise has seriously and for the most part adversely affected both the United States and the underdeveloped countries of the world

Events of recent years, such as the energy crisis, the involvement of ITT in the downfall of Chilean President Allende, and the Lockheed payoffs in Japan, have increased Americans' awareness of a significant and ambiguous force in many areas of their lives—the multinational corporation. Of course, the existence of companies doing business across national borders is hardly new—the Hudson Bay and Massachusetts Bay Companies being only two examples from our earliest history—but their growth and influence here and abroad in the last years has been phenomenal. Richard J. Barnet and Ronald E. Müller in *Global Reach: The Power of the Multinational Corporations* attempt to assess the significance of that growth and influence. In their view, "The rise of the planetary enterprise is producing an organizational revolution as profound in its implications for modern man as the Industrial Revolution and the rise of the nation-state itself."

The most essential feature of these large corporations discussed in Part I of *Global Reach* is precisely their internationality, or, more accurately, their anationality. Many large United States-based corporations such as Gillette, Woolworth, Mobil, IBM, and Coca-Cola now earn more than fifty percent of their profits overseas; but while American firms may have at one time dominated the world market and "still hold a commanding lead," the authors point out that "Global corporations are neither an American invention nor an American phenomenon." Hundreds of American manufacturing interests are now foreign-owned, and the size of the American share of the world market has been shrinking. But the key factor is that the interest and objectives of the multinational corporations transcend national borders, which gives them their revolutionary quality. Quite simply, a company that employs the capital and managerial talent of one country to develop raw materials in another country to be made into components in a third location to be assembled in a fourth and sold in a fifth, ends up owing more allegiance to its own balance sheets than to any of the countries in which it does business.

Moreover, this is not merely a charge of the multinationals' detractors, but a central part of the progressive vision of the corporate leaders themselves, something they proudly claim as the means for future world peace and prosperity. Projecting images of a "World Shopping Center" and the "Global Factory," these world managers, in addition to their capital and technology, offer planning, integration, efficiency, and a shared ideology of consumption and growth as the means to rid the world not only of poverty, unemployment, and crime, but also of the wars that come from "irrational nationalism." What makes the multinational structures forces to be reckoned with is that many of the largest firms already do more business than the GNP's of most nations, and the effectiveness of their anational planning and ideology has left even the most advanced nations ill-prepared to handle or regulate them.

This does not mean, however, that the multinationals' future of unlimited expansion is assured. There are detractors—leftists, labor leaders, smaller competing companies, nationalists, environmentalists. More importantly, the rise of multinationals is built on an ideology of unlimited growth, bigness, and centralization, on values of consumption and a life style modeled somewhat after the United States, and these are all ideas that have to be sold to an increasingly skeptical world. Thus, Barnet and Müller end their first part with a discussion of "The Great Crusade for Understanding," the attempts of the multinationals to convince the world that their view of the future is brighter than what nations of any economic system can offer; they lay claim, in short, to legitimacy.

In Part II, the test of this legitimacy is first measured in the underdeveloped world which Barnet and Müller describe as the "ultimate test of the World Managers' global vision of peace and abundance." Are the

multinationals "engines for development" in the poor third-world countries? The authors' answer is no, when measured by the fairly objective standards of increasing the economic well-being for at least sixty percent of the population. The explanations grow out of the reasons for the corporations' interest in the underdeveloped world in the first place— reasons that form a pattern called the Product Life Cycle. Much simplified, this cycle describes the process by which a major company in a developed country is first driven to export, then to manufacture abroad and eventually to employ "export platforms" (countries with cheap labor where a product is manufactured for use elsewhere). At each stage of this cycle the key factors are the drive for continual growth in an ever-expanding market, the devotion of investment to marketing and advertising techniques, and the emergence of a corporation whose global profits matter more than the profits or losses of any of its subsidiaries.

The reason why the poor countries remain poor or even become poorer, the authors argue, is because the interests of the Global corporations in many ways simply do not coincide with the needs of the underdeveloped country. Basically, for a country to develop, to become wealthy, it needs "capital stock . . . the tangible (and expensive) infrastructures that enable modern developed societies to function and to create more wealth—roads, communication systems, schools, machines, and factories." The multinationals do develop the finance capital (intangible but investible excess wealth) that could create this capital stock. However, it is not left in the underdeveloped country where it is produced, but siphoned off in the form of dividends, royalties, and technical fees, and the local governments often lack either the capacity or the will to reclaim any of this finance capital in the form of taxes, tariffs, or regulations. Other examples of these diverging interests are the cases of several countries importing industrial technology that increased their unemployment, and of others importing the consumer ideology that has the now better-paid workers spending their money on Coca-Cola and transistor radios instead of the nutrition, clothing, shelter, and education they need. But, perhaps most devastatingly, the authors disptue the notion that without foreign capital there would be no investment of any kind in the underdeveloped countries. They point out that the multinationals actually use a great deal of local capital in their enterprises, attracting investment by virtue of their size and potential for success and thereby further extending their control over local economies at less risk to themselves. For Barnet and Müller the solution to these problems lies less in nationalization than in the individual countries waking up to their bargaining power, banding together in some cases in producer alliances such as OPEC, and generally forcing the multinationals to pay back in wealth and divested power more of what they have been taking away.

In the long and somewhat tedious third section of *Global Reach* the authors recapitulate much of what they had previously argued about the multinationals and attempt to show how the United States is becoming "Latin-Americanized"; that is, subject to some of the same abuses of oligopoly from which the underdeveloped countries suffer. Their primary concern is how the large companies make decisions affecting the lives of all of us but are not politically accountable, not only because of their international outlook, but because the traditional monetary, legal, political, and social means of dealing with them are outmoded. The concentrations of financial power in a few banks, and business practices such as transfer pricing (buying and selling at falsely inflated or deflated prices between subsidiaries of a single corporation) and cross subsidizing (using investment power from one "profit center" to expand or dominate in another) have destroyed the classical concepts of the market or at least rendered it ineffective as a regulator. Government regulatory agencies too closely share the viewpoints of those they are supposed to regulate, and labor unions lose their strike weapon when the more mobile corporation threatens to move its plant overseas. Barnet and Müller go even further to describe how the large multinational corporations are affecting the quality of our lives and our environment, turning us into powerless consumers of gadgets, wallowing in pollution.

Regarding solutions to some of these problems the authors are only modestly hopeful and helpful. Much more information through better disclosure laws is a first step for governments to regain some of the advantage the multinationals now hold, and more innovative regulation by international bodies as well as nations, states, and even cities is needed. Ultimately, however, according to the authors, there must be a shift in values, a turning away from wholeheartedly embracing unlimited growth, bigness, centralization, and wasteful consumption as primary ideals, a refusal to measure efficiency by what is efficient for the corporation, rather than what is efficient for humanity generally. By aiming their book at the general public (notes are collected at the end and jargon is scrupulously avoided), Barnet and Müller clearly hope to promote some of these shifts in attitude, and to disseminate some of the knowledge about the multinationals that is prerequisite to combating them. But, after reading their descriptions of the obvious countervailing power of media advertising, it is hard to find much room for optimism.

John Cleman

THE GREAT RAILWAY BAZAAR
By Train Through Asia

Author: Paul Theroux (1941-   )
Publisher: Houghton Mifflin (Boston). 342 pp. $10.00
Type of work: Travel account
Time: September 1973 to early January 1974
Locale: From London through Central Europe, the Middle East, and Asia, returning via the Soviet Union

A vivid, detailed description of the places and people encountered during a circular four-month railroad trip that begins in London and includes much of Central Europe, Turkey, Iran, Afghanistan, Pakistan, India, Burma, Thailand, Malaysia, South Vietnam, Japan, and the Soviet Union

As the passenger railroad in America groans and creaks to extinction, with only a skeletal Amtrak to placate the diehards, it has become an object of nostalgia and idealization—which no doubt helps to explain the surprising popularity of this "travel book." But for the rest of the world railroads provide a very real, if often erratic and chaotic, mode of transportation. Indeed, it is a thesis of *The Great Railway Bazaar* that railroads are the microcosms of the nations they traverse, test tubes in which one finds, in the most colorful and volatile compounds, the essence of the culture: "The railway bazaar, with its gadgets and passengers, represented the society so completely that to board it was to be challenged by the national character."

Besides, trains are great fun to ride, and Paul Theroux is an addict: "Ever since childhood, when I lived within earshot of the Boston and Maine, I have seldom heard a train go by and not wished I was on it. Those whistles sing bewitchment."

Anything is possible on a train: a great meal, a binge, a visit from card players, an intrigue, a good night's sleep, and strangers' monologues framed like Russian short stories. It was my intention to board every train that chugged into view from Victoria Station in London to Tokyo Central; to take the branch line to Simla, the spur through the Khyber Pass, and the chord line that links Indian Railways with those in Ceylon; the Mandalay Express, the Malaysian Golden Arrow, the locals in Vietnam, and the trains with bewitching names, the Orient Express, the North Star, the Trans-Siberian.

But, of course, the quality of the experience depends to a great extent on the receptivity of the passenger. Paul Theroux is the perfect traveler. Although hardly an "innocent abroad"—he had traveled a good deal of the route before, had lived in Singapore for some years, and chronicled the area in his novels (*Jungle Lovers, Saint Jack, The Black House*)—Theroux's sense of wonder is alive, his perceptions are acute, and his wit is sharp. He deftly balances the feeling of a naïve passenger's virginal response to the experience, bizarre and threatening, with the experienced traveler's resourcefulness, experience, and confidence. While there is no reason to doubt the veracity of the account (he even tells one co-passenger that as soon as he was "out of sight" Theroux would "write down what he said . . . and describe his mustache"), the novelist is never out of sight. *The Great Railway Bazaar* is almost like a picaresque novel with Paul Theroux as picaro who not only reacts to events surrounding him, but plays active roles in shaping them.

This novel is similar to a film. Like a first-rate cameraman, Theroux is especially adroit at focusing on the small, relevant details of sight, sound, and texture that instantly capture the essence of the person or place. He can instantly shift from the intimacy of a close-up to the mob activity of a medium shot to the lyrical beauty of a landscape or figures etched in long shot distance:

> . . . At a road near the track a crowd of people fought to look at a horse, still in its traces and hitched to an overloaded wagon, lying dead on its side in a mud puddle in which the wagon was obviously stuck. I imagined its heart had burst when it tried to free the wagon. And it had just happened: children were calling to their friends, a man was dropping his bike and running back for a look. . . .

But it is in the close-up that Theroux is most impressive, because this is where he captures the personalities of individual people. "I sought trains," he states, "I found passengers." For example, he describes his first memorable traveling companion, a man named Duffill:

> Duffill had that uneasy look of a man who has left his parcels elsewhere, which is also the look of a man who

thinks he's being followed. His oversized clothes made him seem frail. A mouse gray gabardine coat slumped in folds from his shoulders, the cuffs so long, they reached to his fingertips and answered the length of his trampled trousers. He smelled of bread crusts.

Looking as he does, Duffill seems like the type who would easily become confused, panic, and get left behind; "Duffill" therefore becomes a word in Theroux's vocabulary: to "duffill" is to miss one's train.

This gallery of fascinating snapshots and the sharp vignettes that capture their characters in action are the most memorable features of the book. "The railway was a factor's bazaar in which anyone with the patience could carry away a memory to pore over in privacy." Admittedly, Theroux goes in for the extreme, the obsessed, the comical, and the grotesque: Sadik, the lecherous Moslem who refrains from visiting Mecca because "once you go to Mecca, you have to make promises—no drinking, no swearing, no women, money to people. . . . Is for old men. I'm not ready"; V. G. Deshmukh, the unsuccessful Indian novelist, who will write 108 unprofitable novels because "Vishnu has 108 names"; Cedric, the pompous Englishman, who will bring order to rural Malaysia by "good old-fashioned caning"; the Indian professor of literature who gives a two-year course in Henry James's *The Golden Bowl*; the "family planners" from Bangladesh who see no contradiction between their work and their own five-plus families, and who lament that they can do nothing until "a census is taken," however long that may be; the Vietnam officials who, in the midst of the war, launch an advertising campaign to bring tourism to South Vietnam.

To be sure, some of these figures and scenes are almost cartoons, but Theroux avoids turning the book into a traveling freak show by carefully relating the individuals to their environments and by always keeping the larger context of the journey fixed in the reader's mind. These colorful characters stand out from their backgrounds, but they remain firmly connected to it.

Theroux's acute sense of place, his ability to evoke quickly and sharply the total ambience of a location with a minimum of vital, concrete details is what gives validity to his cultural generalizations. For example, he sees all of India in the Amritsar railway terminal:

> Indian railway stations are wonderful places for killing time in, and they are like scale models of Indian society, with its divisions of caste, class, and sex: SECOND-CLASS LADIES' WAITING ROOM, BEARERS' ENTRANCE, THIRD-CLASS EXIT, FIRST-CLASS TOILET, VEGETARIAN RESTAURANT, NON-VEGETARIAN RESTAURANT, RETIRING ROOMS, CLOAKROOM, and the whole range of occupations on office signboards, from the tiny one saying SWEEPER, to the neatest of all, STATIONMASTER.

Utilizing all of his skills as a first-rate novelist, Theroux carefully modulates his story, balances the comic with the serious, the grotesque with the beautiful, the purely narrative with the dramatic. He knows when simply to sit back and let his characters perform; he knows when to intrude carefully to influence the events, to react to them, or even to summarize their meaning to the reader. When stimulated to direct commentary, Theroux consolidates his insights with precise and powerful rhetoric:

> . . . the Vietnamese had been damaged and then abandoned, almost as if, dressed in our clothes, they had been mistaken for us and shot at; as if, just when they had come to believe that we were identified with them, we had bolted. . . . The tragedy was that we had come, and, from the beginning, had not planned to stay: Danang was to be proof of that.

Thus, despite his detached pose, Theroux has a deep emotional involvement in the events of his journey. He is no simple chronicler; he is the main character in his own nonfiction novel and, like the central character in any good narrative, he develops. "Travel writing, which cannot but be droll at the outset, moves from journalism to fiction, arriving as promptly as the Kodama Echo at autobiography." The eagerness and openness evident at the beginning of the trip gives way to a weariness and irritation by the end of it. At the start of his journey he calls the view from the train window "a continuous vision, a grand tour's succession of memorable images," but, after four months, that same window "seemed an imprisoning thing and at times took on the opacity of a cell wall."

No doubt this shift in attitude was at least partly the natural result of a long, strenuous trip, absence from wife and family, and the fact that the journey concluded with the longest, dullest stretch, the vast and barren Soviet Union: "It was brown, flat, and treeless, the grimmest landscape I had ever laid eyes on, like an immense beach of frozen dirt washed by an oily black sea."

But, beyond that, it is strongly suggested that his emotional and intellectual faculties have been assaulted too long. The tone of the book moves from genial irony to indignation to black humor that becomes blacker and more grotesque as the trip progresses. Although Theroux finds much to admire in particular individuals, as well as pockets of beauty and purpose, his general conclusions about the various nations are pessimistic and depressing. The meaningless ostentation in Teheran, the death and stench in India, the dull inertia of Burma, the oppression and greed of Singapore, the sexual perversity of Bangkok, the dissection of Vietnam, the mechanistic dehumanization of Japan, the desperate isolation of the Russian landscape—

all this and more leave him with a battered, numbed, and vaguely disgusted sensibility.

It is unclear at the end of the book whether or not Theroux has been cured of his railroad obsession. On the one hand he confesses that he "felt flayed by the four months of train travel: it was as if I had undergone some harrowing cure, sickening myself on my addiction in order to be free of it." On the other hand, however, he ends the book by quoting its beginning: *"Ever since childhood, when I lived within earshot of the Boston and Maine, . . ."* Such addictions are not easy to satiate permanently.

So, whether or not Paul Theroux ever again takes to the rails is problematical. But as a result of this sojourn he has given us a fascinating, exhilarating, depressing, insightful, amusing, sad book that will remain sharply etched in memory for a long time.

Keith Neilson

THE GREAT VICTORIAN COLLECTION

Author: Brian Moore (1921-   )
Publisher: Farrar, Straus and Giroux (New York). 213 pp. $7.95; paperback $1.75
Type of work: Novel
Time: The present
Locale: Carmel, Los Angeles, and Montreal

A fantasy dealing with an obscure assistant professor's dream which comes true in the shape of an elaborate collection of Victoriana that astounds the world and involves the professor in a desperate campaign to preserve his creation

> *Principal characters:*
> ANTHONY MALONEY, an assistant professor of history whose dream materializes
> FRED VATERMAN, a young journalist
> MARY ANN MCKELVEY, Fred's fiancée
> MR. MCKELVEY, Mary Ann's father
> MR. HICKMAN, a business promoter
> DR. SPECTOR, a parapsychologist

"The Imagination may be compared to Adam's dream—he awoke and found it true." So wrote John Keats in a letter to his friend Benjamin Bailey late in November, 1817. In Brian Moore's novel the central character, Anthony Maloney, wakes to the literal truth of his dream: a huge collection of Victorian artifacts and art works piled up in a lot adjacent to the motel in Carmel, California, where he spent the previous night. Adam's dream of the creation of his female companion Eve took on a will and life of its own which ultimately changed Adam's life—to say the least. Maloney's dream has no less powerful an effect on him. The Victorian collection makes him famous overnight. A lonely and divorced assistant professor, he becomes important to psychics, art collectors, and the promoters of extravaganzas and exhibitions. Simultaneously, he is plunged into desperate anxieties that make Adam's expulsion from Eden look like a pleasant journey.

Moore's previous work has explored the dynamics of fantasy and authoritarianism or paternity. Whereas dreams or fantasies are a way of escaping the community of the fathers in his earlier fiction (*The Luck of Ginger Coffey,* 1960; *I Am Mary Dunne,* 1968), the more recent works (*The Revolution Script,* 1971; *Catholics,* 1972) take a more charitable view toward the fathers and scrutinize with cold irony the liberating power of dreams.

In *The Great Victorian Collection,* dreaming is no longer merely evasion or neurosis but rather a clear road to madness and death. Anthony Maloney's pseudocreation becomes an allegory for the media-conscious and fad-oriented mass imagination of modern society, which allows itself to be manipulated by exploiting interests. The autocratic fathers of the earlier books are conspicuously absent—Maloney is dominated by a scatterbrained and cold mother—or transformed into cranks or weak old men who counsel sanity from a distance. Maloney's Collection is periodically picketed by a derelict brandishing a sign that reads "God Alone Can Create Do Not Believe This Lie"; and Mary Ann's father, who is characterized as vengeful and murderous (with incestuous longings for his daughter) by her insipid and paranoid boyfriend, is in fact a loving and gentle parent, who helps his daughter escape from the pathological attentions of both Anthony and the boyfriend, Fred. When Anthony announces that he will not be able to get along without Mary Ann, her father offers the following consolation: "You'll get over it. Fellows like you must be in love with yourselves. Otherwise, why would you dream up things to make the world take notice of you?"

Vanity is an important clue toward understanding Moore's theme. The mere act of dreaming cannot be construed as a human achievement unless it expresses something more than the dreamer's little world, no matter how tortured or neurotically intricate that world may be. Adam's sympathetic imagination gave him another being, Eve. Anthony's solipsistic imagination provides merely a reproduction of his own repressed personality. Moore achieves something of a *tour de force* by identifying that personality with a Collection that provides a historical source for the tawdry stuff on which the collective modern dream is based. There is rich irony in the promoter Hickman's dismissal of most of the Collection as being too esoteric. The "erotic stuff" and the "brothel parlor" are fine, but Hickman has his doubts about the bulk of the Collection, which includes *papier-mâché* easy

chairs, marquetry dressing tables with botanical carvings, red silk sofas, tea sets, ornamental urns, cheval glasses, ottomans, gaming tables, and fireguards, not to mention such technological marvels as the locomotive "Folkstone" originally designed for the Great Exhibition of 1851. Yesterday's ostentation and bad taste become the high culture of today, "a bit over the heads of the general public." Hickman would prefer Maloney to dream another dream, one with greater commercial possibilities. Modestly, Maloney answers that he can only dream what he knows. "And what I know is Victoriana." "Imagine," says Hickman, "if you could materialize real people. That would be a major breakthrough." But Anthony is no Adam, and Hickman and his promoters are left with the dream they deserve.

Does Anthony deserve his dream? His fate seems unduly harsh. Divorced from a petty woman, he is hungry for affection. Mary Ann is attracted to him mainly because of his notoriety, and when he fails to perform effectively as a lover she does not understand his anxieties and assumes that the sexual failure is hers. Anthony's anxieties are attributed to the gradual erosion of the Collection. At first he guards it in his sleep with a dream in which a television camera scans the aisles. But soon he notices that despite all precautions various objects lose their luster and some even begin to look like contemporary reproductions. He begins to fear sleep, which he believes may cause the Collection to disappear. Finally, he cannot sleep and tries desperately to shake the hold that the Collection has on his mind by cavorting with

Mary Ann and Fred in Los Angeles into the early morning hours. After they return to Carmel, Anthony runs off with Mary Ann once more, this time without Fred, to Montreal. It is here, back in his native city, that Anthony has to face his impotency with Mary Ann and loses his last chance at forging a reality strong enough to substitute for his dream.

Left with nothing but his Collection, he finally becomes its prisoner. In an interview with Dr. Spector, Anthony concedes that even if he could dream another dream to free him from the present one, he would probably become its prisoner as well. After this revelation, Anthony's condition continues to deteriorate. Finally, he dies as a result of seeking complete forgetfulness through alcohol and an overdose of drugs. He begins with a terrifying fear of losing the Collection, and ends by succumbing almost gratefully to the oblivion of forgetting it. Hickman and the cartel of promoters are far less vulnerable. They have built a Victorian Village to accommodate all the tourists visiting the Collection. The Village's restaurants, markets, and such shops as the Florence Nightingale Tea Room and the Oscar Wilde Way Out, a "men's-wear boutique," have done so well and become so popular that most tourists confuse the Village with the Collection, and attendance at the Collection Exhibit itself becomes almost negligible.

Brian Moore has written a disturbing fantasy, disturbing not because it forces us once more to confront the shallowness of our materialistic culture (a theme sounded often enough in the last fifty years of fiction), but because it insists on a full reckoning with the illusion that every man has —as the recently popular song puts it, his "impossible dream." Don Quixote had it—the dream of chivalry, a human ideal—and was rendered both noble and absurd in the brilliant light of comedy. But Anthony Maloney is only a psychic curiosity, and his dream a death-in-life. And if he dies a man whose taste for life is so primitive that he can be destroyed by a shoddy dream, we are left with the queasy feeling that his fate could be our own; that our misguided self-love, our trust in the uniqueness of our minds, is based, after all, on little more than the convictions of a century that produced such bric-a-brac as the Marvell Collection of Victorian Toys. What else do *we* know? What are *we* capable of dreaming?

Peter A. Brier

THE GREAT WAR AND MODERN MEMORY

Author: Paul Fussell (1924-   )
Publisher: Oxford University Press (New York). 363 pp. $13.95
Type of work: Literary and cultural history
Time: Immediately before, during, and after World War I
Locale: England, the Continent, and America

A study of the ways in which English and American authors have dealt with the experience of World War I in their writings

Paul Fussell has written a fine and important study of the impact of World War I on the imagination of the English-speaking world, especially as it is revealed in the writings of those who participated in it. Fussell's thesis, which he argues convincingly and with a wealth of example, is that the first modern war taught English-speaking writers a vocabulary which they have since used to describe the meaning of the postwar world. From the waste land of T. S. Eliot's most important poem to the paranoid vision of Thomas Pyncheon's *Gravity's Rainbow,* from the bleakness of Hemingway's *A Farewell to Arms* to the multiple ironies of Joseph Heller's *Catch-22,* the terms with which modern writers have dealt with the experience of modern man in the West have all come from the experiences of men, especially Englishmen, during the years of World War I. The nature of life in the trenches, the horrors of combat, the randomness of death, the stupidity and stubbornness of military leaders, the closeness of home and the foreignness of the war experience, the inadequacy of old concepts and modes of thought to deal with the new situation—all these factors and others, had their part to play in developing the distinctively modern consciousness of recent writers.

Fussell's work is, as well, a description and history of the war itself, which strips away the anonymity of history books and presents the events of the war through the eyes of the participants. Drawing heavily on letters, diaries, war poems, and memoirs of the combatants, as well as on contemporary newspapers, Fussell paints a graphic and often moving picture of the nature of life in the trenches. He contrasts the naïve optimism and idealism of the early days of the war with the growing sense of disillusionment and despair as the war dragged on and casualties mounted; ultimately, the result was a deeply felt sense that the war had become a way of life, and could go on forever. Indeed, in a very real sense, it has; Fussell makes clear that the language which was used to describe World War II was heavily borrowed from the earlier war. Even more important, the quality of life in peacetime has come to be seen in the same terms; the stalemated dance of death, which World War I quickly became, is the perspective through which we view the world in which we now live.

Fussell's first point is that the Great War occurred in a world totally unprepared for its horrors, yet strangely ready to describe them once they were a reality. The war came as a radical intrusion into a relatively stable world, a world whose images of war had been formed long before, in battles fought without the fruits of the industrial revolution. English images of war suggested that it was a noble and heroic business, conducted by the nobility, involving clear-cut battles, retreats, and inevitable victory. Recent English wars had been fought in faraway places, by professional soldiers, against untrained native warriors. This war, fought against fellow Europeans armed with all the weapons which the industrial revolution and modern science could produce, quickly bogged down into a ceaseless struggle over a few miles of territory, a struggle in which there were no real battles, no real retreats, and worst of all, no real victories.

Even so, poets such as Hardy and Arnold had foreseen in their work the irony of the modern age, and the death of joy which the receding of the old civilization must bring with it. They gave Englishmen a vocabulary of horror, of the loss of hope, of the gruesomeness of war which would serve writer-soldiers well in their attempts to deal with their experiences. It was a strangely literary war, and a uniquely literary group of men who fought it. Without the diversions of television and motion pictures, Englishmen of the early twentieth century had turned to literature to enrich their spare time. Soldiers carried with them into battle copies of poetry anthologies which they read in the long days between encounters with the enemy. The Romantics had taught them to notice sunrises and sunsets; the daily routines of mustering at these times of day caused them to remember and use in their writings

the vocabulary of the Romantic writers. The Aesthete movement of the late nineteenth century had prepared them to accept the emotional attachments among soldiers in the trenches, and to celebrate them during and after the war.

The Great War began in innocence; the loss of innocence brought with it the perspective of irony. This is Fussell's overriding concern, that the disillusionment which set in so quickly brought with it a sense of irony often both bitter and humorous which has colored our view of life ever since. The prewar world was one in which words like *intercourse, ejaculation,* or *erection* could be used with no sense of their sexual connotations. History was an unbroken process which led from a clearly understood past through the present into an easily recognizable future. After the war, no word could be used without immediately suggesting all its sexual overtones; history was broken into a past now clouded in doubt, a present intelligible only in ironic terms, and a future which no one could predict with any certainty. Central to this understanding is a scene which Fussell demonstrates occurring over and over in writing about the war; in it, a soldier comforts a wounded comrade, only to discover that he is already dead of wounds unknown to the comforter. Found in a number of immediately post-World War I literary works, this scene has its most famous replay as the central and critical scene in Heller's *Catch-22.*

Most of Fussell's work consists of a detailed catalogue of different ways in which the participants came to see the war. Chief among these is the tendency to draw absolute distinctions between good and bad, friend and enemy, men at the front and men at the rear. Another is the tendency to mythologize the war, to treat it in terms of myth and ritual. On the one hand, soldiers developed a long and elaborate set of superstitions, relics, legends, rumors, miracles, talismans, and wonders. Signs in the sky, miraculous deliverance from death, rumors of enemy atrocities, good luck charms, magic numbers—all these, and others, become the stuff of attempts to deal with the experience of the war. A statue of a Virgin and Child, left hanging precariously from its perch atop a basilica in a town at the front, became the object of mythic predictions about the end of the war; later it became an image of attempts to see the war in terms of redemptive Christian suffering. In either case, the third-rate religious object took on mythic proportions as a sign of the nature of the combat experience. Another unusual group of images brought in to describe the war's meaning was the tradition of the English pastoral; from this came the repetitious use of images of barbed wire as hedges, of songs of nightingales and larks, and of the symbolism of the rose and the poppy. The soldier became a shepherd; the war became a more recognizable and more easily dealt with experience.

Along the way, Fussell stops to consider the major writers of the period, the Englishmen who participated in the war and attempted, both during and after it, to make some sense of it in literary terms. Singled out for special attention are writers both familiar and not so familiar— Siegfried Sassoon, David Jones, Robert Graves, Edmund Blunden, and especially, Wilfred Owen. Each is accorded a careful and sensitive account of his work, and of the vocabublary each developed for recording his experiences. Just as important is Fussell's tracing of the use of their language in the works of later writers, both British and American. He is able to demonstrate convincingly the pervasiveness of their vocabulary and their approach to their experiences in the work of authors writing about World War II, and the world in which we now live.

Perhaps this is Fussell's greatest contribution—to show that our world was created during that first modern war, and that the terms through which we understand it were created then as well. In small details (the fact that the odd hours of closing still observed in British pubs were begun during World War I, and that when American officials described the war in Vietnam as unending, they spoke out of a modern tradition of talking about wars) as well as in major ones (the view of life as a game, as theater, as ironic), the experience of World War I defined not only our world but the terms we use to describe it. The persistence of these facts is at once sobering and reassuring. On the one hand, it documents our sense of unease, our sense of being at war, our sense of the absence of peace; on the other, it suggests the ability of man to find terms, however bitter and ironic, through which to describe and deal with the world in which he finds himself. Fussell has traced a new concept of literary history, and has found new and especially effective ways of demonstrating the continuity of literature in our time. He has helped immeasurably in our attempt to define modernism and thus to understand our peculiar world. For this, and for a rich and moving book, we are much in his debt.

John N. Wall, Jr.

GUERRILLAS

Author: V. S. Naipaul (1932-   )
Publisher: Alfred A. Knopf (New York). 248 pp. $7.95
Type of work: Novel
Time: The present
Locale: An island in the Caribbean

The brutal story of what becomes of a former political activist when he seeks to escape the roles set for him by his past, and what happens to the woman who follows him in his search

Principal characters:
JIMMY AHMED, a local organizer of the masses
PETER ROCHE, a social activist
JANE, his lover

Rarely can one expect an author who deals with related themes in his several novels to produce consistently works that are involving and pointed over his entire career. But such has proven the case with V. S. Naipaul's seventh novel, *Guerrillas*. Although one can predict a wave of novels throughout the balance of the 1970's dealing with previous political activists and what becomes of them when they are separated from their causes, *Guerrillas* will stand out—if not as one of the first, then at least as one of the best. Naipaul has handled the themes of the loneliness of commitment, of involvement, and of exile superbly, but he extends himself far beyond that initial first layer of an examination of what becomes of social and political folk heroes. For, in *Guerrillas,* the hero is a hero no more, except in the eyes of the few who have read of him, and of the even fewer who know or remember him. And the qualities that at first defined Peter Roche as the admirable person he distinguished himself as are the same qualities that prevent him from drowning in either mythification or sloughing off by his contemporaries.

Peter Roche was born into that nebulous land of the racially mixed, yet, he threw himself entirely into the racial injustices abounding in South Africa, lived through his tortures, and published a book relating his experiences. He came to reside in London, where he not only met his lover, Jane, but also realized that he was tired of that rare position that has recognition but concomitant notoriety which deadens the impact of any social change he wanted to effect. He elects to relocate to the Caribbean to work with a local firm, Sablich's, in hopes of bettering the poorer citizens of the island. His infatuation with the idea of working again for the people, but from a different vantage point, drives him to leave abruptly, and Jane, caught up in his romantic enthusiasm, follows closely after him.

But, once on the island, individual souls and characters are magnified, almost as if a new adage has suddenly been invented: you are who you said you were. The heat, the poverty, the futility, and the unknown needle each individual into proving that no matter what changes one may make in his life, no matter where he may go either geographically or socially, people never change.

But, initially this does not seem to apply to Roche, especially when he is seen through Jane's eyes. Likewise, Roche's first impression of Jane seems to be constantly denied, yet it always emerges above what she does and what she allows herself to think of herself: "Everything that was to be known about Jane was clear at their first meeting. He had picked up all the clues; but their relationship was based on his ignoring these clues." Jane, who is referred to only by her first name throughout the novel, is a jaded slut, and anything she does to remove herself from the mundane only reinforces that image. It is through Jane and her sexuality that a major theme of the novel is first mentioned: the mirroring expectation with which others perceive the individual determines to a large extent who that individual will "be." Jane is unable to extract herself from the image that others, particularly Jimmy and Peter, have of her, no matter what guise she assumes, be it spontaneous, coquettish, or domestic. Similarly, and even more significantly, we find later, Peter is unable to extract himself from the image of the anti-*status quo,* the activist, the politically all-knowing.

Jane epitomizes what becomes of sexuality once it is reduced to pure function; similarly, she epitomizes what happens to many contemporary women when they go through the motions of individualizing themselves, seemingly preparing themselves for a male-dominated society without understanding the rationale behind what they are doing. Ultimately, Jane herself is reduced to pure function, and even more specifically, to a mere function within the time confines of the novel. In other words, her entire life has no meaning except for the codified, ritualistic death she fulfills on the island; there is no other justification for her existence. She is not committed, nor does she want to reconcile herself with the real. While in London, for example, she had seen Roche laugh: "Roche laughed, and the corners of his mouth rode up over the receding gums on his molars, which showed long, with black gaps between them. It was like a glimpse of teeth in a skull, like a glimpse of a satyr; and she felt it was like a glimpse of the inner man. . . . This was like a glimpse of a grotesque stranger." Jane cannot accommodate the real.

Jane's life on the island prior to her death is replete with preliminary rituals that are somehow necessary to the final ritual: the flick of her lighter, flip comments about it, excuses for inexpensive jewelry she wears, wantonly detached sexual gestures. But even more important, the fact that she walks to her own murder almost without fear or force indicates that she has virtually no more depth than those ritualistic functions she performs daily. In effect she is those rituals—an uncommitted, unthinking individual given substance only in those actions that allow her to progress from one blistering morning to the next, avoiding the fact that since she is a portion of an imperfect society, what she does is not only similarly imperfect but also morally wrong. The function she serves in providing Jimmy Ahmed an object to destroy, beginning the elimination of what is socially necrotic on the island, is the most meaningful function she fulfills.

Jimmy Ahmed lives in a socially nebulous land as well. In the novel, race, color, and background are objective "givens," and Jimmy is a product of racial mixture. He tries to have himself recognized as a Utopian, ostensibly encouraging young men from the surrounding poor areas to come up to the Commune, Thrushcross Grange, to cultivate the land, to help the poor to help themselves. While encouraging his men to live communally, to defy conventional standards, he, on the other hand, elects to live away from the tin huts where his men dwell, opting for his own home, a sort of transplanted slice of middle-class England—tasteless, cluttered comfort.

In Jimmy's home, Jane notices a photograph of two children whose color reveals that they are obviously his. Yet, the other portion of the photograph (containing the mother?) has been ripped off, obliterated from reality. Although Jane thinks this odd, she is not mentally equipped to think of it as a sign of anything destructive or violently manipulative. After all, Jimmy has told them, "I have no gun. I'm no guerrilla." But with the advantage of hindsight, we see that destruction and violence are precisely what the photograph presages. Jimmy is violent, but he is only selfishly benevolent. He offers to his frenzied male lover the body of his female quasi-lover for mutilation. And, ultimately, we learn that the individuals in his camp are not merely young members of street gangs, but organized guerrillas, and they are organized by Jimmy Ahmed.

There is a pivotal scene in the novel in which the unclear qualities of the characters' personalities become defined and underscored in terms of those mirroring expectations mentioned earlier. The scene is at the radio station, shortly after the riots have died down. An acquaintance of Peter who also runs a radio station asks to interview Peter for his reactions to the disturbances. The atmosphere is inhuman and oppressive, and Peter realizes that he is not being asked for his own views of the situation, but rather to parrot the views that others expect of him. At this point, he realizes that this is the reason why coming to the island was wrong: everyone expected him to respond in a particular way, even Jane, who followed him for the romantic and exotic image she carried of him at the moment. Consequently, it was not he who was to be of use, but rather his image, an image over which he has no control. Peter is quietly enraged, and finally decides he will not respond according to the expectations imposed on him. When Meredith asks him, "Don't you think you've allowed yourself to become the conscience of your society?" Peter responds blankly, "I don't know what people mean when they talk like that."

After this point, Peter Roche, having refused to respond according to the role imposed upon him by those familiar with his past actions, again responds with the immediacy one would expect from someone socially and morally cognizant. Just as he had denied the validity of the oppressive white supremacy of South Africa by defying its codes, so he denies the power of the contorted plans of

Jimmy Ahmed. He drives to Jimmy's home, where he knows Jane has on occasion been alone. Yet when he does not find her there, he senses sickness, the same sort of social sickness he has tried to fight on so many levels before, and he denies its validity by walking away from it. He retreats from what he intuits as a "slaughterground," leaving behind the calling Jimmy. After letting Jimmy know that there are others who know where he is, he walks away and says to himself, "I've just done the bravest thing in my life."

Although Jane is dead and it is likely that Peter knows she is dead, she serves one final function in the novel. Once Peter is back at home and finds Jane is gone, Jimmy telephones him, begging him to come back to see him. But Peter denies not only the urgency Jimmy claims, but the entire *status quo* of life by firmly stating, "We are leaving you alone. I am leaving. I am going away. Jane and I are leaving tomorrow. Jane is in her room packing. We are leaving you here. Are you hearing me? Jimmy?"

The dynamic force behind these words that in essence allows Peter to reshape reality and social order, then, is real. For, in response to this, Jimmy acquiesces simply with the familiar appellation of camaraderie between the two, "Massa."

Bonnie Fraser

THE GULAG ARCHIPELAGO: TWO
Parts III-IV

Author: Aleksandr I. Solzhenitsyn (1918-   )
Translated from the Russian by Thomas P. Whitney
Publisher: Harper & Row Publishers (New York). 712 pp. $15.00; paperback $2.50
Type of work: History and autobiography
Time: 1918-1956
Locale: The Soviet Union

The detailed working of the Corrective Labor Camps in the Soviet Union, their role in the economy of the country, and their work in the formation of the national character

This second book of *The Gulag Archipelago* consists of parts three and four of a projected seven-part history of the prison camps of the Soviet Union. Like Volume I, this volume is compiled both from the author's own experiences and from the sources, written and oral, to which he first gained access in the camps, and continued to receive after his release.

The first volume discussed primarily the process of arrest and transportation to the camps; with the present work, we go inside the camps themselves. Again Solzhenitsyn's approach is mainly historical, beginning with the earliest of the slave-labor camps on Solovetsky Island in the White Sea. Again the author takes pains to show how the history of the camps almost exactly coincides with the founding of the Bolshevik state. He notes an astonishing change in the meaning of a phrase: during World War I, the term "concentration camp" had been used for places of detention for prisoners of war and suspected foreigners, but it was in Russia that it was first applied to camps for a country's own people— a change which occurred in August and September of 1918.

The archipelago was born on Solo-vetsky Island, and it was here that the scheme was first hatched to grind labor out of the prisoners of the camps; the euphemism "Corrective-Labor Camps" was soon born. There is an epic sweep to the first extended story he tells, the building of the White Sea Canal. An unaccountable brainstorm of Stalin, the canal was ordered to be built in twenty months, from September 1931 to April 1933. The project was hurrried on as if it were a military necessity, and indeed the decrees, orders, posters, and so on referring to the project consistently used the metaphor of battle, although there was and is no discernible reason for the urgency with which it was pushed forward. Solzhenitsyn suggests that Stalin simply had camps filled with prisoners from the collectivization of the farms, and decided to kill them off on a job, saving the cost of bullets or gas while at the same time producing something monumental in his honor.

The building of the canal was in keeping with the objective of the camps: nearly complete self-sufficiency. Engineers were needed, so they were arrested; sent to the site to begin work even before surveys had been completed, they found that the canal had to be built without concrete, without iron, without practically anything but what the prisoners could devise from their own labor using native materials. Hence dikes were built of earth, cranes, and locks of wood, and the quotas of labor expected from the prisoners literally worked them to death. The prisoner labor could be easily replaced, as the author notes. He gives an example of one of the quotas: to break up two-and-a-half cubic yards of granite with hand tools, and move it a hundred yards in a wheelbarrow. When things fell behind schedule, the response of the administration was simply to increase work quotas; no one would receive even the skimpy food ration unless the herculean quota was met. Solzhenitsyn points out that the hardworking and conscientious were the first to fall under such a regime, since they could not get enough calories from the punishment ration to replace those expended at work. And unless the quota was fulfilled, they remained on the punishment ration. The best that could be hoped for was slow starvation, but many did not have to wait that long.

Solzhenitsyn estimates that during the first winter of construction, 100,000 prisoners died. But the canal was finished on schedule, apparently for propaganda purposes more than anything else. In almost a denouement to the story itself, he tells of visiting the canal after his release from prison; it was nearly empty of traffic, and he considers why it was built. Not for commerce, since there is nothing to haul on it; not for moving the Soviet fleet from the Baltic to the White Sea, because the canal is too shallow to permit the passage of warships. Therefore the suggestion

that it was a simple way to reduce the camp population becomes ever more plausible.

There are two especially important points about the Labor Camps that are driven home again and again. The first is the corrupting influence the system had and has, both on the largely innocent inmates, and on the relatively free population of the country outside the camps. The whole system of the camps acted, even if not designed to do so, to crush efficiently the kind and honest, and to reward the cruel and treacherous. It seems unbelievable to read that only thirty-seven police guards controlled the hundred thousand or more workers on the White Sea Canal project, until we realize that the prisoners were actually guarding themselves. Besides the "trusties" with rifles, prisoners who did not hesitate to shoot others attempting to escape, the whole pseudomilitary organization worked as an effective instrument of oppression; spies and stool pigeons were everywhere, and the quota system worked inexorably here, too. Whole brigades would have their rations reduced for failure to fulfill the demanded tasks. Once the conscientious had died behind their wheelbarrows, the impossible quotas made cheating a matter of self-preservation.

The constant wariness and suspicion of the camps mirrored the larger society of which they were part. In the fourth section, Solzhenitsyn talks about the effect of the Archipelago on the spirit, and some of the most moving passages concern the turmoil of ordinary decent husbands and wives caught in a dilemma of how to raise their children: to speak the truth in front of them and risk exposure, or lie to them and corrupt both themselves and the children. Thus "free" children suffered spiritually from the concentration camp mentality begun in the labor camps and enforced by their threat, while those children confined in the camps were turned into savages.

The children are the subject of an entire chapter, and in their numbers might have taken up a greater part of the book if space were given proportionally. From 1935, the punishments of the Criminal Code were applied in full to all from twelve years of age. They learned very quickly, once in camp, that the strong survive at the expense of the weak, and they operated on that principle.

There are some, of course, both children and adults, who were not corrupted: Solzhenitsyn tells the story of two of these at the very end of the fourth part. He himself enumerates some of the real advantages that the labor camps offered to gain the kind of freedom that cannot be taken away; he notes that each prisoner faced at some time or another a decision over whether he would do anything, take any step, to survive. Those who answered no, those who were ready to die rather than adapt themselves entirely, found a real freedom. Since they no longer feared death, their captors' strongest hold on them was useless.

In the midst of wave after wave of human suffering on a national scale, the reader finds here and there instances of biting humor, as the second great point of Volume II is made: a fierce humor rises to the surface again and again as the essential uselessness of the vaunted labor done in

the camps becomes clear. In the stories of the great projects undertaken and completed, one receives an impression of a vast country crisscrossed by railroads that run from nowhere to nowhere, by canals that serve neither economic nor military function. All the blood-stained works serve no more practical purpose than if they had been designed to write Stalin's name across the country so that it would be visible from the moon. Beside these wasted artifacts, the labor camps produced swindling and deceit on a monumental scale, as falsified results swelled the greater at each successive level of administration. We are left with the uneasy feeling that the camps confirm what George Orwell wrote in *Nineteen Eighty-Four,* that they existed solely as an exercise of power, as a means of instilling in the population the same paranoia that was nurtured in the highest echelons by the supreme leader. Finally, the camps existed as a training school for the brutal, the unquestioning, and the subservient.

Solzhenitsyn tells the story of these proving grounds for the absurd in a sort of dialogue between himself and the architects of the system. He interrupts the documents and decrees that produced it, inserting comments and asides of his own, reminding us of what we cherish as the ground rules of civilized behavior in order that we not become overwhelmed and dulled by the atrocities he recounts. He rightly calls the whole work "An Experiment in Literary Investigation," since it is in a real sense *literary*: here the methods and objectives of satire are applied not to fiction but to history.

Walter E. Meyers

HERE AT THE NEW YORKER

Author: Brendan Gill (1914-   )
Publisher: Random House (New York). 406 pp. $12.95
Type of work: Autobiographical memoir

A highly entertaining and informative account of one of the most successful American magazines by one of its longtime writers

Published on the fiftieth anniversary of the *New Yorker*'s founding, which occurred in February, 1925, *Here at the New Yorker* is Brendan Gill's memoir of the magazine and of his nearly forty years of mainly happy association with it, along with a few backward glances at his pre-*New Yorker* life. His announced aim suggests the nature of both the content and the tone of the book: "I will try to cram these paragraphs full of facts and give them a weight and shape no greater than that of a cloud of blue butterflies." He gives facts in abundance—about editors, writers, artists (as the *New Yorker* cartoonists are called), working conditions, disagreements, hiring and firing, editorial standards—but there are opinions and impressions too, both Gill's and those of the men and women he has known and worked with. And what a group they are—Harold Ross, E. B. White and his wife Katharine, James Thurber, William Shawn, Alexander Woollcott, Dorothy Parker, Wolcott Gibbs, St. Clair McKelway, Robert Benchley, Peter Arno, Saul Steinberg, and many others. Some have long been dead, but they briefly live again as Gill recalls them.

The *New Yorker* has had only two editors in its fifty years: Harold Ross (1925-1951) and William Shawn (1952-   ). Having worked so long under both, Gill frequently contrasts the men themselves, their very different editorial management of the magazine, and their relationship with the writers and other workers. The semi-educated, explosive, profane, crude, rambunctious, exasperating, and yet amusing Ross became known to the general public several years ago through James Thurber's *The Years with Ross*. Brendan Gill adds to the portrait of Ross in some of the most diverting passages in *Here at the New Yorker*.

The reader may well wonder at times how the magazine succeeded with such an editor. (Gill credits E. B. White and Thurber with supplying much of the special blend of humor and sophisticated satire that helped the magazine to gain acceptance in its early years.) Ross was "aggressively ignorant" and deficient in reasoning power: ". . . he could get from A to B and even to C, but he could rarely reach D. . . ." He was obsessed by facts, and clung to them "as a shipwrecked man clings to a spar." He was a mass of contradictions, "at once brave and timid, cruel and tender-hearted, shy and overbearing." He tried to control his rough language around women, but he spewed billingsgate around men, with whom he felt more at ease. Although a reckless gambler at poker and other card games and so careless about fiscal matters that one of his assistants was able to embezzle $70,000 before the theft was discovered by the magazine's business department, Ross yet cautioned young Gill, "You don't know a goddam thing about money." The ulcer-ridden Ross must often have been hard to put up with, but he had his problems, as Gill says, "playing father-uncle-brother-guardian-nurse-maid-confessor" to the troubled and troubling group who helped him get his magazine out in the early years. Long afterward, Gill once heard him say, "What I'm running here is a goddam bughouse. Not a man in the place without a screw loose." Gill reveals many of Ross's crudities and personal idiosyncrasies, but he obviously holds him in affectionate memory and admires what Ross did: "He saw his job as encouraging people more talented than he to do their work better than they had hitherto known how to do it, largely by being harder on themselves than they had been accustomed to be."

William Shawn (originally Chon: "I made the mistake of thinking I might become a writer, and I wanted to be taken for an American and not a Chinese"), who had been associate editor of the *New Yorker* since 1939, became editor a few weeks after Ross's death in December, 1951. Shawn differs from Ross in almost every respect except in his determination to keep the high editorial standards set by his predecessor. Ross was noisy, gauche, argumentative, belligerent, foulmouthed; Shawn is a quiet, cultured, polite gentleman at all times who does not argue with his writers but through "gently probing cross-examination" seeks to learn what they have meant to say and, with "silences, hesitations, sidelong glances of his very blue eyes," en-

courages them to say it better. During World War II the *New Yorker* began to lose its early parochial character and increasingly developed a national and an international outlook. According to Gill, Shawn was responsible for this broadened view, which has continued since he assumed the editorship. Gill sees Shawn as an ideal editor who desires no personal fame but only to continue issuing a magazine of high quality for a comparatively select group of readers capable of appreciating its particular character.

At the outset of his book Brendan Gill declares himself a happy man because for most of his life he has been doing just what he wanted to do. His happiness appears to be ingrained, but the circumstances of his early life were favorable. Although he lost his mother when he was seven, he had a father who, through hard work as a physician and through wise investments, became a millionaire and shared his money with his five children as they were growing into maturity instead of waiting to will it to them upon his death. Dr. Gill was very proud of his son's *New Yorker* writing. Gill married young and apparently has enjoyed being a husband and father. He admits to having spent a good part of his European wedding trip typing on his first novel while his pretty wife went sight-seeing alone. The mention of several parties in one or another of the Gill homes over the years suggests, however, that Mrs. Gill has not resented her husband's devotion to his writing and has even welcomed his *New Yorker* friends and co-workers despite their eccentricities.

Gill confesses to snobbery which

prevented his meeting in youth a number of famous authors he now wishes he had sought out. He did meet Robert Frost and Sinclair Lewis, in both of whom he was disappointed. Through his work at the *New Yorker* he has met many writers and artists of whom we get glimpses through scenes and anecdotes. With some of these he has had lasting friendships.

Here at the New Yorker is highly entertaining throughout not only because of Gill's effortless style and great fund of recollections, but also because it includes a large number of illustrations that, especially for long-time readers of the *New Yorker,* satisfy curiosity or stir memories of past pleasures with the magazine.

Henderson Kincheloe

THE HOLOCAUST AND THE LITERARY IMAGINATION

Author: Lawrence L. Langer (1929-   )
Publisher: Yale University Press (New Haven, Conn.) 300 pp. $12.50
Type of work: Literary criticism
Time: Post-World War II
Locale: Central Europe

A study of the "Literature of Atrocity": imaginative works written about the nature and effects of the Nazi Holocaust

All "literary revolutions" can be traced back to shifts in man's perception of his own essence, the nature of the world he lives in, and the meaning of his existence. Whether recognized at the time or not, these alterations in basic cultural assumptions are produced by great political, historical, scientific, or theological events (such as new ideas, inventions, movements, wars), although the immediate effects may not be consciously and generally felt for a long time.

Such a shift in perceptions and assumptions occurred in the wake of World War II, and the impact has been immediate and deep. For example, as Norman Mailer discussed in his essay "The White Negro," the fear of death by the atomic bomb or the gas chambers of a concentration camp—a death particularly devoid of dignity, choice, or meaning—has become rooted in the unconscious mind of almost everyone. Whether overtly or not—whether the artist was even aware of it or not—most of the important writing that has been done since the war has reflected this new attitude, and the best critics have attempted to articulate the implications of it as embodied in recent fiction, poetry, and drama.

However, for reasons both obvious and subtle, relatively little has been written specifically about the central events which have provoked this shift in moral vision; and the Holocaust, Hitler's attempt to exterminate the Jewish race, has perhaps been the most neglected of these crucial events, both by the creative artists and by the literary critics. Nevertheless, despite the many psychological and artistic problems involved in treating the subject, a small body of impressive work has been stimulated by the Death Camps. But, although individual works have been reviewed, no previous attempt has been made to study them systematically and comprehensively. Professor Lawrence L. Langer has accepted the challenge. In *The Holocaust and the Literary Imagination* he attempts not only to discuss and compare individual writings, but also to present an overall view, to define the works as a genre ("The Literature of Atrocity"), and to work out an "aesthetic" for that genre.

The basic paradox that has made artistic treatment of the Holocaust almost impossible lies in the contradictory fact that, while the events actually happened, they are nevertheless beyond human comprehension. Writers such as George Steiner felt that after 1945, artists would never again be able to exceed, through imagination, the scope or intensity of what had happened in reality. Or, to put it more concretely: ". . . no creature of the imagination could compete for dramatic impact with the real figure of Ilse Koch. Nor can any universalized image elaborate on the concrete and essential truth of the lampshades made from human skin." Thus, the reality of the concentration camps, however fully documented, remains incomprehensible to the "uninitiated" reader. Even the survivors themselves, as Elie Wiesel noted, have difficulty in believing in the reality of their own past experiences. This is why documentary accounts (for example, Peter Weiss's *The Investigation*) or literal autobiographies have failed to transmit the truth of *l'univers concentrationnaire*; instead, they often merely overpower the consciousness with horror without revealing any new insights.

Importantly, the Holocaust was not only too extreme and bizarre to describe, but it also refuted all the moral, philosophical, psychological, and artistic assumptions that have been basic to modern Western culture—that life is a meaningful experience, the human being is a rational, understandable creature, and language is a valid means of communication. The death camps made it impossible to believe in humanity, rationality, or meaning, either as ultimate realities or even as practical alternatives. And perhaps even language, debased by Nazi perversions and dwarfed by the magnitude of the events, had lost the capacity for serious artistic expression.

However, while the artists themselves shared many of these depressing conclusions, their feelings were too strong and their need to communicate the experience too intense

not to make the attempt. In general, they found their answer where serious artists have always found it: in a selective distortion, a reshaping of reality to make it palatable and permanent. But, given the extremity of their subject matter, they had to find new and more extreme modes of distortion.

This is not to say that the Literature of Atrocity has no relationship to the larger literary tradition. Langer cites Shakespeare, Dostoevski, Kafka, and Faulkner, among others, as important thematic and artistic forebears. But he also uses these classic predecessors to clarify the differences between pre-Holocaust writing and the Literature of Atrocity. For example, the depths of despair and madness in *King Lear* have their clear echoes in atrocity literature, but Hamlet's "To be or not to be" is more rhetorical, more of a philosophical argument, than a traumatic emotional experience dramatically reproduced. Likewise, Ivan Karamazov's lament over suffering meted out to innocent children is powerful, but essentially theoretical, while Ilse Aichinger presents children as real victims dying in real death camps. Franz Kafka's vision is at best a prophetic hint of the Holocaust: "An intricate maze leads from the claustrophobic Law Court Offices to the gas chambers, and though winding corridors may indeed connect the two, neither Joseph K. nor his creator ever trod them." William Faulkner emphasizes the unreliability of the past and its ambiguous influence on the present and future; Heinrich Böll, André Schwarz-Bart, and Jorge Semprun demonstrate the power of a memory that is too reliable, a past that refuses to be ambiguous, and a future without shape or meaning.

After stating these overall problems, Langer goes into extended, in-depth discussions of the separate works. The cumulative result of his analyses is not so much to establish an aesthetic for the genre as to describe its strategies. Because the events were too enormous and terrible to be believed in a realistic presentation, these authors relied on indirection, innuendo, grotesque-comedic exaggeration, dreams, and metaphors. Because rational man cannot comprehend such atrocities, the events were frequently narrated by children; because human values collapsed under the pressure of the Holocaust, the bestial side of man predominated until it became difficult to distinguish men from animals. Because the intellectual and moral standards of the "normal" world were no longer operative, madness became the norm. And because the progress of humanity in chronological time collapsed, conventional notions of sequence and time were discarded. Thus, the Literature of Atrocity distorts the awful world it describes in order to communicate it more directly to readers at visceral levels that connect to their experience, even if indirectly, subjectively, and subconsciously.

For example, Elie Wiesel (*Night*) avoids the pitfalls of autobiography by creating a nightmarish landscape, grotesquely simplified characters, and bizarre, heightened scenes, narrating the story from the viewpoint of a boy coming of age. The reader is forced to identify with this innocent hero as he is introduced not to life, but to death's imminence. The form

is, in fact, the classic *Bildüngsroman,* or novel of education, initiation, and development, but with a vicious twist—what the boy learns is that human values have collapsed, life is meaningless, and there is no future for him to face. This inverted *Bildüngsroman* became a popular form among artists of atrocity.

Jerzy Kosinski (*The Painted Bird*) approaches the Holocaust indirectly by creating a primitive peasant world of superstition, animalistic perversity, and arbitrary, vicious, spiteful cruelty. He underscores the bestiality of this existence by presenting powerful, vivid symbols, metaphors, and quasi-religious rituals. Like Wiesel, Kosinski narrates the action through the eyes of a frightened child who ultimately becomes more cruel and perverse than his tormentors. Ilse Aichinger (*Herod's Children*) offers a society of children who imitate in their games the violent world that systematically murders them. Ladislav Fuks (*Mr. Theodore Mundstock*) demonstrates the self-destructive absurdity of trying to deal rationally with the Nazi horror. Jakov Lind ("Soul of Wood"; *Landscape in Concrete; Ergo*) carries this further by postulating a world in which schizophrenia is the norm and only cruelty and power have any real validity. And finally, time itself is fragmented and reorganized in the works of Heinrich Böll (*Billiards at Half-Past Nine*), André Schwarz-Bart (*The Last of the Just*), and Jorge Semprun (*The Long Voyage*), as they juxtapose the prewar world of "normality"—which still conforms to the reader's own experience—against the horrific new reality of the *l'univers concentrationnaire*. This radical comparison forces the reader to view both the old and the new in a different perspective.

Langer has probably attempted to do too much in this one book; the subject and its implications are too large and complex for one volume. At times he seems to bend his aesthetics to fit his selection of books, and one could question some of his particular choices (why Heinrich Böll and not Günter Grass?). But these are very minor criticisms. Like the genre he delineates, Langer forces us to reencounter a reality that we would probably like to forget, but which has left deep and permanent psychic scars on us all. He has written an impressive, important critical book that is central to an understanding of the moral and intellectual forces which shape the world we live in.

Keith Neilson

A HOMEMADE WORLD
The American Modernist Writers

Author: Hugh Kenner
Publisher: Alfred A. Knopf (New York). 221 pp. $8.95
Type of work: Literary criticism

An attempt to prove the thesis that twentieth century American literary values owe amost nothing to European models and influences by a prolific, erudite, and controversial American critic

One of America's more prolific critics, Hugh Kenner has produced another book in his life's work of cataloging and dissecting the twentieth century experience. As always, his range of relevant and irrelevant data is formidable and fascinating. Since 1951, he has written ten critical works, any one of which would have satisfied a mere academician. Obviously Kenner writes as he does because, like the artists he studies, he is a man obsessed with creation. His two studies of Ezra Pound (*The Poetry of Ezra Pound* and *The Pound Era*) are erudite, challenging, and sometimes outrageous. Even when one cannot agree with Kenner, one is always delighted that Kenner has had his say, for he can use the language as few critics are able. His studies of Eliot (*The Invisible Poet*), Beckett (*Samuel Beckett*), Lewis (*Wyndham Lewis*), and Buckminster Fuller (*Bucky*) are eminently readable. All of his subjects are artists involved with creating new modes of perceiving the world. Principally, they are internationalists. In his most recent work, *A Homemade World,* Kenner examines the American artists who remade the language of poetry and prose for the homefolk whether they wanted it or not. "Language defines what we can perceive, what think, what discuss. A fifty-year re-shaping of the American language is the topic of this book."

It is Kenner's thesis that the homemade world of American literary values was created by Wallace Stevens, William Carlos Williams, Marianne Moore, Scott Fitzgerald, Ernest Hemingway, and William Faulkner during the period when T. S. Eliot, James Joyce, and Ezra Pound were reinventing the international world of literature. It is a homemade world, the dust jacket tells us, "scarcely at all indebted to European precedents and models." Immediately the reader's suspicion begins to rise. As always with Kenner, his thesis is somewhat outrageous and not infrequently carried by rhetoric, and the reader must balance the thesis with his own knowledge of the European impact on these writers. If one knew nothing of American literary history in the twentieth century, *A Homemade World* would not be the place to begin. But what Kenner has to say is important and well-presented. The common interest of these writers in the limits and possibilities of language, in the way we see the world, and in the fictional order we impose upon it in the form of art, has not been sufficiently defined or measured. Kenner's work is another beginning. Much of it is intuitive, and it will be left to younger men to work out the rigorous proofs and the corollary theorems, qualifying and expanding. What Kenner says of the writers he examines applies equally to his own work: "Purity of intention lies at the center of American achievement; it will cover . . . a multitude of lapses."

His chapter on F. Scott Fitzgerald, "The Promised Land," is Kenner at his best. Focusing on *The Great Gatsby,* Kenner gives more new and interesting insights into that much-belabored novel than many Fitzgerald critics have been able to do in four times the space. While Joyce and Eliot and Pound dug back to European and primitive roots for their myths, Fitzgerald found his myth—the American Dream—in his own back yard. The myth of America, Kenner knows, has always been its strength. From the very beginning, the sixteenth century imagination had to make the "enormous effort of imagining that a second world, a New World, could exist." America is one of the major feats of the imagination, and all romantics, Fitzgerald included, have had to reinvent it for themselves. Very neatly tying Jay Gatsby (*nee* Jimmy Gatz) into his forerunner, Horatio Alger, Kenner describes the necessity of conceiving the goal before Gatsby can pursue it. The first act of pursuit is the act of the imagination—of reinventing the promise of America in such a way that it is worth the pursuit. Gatsby pursues the same romantic dream that Alger pursues through his life as it was described in *Alger: A Biography Without a Hero.* Kenner then notes that this biography itself was invented by a journalist. It does not seem to matter. All dreams are in-

vented. But, Kenner notes in one of those rhetorical tricks, "there is something about Alger . . . that turns fertile minds toward fraud." That statement somehow encompasses Alger, Fitzgerald, the fraudulent biographer, and Jay Gatsby—all in one neat paradigm. Gatsby, like his creator, had to invent a new world, rich and various, limited only by his ability to imagine it. If Gatsby's dream seems shallow today, the background of its dreamer was shallow. Jay Gatsby and Scott Fitzgerald are both half-educated; they have read just enough to wonder and not enough to become jaded. Their dream could only happen in America. No European would have thought it worth the effort. What matters is "intensity of intention . . . purity of vision."

Kenner's treatment of Hemingway is equally intuitive and useful. He has the uncanny ability to draw together tangential forces, pinpointing inter-relationships that others will have to prove conclusively, but which Kenner has said first, somehow knowing without the rigorous proof. For example, he draws together Gertrude Stein, the young Hemingway, and the silent movies of the 1920's into a progression, relating them on the one hand to Eliot's objective correlative and on the other to the new audience trained by the camera to see things in a different way. In just a few pages Kenner goes deeper into the stylistic relationship among these three forces than any have dived previously. The Stein-Hemingway relationship is one of the clichés of modern criticism; no one, however, has been able to demonstrate the exact nature or extent of influence. Kenner astutely relates both writers to the dramatic and cinematic principles of the silent film. Once Kenner has said it, the relationship is obvious: "In the 1920s the most pertinent influence on the narrative art was surely realizing the public's newest habit: it was starting to go to the movies. This was to mean, eventually, the obsolescence of a whole order of fiction."

Kenner also says well what has been previously little noticed: Hemingway's roots in the nineteenth century. Kenner sees Hemingway's view of life as belonging "to the years in which Yeats's mind was formed, the late years of Walter Pater's nineteenth century. His model for the perfection of a style is the perfection of a life." Style and "not thinking" are the Hemingway techniques for dealing with life, but Kenner misses part of the point. Yeats and Pater are misleading. Hemingway's roots are nineteenth century, but Oak Park, Illinois, nineteenth century. His characters may be citizens of the world, but their values never stray very far from home. Although Kenner does not say this, the point drives home his whole thesis: these new writers were inventing a new American tradition out of home-grown materials. What Kenner does see more clearly than anyone else is the recognition by these writers of the arbitrary nature of language. Language is external to the speakers who use it. It can be reinvented by the author for his own uses. Style need not be inherited; it can be elected.

Kenner's sense of American poetics is perhaps even more astute than his insights into fiction. The most valuable part of *A Homemade World* deals with the poetry of Stevens, Williams, Moore, and Zukofsky. His analysis of the reaction against Eliot's *The Waste Land* by the American poets of the 1920's is brilliant. Williams, Kenner says, realized that Eliot's poetics achieved eloquence at the terrible cost of rejecting American immediacies. It was the poetry of the past remade, not a new poetry. Using the much-discussed "Red Wheel Barrow" poem, Kenner demonstrates Williams' focus on words, the nature of language, the process of creation, and the homemade philosophy of the object. What Kenner does so well is to take the clichéd art object and make the reader see it new. His analysis of "Thirteen Ways of Looking at a Blackbird," makes new sense out of over-explained material. Kenner relates Stevens to Wordsworth to nature poetry to landscape painters, showing how Stevens is reinventing the world in his own language, a fictive world in which the painter "has developed the only feasible relationship of the sole man to the mute universe." Kenner's analysis of Marianne Moore is equally interesting, bringing seemingly disparate knowledge to bear. What Kenner does well here is to see these poets in their own light and not in Eliot's. He grants them their premise that there are other poetics and that the American grain may be reinvented by anyone at any time, providing he has the skill and the imagination.

For all its brilliance, *A Homemade World* is flawed. Kenner's analysis of Faulkner does not match the level of his insights into Hemingway and Fitzgerald. This flaw seems glaring, for Faulkner is the most homemade writer of them all. Sometimes Kenner's rhetoric defeats him;

there are more "vectors" vectoring in this book than some will like. Only Kenner could bring Nick Carraway, Henry James, Abe Lincoln, Ezra Pound, the Brooklyn Bridge, movies, actors, photojournalism, *Time,* William Carlos Williams, Pop Art, Andy Warhol, Expo 67, and *Playboy* into a single paragraph. But the incredible thing about this hat trick is that sometimes the author can pull it off. It is a style to be marveled at, but not imitated. If the book sometimes stretches its thesis, most readers will forgive Kenner, for what he has to say is worth hearing, even if one disagrees with him. He is valuable for his insights, but he is equally valuable for the questions he raises in the mind of the reader.

Michael S. Reynolds

HUMBOLDT'S GIFT

Author: Saul Bellow (1915-   )
Publisher: The Viking Press (New York). 487 pp. $10.00
Type of work: Novel
Time: The late 1930's to about 1972
Locale: Chicago, New York City, Madrid, Paris

A novel which questions the place of the artist-intellectual in contemporary America through the attempt by Charlie Citrine to come to terms with the death of his former friend and mentor, Von Humboldt Fleisher, who had promised so much but accomplished so little

> *Principal characters:*
> CHARLIE CITRINE, the narrator, a Pulitzer Prize-winning author of popular histories and biographies
> RENATA KOFFRITZ, his present girl friend
> DEMMIE VONGHEL, his fiancée, who is lost in a plane crash in the Amazon
> DENISE CITRINE, his former wife
> JULIUS (ULICK) CITRINE, his wealthy brother, a successful financier
> VON HUMBOLDT FLEISHER, a once-promising poet who dies in poverty and madness
> KATHLEEN TIGLER, Fleisher's former wife, and his heir along with Charlie
> RONALD CANTABILE, a small-time gangster
> PIERRE THAXTER, a crack journalist, slated to be editor of *The Ark*

In his eighth novel, Saul Bellow explores the predicament of the intellectual in contemporary America with acute sensitivity. Cursed with more consciousness of the human condition than he can easily bear, but powerless to change those conditions that make our society a cultural and moral desert, the typical Bellow hero (or anti-hero) articulates his anguish endlessly as he seeks to discover some accommodation with an intolerable world. Charlie Citrine, the narrator of *Humboldt's Gift,* perhaps goes further than any previous Bellow character toward finding the inner peace which will put his anguished spirit at rest.

When we first encounter Charlie, he is at the height of his success as a writer of popular histories and biographies. Though he once wrote a moderately successful Broadway play—from which a very popular film was adapted—he has long since given up the vagaries of creative writing for the easy success of his popular works. Not surprisingly, Charlie can measure his success only in material terms: his $18,000 Mercedes Benz, his exclusive apartment and luxurious wardrobe, his bank account and investments, and even Renata, his voluptuous and expensive girl friend. Along with these symbols of having "made it," Charlie is most characterized by his personal vanity. Refusing to grow old gracefully, he daily risks heart attacks to play racquetball against superior players, justifying his athletic activity on the grounds that it makes him seem younger than his years. Charlie's ego requires constant appreciation of his physical and material condition, especially from the young women in his life.

Charlie's empire, however, is under siege. Some weeks before the opening of the novel, Charlie had lost heavily to Ronald Cantabile in a poker game, and, suspecting his opponent of cheating, had stopped payment on the check written to cover his losses. After several futile attempts to collect the debt, Cantabile destroys the Mercedes with a baseball bat as a warning to Charlie. On the same day that his car is destroyed, Charlie's former wife, Denise, takes him to court in a support suit with the result that he is ordered to post a bond of two hundred thousand dollars, a sum which wipes out his assets. In the course of the novel, Renata, perceiving that Charlie is fast losing solvency, runs away to marry a rich undertaker, thus stripping Charlie of the last symbol of his material success.

The action of the novel, much of which is concerned with Citrine's involvements with Cantabile, Renata, and Denise, is played out against Charlie's memories of his former idol, Von Humboldt Fleisher. In the late 1930's, Humboldt had published a book of poems of sufficient quality to win him instant fame and the expectation by the literary establishment that he would become the major American poet of his generation. Charlie, then a student at the University of Wisconsin, was so taken with Humboldt's work that he gave up his studies to journey to New York to sit at the feet of this new master. For several years Charlie and Hum-

boldt were close, their friendship eventually leading to simultaneous appointments at Princeton. While at Princeton, Humboldt tried to arrange an endowed chair in poetry for himself, and when that failed he began to disintegrate into manic-depressive madness. Charlie drew upon Humboldt's personality to create his Broadway play, which offended Humboldt and added to a growing estrangement between the two friends. Charlie and Humboldt do not meet for several years; then, two months before the poet's death, Charlie sees him on the street in a deplorably shabby condition and hides to avoid a confrontation. To Charlie's surprise, Humboldt, having recovered lucidity before his death, leaves Charlie a legacy in his will of a screenplay based upon Charlie's life.

Ronald Cantabile improbably becomes, in the course of the novel, the figure who prepares Citrine to accept Humboldt's gift and who, indirectly, teaches him its value. First, however, he comes virtually to dominate Charlie's life in his demand for satisfaction of the poker debt and retribution for the accusation that he cheated at cards. Following his destruction of the Mercedes, Cantabile twice subjects Charlie to the ignominy of publicly paying the debt so Ronald's gangster friends will have no doubt that he has won the argument. After forcing payment in this manner, Cantabile shows his contempt for Charlie's money by leading him out on the girders of an unfinished skyscraper where he throws the money to the winds. As Citrine recalls, "it occurred to me that yesterday Cantabile had taken me up to a high place, not exactly to tempt me,

but to sail away my fifty dollar bills
. . . . He seemed to feel that yesterday's events had united us in a near-
mystical bond." Underscoring the significance of the relationship with Cantabile, Charlie later says of him, "he
was a demon, an agent of distraction.
His job was to deflect and misdirect
and send me foundering into bogs."
Cantabile accomplishes his purpose
by constantly tempting Charlie to become involved in shady schemes to
make money, to have his ex-wife
murdered, or otherwise to improve
his fortunes by allowing the gangster
to act as his agent. Cantabile's final
temptation involves having Charlie
cash in on Humboldt's gift, but Charlie
resists him.

The scheme to which Charlie does
devote himself and his money is the
plan to publish *The Ark* under the
editorship of Pierre Thaxter. Charlie
fears that art and culture are dying
in America, and he conceives the
journal to save them. "In *The Ark*,"
he says, "we were going to publish
brilliant things. . . . Everything possible must be done to restore the
credit and authority of art, the seriousness of thought, the integrity of
culture, the dignity of style." Unfortunately for Charlie, Thaxter
proves more of a con artist than an
editor, so the journal never comes
out. Increasingly, Charlie comes to
recognize—as had Humboldt before
him—that there is no place for culture or the artist in this country, because "Americans had an empty
continent to subdue. You couldn't
expect them to concentrate on philosophy and art as well."

Charlie is himself a victim of the
American conflict between materialism and art. In his youth he had

promise, "but this early talent or gift
or inspiration" had been "given up
for the sake of maturity or realism
(practicality, self-preservation, the
fight for survival)." But, at the time
of the action, these qualities are
"edging back," so that Charlie, seeing himself as an awakening Rip Van
Winkle, can say,

> I was lying stretched out in America,
> determined to resist its material inter-
> ests and hoping for redemption by art.
> I fell into a deep snooze that lasted for
> years and decades. Evidently I didn't
> have what it took. What it took was
> more courage, more stature. America
> was an overwhelming phenomenon,
> of course. But that's no excuse, really.
> Luckily, I'm still alive and perhaps
> there's still some time left.

Humboldt's death and his gift serve as
the catalysts for Charlie to redirect
his life to seek once again the values
of his youth.

As Charlie attempts to sort out his
life, the example of Humboldt's failure
becomes increasingly important to
him. He comes to realize that he had
"sinned against Humboldt," and that
"Humboldt was never more sane and
brave than at the end of his life. And
I had run away from him . . . just
when he had most to tell me." Humboldt represents for Charlie the poor
estate poetry enjoys in American life
compared to "ancient times [when]
poetry was a force, [and] the poet had
real strength in the material world."
On the other hand, Humboldt is somewhat responsible for his own fate
because

> . . . he threw himself into weakness
> and became a hero of wretchedness.
> He consented to the monopoly of
> power and interest held by money,

politics, law, rationality, technology because he couldn't find the next thing, the new thing, the necessary thing for poets to do.

In his final message to Charlie Citrine, Humboldt confesses that his anger toward his former friend was "because you thought I was going to be the great American poet of the century . . . but I wasn't." Having so failed, Humboldt degenerated into madness, but he rose from the wreck of his own life to offer Charlie the chance to find "the new thing, the necessary thing for poets to do."

In his screen treatment of Charlie's life, Humboldt sums up Charlie in these words:

To the high types of Martyrdom, the twentieth century has added the farcical martyr. This, you see, is the artist. By wishing to play a great role in the fate of mankind he becomes a bum and a joke. A double punishment is inflicted on him as the would-be representative of meaning and beauty. When the artist-agonist has learned to be sunk and shipwrecked, to embrace defeat, and assent nothing, to subdue his will and accept his assignment to the hell of modern truth perhaps his Orphic powers will be restored, the stones will dance again when he plays. Then heaven and earth will be reunited. After long divorce.

After resisting Cantabile's final temptation to capitalize on Humboldt's gift, Charlie renounces his former life and vows to "take up a different kind of life" in Europe. Leaving the materialism of America behind, he presumably goes to seek the "thing for poets to do," and to follow Humboldt's admonition that "we are supposed to do something for our kind."

William E. Grant

I WOULD HAVE SAVED THEM IF I COULD

Author: Leonard Michaels (1933-   )
Publisher: Farrar, Straus and Giroux (New York). 188 pp. $7.95
Type of work: Short stories
Time: The present
Locale: New York City

An avant-garde collection of stories, anecdotes, and sketches concerning the experiences of Phillip Liebowitz, a Jewish intellectual and would-be writer in New York City

Turning the pages of Leonard Michaels' *I Would Have Saved Them If I Could* for the first time is like pulling petals off the daisy—"I like it," "I don't like it." After reading further, your reactions escalate—"I love it," "I hate it," "I *love* it!" "I *hate* it!" At the end, with all the petals pulled, you *think* you liked it, even loved it, but you are not absolutely sure. Michaels' second book of inter-related short stories (following *Going Places,* 1969) has left you disturbed, irritated, amused, and provoked in an uneasy combination; making critical sense out of these reactions is a difficult proposition.

Such difficulty is understandable, since the book is a complicated mixture of stories, anecdotes, sketches, fragments, jokes, and statements, some as long as typical short stories, some as short as a single line. The mood shifts frequently from sober to matter-of-fact to ironical to manic to mundane to gross to lyrical. The book is a kind of extended verbal montage that assaults the reader's sensibilities, provokes his intellect, and forces him to put the pieces together for himself. This do-it-yourself approach will either stimulate the reader or annoy him, and probably accounts for the widely differing critical responses which the collection has evoked.

At the end of one short piece en-titled "Storytellers, Liars, and Bores," the book's "hero," Phillip Liebowitz, dreams that a room is

. . . full of light, difficult as a head-ache. It poured through plankton, a glaring diffusion, appropriate to the eyes of a fish. Broken nose appeared, swimming through the palpable light, her mouth a zero. "Have you been in-troduced to Kafka? He's here, you know." I followed her and was intro-duced. He shook my hand, then wiped his fingers on his tie.

This passage identifies the primary influence upon the work, while Kaf-ka's gesture, as dreamed by the nar-rator, underscores the book's comic ambiguity. *I Would Have Saved Them If I Could* is another road map for the post-Kafka, post-World War II world. If life is basically absurd, character no more than a locus of consciousness, and living merely the experiencing of a sequence of sensory stimuli loosely organized and given a shape by the perceiver, then it is appropriate for a work of art to come to the reader in apparently random fragments. Logical cause-and-effect plots, believable character-izations, authentic environments, se-rious ideas, a clear distinction be-tween the real and the unreal—all of these elements are false to the reality of the contemporary world.

In the mode of his immediate forebears and contemporaries, such as Borges, Barthelme, Barth, and Sukenick, Michaels offers his vision in a form appropriate to the chaos of the world about which he is writing.

This may make the book sound more arbitrary and diffuse than it actually is. Even though he had abandoned the more obvious linear plot line and the well-rounded character, Michaels does, like many of his contemporaries, keep a firm, if indirect, control over his narrative. Three things give this book an overall unity: the setting, a vision of New York City that is both scrupulously realistic and grotesquely nightmarish; the themes, a number of attitudes and ideas that persistently crop up in the various fragments; and, most important, the character of the unconventional hero.

The narrator, Phillip Liebowitz, is a Jewish intellectual living in New York City, a would-be writer and product of the 1950's who gropes through the city seeking meaning, sex, and stability, a classical *schlemiel,* but one who kicks back when he can. And, although the *avant-gardists* have shaped Michaels' fictional techniques and philosophical attitudes, much of the narrative substance is in the mode of such Jewish novelists as Bellow, Roth, and Malamud. One central strain in the book involves Liebowitz's love-hate relationship with his Jewish heritage; although only presented in glimpses, Phillip's mother is identical to Portnoy's (" 'How do you feel?' My mother said, 'Like a knife is pulling out of my liver' "). The first story in the book, "Murderers," recounts how Phillip gathers with a group of boyhood friends on a precarious rooftop perch to watch the Rabbi copulate with his wife. At the moment of greatest excitement, the youngest of the boys falls to his death, and sex, violence, and Judaism become interrelated as they are throughout the volume.

After this conventional opener, Michaels presents a series of fragments, collectively titled "Eating Out," which gives the reader glimpses of the experiences that have shaped Phillip from his early frenzy as a playground basketball player (basketball prowess guaranteeing sexual conquest), to the shocking, perverse murder of a homosexual friend in the apartment above him (as he turned up the radio "loud enough to interfere with his pleading"), to a highly subjective interview with a psychiatrist. Thus Michaels establishes his pattern. More or less conventional, if bizarre short stories ("Murderers," "Getting Lucky," "Storytellers, Liars, and Bores," "Reflections of a Wild Kid," "Hello Jack," "Some Laughed," "The Captain") are juxtaposed against montages of impressions, experiences, images, and short anecdotes ("Eating Out," "In the Fifties," "Downers," "I Would Have Saved Them If I Could") and unified in the sensibility of the narrator-hero (anti-hero).

All of the stories are not of equal seriousness. Among the more traditional stories, three are simply funny —lively, ingenious, and laced with a bitter irony: "Getting Lucky," "Reflections of a Wild Kid," and "Some Laughed." "Getting Lucky," a funny little sexual parable, might be classified as "hip" O. Henry. Riding the New York subway as usual one morning, Phillip feels himself being masturbated by unknown hands. He reacts with pleasure rather than alarm, not so much from the physical stimulation, but because "Liebowitz was a native New Yorker, with an invulnerable core of sophistication. He realized suddenly that he felt—beyond pleasure—hip." But his reverie is shattered when he later discovers that the author of the act, a high school girl "stinking perfume, dreaming of the sun," is actually a crude transvestite. In "Reflections of a Wild Kid," Phillip finds himself trapped in an old girl friend's bedroom while she entertains her fiancé, a dull Extension College Professor, in the living room. Needing desperately to urinate, Liebowitz uses a window to relieve himself; the professor is subsequently arrested for the act, and Phillip takes over the girl. In "Some Laughed," which might be subtitled "Publish or Perish," the professorial victim of the previous story, one T. T. Mendell, turns into a winner when he gets his "scholarly work" accepted for publication after numerous nasty rejections; the story is an excellent satire on the vagaries of scholarly mediocrity and academic politics.

The most effective of the montages —probably the only one that can stand by itself outside of the collection—is "In the Fifties." Here, with precision, verbal wit, deft and sometimes vicious irony, and most important, a perfect selection of relevant details, Michaels evokes not only the events of the decade, but also its spirit. He recaptures the subtle desperation of the young which lay beneath their material excess and stylistic pretensions ("A lot of young,

gifted people I knew in the fifties killed themselves. Only a few of them continue walking around"). It is in this section that Michaels most forcefully demonstrates that power of compression which gives some of his shorter segments the sound of lyric poetry.

"I Would Have Saved Them If I Could," the title piece of the volume, is more ambitious, although less effective. The most difficult piece in the volume to categorize, it can probably be called an extended meditation on death, meaning, and ambiguity. Fragments of personal and familial experience are interlaced with art works, historical incidents, reminiscences from literary and political figures, snatches of poetry, and the narrator's puzzled, ironical attempt to make sense out of it all. In this collection of fragments, the author suggests an intellectual context for the sense of absurdity that pervades the other stories. He freely introduces and comments on his intellectual mentors past and present, sometimes seriously, sometimes ironically (Borges, Marx, Byron, Kafka, Heraclitus, Hegel, Nietzsche, Wordsworth, Dostoevski, Stevens). At the center, a romantic vision of death—the ecstasy of Jacomir Hladík in the face of Nazi torture (see Borges' "Secret Miracle"), Bonnivard in Byron's *The Prisoner of Chillon*, Dostoevski's condemned man story, Jesus' crucifixion, Wallace Stevens' line "Death is the mother of beauty"—is contrasted with the brutal fact of it— his relatives murdered in the Holocaust, Byron's description of an execution. Perhap's Michaels' whole argument is best summarized in one short section, "The Screams of Children," titled after the sound of Jewish children screaming on the trains that were taking them to death camps.

Michaels is most brutally effective when he treads the line between realism and nightmare, suggesting, through a judicious use of precise details combined with a carefully distorted and heightened atmosphere, a world that is both recognizably commonplace and thoroughly demonic. "The Captain," which concludes the collection, is his most powerful synthesis of the real and the surreal— as well as being his funniest story. The "captain" of the title is Phillip himself as he compares his quest for a lucrative job in publishing with one of the tests of manhood and courage faced by "a young captain in a novel by Conrad." Phillip's test is to get the job by sufficiently impressing his potential employer at a posh Sutton Place dinner party. The party guests are rich, bored, and sophisticated. Their violence, perversity, and bestiality pervade the atmosphere. A prominent plastic surgeon named Swoon beats another guest to death in one corner. Mr. Stanger, the boss-to-be, fondles Phillip's wife Mildred on a couch all evening. The black servants urinate in the coffee. Phillip gets the position largely through a sequence of progressively perverse sexual encounters, first with his boss's wife, then the boss's daughter, then with the wife again in a sado-masochistic routine featuring chains and stuffed animals (they are in a trophy room nicknamed "the zoo"). Phillip wins everything; he gets the job, the boss's women, and his own wife's approval (they make love in the cab en route home) in what is certainly one of the most grotesque and hilarious inversions of the Horatio Alger story since Nathanael West's *A Cool Million*.

Michaels has been criticized for not expanding his talent into a full-length novel; but such a criticism misses the point. If and when he does write a novel, it will probably be as apparently diffuse and haphazard as *I Would Have Saved Them If I Could,* which has the single quality most important in a novel: it provides a coherent aesthetic experience. It is not always a pleasant experience, but it is a stimulating, provocative, and often funny one. Any writer who depends so much on innuendo, linguistic precision, image and metaphor, and appropriate subjective responses, demands much of his readers. He will also "miss" more often than the writer who has a solid, realistic context for his narratives. Michaels has his share of misses in this collection: it is sometimes excessive, pretentious, forced, and frivolous. But the reader who is sensitive and sympathetic toward Michaels' disturbing, funny, ambiguous vision will find in *I Would Have Saved Them If I Could* volumes of experience and insight compressed into one thin book.

Keith Neilson

IN THE BOOM BOOM ROOM

Author: David Râbe
Publisher: Alfred A. Knopf (New York). 113 pp. $5.95
Type of work: Drama
Time: The present
Locale: Philadelphia

A naturalistic play in the tradition of Stephen Crane and Frank Norris

Principal characters:
CHRISSY, a go-go dancer
HAROLD, her father
HELEN, her mother
GUY, her homosexual neighbor
AL, an ex-con; Chrissy's lover and, later, her husband
RALPHIE, Al's strange friend
SUSAN, another go-go dancer

In The Boom Boom Room is David Râbe's fourth play. Like his Vietnam trilogy (*The Basic Training of Pavlo Hummel, Sticks and Bones,* and *Streamers*), it was produced by Joseph Papp at New York's Lincoln Center. As Papp's discovery, Râbe has had the advantage of intelligent casts and brilliant staging. Critics have taken him seriously from his first opening night, and he has not disappointed them. His plays should be seen rather than read, but even in script form, Râbe creates a violent, frequently cruel world of small-time losers with whom the reader has little in common. Râbe never gives in to sentimentality in his characterizations, never attempts to make a myth of his common people. If the reader feels sympathy for them, it is because he recognizes in them, perhaps, his own darker instincts.

The central character of the play is Chrissy—a shallow, gum-chewing go-go dancer whose only redeeming feature is her desire to put a little order in her life. This attempt is doomed by her past, by her parents, by her immediate environment, and by her inarticulate shallowness. But she is mostly doomed by the models of female behavior that she finds in her culture. She can never duplicate the beauty that she envies on the pages of fashion magazines. Her pathetic dream is to appear in the centerfold of *Playboy*. She fantasizes her-airbrushed, or riding topless on the beach—an American Venus.

Chrissy lives in the cheap, blue-collar world of beer bellies, casual prejudice, and disco music, which she takes seriously, desperately trying to understand the words of the songs to which she does the Jerk, the Pony, and the Philly Dog. Harold, her father, worries only about his missing prostate gland and his daily ration of pain and disappointment. Living nostalgically in the past of his youth, he remembers sadistic incidents with pleasure. Chrissy's mother, Helen, has long ago given up trying to change Harold; his sadism is no more remarkable than the evening news. Both have given up on the Dream. They drag out their meaningless lives in a moral and cultural wasteland where the only pleasure is pain. But even pain can no longer excite Harold, and the possibilities are limited.

As he tells Chrissy, "It's hard to drownd a rubber duck."

Chrissy's apartment neighbor, Guy, is a homosexual sperm donor who offers her a sympathetic relationship which would include matching bunny suits; he, too, would like to be on a *Playboy* centerfold. The alternative to Guy is Susan, a lesbian go-go dancer. Chrissy cannot accept either offer, but neither is she able to find a meaningful sexual relationship. Eric, a college graduate, is her only hope, but he wants to worship her and then have something to confess to the kindly old priest in the Sunday confessional. All of the people in Chrissy's life are narcissistic; each wants to feed his ego off of her. Only Chrissy wants to create beauty in her dancing for others to see.

Set in the cheap, flaccid underbelly of Philadelphia, the play alternates wistful humor with painful experience in an atmosphere which is simultaneously real and surreal. The characters are hybrids in the naturalistic tradition of Crane, Norris, and O'Neill; much of the pain and violence could have come out of *McTeague*. Surreal events are presented with realistic touches. For example, Al and his wierd friend, Ralphie, wander into Chrissy's life after seeing her dancing in the Boom Boom Room. They are wanderers, ex-cons to whom life hasn't changed since they served in World War II. The way in which they move into Chrissy's life is a nightmare. Her simple acceptance of them is beyond the rational level. Her only worry is to find her diaphragm.

Desperately trying to make some sense of her life, Chrissy takes Al first as a lover and then as a husband.

The action alternates by jump-cuts between her apartment, the Boom Boom Room, and her parents' house. Driven by her need to understand her sexual identity, Chrissy is barely able to understand the need itself. She does not have the words or the framework to articulate her own confusion, much less to make sense of it. Society offers nothing to sustain her. Religion plays no part, except in parody. The family that raised her provides only nightmares. Pathetically she reads the astrological columns in the daily papers. When Susan disappoints her, she is only able to say: "You are not a perfect Leo like I thought. You are screwing up the universe, Susan!"

The best advice Chrissy can get from her mother is to reach a man's heart through his stomach. Her father, a seedy version of Willy Loman from *Death of a Salesman,* dreams of planting a city garden. Unable to function sexually after his prostate operation, Harold is left with the fond memories of his youthful sexual prowess. In this play, all sex leads to violence, and the past repeats itself endlessly.

As Chrissy's memories unfold, she becomes gradually aware of early sexual pain that has warped her life. In the opening scene, Harold fondly remembers beating her as a child. Later she accuses him of having fed her vodka in a baby bottle, in a drinking contest with her cousin. Harold feels no remorse, only disappointment in her performance. He complains that it had been no contest; the other baby had been older. "We'd been drinking and listening to baseball on the radio. It was the World Series on the radio. The Yankees won it." When Chrissy reminds him that the vodka sent her to the hospital, he simply replies that her mother had said it would not hurt her.

Chrissy's relationship with her mother is no better. The girl half knows that her mother had wanted to abort her as a fetus, not wanting to disfigure her body. When Chrissy accuses Helen of this desire, her mother replies that she did not want Chrissy dead, just to be rid of the "thing" inside her. She had just bounced a little trying to abort. She had aborted others before. This time she hadn't tried as hard as she might have. Certainly she wanted Chrissy. The daughter is horror-stricken.

This confirmation comes on top of Chrissy's realization that as a child she had been sexually assaulted by either her father or her uncle, perhaps by both. She retains the nightmare of the man leaning over her child's bed, assuring her that it won't hurt. The dual recognition of abuse and rejection is too much for Chrissy to bear. Leaving her parents, she turns to Al, who is her father revisited. The past is repeated in pain and degradation. She marries Al, who in turn beats her as her father had done. He too becomes a Willy Loman, unable to find his way off the expressway, driving mindlessly for hours in the snarl of traffic.

In an attempt to strike back at Al, Chrissy plays on his blue-collar fear of blacks. She threatens to have affairs with huge, black men, filming the events to torture Al. In a fit of violence, he begins to beat her sadistically. She pleads with him not to scar her face, not to hit her stomach. Like her mother, it is her body she worries about. The violence becomes

a form of communication. but the message is not pretty. In a parody of the violent dances she does in her go-go cage, Chrissy is battered about the room. The earlier words of Susan haunt the scene. She had given Chrissy instructions on the proper way to dance the Jerk: "You come down. Sudden. Contraction. See. As if you've been hit in the stomach."

There is a jump-cut to a sleazy New York topless bar where Chrissy is being introduced in a mask to hide the scars of Al's beating. She is topless. Here is the final visual metaphor of Râbe's allegory: the anonymous, naked female body displayed before voyeurs. This is the dark side of the sexual dream that rots at the core of America. Beneath the entire play is the running correlation between brute sex and brute beating. The phrase "cut your heart out" recurs. Al was stabbed in the heart as a child; Chrissy threatens to cut Guy's heart out; Susan tells Chrissy the world is full of people who will cut her heart out. Chrissy lives in the bleak, surreal world of blue-collar America from which the spiritual heart has been cut out. There is no possibility for love or dreams. Whatever may have once been there has been made cheap, inarticulate, and violent.

Râbe is working in the tradition of Artaud and Genet with an Americanized version of the Theater of Violence. But, whereas Artuad believed that by staging pain in the theater setting, the need for real pain could be transcended, Râbe's violence provides no cathartic release; the final scene does not allow the viewer to rise above the brutality of the Boom Boom Room.

Michael S. Reynolds

JOURNEY

Authors: Robert Massie (1929-   ) and Suzanne Massie
Publisher: Alfred A. Knopf (New York). 413 pp. $8.95; paperback $1.95
    (Warner)
Type of work: Biography
Time: 1956-1974
Locale: Principally New York City; Irvington, New York; Deer Isle, Maine; and
    Paris, France

*The story of a boy afflicted with hemophilia and of the heroic struggles he and
his parents must endure in order to cope with it, by the authors of* Nicholas and
Alexandra

> *Principal personages:*
> ROBERT K. MASSIE, JR. (BOBBY)
> ROBERT K. MASSIE, his father
> SUZANNE MASSIE, his mother
> SUSANNA and
> ELIZABETH, his sisters
> JIM GREENLAW,
> ALFRED GREENLAW, and
> DAVEY GARDNER, friends in Maine
> SVETLANA UMRICHIN, Suzanne's Russian teacher
> PRINCESS OLGA OF YUGOSLAVIA and
> JOE DOWNING, friends in Paris
> MARIO T. BISCORDI,
> LEE ENGEL, and
> FRANCOIS JOSSO, physicians

Catastrophic illness is an eventuality for which, although most of us dread its possibility, we can never really be prepared. When it strikes, it usually does so without warning and the afflicted family is precipitated into a state in which security simply ceases to exist. Physical, emotional, and financial resources are quickly exhausted; insurance plans are never adequate in such a contingency; the entire pattern of existence is radically altered. If the disaster is a terminal illness of limited duration there is always the possibility that surviving members can recover and return to a more normal life. If, however, it is a chronic illness that is not inevitably fatal, the altered pattern must of necessity become permanent, and perpetual crisis must somehow be endured. Circumstances are worsened if the ailment is one little understood by the general public.

Journey is the chronicle of one family that received such a visitation and eventually found the strength required to cope with it. It is a painful record and a moving testimonial to those who can adapt to impossible situations, accept the almost unendurable, and somehow cope with continuous emergencies one day at a time.

Bobby, the son of Robert and Suzanne Massie, was born in 1956. When he was six months old his parents noticed that he bruised easily, often for no apparent reason, and found that a blood-test puncture refused to stop bleeding. The diagnosis: classical hemophilia.

Hemophilia is the result of a hereditary genetic disorder in which blood fractions that promote clotting are absent. In some forty percent of the cases there is no previous history of the disease; Bobby was one of these. The defective gene, whether handed down or produced by mutation, is then carried only by females, while the disease itself is passed only to their male offspring. That it is often called a disease of royalty is due to Queen Victoria, who was a carrier and passed it to her daughter Alexandra. Alexandra married Nicholas, Tsar of Russia. Their son, the Cesarevitch Alexis, was born with hemophilia and was probably its most famous victim, although he died by violence and not from his ailment.

Although hemophilia is not excessively rare, it is not familiar to most people, who think of the hemophiliac as one who may bleed to death from the merest scratch. Actually, such a scratch could bleed indefinitely if left unattended, but it can be stopped by a bandage. The hemophiliac's real danger is from internal bleeding. These hemorrhages occur without warning and can be arrested only through massive transfusions of fresh blood, fresh frozen plasma, or the more recently developed fraction concentrates. If they occur repeatedly in joints, one of the vulnerable areas, the result is bone erosion and severe crippling; if they occur in the throat or brain they are usually fatal. The internal bleeding, especially in joints, causes excruciating pain, and the amount of blood required for survival is enormous. The death rate among victims is high. Twenty years ago only fifty-four percent of them reached five years of age, and of those who did, only eleven percent achieved maturity. The odds are much more favorable today because of technological advances, but the expenses incurred are truly staggering.

This was the trial that confronted Robert and Suzanne Massie. Every aspect of their lives was changed and the years that followed were a nightmare of emotional and financial pressure, constant anxiety, perpetual strain, crushing fatigue. In such situations the available resources of friends and relatives are soon depleted. Neighbors are reluctant to help out in areas where they fear the unknown and feel they may do more harm than good. The family inevitably becomes isolated: others have lives of their own that cannot be neglected on a continuous basis and there is a limit to the portion of themselves that can be given. Their eventual withdrawal is seen as betrayal or indifference. The callousness so often noted and resented in hospitals and the medical profession is occasionally sadism, but more often it is a form of protective armor: if the persons concerned became emotionally involved with every patient, their objectivity and efficiency—and sanity —would soon be lost. They must tread a fine line between compassion and detachment, and they are not always successful; they are often bone weary too. Such explanations mean little to frantic parents whose child is suffering in a place where no one seems to care. All facilities, it seems, are designed for people without handicaps. Strangers are tactless and often think the bruised child is a victim of parental beatings.

Journey is the joint effort of Robert and Suzanne, who have written separate chapters so that their personal reactions and viewpoints would remain distinct. Those written by Suzanne are deeply distressing. She has made no effort to minimize or conceal the anguish that was felt, and it is through a cry of pain that we see how terrible the ordeal really was. At one point she contemplated suicide, and realized that some strong mental discipline was necessary to preserve her sanity. She had always felt a strong affinity for the Russian people and determined to learn their language. Her studies with a Russian family who lived in Nyack, not far from her home in Irvington, New York, were brightened by their calm acceptance of Bobby. As she observes, the Russians have a history of misfortune and disaster and much of their strength is derived from learning to live with it.

Robert, whose role was necessarily that of provider, writes with a quiet restraint that does not mask his sensitivity. He became a professional writer and worked for several magazines, principally *Newsweek*. The strain of meeting uncertain schedules, commuting to his work, and dealing with emergency situations at night was enormous. To preserve his own sanity through mental discipline he undertook a thorough study of his son's malady; as a result, *Journey* embodies a lucid, detailed introduction to the disease itself and should help to correct many popular misconceptions.

During these years Bobby continued to grow and develop. They were years of pain, of sleepless nights, of frequent trips to the hospital; at the same time they were years in which he and his parents learned to meet the various challenges with which they were faced. Robert learned to give the transfusions at home; an intercom system was established between their home and the local school so that Bobby could participate during the periods when he was bedridden. A decision was made that since there was no way he could be protected against all contingencies his childhood should be made as normal as possible. Summer holidays were spent happily at Deer Isle, Maine.

The Massies are more fortunate than many victims of catastrophic illness in that Bobby's disease furnished them with the means to fight it. Suzanne pointed out that a book on the Romanovs should be written and that it was one that only the parents of a hemophiliac child could write. A three-year family commitment followed; the result, *Nicholas and Alexandra,* was a combination of Robert's careful historical research and Suzanne's deep understanding of the Russian character. It was a best seller, and it enabled them to live in France for four years—a place where Bobby could be educated in a school that concerned itself only with intellectual development, and where the blood fraction concentrates he required were available at a price his parents could pay.

This matter of astronomical expense is one which Robert explores thoroughly. As he points out, most nations today have some form of protection for families who are confronted with catastrophic illness. The United States does not. Insurance companies, which are profit-making organizations, exclude them; only group plans provide assistance and it is limited in extent. Blood is treated as a commodity, and the American Red Cross, who could produce the concentrates cheaply on a nonprofit basis, has instead entered into an arrangement with a commercial firm; prices are maintained at a level acceptable to the drug industry. He refutes the common objection to national health insurance by pointing to France, where doctors do not work for the government. Instead it is up to the patient to pay his physician and then obtain remuneration, provided on a sliding scale based on severity of the affliction, from the local social security office. The services and materials needed to fight catastrophic illness are free.

Journey is both disturbing and inspiring. As a biography it is necessarily devoted largely to peripheral struggles that made the survival of its subject a possibility. One very disturbing aspect is its portrayal of the shattering effect illness can have on those closest to it. Equally disturbing is the knowledge that such experiences are devastating enough, physically and emotionally, without adding the unnecessary burden of financial ruin.

Today young Robert Massie is fully grown. He is a remarkable young man, active physically and brilliant mentally, as much a master of his physical handicaps as it is possible to be. His illness is not cured and its ravages are not eradicated, but he and his parents have nonetheless conquered it. This book is a rare tribute to the human spirit and to what it can accomplish.

John W. Evans

J R

Author: William Gaddis (1922-   )
Publisher: Alfred A. Knopf (New York). 726 pp. $15.00; paperback $5.95
Type of work: Novel
Time: The present
Locale: New York City

A satirical and stylistically eccentric portrayal of the world of contemporary big business

> *Principal characters:*
> J R VANSANT, an eleven-year-old schoolboy and business tycoon
> EDWARD BAST, a composer and employee of J R
> JACK GIBBS, a teacher at J R's school, author, and employee of J R
> MRS. JOUBERT, J R's teacher

J R is an extraordinarily difficult novel, especially for a reader accustomed to traditional narrative structures or, for that matter, traditional syntax and punctuation. It comes as Gaddis' second work, twenty years after *The Recognitions,* which was largely attacked by critics and only gradually became something of an underground classic among a small circle of Gaddis enthusiasts. This first novel is now generally recognized as a work of major significance marking subsequent trends in fiction and belonging to the first rank of fiction in the decade of the 1950's. It, like *J R,* was unusually, perhaps excessively, long, dense, and ambiguous. There is no doubt that its poor reception played a strong role in the formation of *J R,* and one may suspect that the reception accorded *J R*—it was a major book club selection—was in part based on the desire to render Gaddis his due. Yet *J R* is, if anything, more difficult and more controversial than *The Recognitions.*

The novel consists almost entirely of dialogue—no stage directions, no indication of who is speaking, no connective tissue. The characters are not described, nor is there a narration of events, simply a sea of talk, in which the reader must attempt to distinguish the characters by tone of voice, mannerisms, and fixed ideas. There are dozens of characters, mostly minor, who engage in these conversations, often on the telephone, in which case one voice may be lost, often while other characters are talking in the same room. All of this is delivered seemingly without organization, verbatim, along with interruptions from the radio and the printed word. Much has been made of Gaddis' uncanny ear for the cadences of modern speech, filled with jargon and cliché, illiterate and ungrammatical, and as often as not communicating only the speaker's inability to think or to comprehend his own subject matter. People constantly talk past one another, never really listening, talking almost desperately as if to block a great void which threatens to engulf them. *J R* is a virtuoso novel of speech, and it is not long before one realizes that Gaddis' prime target in this novel of the business world is contemporary speech itself, the utter debasement of the language by the media, by government and business, by the invasion of pseudo-science which tries to dress up pedestrian thought—"he structured the material in terms of the ongoing situation to tangibilitate the utilization potential of this one to one instructional medium. . . ."

This technique owes much to the stream of consciousness novel, and particularly to Joyce, although Gaddis claims never to have read *Ulysses*. As a merciless satire of the age of jargon in which we live it is often hilarious, but when carried to the length of more than seven hundred pages, the humor turns bitter, and the reader, stupefied by the sheer mass, may experience something like aversion therapy, becoming unable ever again to read a government document or listen to a speech without acute distress.

It is undeniable that this technique, however brilliant in itself, is also the main problem of the book, since the average reader and even some critics find their attention span inadequate to absorb more than a few pages at a time, and eventually the lack of variation in tone becomes oppressive, as Gaddis pours forth an endless stream of this noncommunication. One reviewer called the novel "an autistic triumph." On the other hand, the technique is not an end in itself, but serves to create a verbal counterpart of the disordered and valueless world it describes; and gradually, through the sea of verbal pollution, the story and the characters emerge, creating a satirical vision verging on the surrealistic, wildly funny at times, at times bitter, and in the end touching as well.

J R Vansant is an eleven-year-old sixth grader in a school on Long Island, whose teacher, to give her charges the actual experience of American business, organizes a field trip to Wall Street, where the class buys one share of common stock. J R is fascinated by this taste of the great world, and embarks upon a madly improbable business career based entirely on mail order catalogues and coupon offers. He runs his growing enterprise from a telephone booth, stuffing a handkerchief (dirty, of course) into his mouth to age his voice. He is barely literate, but with a peculiar literalness of mind he works all the ploys of the business world to form a conglomerate of bankrupt corporations held together by deficit financing, tax write-offs, stock options, futures, and whimsical transactions, such as his initial purchase of 9,000 gross of Navy surplus wooden forks, which he then sells to the Army. The real estate he buys and sells is worthless, and in a particularly malicious concatenation, J R acquires a drug company, a chain of nursing homes to serve as an outlet for the drugs, a funeral parlor to service the nursing homes, and finally, a cemetery. *J R* is the great American Horatio Alger success story updated and perverted, and the perversion extends beyond the business world to engulf all the institutions and values of our society as it is portrayed here.

J R Corporation includes a company that publishes textbooks interleaved with advertising pages, but the school out of which he comes is little better; the president of the school is also a bank president, and the school is run by coaches and staffed by demoralized teachers armed with all sorts of educational gadgetry.

The world of education is infected with the same collapse of language as is elsewhere evident, and the omnipresence of money as the central or rather sole value is in evidence here as well. Education is replaced with public relations, political strategy, and funding questions as the prime interest of the school, and mechanical devices are preferred to live intellectual exchange, because they are so much more easily manipulated. Almost inevitably, the institution becomes self-aggrandizing, and, cancerlike, diverts the energy from its real purpose to feed the institution itself.

The center of this world is not the school, however. J R rapidly acquires a corporation headquarters—a dirty tenement on East 96th Street, with leaky water faucets, telephones that ring constantly, a radio buried among the piles of junk, and a varied crew of assistants, live-in parasites, and government regulators who snoop about. Rhoda, who will sleep with anyone, inhabits the place, and it is populated as well by two of the more touching figures in the novel, Edward Bast, a composer, and Jack Gibbs, a teacher of social studies at J R's school, supposedly working on a "social history of mechanism and the arts" entitled *Agape, Agape.* He hasn't looked at his manuscript in sixteen years. It is Gibbs who seems the most human of the characters, perhaps because he is closest to Gaddis himself; the parallel between the two author figures is unmistakable. Gaddis indeed quotes from reviews of his first novel, and the failed artists who rail against the commercialism of the arts in the contemporary business world are linked to the theme of

the debasement of language; society is destroying both the artist and his medium, while the illiterate and unprincipled thrive in a cacophony of greed. Gaddis is undoubtedly speaking from experience when he lets Gibbs lament that most potential readers would rather go to the movies.

Gaddis has claimed that his royalties average only $100 a year for *The Recognitions,* and he has earned his living writing speeches, scripts for industrial films, and public relations for a drug company, all of which may explain somewhat the intensity of his satire, as well as his expertise. It is this personal relationship of Gaddis to his subject, not merely in the figure of Gibbs, but in all the characters marooned in the isolation of empty words, that the novel has its ground. It is from here that the brilliant technique and the seemingly interminable extension of the satire receive their life and their value. Gaddis moves from the satirical to the tragic in this world, which for all its madcap insanity bears such clear relationship to the phenomena that we see around us—the manipulation of language devoid of moral content; the concealment of gross and palpable wrongdoing behind euphemism and the direct lie; and the self-perpetuating tendency of institutions, which supplant their original function and may even work counter to that function.

While the size of the novel and its demanding technique may place it beyond the average reader, the importance of the theme and the brilliance of its execution make it one of the significant works of recent fiction.

Steven C. Schaber

JULIA AND THE BAZOOKA

Author: Anna Kavan
Publisher: Alfred A. Knopf (New York). 155 pp. $6.95
Type of work: Short stories

Fifteen poetic and haunting stories which probe the lonely, hallucinatory worlds of their drug-addicted protagonist, all of whom are facets of the author's own personality

The bazooka of the title is the syringe used to give oneself a shot of heroin. It is difficult to separate these strange and brilliant stories from their author, for they are visions which stem directly from her own experiences. Although they might be classified as nightmares, they also are autobiographical. The drug addiction of Anna Kavan is helpful to an understanding of the stories and much of her other work, but ultimately these pieces—like all literature—must stand on their own as works of art. These fifteen stories can do this very well; they are hard and brilliant as ice, composed in a dazzling, yet sensitive, prose, and they present a glimpse of a world rarely encountered in fiction. *Julia and the Bazooka* is a masterpiece and will endure on its own merits, aside from the unusual biography of its creator.

The reader will not find "realism" in these stories, but rather a kind of heightened reality, a world in which human beings are so sensitive that their nerve endings seem to hang out. It is a world in which the female protagonists are always seeking escape from pain, both physical and mental. Often, the only escape is in a high-powered motor car; sometimes, it is only to be found with the aid of the "bazooka." Frantically, the heroines seek release from their torments, seek

an escape from their excessive vulnerability; they cannot cope with the world, and human relationships are too painful for them. They suffer from an agonizing loneliness, yet the presence of other human beings only increases the suffering. The plight of these women is, in many respects, the plight of all men and women in the modern world, and by writing so blazingly about her own consciousness, Anna Kavan has uncovered the torments that besiege all human beings.

On the surface, these startling and brief stories seem only to reflect a weird, if thrilling, realm of drug addiction and heightened consciousness bordering on madness. They expose thirty years of seesawing stability and chaos in the life of a brilliant English writer: it is a life of ever-present drugs and suicide attempts interspersed with stays in hospitals, productive work, and marriages. But the stories also penetrate the dark regions of human consciousness and perception, the areas of reality which most men and women fear to confront. Kavan has risked everything in her stories, confronting the panic which all of us feel in the dark nights of our souls. At the same time, a tender beauty pervades many of the stories, a vision of the splendors just beyond mortal reach. It is as if she has captured with her remarkable prose the aura which is said to surround each human being. Inanimate objects come to life in her narrative, animals speak, and dreams mingle with everyday life. The seductive despair inherent in the human condition is laid open with brutal toughness, and the violent core at its heart is exposed.

The first story, "The Old Address," begins, significantly, with the narrator-protagonist leaving the hospital. The world seems insane to her, "delirious, ominous, mad." *She* was hospitalized because of her abnormality, because of her drug addiction, yet the "sane" world is a violent, bloody place, perhaps far more mad and dangerous than she is. Is it the vision of this woman which is warped, or is it the actual world? There is no answer offered to this question, yet the attitude of the author is never in doubt. The heroine is locked in a nightmare of violence, but the core of this nightmare is the real world.

A sense of loss pervades many of the stories; moods of gentle melancholy alternate with violent, passionate cries for help. One of the most sensitive and lovely pieces is "A Visit," which tells of a painter living alone on the edge of a jungle and the nighttime visits of a leopard which seems to have a special message for her. It reminds her of freedom, of a wild and beautiful existence which she has never known, or, perhaps, once knew and then lost. Is the loss which Kavan's heroines share chiefly a loss of freedom? The author's "message" is always implied; as in all first-rate art, these narratives avoid spelling out moral lessons or sociological conclusions, but, rather, present visions of the human condition with all its contradictions and complications.

Kavan's use of images and metaphors is among the most effective in recent fiction. In "Fog," for example, a woman driving alone encounters a world in which people look like dummies stuffed with clothes, their faces like Japanese masks. These horrible, inhuman creatures are all-powerful, like robots, because they feel nothing; it is only those mortals susceptible to human emotions who are vulnerable. The fog becomes a symbol of the poison of the modern world; it spreads throughout the book, drifting from the pages of that one story to invade the territory of the others. It is also a symbol of an all-consuming boredom which Kavan's heroines all share.

In "Experimental," the protagonist takes a temporary lover to alleviate her boredom, but discovers that she is even more bored with her lover than without him. In the end, she is left alone. In "The World of Heroes," the protagonist seeks to escape her loneliness and boredom through her compulsive relationship with race car drivers, but she again ends up alone. The fearless, nomadic, "elegant" world of professional race driving provided no more than a temporary refuge from the terrors which pursued her. In "The Mercedes" an automobile again is a symbol of escape. A brilliant doctor and his mistress, the protagonist, plan continuously for the expensive cars they someday will buy, but in the end a phantom automobile carries away the doctor, leaving the woman alone. The stories consistently conclude with the female protagonist left alone, isolated, in a hostile world. One must endure the boredom of strangers or the boredom of existence alone; either way, one is ultimately lonely and bored, so perhaps there is no real choice, after all.

Some of the stories were no doubt written in periods of acute depression, perhaps even while under the influence of drugs, yet they are brilliantly crafted and highly polished pieces of prose composition. In no way can they be considered as the excrescences of a dope-crazed mind. Unlike some of the writings of the fashionable narcotic-influenced writers of recent years (William Burroughs, for example), these stories have been subjected to rigorous intellectual and artistic standards; their vision and style call to mind the masterpieces of writers such as Kafka, Borges, and Beckett. The author's discipline, clarity of style, and relentless logic triumph over any mere sensationalism of subject matter.

Throughout this volume, from "The Old Address" to "Julia and the Bazooka," which closes the book, a climactic moment of extreme feeling pulls together the disconnected threads of the protagonist's consciousness. Kavan shares with James Joyce the belief that a story should end with a fragmentary clue into the meaning of life as a whole, and she provides the reader with that "insight into individual lives" which Joyce felt was the object of serious writing. Taking apparently trivial stimuli, capturing revelations in midflight, with an amazing and startling psychological precision, the author shares with the reader her own mystical vision, linking the beholder to the object beheld. She never yields to that temptation of the minor writer, to turn away from the object of emotion and describe the emotion instead.

Julia and the Bazooka will probably not appeal to a large audience, since it deals with sordid and unpleasant subjects and with unusual states of mind. The symbols are rich and luminous, but they are not always easy to follow. But for the reader willing to risk traveling in the regions of the unknown, for the reader who dares to probe into the heart of darkness and to confront his or her own inner spaces as revealed by an author's skill, this book will be a thrilling and rewarding experience. It is a book that one cannot read and forget.

Bruce D. Reeves

LAMY OF SANTA FE
His Life and Times

Author: Paul Horgan (1903-   )
Publisher: Farrar, Straus and Giroux (New York). Illustrated. 523 pp. $15.00
Type of work: Biography
Time: 1814-1888
Locale: France, Italy, Mexico, and the United States, especially Cincinnati and
Santa Fe

*The story of the sacrifices and successes of a leader of the Roman Catholic
Church during pioneer days in the West*

> *Principal personages:*
> JEAN BAPTISTE LAMY, Archbishop of Santa Fe
> JOSEPH PRIEST MACHEBEUF, his friend and associate
> MARIE LAMY (SISTER FRANCESCA), his niece
> MARGARET LAMY, his sister
> ARCHBISHOP JOHN BAPTIST PURCELL, his superior
> JEAN BAPTISTE SALPOINTE, his successor
> JUAN FELIPE ORTIZ, his enemy, a Mexican rural dean
> MARY MAGDALEN, Mother Superior in Santa Fe
> GENERAL LEW WALLACE, Governor of Santa Fe
> JAMES S. CALHOUN, U.S. Territorial Governor
> FATHER JOSE MANUEL GALLEGOS, Lamy's New Mexican rival
> BISHOP JOHN MARY ODIN, Lamy's companion from Galveston

Paul Horgan, a Roman Catholic by faith, was born in Buffalo, New York, grew up in Albuquerque, and became established as a New Mexican regional writer with his trilogy *Mountain Standard Time,* as well as with his numerous other novels, plays, and short stories. Horgan knows his territory, having not only lived there most of his life, but having also taught at the University of New Mexico, and served in the U.S. Army in the area in which he centers his recent biography. In addition to his fiction, he has written a considerable body of historical and biographical works based on the region. In 1927, Willa Cather published her classic, *Death Comes for the Archbishop,* introducing Archbishop Marie Latour who "died of having lived." After a half century of research, Horgan res-

urrects Latour here, in the person of the real-life archbishop, the quixotic Jean Baptiste Lamy; at the same time, his fellow priest, Joseph Priest Machebeuf, reminds us of Cather's Joseph Vaillant.

The book begins as the twenty-five-year-old Lamy is stealing away from Riom in central France with the older Machebeuf, whose family will not let him run away to America. The two men vow they will always work together. With fourteen associates they leave Paris on July 9, 1839, landing on Long Island in August and reaching Cincinnati nineteen days later. At that time, Ohio's population of about a million was so anti-Catholic that priests had to wear lay clothing to carry on their duties. Fellow priests in the city were too busy proselytizing to help the pair much with their English, so they were largely self-taught.

Because of the illness of Machebeuf's father, his family urged the remorseful priest to return to France, but church activities in the towns he and Lamy were then serving confined their traveling to fund-gathering in St. Louis and Canada until the father succumbed in 1844. When family affairs finally demanded the priest's presence at home, he extended his travel to Rome, where he reported to the Pope on their work and was assigned eight nuns to help them in their effort.

When Lamy's own father died two years later, he returned to Riom, from which he brought back his sister Margaret and his niece Marie. Back in America he took out American citizenship papers, and shortly afterwards was transferred to Covington, Kentucky, across the river from Cincinnati.

As Horgan explains, 1848 was the year when hordes of Irish immigrants began fleeing the potato famine, flocking to America and spreading across the continent, thus increasing the labors of the priests. A meeting of American Catholic authorities met in Baltimore and decided to appoint new administrators, especially for the Western area coming into prominence after the Mexican War of 1846 and the Gadsden Purchase. From among the many nominations, "Joannes Lamy of the Diocese of Cincinnati" was selected, and in July, 1850, Pope Pius IX issued a papal bull appointing him bishop with headquarters in Santa Fe. Still sickly and uncertain, Lamy invited Machebeuf from Sandusky to accompany him as Vicar General, and, remem-

bering their oath of companionship, Machebeuf agreed. Lamy was consecrated bishop in St. Peter's Cathedral, Cincinnati, in October, 1850, in ceremonies described in detail in four pages of Horgan's biography.

The two friends planned to travel by way of New Orleans and the Mississippi so that Lamy might leave his sister in a New Orleans convent for training, and so that they might have more time to work on learning Spanish. Part III, "To Santa Fe, 1850-1851," describes their journey, and the chronicler comments that perhaps their hardships were training for the tribulations that awaited them. First they were shipwrecked at Galveston, and Lamy lost his carriage and all his belongings except his trunk of books. From Bishop Odin, who sheltered them, Lamy got warning of the enmity and opposition he might expect from dictatorial clergy too long enjoying an easy and unsupervised living; Odin suggested he hasten to Santa Fe to "secure his throne," then travel to Spain to learn Spanish and gather associates to help him. Instead, Lamy wrote to Paris to the Society for the Propagation of the Faith for 5,000 francs to replace his losses, then joined a caravan of merchants for San Antonio, leaving Machebeuf to follow later.

For the next 350 pages, we read of one catastrophe after another. By the time Machebeuf caught up with him, bringing news of the death of Sister Margaret in New Orleans, Lamy was in bed with a sprained leg, suffered when his borrowed carriage overturned during circuit riding through army posts and outlying settlements. It took until May to recover. To help him continue on to El Paso, General

Harney temporarily assigned him to the army caravan heading for the upper Rio Grande, so that he might draw free rations for the trip.

From El Paso, the priests used El Camino Real, the old Spanish road in use since the seventeenth century. Everywhere they were enthusiastically welcomed, with flowery arches and Spanish shawls spread at church entrances, along with other tokens of hospitality; nevertheless, the astute new bishop saw that the zeal and piety of the people lay only on the surface, and correctly judged their priestly guides lax and arrogant.

On Sunday, August 9, 1851, Lamy's group approached Santa Fe, established ten years before the Pilgrims landed. Five miles from town they were met by a crowd with U.S. Territorial Governor Calhoun in his carriage, to accompany them the rest of the way; musicians playing a fandango, the only religious music they knew, led them to the humble adobe cathedral of St. Francis.

The rest of the book largely concerns the priestly quarrels and refusals to cooperate in what Horgan terms Lamy's "Desert Diocese." Bishop Odin had warned Lamy against the antagonism of fellow Catholic administrators afraid of losing their sinecures. The truth behind his warning soon became evident. Lamy was in charge of a territory sixteen times the area of his Ohio parish. Most of the bishops, enjoying a comfortable living from their excessive charges for every service, refused to work together in the best interests of their flocks, lapsing instead into bitter fighting among themselves. When Bishop Zubiría of Durango protested the new alignment

of territory, for example, it required ten years of letter writing and several trips to Rome to force his agreement. However, Gallegos of Albuquerque then brought false charges against him and ran for Congress solely to be able to launch attacks from Washington. Meanwhile, Ortiz, the rural dean, led a group of rebellious churchmen until he was removed from the fight by apoplexy. One man waylaid him in his travels, another shot at him in his bedroom; but Lamy persisted in his efforts to untangle complex churchly affairs. He also pursued projects such as the construction of a new cathedral of native stone built around the cathedral's mud structure; the smaller building was demolished just before his death. Meanwhile, Lamy was building a hospital and schools for the Indian boys and girls.

Lamy had many trials to bear: his sister died in New Orleans; cholera killed his helpers; one priest was poisoned at the altar; and attacks by marauding Apaches and Comanches killed others. But the bishop never neglected his duties, and his efforts were rewarded by promotions. Horgan describes his silver anniversary celebration, at which he was given the archbishopric and the pallium, a collar of white wool, symbolic of his participation in the Pope's supreme pastoral office.

But years of toil had wearied him. He sought rest in Villa Pintoresca, a small home and garden in a canyon three miles from Santa Fe, from which he walked every day to the cathedral. Finally in 1880 after repeated unsuccessful requests to the Pope for a coadjutor to compensate for his failing strength, he became seriously ill, and for five weeks the city expected to hear of his death. But he recovered enough to perform his duties for the 100,000 people in his care and to answer the many calls upon him by dying parishioners. Finally came the Vatican agreement with his request for a Jesuit priest helper with long experience in the land. He was authorized to name Bishop Jean Baptiste Salpointe as his successor, and permitted to retire. But first he made one more trip to upper Mexico, traveling ten thousand miles and confirming 35,000 people before returning to Villa Pintoresca. The farewell ceremonies, says his biographer, praised him for leaving 238 churches where only sixty-six existed upon his arrival in 1851. He had increased the number of priests from twelve to fifty-four; colleges had doubled in number and schools had tripled; and his parish now had hospitals and orphan asylums.

On February 7, 1889, a message reached Santa Fe from the seventy-two-year-old archbishop at his villa, who was suffering from a cold and requested conveyance to the city. The cold turned out to be pneumonia, however; and when all the church bells rang on the morning of the thirteenth, the saddened city knew that they tolled for their devoted archbishop.

Willis Knapp Jones

THE LAST VALLEY

Author: A. B. Guthrie, Jr. (1901-   )
Publisher: Houghton Mifflin Company (Boston). 293 pp. $8.95
Type of work: Novel
Time: 1922-1946
Locale: A small town in one of the cattle counties of western Montana

The fifth novel in a series about the American West, The Last Valley *depicts the effects of the twentieth century on the land and its people*

Principal characters:
>BENJAMIN ASWELL TATE, a newspaper publisher
>MARY JESS, his wife
>MATTIE MURCHISON, a young widow
>MACALESTER CLEVELAND, a retired newspaper publisher
>MORT EWING, a local cattle rancher
>BENTON COLLINGSWORTH, local school superintendent and
>   Ben's father-in-law
>FRANK BROBECK, local sheriff and Ben's friend

For a quarter of a century and more, A. B. Guthrie has been acknowledged as one of the great regional writers in American fiction. His saga of the American West has been carried through five novels: *The Big Sky* (1947); *The Way West* (1949), which earned Guthrie the Pulitzer Prize for fiction for 1950; *These Thousand Hills* (1956); *Arfive* (1971); and the most recent novel, *The Last Valley,* which the author has said is likely to be the final book in the series, as its title implies. The series gives a fictional account of the West from the 1830's to the end of World War II, from the opening of the country early in the nineteenth century to its facing of problems induced by civilization in the twentieth century.

The setting of *The Last Valley* is a small town in western Montana, the same fictional town which gave the title to the preceding novel in the series, *Arfive.* Into the town of Arfive, shortly after World War I, comes young Ben Tate, a man from Ohio who served as a captain in the army during World War I and then studied for a time at Harvard. He buys the Arfive *Advocate,* the local newspaper, with his savings, and settles into the community to become a part of its life, marrying a local girl, becoming influential in the local affairs, and struggling with his own and the community's problems.

The novel is divided into three parts. The first part, set in the 1920's, centers around the emergence of hollow superpatriotism in that era. Local people, caught up in their own fervor, bring in an out-of-state speaker who unsuccessfully attempts to sway the citizens of Arfive to start a witch-hunt against their fellow citizens who might be, to use the term of the time, Bolsheviks, Communist-inspired revolutionaries seeking to undermine America and its democratic institutions. Targets of the outsider's attack include Ben Tate, the local newspaper publisher, who has tried to oppose what he sees as dangerous in the superpatriotism, and elderly Benton Collingsworth, the well-educated local school superintendent. The incident serves as a focal point for a narrative which relates realistically what life was like at the time in western Montana. Ben Tate, as a newcomer, learns (as does the reader) about life in the town and the surrounding county. From the three most influential men in the community he derives valuable lessons: Macalester Cleveland, retired publisher of the *Advocate,* advises him to keep his integrity; Mort Ewing, a successful cattleman, advises him to be cautious of so-called progress; and Benton Collingsworth advises him to avoid becoming too parochial through adopting the coloration of the community. From two women, too, Ben learns. He falls in love with well-educated, cultured Mary Jess Collingsworth, who accepts his proposal of marriage, and he receives lessons in women and physical love from a young widow, Mattie Murchison, his landlady's daughter.

The second part of the novel centers around the death of a bear, a cantankerous old grizzly who lives in the mountains west of Arfive, and the death of a man, a convicted murderer who is hanged in the town. These two events occur in the 1930's and furnish focal points for this section of the novel. Ben Tate and Jap York, the latter a hunting guide, track down the grizzly after it has been wounded by a thoughtless third member of their party. Tate and York finish off the bear, but the bear also kills the guide. Beast and man represent the older, the natural West, which is being crowded out by civil-

ized man. The other event is the hanging, which is a public event, complete with numerous official invitations from the sheriff; the hanged man is a drifter who strangled the weak, handicapped operator of a bar in Arfive. In this section, both Ben and the town have grown older and more prosperous. Problems of the 1930's are related, along with the not entirely successful solutions to those problems. The town prospers, with growing pains, through the construction of a flood-control dam on the nearby Breast River. Funds from the Public Works Administration program of the Franklin D. Roosevelt era create the dam, but the influx of money and jobs brings its own problems, such as unsavory characters who come to the community temporarily to take advantage of the local people and the honest workers and their families. Even the dam itself appears a mixed blessing, for its ability to control floodwaters is questionable, and it initially provides no program for the irrigation of farmland.

Part Three of *The Last Valley* centers around a flood which threatens to destroy the dam on the nearby Breast River and flood the town. Events in this section occur immediately after World War II. The town of Arfive has changed, as have its people. Streets have been paved, but trees are gone from the main street. The town is prosperous, but the automobile and changing buying habits have ended once-thriving businesses, such as the general store and the men's haberdashery. In the surrounding county, good grazing land has been tilled temporarily to grow grain for the war effort, only to be left after the war to sprout weeds instead of the native grasses, which do not return. Ben discovers, with the advent of the flood threat to the town, that he has become one of the handful of citizens in the community to whom people turn in emergencies, as they seek out clear-thinking men of action. The leaders of the community when Ben Tate came to it a quarter of a century before have grown too old or have died; it is Tate's generation who have taken the places of responsibility. New problems, in addition to the flood threat, have emerged. Summer fallowing of land has become a danger; the practice in the county of planting grain every other year appears to be endangering the cropland by bringing mineral salts, including alkali, to the surface. Also, irrigated farms, too small to provide a good living, are reducing their operators to near-poverty. But, as Ben sees it, the land endures, with him a part of it, despite time and change.

The Last Valley is a novel about people, as well as about a region. Ben Tate, his family, his friends and acquaintances, are all shown growing older, learning about life: about its sorrow and disappointments, its happiness and successes. A. B. Guthrie demonstrates through his characters how each generation in its turn matures, faces its responsibilities, grows old, and dies. He shows how life brings its surprises, uncovers long-kept secrets, and forces people to see themselves in new ways. At one point in the novel, for example, the inheritance of a ranch by an elderly woman reveals the fact that many years before she gave birth to a child by the rancher, having chosen him, rather than her worthless husband, to father the infant. Ben, disappointed for many years by his literary wife's unwillingness to bear children, discovers after two decades that he has fathered a son during a brief affair with Mattie Murchison when he first came to Arfive. The son, now a young journalist, seeks advice from Tate, much as Tate had sought advice a quarter of a century before when he came to the town as a young man.

Both characters and setting come alive in *The Last Valley*; as a successful regionalist, Guthrie has caught the spirit and character of the land and its people. In a prefatory note, he apologizes unnecessarily for liberties he took in creating this novel—liberties, as he calls them, taken for the sake of the artistic quality of the work. Guthrie points out that his dam on the fictitious Breast River is a composite of at least two specific structures; that his hanging is a year off date from the original incident; that the great flood of Part Three occurred in 1964, not eighteen years earlier; and that saline seep, a growing agricultural problem in the 1970's, was not identified, perhaps not even recognized, until a decade after the closing events of his novel. Guthrie need not apologize for such alterations of history, however, for he wrote as a novelist, not as a historian. Only those who fail to understand the difference between fiction and history could charge him with a fault. He wrote to give a sense of the grandeur of the country, a sense of the enduring qualities of the land and the people he knows and loves, and he has succeeded admirably.

Gordon W. Clarke

LETTERS HOME
Correspondence, 1950-1963

Author: Sylvia Plath
Edited by Aurelia Schober Plath
Publisher: Harper & Row Publishers (New York). 502 pp. $12.50
Type of work: Letters

A revealing collection of posthumously published letters edited by the poet's mother

Letters Home should not be read as literature, since, had Sylvia Plath not written the letters, they would not have been published. Because Plath has become the model for the female confessional poet in America, however, these letters will be read as her biography. Edited by her mother, the correspondence covers the period from 1950, when Sylvia went off to Smith College as a freshman, to 1963, when she held her head inside a London gas stove to end her life. Since 1963, a Plath cult has proliferated in the slick female magazines that she herself loved so well. That cult will be disappointed by these letters, for neither do they support Sylvia's sainthood nor do they substantiate the villainy of her father or her husband, Ted Hughes. If Sylvia was a victim, she was a victim of the same 1950's success myth that drove talented males into advertising and law firms.

From the earliest letters, patterns appear which continue to the very end. Plath was ambitious, talented, and success-motivated. Before she was out of high school she had been published in *Seventeen,* a magazine she studied in order to write in its style. Her mother, widow of a Harvard professor, wanted only the best for her children. Even without wealth, she managed to send Sylvia to Smith, and Warren, her son, to Philips Exeter Academy and then to Harvard.

Scholarships came to both children. At age seventeen, Sylvia could write: "I want to be omniscient. . . . I think I would like to call myself 'The girl who wanted to be God.' " A year later she wrote home: "I just can't stand the idea of being mediocre." She never was. At every stage of her career, important people recognized her talents and encouraged her writing. At Smith, Alfred Kazin gave her critical advice and praise. In 1955, she shared the first prize in a writing contest judged by John Ciardi, who said of her: "She's a poet. I am sure she will go on writing poems, and I would gamble on the fact that she will get better and better at it. She certainly has everything to do it with." Even when she received rejections, she frequently got hand-written letters from the editor encouraging her work. To those who never see so much as an editor's initial on the rejection slip, Sylvia Plath looks like a *wunderkind* indeed.

But like so many talented children coming of age in the 1950's, she was never satisfied with her successes for long. Each new endeavor was treated as a new beginning, as if she had accomplished nothing previously. Each new beginning was wrought with the anxiety of failing. Over and over in the letters, one sees the young poet discounting a new effort before she has faced it. She was anxious before she began Smith College—anxious about dates, about roommates, about her talent. Her first summer job as a live-in baby sitter was anxiety-ridden. She was always afraid that others would see that she had failed to meet her own expectations. In her class work she was always surprised that she did as well as her professors said she had; she almost did not believe them. At no point in her career did she feel really adequate to the task before her.

Sometimes the anxiety grew so far out of proportion to the cause that it became neurotic. During her junior year she became suicidally depressed by her physics course: "I am in a rather tense emotional and mental state, and have been tense and felt literally sick for about a week now . . . . The crux of the matter is my attitude toward life—hinging on my science course. I have practically considered committing suicide to get out of it, it's like having my nose rubbed in my own slime . . . it is obsessing all my life."

What the letters document rather well are the events leading up to her first attempt at suicide in the summer of 1953. In June, 1952, she had won the $500 prize in *Mademoiselle*'s college fiction contest. The following spring, she was selected as a guest editor for the August issue of that magazine. During her frantic month in New York, she edited manuscripts and interviewed Marianne Moore and Elizabeth Bowen. When she returned home, her mother informs us, she was gaunt and anxious about the summer creative writing course at Harvard where she had hoped to be in the class taught by Frank O'Connor. When she was told that she had

not been selected, she took it very hard; her previous successes did not offset this rejection. Unfortunately, there are no letters at this point; we have only her mother's account: "She finally began to talk to me, pouring out an endless stream of self-deprecation, self-accusation. She had no goal, she said. . . . She had injured her friends, let down her sponsors." After electric shock treatments which were prompted by her slashing her legs with a razor, Sylvia managed to swallow a bottle of sleeping pills after climbing under the foundations of the house. Three days later she was found, sick but alive. She had vomited most of the pills. In a letter written that December, she gave a number of reasons for the suicide attempt, reasons which focused on her sense of failure and her fear of insanity. One cannot tell if the letter is art or reality. Like all confessional writers, Plath fictionalized her life—as seen, for example, in *The Bell Jar,* which she accurately assessed as a potboiler. There is frequently the suspicion in the letters that she is dramatizing her life in the letters as if she were trying out events for her poetry and fiction. We will never be sure.

What we can be sure of is the way she equated publication with money, and money with success. When she won a third place in *Seventeen*'s fiction contest, she said: "it does mean $100 (one hundred) in cold, cold cash." The poetry prize she won at Smith in 1954 carried a $20 award, which she equated with a pair of new shoes for a wedding. In a balance sheet compiled in May, 1955, Sylvia wrote home that she had either won or earned $470 from her writing, including publications in *Vogue, Atlan-*

tic, and *Mademoiselle*. "Now can pay all debts and work towards coats and luggage." A year later she got her first acceptance from the still prestigious *Poetry* magazine: "Do you know what that means! First, about $76." Money rings true throughout the letters. There was always the worry that there would not be enough, and when there was enough, she converted it into new clothes, a good meal, a short trip, or a luxury, however small.

One of Plath's driving ambitions that echoes throughout the letters home was her desire to publish fiction in the *Ladies' Home Journal*. In 1953, she said she wanted "to hit the *New Yorker* in poetry and the *Ladies' Home Journal* in stories"; four years later she was still sending manuscripts to that magazine. As late as 1960, she wrote, "I'll have a story in the *LHJournal* or *SatEvePost* yet." It was not until she was at work on the *Ariel* poems, having finally discovered her own voice, that she was able to tell her mother: "Now stop trying to get me to write about 'decent courageous people'—read the *Ladies' Home Journal* for those!" When she no longer valued *LHJ,* she had indeed lost her sanity—by the standards of the 1950's. It was only then that her art burned with the intensity that frightens the reader; it was only then that she forgot that she was writing for money.

The letters document Plath's marriage to Ted Hughes in copious detail. As a college junior, she had said: "I want a man who isn't jealous of my creativity in other fields than children. . . . Graduate school and travel abroad are not going to be stymied by any squalling, breastfed brats." Three years later she was literally consumed by Ted Hughes. She made a religion of him which was as intense as her poetry was to become. Hughes liberated her from many of her American success values, taught her a new poetic language, and fathered two breastfed children, both of whom she wanted very much. They met in 1956 while she was in Cambridge on a Fulbright scholarship. Her letters overflow with her devotion to this dark, earthy writer whose experience was so different from her own. She told her mother that he was her male counterpart, and she was almost right. He was, if anything, her alter ego, her anti-self. They started out even in 1956. Both were intensely devoted to writing; both published (he in a more minor way than she); both were ambitious. Six years later, Ted Hughes had a solid book of verse out in America and England, a verse play produced on the BBC, a children's book published, and had become a familiar voice on the BBC. Sylvia Plath had one book of verse out in England (*The Colossus*) and two children who were taking up most of her time. At a Faber cocktail party, Sylvia watched while Ted had his picture taken with T. S. Eliot, Stephen Spender, and Louis MacNeice—all Faber poets; but Sylvia was there merely as Ted's wife. In August, 1962, the Hugheses separated, ostensibly because of Ted's infidelity. But one suspects that Sylvia would have left him anyway. "Living apart from Ted is wonderful—I am no longer in his shadow, and it is heaven to be liked for myself alone, knowing what I want."

Sylvia Plath, scholarship winner, Fulbright winner, Yaddo recipient,

New Yorker poetess, prize winner, and writer who had been recognized as talented by many of the best writers of her time, wrote in 1963: "It is the *starting* from scratch that is so hard." There are those who grieve her suicide as a terrible waste that could have been prevented. What the letters show is that sooner or later she would have found a way, for each event was a new beginning that no previous success could bolster.

Michael S. Reynolds

THE LETTERS OF BERNARD DEVOTO

Author: Bernard DeVoto (1897-1955)
Edited with an introduction by Wallace Stegner (1909-   )
Publisher: Doubleday and Company (New York). 393 pp. $10.00
Type of work: Letters
Time: 1920-1955
Locale: U.S.A., mostly the East Coast

A collection of letters covering DeVoto's career as author, critic, historian, conservationist, and cultural gadfly

With the editing of *The Letters of Bernard DeVoto* Wallace Stegner completes the labor of love begun last year with his excellent, thorough biography of DeVoto, *The Uneasy Chair.* The collection succeeds admirably in touching many moods and attitudes; however, the modest number of selections and the wide range of subjects and recipients do not allow the reader to delve very deeply into any single area or relationship. Aside from historian-friend Garrett Mattingly, who received seventeen letters, and political ally Adlai Stevenson, who received five, no one gets more than three, and the remainder are mostly single correspondences. The collection conveys breadth rather than depth; we are most impressed by the range and variety of DeVoto's concerns, the intensity of his feelings, the scope and precision of his knowledge, the firmness of his convictions, and the deftness of his wit—as well as his idiosyncrasies and the quirkiness of his affectations.

In order to capture this breadth and variety Stegner arranges the letters topically rather than chronologically "so that the letters on the same subject may be read together." The topics do, however, follow a rough chronology, with his earliest concerns presented first and later preoccupations coming after. Within each subject area, the letters are arranged by date, so that a reading of the letters from cover to cover offers both a general overview of DeVoto's thought, and a sense of the progress of his life.

The nine topic areas cover every aspect of DeVoto's life. In "Self-Scrutiny" (1922-1944), Stegner traces his early decisions and indecisions, his recovery from a nervous breakdown, his brief teaching fling at Northwestern University, and his marriage to Helen Avis MacVickar; in "Education" (1928-1948), he presents his general ideas on education, learning, teaching, and the institutions which encourage—and discourage—them. "The Mark Twain Estate and the Limits of Patience" (1928-1946) chronicles his mounting frustrations as Mark Twain's unpaid editor and popularizer; "Controversies, Squabbles, Disagreements" (1936-1950) describes the controversies he stimulated by challenging the "literary establishment" of his time; and "Certain Inalienable Rights" (1929-1955) surveys his life-long crusade for freedom of expression, from early fights with Boston's Watch and Ward Society to broadsides against J. Edgar Hoover and Senator Joseph McCarthy during the 1950's. In "The Literary Life" (1934-

1954), the author pictures DeVoto as the professional writer—his experiences, intentions, accomplishments, and attitudes; in "The Writing of History" (1933-1953), he tells of the problems and difficulties, both with material and with the "history establishment," encountered by DeVoto while writing the books that probably represent his finest works; and in "The Nature and Nurture of Fiction" (1934-1949), he explains DeVoto's theory of writing and speculates on the relationship between creativity and human psychology. The final section, "Conservation and the Public Domain" (1948-1955), dramatizes DeVoto's last and most vigorous fight—his battle against special interest groups to preserve as much of America's natural beauty as possible for all its citizens.

One of the major points in Stegner's biography is that the private man was far different from the public figure. The letters demonstrate this convincingly. Most of them can be roughly divided into three types: letters to good friends, which are long, entertaining, laced with self-irony, and affectionate; responses to interested, sympathetic questioners, which are careful, intelligent, thorough, and concerned; and letters to antagonists, which are sharp, accusatory, sarcastic, and frequently bitter. The composite picture is that of a loyal, devoted friend, a serious, sympathetic adviser, and a tough, sometimes even nasty, opponent.

Most of DeVoto's basic attitudes, as well as his personal insecurities, can be found in the earliest letters. The correspondence begins after DeVoto has pulled himself together following his postgraduate break-

down. "I am here," he wrote friend Melville Smith, "not to teach English [at Northwestern University], but to make myself over from the debris that remains." That he succeeded in doing so is clearly indicated in subsequent letters that touch (but only touch) on his marriage, his pleasure in teaching and irritation at the bureaucratic frustrations that went with it, his beginnings as a writer and the development of those professional attitudes that were to characterize his work all his life.

The bureaucratic frustrations encountered at Northwestern were only a warm-up for his encounters with the two institutions that were to stimulate his creativity while taxing his patience and endurance: Harvard University, whose English Department kept him on tenterhooks for several years, and the Mark Twain Estate, which hired him as the (unpaid) editor of Twain's papers and then denied him the right to publish many of Twain's most representative writings. Pettiness, shortsightedness, and plain stupidity (from DeVoto's point of view) forced him to break with both institutions, but both powerfully influenced the shape and substance of his life.

DeVoto's natural prowess as a teacher, demonstrated in Stegner's biography, is underscored in these early letters and reinforced in the later ones. One wonders what would have happened had DeVoto's quest for permanence at Harvard not foundered on the vagaries of academic politics and the skepticism of President James B. Conant. Contact with Mark Twain's works crystallized DeVoto's ideas about America and especially about the West, which were later realized in his historical epics.

Twain was the pivotal figure in DeVoto's initial attack on the literary-cultural establishment and its view of American life. His first important work, *Mark Twain's America,* was a direct counter to Van Wyck Brooks's *The Ordeal of Mark Twain,* and, while particular critics and books changed, the basic opposition evident in that clash remained central to DeVoto for the rest of his life.

The primary enemies during the first twenty years or so of DeVoto's career were the "abstractionists"— those who looked at life "theoretically" and then presented their distorted, abstract vision of reality as "Life." In the 1920's and to a certain extent beyond, the main adversaries were the literary "aesthetes" and "elitists," led critically by Brooks and creatively by such spokesmen as T. S. Eliot, Sinclair Lewis, and Ernest Hemingway, who denigrated the American experience and dismissed the average middle-class American as crude, stupid, and greedy. In the 1930's the "abstractionists" became Marxists, and DeVoto reacted with a mixture of haughty disdain and comedic irony to the spectacle of those same literary evangelists who had preached aesthetic and elitist separation in the 1920's suddenly claiming "solidarity" with the workers in the 1930's.

Against such opponents he was almost merciless on the printed page in such essays as "A Generation Beside the Limpopo" (1937) and books like *Mark Twain's America* (1932) and *The Literary Fallacy* (1944), although he remained cordial and conciliatory in person. It is clear from his letters that scrupulous objectivity was not a DeVotian absolute; he overstated his case with malice of forethought. He saw himself not as a detached observer, but as a committed redresser of balances. As he admitted to Catherine Drinker Bowen in a letter, he intentionally overstated the points made in his *Mark Twain's America,* intending to revise it to a more reasonable form later, after his battle with the "Brooks—Frank—Mumford—Lewisohn system" had been won. His tactic, therefore, was

> . . . to make a lot of mess on the floor, splatter blood and marrow on the walls, and give portions of the book a distinct resemblance to an abattoir, but it had to be done.

He even hesitated to meet his opponents face-to-face lest that blunt his rhetorical stridency. "It seemed to me important," he wrote his primary literary foil Van Wyck Brooks, "that the edge of difference not be dulled by any discovery that it was pleasant to spend an evening talking and drinking together."

Yet DeVoto was frankly amazed when such diatribes provoked equally strong responses. "His principal weakness as a controversialist," Stegner suggests, "was that he did not understand that words like 'fool' and 'stupid' might be taken personally." And for such a vituperative polemicist, DeVoto seems to have had a rather thin skin himself. While he called others fools and incompetents rather freely, he reacted with bitterness and a righteous indignation that bordered on the comic against what he called "personal abuse" by those out of sympathy with his views and person.

On the positive side, DeVoto celebrated the America that his literary antagonists denigrated. "I burst with creative criticism of America—I have at last found a kind of national self-consciousness," he wrote to Melville Smith in a 1920 letter that Stegner uses for the book's epigraph. To Catherine Bowen he said that "American history . . . is the most romantic of all histories. It began in myth and has developed through three centuries of fairy stories." This impulse became embodied in the three books that represent the culmination of his career: *The Year of Decision: 1846* (1943), *Across the Wide Missouri* (1947), and *The Course of Empire* (1952).

In terms of his running battle with the artistic establishment, his vindication came, he proclaimed, with the example of that America so maligned by his opponents rising up as a people to fight and win World War II. DeVoto can hardly contain his glee at the sight of such antagonists as Van Wyck Brooks and Archibald MacLeish recanting their errors with patriotic fervor.

But if the 1940's saw DeVoto's vision of America's greatness realized, the late 1940's and early 1950's saw it flounder and dissipate. With the literary wars behind him, DeVoto took on two new opponents who proved to be powerful, tenacious, and infinitely more dangerous—those who would destroy our natural resources and those who would destroy our personal liberties.

DeVoto's love of American history and especially of the West ultimately led him to a personal exploration of the country, and he became aware of the many threats to the environment, especially by lumbering, stock, and mining interests. Long before it was politically and socially fashionable, DeVoto became a dedicated conservationist and channeled all his polemical talents—especially through the avenue of his "Easy Chair" column in *Harper's*—into the struggle to prevent these big special interests from destroying what modest protections the Western lands possessed. His letters graphically describe his large frustrations and small victories in the cause. One of the sad aspects of DeVoto's life is that many of the battles he initiated were not won until after his death.

DeVoto's agitation against the vitiation of civil liberties during the McCarthy era was even more disheartening. He had, of course, been an uncompromising advocate of free speech and civil rights from the outset of his career. But he had always believed that as long as honest men fought for their rights, these ideals would survive. In the 1950's he came to doubt seriously that optimistic view. He took little satisfaction from the fact that his ex-enemies were now victims and that he had become their defender. DeVoto felt that the America which had demonstrated drive, courage, endurance, and idealism in defeating the totalitarians abroad had, in a few short years, turned into a petty, grasping, shallow nation of complaisant cowards. Given his lifetime as a strident advocate for the American character, his last comments prior to death, written to old friend Garrett Mattingly, are especially poignant:

. . . The American people would not adopt the Bill of Rights now, they don't want it. . . . The moral of our time is that the U.S. can be respected when it's scared—when it's scared about tonight's supper & next week's rent. . . . We are so God damned rich that we aren't worth hell room. I doubt if we ever will be again.

There are too damn many Americans and the Americans are too gutless. I don't know how I acquired the delusion I wrote several books about.

As a collection of letters this volume has flaws. One needs *The Uneasy Chair* as a cross reference; the volume does not stand alone. Stegner has been so scrupulous about not intruding himself into the text that he makes only the most sketchy textual comments and footnotes. The reader is frequently left up in the air: "What happened to that request?" "How did the situation come out?" "Did 'X' carry out his threat?" —and so on. Furthermore, Stegner's topical organization is perhaps a bit arbitrary and fragmented; it prevents the reader from ever getting a solid sense of DeVoto's overall development.

But even with these shortcomings, *The Letters of Bernard DeVoto* is a fine personal record of one of this country's most colorful and challenging literary and cultural forces, a man who fulfilled his ambition

> . . . to do good work, to do work in which I may take some satisfaction and my friends some pleasure; at the utmost . . . to put something on the record that will not easily be dislodged.

Keith Neilson

THE LETTERS OF VIRGINIA WOOLF
Volume I: 1888-1912

Author: Virginia Woolf (1882-1941)
Edited, with an Introduction and notes, by Nigel Nicolson and Joanne Trautmann
Publisher: Harcourt Brace Jovanovich (New York). 531 pp. $14.95
Type of work: Letters

This first volume of a projected six-volume collection of the novelist's letters contains those letters written during the first thirty years in the life of Virginia Woolf (then Virginia Stephen)

Although this first volume of *The Letters of Virginia Woolf* ends midway through the author's life, Woolf's career as a novelist had scarcely begun by that time. The volume takes her from childhood to her thirtieth year—to her marriage and to her ultimate assertion of her vocation as she completed her first novel; five more volumes will be required to encompass the correspondence of her later years. Obviously, as her reputation and her associations grew, her letters tended to be filed and kept. But there is enough information in the 638 letters of Volume One (about 3,800 survive in all) to sketch a portrait of the artist as a young woman.

Deaths in and out of the family, nervous breakdowns, travel on the Continent and changes of address in England, flirtings and proposals, crushes on older women, social confrontations, teas, dinners, dances, and extended visits—those events which typically took up much time in the lives of the upper middle class— were familiar trappings of Virginia Woolf's life. The letters, of course, are concerned with those trappings, but they also give constant evidence that Woolf was an extremely hardworking writer; one wonders where she found the time.

From her first twenty years, only forty-one letters remain, most of them addressed to brother Thoby (at Cambridge), half-brother George Duckworth, and cousin Emma Vaughan. The Stephen children were forever nicknaming one another: Virginia signed herself "Goat," addressed George as "my dear old Bar," and saluted Emma as "beloved Toad," "dearest Todkins," or "dearest Reptile." As one might expect, these letters contain little beyond the bright, intelligent chatter of a bright, intelligent child and adolescent. There is a hint also of youthful intolerance and snobbery, though there are clear indications that Virginia scarcely felt that she was the center of society: "We aint popular—we sit in corners and look like mutes who are longing for a funeral. However, there are more important things in this life." One important thing was the discovery that she could "really *enjoy* not only admire Sophocles"; another was her decision to enlist in the "company of worshippers" of "the great William." Hauntingly, in light of her later mental problems, we find this passage: "This world of human beings grows too complicated, my only wonder is that we don't fill more madhouses: the insane view of life has much to be said for it—perhaps its the sane one after all: and *we,* the sad sober respectable citizens really rave every moment of our lives and deserve to be shut up perpetually."

The letters of 1902 and 1903 record the lingering death by cancer of the author's father, Leslie Stephen. On some days, she wrote, he "looks so well, and one can't believe that it is true. It is a strange pause." He grew weaker, stronger, then "very weak," then "steadily weaker." Guilt followed: "He was so lonely often, and I never helped him as I might have done." Of all the children it was Virginia who felt Leslie's death most intensely. Apparently a special bond had been established between father and younger daughter, and she mourned the loss of companionship: "He said he didn't mind dying for himself, but he should like to see a little more of the children. He feels, I think, that we are just grown up, and able to talk to him—and he wants to see what becomes of us."

It was to Violet Dickinson that she confided these feelings. Violet, tall (six feet, two inches), gawky, daughter of a squire, granddaughter of Lord Aukland, was, according to the editors, adored by all who knew her. She was a woman to whom Virginia could give and from whom she could demand affection, and could reveal, in the process, a fascinatingly ambivalent set of reactions to the world around her. She was both mocking and loving, defiantly independent and defiantly dependent. In the Violet letters she signed herself a "devoted Sparroy," a "little Wallaby." According to one letter, "My Wallaby paws stick to the paper as I write—and my letters are convulsive. Write to me, and tell me that you love me, dearest." She could openly complain,

"When you next write put some affection in your letters. . . . I always do." She could consciously delight in having a correspondent with whom she could be open and avoid pretense: "That's why I get on with you isn't it?" She insisted: "With no one else shd. I dare to behave so badly."

The mental breakdowns that were always just around the corner do not, of course, appear very often in these letters. The first breakdown occurred after the death of her mother in 1895, when she was thirteen; there was another in 1904, after the death of her father. "All that summer she was mad," according to Quentin Bell, her biographer. It was then that Violet revealed the reality, the depth, and the sturdiness of her friendship, taking Virginia to live with her for three months under the care of three nurses. We hear from the victim only after she has returned to herself: "It is the oddest feeling, as though a dead part of me were coming to life. . . . All the voices I used to hear telling me to do all kinds of wild things have gone." Every moment of her life had become "an exquisite joy." During two rest cures at a mental nursing home, she did produce several letters: time passes slowly; she yearns for intelligent conversation; but she promises to be "very reasonable." Nevertheless, she cannot help releasing her puckish humor: "One of the patients, a Miss Somerville, has periods of excitement, when she pulls up all the roses and goes to church. Then she is silent for weeks. She is now being silent." Reading the epistolary evidence, the editors feel that the bouts of insanity may have had positive results. After each breakdown, they insist, her mind was clearer than before. "Each time she recovers from one of her early attacks, she seems slightly more mature. Her handwriting improves: she drops childish expressions."

They may, in fact, be correct, for it was after her recovery from her attack in 1904 that she made her first tentative moves in the direction of literary journalism. Her first productions appeared in the women's supplement of the *Guardian,* a weekly London newspaper for clerical readers. Shortly after, other publications were added, including *The Times Literary Supplement.* She wrote reviews, articles, essays, obviously enjoying the work and enjoying also the money she earned. In the tradition of reviewers everywhere she felt compelled to complain about the results: "I spend 5 days of precious time toiling through Henry James' subtleties . . . and write a very hardworking review . . . then come orders to cut out quite half of it. . . . I cut two sheets to pieces . . . and so sent the maimed thing off—with a curse." But, she also insisted, "I cant help writing—and there's an end of it."

Settled with her brothers, Adrian and Thoby, and her sister, Vanessa, into 46 Gordon Square, Bloomsbury, and feeling thoroughly at home there, she widened the scope of her activities. In November, 1905, she tallied her responsibilities for Violet: "I have had such a run of work as is not remembered for I cant say how many years; books from the Times, the Academy, the Guardian. . . ." Vanessa had started a club of people interested in discussions of artistic matters, the group meeting on Fridays; and "then we have our Thursdays" (these meetings were the nucleus of the Bloomsbury gatherings); and on Wednesdays, Virginia taught a class at an evening college for working people: "It is I suppose the most useless class in the school." Growing busier and busier, Virginia had less time (and less need) for corresponding with Violet; her letters to the older woman grew shorter with the passing of the years.

One reason for this slackening of their friendship was that she became increasingly absorbed in her first novel (called *Melymbrosia,* but published ultimately as *The Voyage Out*) through the period covered by these letters. For years, she had been leading up to this production. We hear of a number of comic lives and descriptive essays of people, events, and places, many of them lost. In a November, 1904, letter to Violet, she bemoaned the fact that her "precious MS. book, which should have given me hints for dozens of articles is lost in the move" (to Bloomsbury). We finally hear of the novel in an October, 1907, letter, again to Violet: "My writing makes me tremble; it seems so likely that it will be d------d bad—or only slight. . . ." It began to fill her mind: "I can think of nothing but my novel." Nevertheless, the reviews and articles continued to pour out. Her spirits rose and fell with the progress of the novel, but she asserted quite stoutly that she would "carry through Melymbrosia, and I believe I care less than ever before for what people say."

Interestingly, it was Clive Bell, married to Vanessa, who now became Virginia's confidante. At first Virginia was resentful of Bell because the marriage had, of couse, separated her from Vanessa. But when Vanessa withdrew into domesticity, Virginia and Clive became fast friends and conducted an extended flirtation that found expression in the letters. "Why do you torment me with half uttered and ambiguous sentences? my presence is 'vivid and strange and bewildering.' I read your letter again and again, and wonder whether you have found me out, or, more likely, determined that there is nothing but an incomprehensible and quite negligible femininity to find out." In a more open statement, she wrote: "I am really shy of expressing my affection for you. Why? Do you know women?" The tone of the letters to Clive was generally more serious than that of the missives to Violet. To him she could confide: 'I thing a great deal of my future, and settle what book I am to write—how I shall reform the novel and capture multitudes of things at present fugitive . . . ." To Clive she sent the first one hundred pages of her novel, receiving extended criticisms that are quoted by Quentin Bell in an appendix to his biography.

By the time she finally committed herself to a man, Leonard Woolf, Virginia had already had several unsatisfactory proposals. She had, in fact, accepted one—from Lytton Strachey, whose proclivities were not basically heterosexual (Virginia and Lytton shortly came to their senses). Most of her comments about marriage and children—as she experienced them in the household of her onetime confidante, Madge Vaughan, and of her sister, Vanessa—are dispirited and pessimistic: "Lord! What it must be to have a child!" Finally, after much twisting and turning, she accepted Woolf. In him she apparently saw "someone to make me vehement." Interestingly, this was the quality she had attributed to Violet Dickinson: "I like something stronger tasting— like my Violet"; "I like you because your vicious. Entirely vicious." With Leonard she wanted everything, including children. She never had the child, but she did complete the book.

Max Halperen

LIFE HISTORY AND THE HISTORICAL MOMENT

Author: Erik H. Erikson (1902-   )
Publisher: W. W. Norton and Company (New York) 283 pp. $9.95
Type of work: Essays

A collection of essays, book reviews, and lectures in which the author discusses his understanding of the nature of psychiatry and the place of his work within it

Erik Erikson is perhaps the most well-known and influential of American students of Freud. In a long and distinguished career of analysis, teaching, and writing, he has brought his understanding of Freudian analysis to the attention of vast numbers of patients, students, and readers in both the professional and general publics. Best known for his books on the mental histories of Martin Luther and Gandhi, Erikson's most important contribution to the theory and practice of psychoanalysis has been in his development of a growth model for the progress of the human psyche. Moving beyond the Freudian model, with its emphasis on childhood traumas, Erikson, in his *Childhood and Society,* posits that everyone moves through a series of mental and emotional crises which must be resolved if the individual is to grow toward maturity. The advantages of this model are manifold; it enables an individual to see his emotional difficulties as opportunities for growth, while it makes possible the understanding of life as a long process of growth, divided into discrete stages with specific issues to be dealt with at each stage. Erikson is the father (perhaps unwillingly in some cases) of many of the American adaptations of Freudian theory and practice.

His best-known contributions to the popular understanding of psychoanalytic theory, however, have come with his studies of historical figures. His study of Luther's adolescence (*Young Man Luther*) and Gandhi's maturity (*Gandhi's Truth*) have brought him a wide readership, as well as public acclaim and numerous awards. The praise has not been total, however; both books have been criticized for their use of the tools of analysis on historical figures unavailable for interview, and for their applications of psychiatric insight to the actions and teachings of such important figures in the history of ideas. Freudian theory is always open to the charge of reductionism; many have felt that Erikson reduces the beliefs of such figures to the level of infantile crises. In so doing, critics argue, the independent truth or falsehood of those ideas is belittled. But such argument is itself the result of misunderstanding Freudian, and Eriksonian, thinking; Erikson's work stands on its own as a valid means of understanding the events of the past and the motivations of the important figures of history. If our purpose in the study of the past is to understand not just what happened, but how and why it happened when and in the way it did, then we are indebted to Erikson for providing us with another means of getting at the truth which the past holds for the modern student.

For these reasons, the volume *Life History and the Historical Moment* is a valuable addition to the shelf of

Erikson's works. A collection of book reviews, essays, and lectures, some printed earlier but here given wider and well-deserved readership, this work presents us with a more informal Erikson reflecting on the history of Freudian analysis, the development of his techniques for investigating the past, and some aspects of the contemporary scene, from student rebellion to women's liberation. The style here is relaxed, often conversational; we see Erikson the man reflecting on himself and on his lifelong involvement in what is perhaps the most important intellectual movement of the twentieth century.

It is appropriate that such a work begin with a backward look. The work is divided into three sections. The first, entitled "Backgrounds and Origins," consists of a long essay and two book reviews. The essay is a lengthy autobiography; written originally for a symposium on important ideas in twentieth century science, it presents a warm portrait of the man himself, while it traces his early years, his involvement with the circle around Freud, his journey to America, and the progress of his work in a variety of clinical and academic settings. Even more important, perhaps, is the fact that the essay is written as an attempt to clarify Erikson's definition of the "identity crisis," a key concept in his thinking which has entered the vocabulary of all Americans, especially those with adolescent children. What comes across is the honesty of the man—his ability to see himself clearly and to talk about himself without illusion. Freud began his work with self-analysis; Erikson exemplifies the fact that Freud's disciples have continued in this tradition.

The second part of this first section consists of two book reviews which also take Erikson back to the founding days of Freudian theory. The first review is of a collection of letters written by Freud to Wilhelm Fliess, a close friend and confessor to Freud in the days during which Freud began to develop his theories of human personality. A fascinating review of a significant work, this essay is a small example of the use of Erikson's psychohistorical method. Through a careful reading of Freud's letters, Erikson is able to reconstruct for us the psychological dynamics of Freud's relationship with his friend, and to suggest its importance for the development of Freudian theory. The second review is of the psychobiography of Woodrow Wilson, written jointly by Freud and the American diplomat William C. Bullitt. Erikson's review of this work is highly critical; if the first review reveals his ability to be objective as well as loving about the founder of his profession, the second demonstrates that to Erikson, Freud was easily capable of error and of bad judgment. Erikson demonstrates the questionable history of this book; mostly the work of Bullitt, it also reveals many of Freud's prejudices and blind spots. To Erikson, a student deeply indebted to Freud, this work is an embarrassment, but one he finally turns to an advantage. As a practitioner of the psychohistorical method of approach to the past, Erikson sees this work as a reminder of the difficulties which such an approach to history entails for the investigator.

The second section of the book, entitled "In Search of Gandhi," is made up of two essays which grew out of Erikson's studies leading up to the publication of *Gandhi's Truth.* The first, "On the Nature of 'Psycho-Historical Evidence' " is an account of the beginnings of Erikson's interest in Gandhi. It is, as well, an essay descriptive of the method of historical research practiced by Erikson in this book and in the earlier *Young Man Luther.* The author describes his search for evidence, his methods of evaluating that evidence, and the development of his models for understanding what he has learned from his research. The second of the two essays in this section is entitled "Freedom and Nonviolence," and was originally given as the T. B. Davie Memorial Lecture at the University of Cape Town in South Africa. Growing out of his studies into the nature of Gandhi's devotion to nonviolence as a force for political change, Erikson's lecture is given special force by Gandhi's own close links with South Africa and by the fact that students at the University were soon to resort to nonviolent protest of the racial policies of the South African government.

The third and final section of the book, entitled "Protest and Liberation," is, perhaps, the section of the book of most interest to the general reader. It consists of three essays, each of which treats a major aspect of the social changes wrought in American life by the events of the 1960's. The first, entitled "Reflections on the Revolt of Humanist Youth," is perhaps the most dated piece in the whole volume. Erikson attempts to discover the roots of adolescent rebellion in the 1960's and to make some predictions about the nature of future society based on his analysis. While his view of the future may yet

be right, it is clouded by the fact that the rebellion on which it is based has, at least outwardly, subsided. The second essay is more relevant; entitled "Once More the Inner Space," it surveys the traditional Freudian concept of woman in light of the movement for women's liberation. Perhaps its most interesting point is that the concept of penis envy, with which many leaders in the woman's movement take issue, has its male counterpart in what might be called womb envy. Men, angry that they are unable to bear children, may attempt to crush their feminine natures and thus distort their personalities in response. Erikson maintains that biology must have some role to play in the development of personality and destiny, even as history and social circumstance have theirs. The final piece in this section, and in the volume, is entitled "Psychoanalysis: Adjustment or Freedom?" This essay is a response to the criticism of Freudian analysis which claims that it attempts to make all people the same by adjusting them to fit an artificial norm; it defends the usefulness of Freudian theory and its developments for the freeing of men and women to do what they want to with their lives.

Erikson's work has always been a testimony to the importance of psychoanalysis for the modern world. This book is, finally, an affirmation of faith in that proposition, as well as effective proof of it. In the hands of men like Erikson, the essential concepts and methods of Freudian analysis continue to reveal their value in illuminating our world and freeing us for creative participation in it. *Life History and the Historical Moment* is a valuable guide to the history of the psychoanalytical movement, as well as an important commentary on the moment in which we now live. More importantly, it is a significant testimony to the value of Erik Erikson as a man who has given us the tools for understanding both our lives and our unique time in the history of man.

John N. Wall, Jr.

THE LITTLE HOTEL

Author: Christina Stead (1902-   )
Publisher: Holt, Rinehart and Winston (New York). 191 pp. $6.95
Type of work: Novel
Time: Shortly after World War II
Locale: Montreux, Switzerland

A novel of interactions among eccentric characters residing at a small hotel in Switzerland

Principal characters:

MME. BONNARD, the proprietor of the Swiss-Touring, a tourist hotel

ROGER BONNARD, her husband and co-proprietor

MRS. TROLLOPE, a middle-aged Englishwoman who has lived mainly in the East

MR. WILKINS, her "cousin"; actually her lover

PRINCESS BILI, an American, and the rich widow of an Italian nobleman

MME. BLAISE, a Swiss housewife and drug addict

DR. BLAISE, her husband

THE MAYOR OF B., a half-mad Belgian

MRS. POWELL, a patriotic American expatriate

MISS ABBEY-CHILLARD, an Englishwoman and a permanent invalid

The Little Hotel begins with the voice of Mme. Bonnard, the voice of a preoccupied, lonely, somewhat callous woman who finds it is part of her job as proprietor of the Swiss-Touring to become privy to the inner lives of the guests at her small fourth-class establishment in a resort town on the shore of Lake Leman. Dealing with the confidences of the guests is one of her challenging problems, like dealing with the servants, or with her husband Roger, or with the police when irregularities occur.

Everything interests her, everything gives variety and color to her life, but nothing interests her unduly. "If you knew what happens in the hotel every day! Not a day passes but something happens," she begins, but it is hard to feel enthusiasm in her vague clichés. Yesterday, she says, a former guest, who has frequently called to pour out her joy and sorrow over her son and daughter-in-law, telephoned to tell her something tragic. The daughter-in-law was dead (a suicide? murdered?), the son had left home or was dead, too—but because of a language difficulty, Mme. Bonnard never quite got the straight of the story. Madame is busy; her head often aches; and although she is amused and even sympathetic, she is not really touched. She doesn't quite understand the human language. Her voice ranges from flat and impersonal to sharply satirical. Often she is impatient or even dictatorial.

Mme. Bonnard is lonely but never self-pitying. She has a five-year-old son, but he is always in the background, and her affection for him remains concealed. Some time ago she had a girl friend with whom she shared secrets; then she was happy. But once you marry, she says, you can't expect to be happy anymore.

Her husband Roger is practical and serious; he worries about the behavior of the guests and about the police and about being cheated. Often he spies on the guests while pretending to move furniture or fix a radiator. He chain smokes and has nervous fits and gets blue. Mme. Bonnard's best friend Julie is trying to attract Roger, who goes out quite a bit alone at night. All these details emerge from Mme. Bonnard's accounts, but Roger's real self remains hidden. His wife finds it interesting to be married and to try to keep a husband. She seems to look on him as a project.

Madame is just twenty-six, but seems much older; occasionally she has a good laugh with the servants or a fit of temper with Roger, but usually she seems settled and serious. To her, the elderly guests at the hotel are as irresponsible and disorderly as schoolchildren, and she runs the place like a schoolroom with plenty of rules and an insistence on order.

Mme. Bonnard has a fondness for the hotel servants, but she sees them as difficult and jealous and unreliable. If they dislike a guest, as they dislike the "Admiral," a commanding Englishwoman who is old and poor and does not tip, they spill food and give careless service. Francis, the French chef, insults the German and Italian servants. Charlie, the charming, broken-down handyman, seduces schoolgirls.

But it is the semi-permanent guests at the Swiss-Touring who are most troublesome and receive the most attention in Mme. Bonnard's narrative. The Mayor of B., for example, thoroughly delighted Mme. Bonnard at first. He was an expansive Belgian who bought champagne for the servants. He had come, it seems, for shock treatments at a local mental hospital. Soon he began to complain about Germans whom he imagined to be all over the hotel and poisoning his food. Finally, after running around town naked one night, he had to be locked up and then put on a train for Belgium; but he stole away from the train in France. Despite his fears and his peculiar habits, Mme. Bonnard sees him as a sympathetic, fun-loving man. But her objective view of this sample of the human comedy distances the reader and prevents him from perceiving the Mayor as a real human being.

The Mayor's lunatic fear of the Germans is counterpointed by other guests' fears of the Russians, fears which they discuss at length, especially when Mrs. Powell is in residence. Since inheriting her husband's fortune thirty-nine years ago, Mrs. Powell has traveled abroad to avoid United States income taxes. Though she never sees the United States, she is intent on aiding it in a last-ditch stand against the communists.

Gradually from Madame's interlaced stories and character sketches, a view of the principal guests emerges. Though not all expatriates, most are; all tend to be long-term residents at the Swiss-Touring because of problems with governmental money controls. Mme. Blaise, who is Swiss, is trying to lay claim to the property of enemy aliens which was entrusted to her and which has been sequestered in the United States. Miss Abbey-Chillard is unable to get money out from England, despite medical certificates that her chronic invalidism requires residence abroad.

Mrs. Trollope is gradually transferring funds from England, which she turns over to her "cousin" Mr. Wilkins to transfer from one currency to another. Some of the guests are poor, but most are not; they simply have money problems. Aging, dislocated, nervous, they stay on at the Swiss-Touring because it is cheap. They fuss at the servants and get on one another's nerves. Their lives are drab and pathetic, enlivened at first by little complaints of ill health or stolen property and small quarrels. But gradually it appears that for some, love and its difficulties are still of paramount importance.

In presenting life at the little hotel through the eyes of Mme. Bonnard, Stead has not been able to avoid a certain flatness, which pervades the book. Even though she changes point of view before the middle, the tone cannot change much, and the characters, who are riddled with faults and inadequacies, never become sufficiently vivid to grip the reader.

Less than halfway through the novel, Mme. Bonnard's voice fades away, and the narrative becomes third-person. Now the guests become more themselves, and the satire bites deeper and is mixed with more authentic emotion. The long central scene of the novel is a dinner party in a hotel, given by Mrs. Trollope and Mr. Wilkins. Guests are the Princess Bili, an American widow of an Italian nobleman, and owner of a dreadfully irritating little dog, Angel; Dr. and Mme. Blaise; and an English couple. A dispute over the women's dress, an orgy of ordering food and wines, a great deal of small talk are the surface under which raw tensions reveal themselves. Mme. Blaise, whose husband brings her drugs when he visits her from Basel, is convinced her husband is having an affair with their housekeeper. Mrs. Trollope, while living in the East, took Mr. Wilkins as a lover; finally she became divorced from her husband only to find that Mr. Wilkins would not marry her. Now she has become deeply unhappy because of Mr. Wilkins' indifference. Her children are alienated from her; other guests condescend to her, thinking she is Eurasian. Mr. Wilkins, a selfish bachelor much attached to a mother and sisters he never sees, has promised his mother never to marry. More and more he makes Mrs. Trollope feel pathetically lonely, neglected, and hopeless. She finds a friend in the domineering Princess Bili, who intends to whip Mr. Wilkins into line before she goes off to South America with a much younger man. Like Dr. and Mme. Blaise, Mr. Wilkins and Mrs. Trollope are separated by years of emotional discord, but are held together by long-term ties as well as resentment of the other couple's behavior.

In this section, Stead's surgical knife peels away outer coverings to show nerves and hearts. The sharp satire and the collisions of lives are a good deal reminiscent of those in Katherine Anne Porter's *Ship of Fools,* as is the technique (long familiar, however) of bringing together various characters and having them play out their interwoven stories. The anguish and selfish cruelty of the characters are quite powerfully displayed, yet even after reading the book, one is not inclined to call the characters by their first names. Christina Stead, an expatriate herself for many years, living in England though born in Australia, never succeeds in making her personages truly sympathetic, despite a fine style and excellent ear for dialogue. Their Chekhovian discourses lack the poignancy and humor of Chekhov. Characters struggle and complain but remain ineffectual and dull. Nor does their eccentricity render them really entertaining. Of Miss Stead's eleven previous novels, *The Man Who Loved Children* is best known and most praised. *The Little Hotel,* however, is artistically superior to the earlier work.

Mary C. Williams

THE LONELY HUNTER
A Biography of Carson McCullers

Author: Virginia Spencer Carr
Publisher: Doubleday and Company (New York). 600 pp. $12.50
Type of work: Biography
Time: 1917 to 1971
Locale: Southern and Eastern United States and Europe

A just and sympathetic definitive biography of an outstanding recent American writer

Recent biographies of American literary figures are chiefly remarkable for exposing their subject's awesome character failings. Carlos Baker's *Ernest Hemingway: A Life Story* reveals no *machismo* artist, but a self-indulgent bully who tried to destroy anyone he could not dominate. Mark Schorer in *Sinclair Lewis* portrayed a sick, whining man, whose hatred of humanity grew to morbid proportions as the years passed. Lawrance Thompson's biography of Robert Frost uncovered a gnarled old man who was no rude tiller of the soil and simple, patriotic voice of the people, but a sadist of psychotic proportions. Virginia Spencer Carr's *The Lonely Hunter: A Biography of Carson McCullers* may have halted this biography-by-assassination trend. Professor Carr treats McCullers with sympathy, understanding, and justice. What emerges in this lengthy, painstakingly documented study is the definitive portrait of a contradictory and intense human being. Carson McCullers was every bit as eccentric in real life as any of her vibrant, Gothic creations.

While she possessed neither William Faulkner's grand design of human interaction, nor Flannery O'Connor's penetrating philosophical vision, McCullers did write several novels and short stories set in the South which have become modern classics. Her first novel, *The Heart Is a Lonely Hunter* (1940), is a powerful story about a young girl's search for identity, and a deaf mute's search for acceptance. The setting is a small town in the Deep South, but the book's meaning, its interrelated themes of anguish and joy bound together by humor and the grotesque, transcend its location. *The Heart Is a Lonely Hunter* shows McCullers' command of precise language, ability to dramatize scenes, and insight into human nature. *Reflections in a Golden Eye* (1941) is a deeper penetration into the grotesque possibilities inherent in human relationships. *The Member of the Wedding* (1946) returned to the theme of adolescent feelings with as much perception as *The Heart Is a Lonely Hunter*. McCullers' last novel, *Clock Without Hands* (1961), is more abstract than her earlier work and has received less critical acclaim. However, *The Ballad of the Sad Café and Collected Short Stories* (1955) has been acclaimed as one of the very finest fiction anthologies ever assembled. Clearly this is no great body of major work, but Carson McCullers should be measured by the quality of what she wrote, which is considerable.

Carr's contribution to understanding McCullers is primarily biographical, not an estimation and analysis of her literary works. Normally, such an emphasis would be questionable at best, an invasion of privacy and the past to follow that Gothic notion that the dead owe us both their secrets and a living. Carson, however, turns out to be a rewarding subject. Her personal life was not only highly interesting, but instructive; her professional career was an important chapter of recent literary history. Carr's research is so thorough that serious students of McCullers' writing cannot help but find many passages in this biography that illuminate her writing. Carr consistently presents opposing views and contradictory evidence in an effort to document her subject's life rather than shape information to create an easy thesis and judgment.

With care and thoroughness, Carr debunks the public image of Carson McCullers, prodigy author and vulnerable, wounded writer. A good deal of work went into the fabrication of this image. The publicity picture of Carson upon the appearance of *The Heart Is a Lonely Hunter* revealed a round-faced adolescent girl with pug nose, small mouth, and scattered bangs looking all of fifteen years old. Carson was actually almost twenty-four, already a chain smoker, hard drinker, and deeply involved in several romantic entanglements. Projecting an aura of the genius who needed assistance, especially from older, established males, McCullers found very valuable. Sponsored by Louis Untermeyer and others, she gained entrance into the highest literary circles. During the 1940's, she

could count on paid summers at the Bread Loaf Writers' Conference or the Yaddo Colony, and she received two substantial grants from the Guggenheim Foundation. Carr reveals that during the 1950's and 1960's, Carson, while never wealthy, could effectively use her charms on those in a position to produce dramatic and movie versions of her prose works.

In reality, Carson was no hurt dove, but, in Carr's words, an "iron butterfly." True, she was painfully shy, introverted, and the victim of an inordinate number of debilitating physical illnesses. Throughout her life McCullers was plagued by serious respiratory ailments and alcoholism. At age thirty she suffered the first of several strokes which eventually paralyzed her left side. She underwent a mastectomy and numerous surgical operations for severe arthritis. Severe nervous tension was a constant McCullers characteristic. In spite of such handicaps, however, she possessed an iron will and unflagging determination. She was a highly contradictory personality, typically affecting people in opposite ways. Carr must be credited for establishing a clear and balanced portrait of a person whom almost everyone regarded as either a bitch or a saint.

Carr's problems do not end with the divided view of how others saw Carson McCullers, for her personal life was also contradictory as well as unconventional. Carson was an intense human being, capable of loving to the fullest either men or women. Carson's most passionate relationship was with Annemarie Clarc-Schwarzenbach, an adventurous, wealthy Swiss expatriate who, in turn, was enamored of Thomas Mann's daughter, Erika. Annemarie had lived the life of luxury and high adventure that Carson had dreamed of as an adolescent. According to Carr, Carson imitated and worshiped the women she loved, but these women seldom reciprocated with similarly intense feelings. McCullers' passion for women was an important aspect of her being that apparently everyone close to her recognized and accepted, except her husband.

James Reeves McCullers, Jr., grew up in Wetumpka, Alabama, the star athlete and writer of his high school class. Reeves met Carson in 1935 when he was stationed as an Army enlisted man at Fort Benning, near Columbus, Georgia, Carson's home town. In the early days of their relationship and marriage, Reeves shared the same high aspirations to be a novelist that his wife had. But with Carson's publication of *The Heart Is a Lonely Hunter* in 1940 and its subsequent success, Carson and Reeves became distant. Reeves provided a protective and competent masculine presence, and this Carson greatly needed. She did not need, however, Reeves's suspicious and sometimes dishonest nature; nor did she wish to be sexually involved with him. Intimidated as the husband of America's finest young woman novelist, puzzled and then terrified about their personal problems, Reeves found consolation, or at least attention, in alcoholic bouts of depression. Carson had become devoted to alcohol a little earlier when her relationship with Annemarie terminated.

Reeves and Carson had an unusual relationship, to say the least. They were married, divorced, remarried, and then separated before Reeves's suicide in 1953. Besides all the other problems, Reeves simply could not keep up with Carson's pace in acquiring famous new friends and gathering fame. Failure in his writing career and in his relationship with Carson, whom he desperately needed, weighed heavily upon him; his sexual failure with his wife led him to question his own masculinity. Eventually he fell in love with David Diamond, a composer who felt an unrestrained passion for *both* the McCullers. Carson took the news of a Reeves and David liaison very badly. According to Carr, Carson felt that Reeves could have sexual relations with anyone he pleased since she had so little to give in this area of their relationship; but he was not to fall in love with a mutual friend. Through periods of intense fulfillment and intense jealousy, these three remained close friends for years.

Carr argues that an insight into Carson's bisexuality provides meaningful insight into her personality and creative powers. This deep need and ability to love both women and men gave Carson the insight for her fine character portrayals and her profound understanding of human relationships, especially when they formed triangles. In this kind of interaction Carson felt that the selfish bonds of identity were replaced by empathy with others, what she called "the we of me." As the paralyzed victim of a stroke, Carson had a real understanding of alienation and the grotesque. Carr also establishes Carson's fixation on frustrated female adolescents. Tall, thin, and very youthful looking until her later years, Carson typically scorned dresses, preferring jeans and a man's white shirt; this outfit added to her unforgettable personal appearance and manner.

One of the most intriguing episodes in *The Lonely Hunter* concerns Carson's involvement in 1941-1942 with an artists' commune in Brooklyn. Living apart from Reeves at the time, Carson loved the disintegrating Old World neighborhood and the vast number of creative people who passed through this area under the Brooklyn Bridge. The commune was organized and run by W. H. Auden who ruled with what might charitably be called a very firm concern. Carson's friend Louis Untermeyer was in residence, as was George Davis, the owner and a noted conversationalist. When Gypsy Rose Lee joined the house, the whole tempo changed. Miss Lee was not only the most famous "interpretative dancer" of her era, but a warm and very literate human being. Carson was entranced. Eventually, several of Auden's friends moved in, including the poet Louis MacNeice, composer Benjamin Britten, and a talented tenor named Peter Pears. A magazine of art and criticism, *Decision,* was planned and printed at the commune on 7 Middagh Street. The place was filled with excitement and confusion, but with all the drinking, parties, and all-night conversations, there was hardly any time for serious creativity. When Auden left for a teaching position at the University of Michigan, the commune folded. It had been a refreshing, stimulating experience, a community of displaced refugees during the hysterical early war days, but finally everyone wanted to resume his own work.

In *The Lonely Hunter,* Virginia Carr, by her thorough research and very readable style, significantly illuminates Carson McCullers the person and Carson McCullers the writer. The story is often not a pretty one, and there will probably always be unanswered questions about this talented and enigmatic individual. Yet, Carr explains her subject with such sensitivity and honesty that general readers can be grateful for a fascinating "life and times" account, and scholars will be able to spend years analyzing a mass of new data brought to light.

Patrick Morrow

LOOKOUT CARTRIDGE

Author: Joseph McElroy (1930-   )
Publisher: Alfred A. Knopf (New York). 531 pp. $10.00
Type of work: Novel
Time: The present
Locale: London, New York, Corsica, Wales, Stonehenge
   An elaborate intellectual mystery, filled with symbols, allusions, and often vivid portraits of the violence of the modern world

> *Principal characters:*
> DAGGER DI GORRO, an American amateur film maker, living in England
> CARTWRIGHT, an American businessman and amateur film maker, living in England
> LORNA CARTWRIGHT, his wife
> JENNY CARTWRIGHT, his nineteen-year-old daughter
> WILL (BILLY) CARTWRIGHT, his younger son
> SUB, Cartwright's boyhood friend
> MONTY GRAF, British friend of Cartwright
> CLAIRE, Cartwright's American contact

Set mainly in London and New York, *Lookout Cartridge* concerns a film made by two Americans living in England and the forces that are threatened by the film and by Cartwright's diary of its shooting, as well as by his inquiry into why the film was destroyed. But the plot of this long and demanding *tour de force* is merely an excuse for the stylistic and philosophical gymnastics of the author. The question is whether the reader is willing to follow narrator Cartwright's obsessive mental process as he puts fragment after fragment of information together to find out what others think he already knows—and why it is valuable enough for them to threaten his daughter's life for it. The story's clothesline of suspense, hung here and there with tough situations and tougher talk, is conventional, but McElroy brings a certain amount of freshness to his contemporary imagery, including that of film cutting, the supernatural, scientific toys, and the jargon of the modern world. There are glints of comedy beneath the calculated convolutions of the novel's language, but *Lookout Cartridge,* like Pynchon's *Gravity's Rainbow* and other recent novels, obtains its symbolic and allusive formulae from science and technology rather than from literature and art. It is a special kind of game that only the initiated can play.

   The author has a fine sense for detail, for observing the minutiae of everyday life. He fills his narrative with closely observed descriptions of street scenes, with sudden glimpses of contemporary life styles. But his characters are stylized to the point of flatness; they are puppets, manipulated for the plot, rather than full-bodied men and women who cause the plot to happen. The reader cannot believe in them as human beings or care about their fates. Possibly the author has done this deliberately, believing that the time has come to leave the traditional novel with its emphasis on characterization behind. But to capture the emotions of the reader, a novel must be more than an ingenious jigsaw puzzle of elaborate metaphors and clever symbols. For all of its intellectual artifice, this book does not deeply engage the reader's sympathies. One admires it as a construction, but one remains essentially aloof from it.

Diary and memory work together in the narrative, and sometimes at odds, trying to reconstruct the past, to find the reality of life. The diary and memory, and the fragmented and mostly destroyed movie which are their subject, belong to Cartwright, the protagonist of the plot. Memory is perhaps the real subject of *Lookout Cartridge,* for everything important seems to have happened in the past, and the necessity which drives Cartwright is that of recalling this past. "Bring back a memory," his daughter Jenny tells him, when he travels.

Also at the heart of this unusual novel is the scientific tradition as it is embraced in science fiction, in industry, and in the popular imagination. There is a revolution at work in the world, the characters agree, but it is more scientific than social. "Are you part of the film-making revolution?" Cartwright asks some young film makers, but he is told that anyone who *is* part of the revolution would not have to ask. The narrator-hero tells his children the tale of "Beauty and the Computer." The connections in the novel, flashing and vanishing almost at random, suggest the alternating connections of a vast computer. Little attempt is made to hold the reader's interest through conventional methods; like a switchboard ablaze with signals, the novel hurls fragments of conversations and brilliantly illuminated but tantalizingly brief scenes at the reader, who can only struggle to unify these images into a meaningful whole. The scraps of incident and shards of memory do eventually add up, but one person's summary might be quite different from somebody else's. The novel is like a fun house mirror, reflecting the viewer as well as the author and his characters.

One of the foremost themes in this book is that of violence in the modern world. Near the opening of the novel the reader is deliberately shocked by a scene of gratuitous violence. The selfish callousness of the contemporary citizen is shown when the narrator witnesses the accidental stabbing of a man in the street with a car radio antenna and, after watching the man collapse in a pool of blood, wanders into a camera shop to look for a new camera for his daughter, apparently undisturbed by what he has witnessed. Cruelty, various forms of brutality, and the constant bombardment of mechanical violence give the novel a kind of nervous vitality, but at the sacrifice of sympathy. No one in the novel emerges as genuinely admirable or sympathetic.

Like the novels and stories of Thomas Pynchon, Donald Barthelme, and John Barth, *Lookout Cartridge* is a novel to study, a novel written for academics to explore rather than for the general reader to read. The book is filled with devices to make it seem *avant-garde,* such as not using quotation marks around the dialogue and breaking into the action with random thoughts and disjointed phrases. However, difficulty or obscurity is no guarantee of either profundity or quality. Fascinating as this novel often is, the author seems to have deliberately set out to construct a puzzle rather than a coherent narrative. The reader follows the ironies, follows the coincidences which dot the story line, such as it is, and suspends disbeliefs as the hero battles obscure and menacing forces, but despite the energy put into the tale, it is never quite convincing.

Influenced as the book is by the movies, it is possible that it was inspired, at least indirectly, by the several movies dealing with the notorious underworld figure Dr. Mabuse, directed in the 1920's and 1930's by the great German film maker Fritz Lang. Certainly, the technical pyrotechnics of the novel suggest the dazzling genius of the movies, and the tale of the power-hungry Mabuse and his many faces and vast organization has many similarities with *Lookout Cartridge.* In this century, novelists and movie makers both seem fascinated by the subject of great, hidden powers which are striving to take over the world. These organizations are seldom clearly defined, but their presence is *felt,* and more than a few protagonists have suffered at their hands. Actually this startlingly *avant-garde* novel is part of a pattern in twentieth century narrative fiction, both cinematic and novelistic.

The novel suggests a montage of countless movies of the past and present and future, a splicing of scenes and film clips and newsreels into a dazzling but not always coherent whole. The labyrinthine narrative tracks Cartwright's efforts to separate occurrences from imaginings, splicing together at random figures and scenes enigmatically recalled, including Welsh hippies around a bonfire, an art-gallery intrigue, an Olympian softball game, and assorted acts of grotesque violence. In the end, Cartwright has gained a kind of wisdom, possibly, about himself and the truths which rule mankind, but these visionary axioms, for the most part, escape the reader. The scenes of violence and grotesque comedy linger longer in the reader's imagination than the bits of wisdom thrust forward along the way. McElroy should trust more to his talents for describing characters and their actions than to his predilection to philosophize.

Ultimately, it is the nature of truth which is being explored in *Lookout Cartridge.* Ironically, in this age of great scientific and technical skills and massive information retrieval systems, of mass media and instant communications, truth is more elusive than ever. We cannot look to scientific advancements or to technical growth to help us find truth, any more than we can look to movies or other giants of communication. The only place where we can and must look for the truth is in ourselves. All of us, like Cartwright, race through life, searching for the answer, but the end of the steeple chase is within us. Actually, the message, if such it is, of this dazzling and experimental novel, is almost conventional, unless the message *is* the medium.

Bruce D. Reeves

THE LOST HONOR OF KATHARINA BLUM

Author: Heinrich Böll (1917-   )
Translated from the German by Leila Vennewitz
Publisher: McGraw-Hill Book Company (New York). 140 pp. $7.95
Type of work: Novel
Time: February, 1974
Locale: Germany, possibly Bonn

The story of the destruction of an intelligent, sensitive, and morally pure woman by a corrupt and amoral society

Principal characters:
> KATHARINA BLUM, a self-employed housekeeper and caterer
> HUBERT AND GERTRUDE BLORNA, her employers; the former, also her lawyer
> ELSE WOLTERSHEIM, her godmother and friend
> LUDWIG GOTTEN, the man Katharina meets at a dance and falls in love with
> ALOIS STRAUBLEDER, an eminent industrialist, a friend of the Blornas and would-be lover of Katharina
> WERNER TOTGES, reporter for the *News*

The Lost Honor of Katharina Blum by Nobel Prize-winner Heinrich Böll is a complex study of the quality of human life in the world today. The novel's subtitle, "Or: How Violence Develops and Where It Can Lead," indicates its primary thematic concern; it is an investigation which eventually involves all aspects of society.

The primary level of the plot is almost a traditional murder mystery, a genre generally equated with sex and violence presented in a sentimental and sensational manner. The attitude of this narrator, however, differs obviously: there is a detached, objective, repeated desire to avoid the usually overplayed blood, guts, and sex, and an insistence upon accuracy of fact and detail. In addition, the reader is immediately told the bare facts of the murder and the identity of the murderer, who turns herself in only a few hours after the crime. The focus of the novel becomes, then, not the traditional "Who did it?" but "Why was it done?"

With such a focus, the character of the murderess, Katharina Blum, assumes major importance in the final impact of the novel. Katharina is almost an archetypal dream: the poor but virtuous girl who, because of her own intelligence, drive, and virtue has achieved an independent financial status, an apartment she owns, a business she owns, and the respect of all who know her. Married early to escape her family home, Katharina left her husband because his attitude toward her compromised her sense of human dignity. Although considered attractive by the socially and economically powerful men she meets in her profession, like Clarissa, she holds herself morally pure for the man she can truly love.

When Katharina accidentally meets Ludwig Götten at a dance the night before Carnival, they immediately and totally fall in love. Unfortunately, he is sought by the police, who trace him to her apartment. Her assistance in his escape, the arrests of both at different times, the attendant publicity, the murder, the couple's determination to reunite after their prison terms—these events form the basic plot around which the thematic concerns are structured. Although the plot may be reminiscent of a soap opera, as in all great works the telling difference comes in the reverberations, in the treatment of problems inherent in human nature, and in the conflict between the individual's sense of values and self-worth and the amoral or corrupt social system.

The honorable but defenseless world of Katharina is impinged upon first by police suspicion, then by the press accounts of her "lost honor." As the obscene phone calls and mails mount, as the newspaper's stories grow more lurid, referring to her as a whore, a Communist conspirator, and the murderer of her mother, Katharina's self-control breaks in a frustrated act of violence: she smashes things on the walls of her immaculate, once-treasured apartment. As public insults against her morality and invasions of her privacy —encouraged by the *News*—increase, the almost inevitable result of outrage and frustration occurs: the act of utmost violence, murder. Premeditation is not proven; provocation is. With no one else to protect her honor, the act, as stated in the opening of the novel, seems "not inexplicable, but almost logical." From beginning to end, Katharina has no moral misgivings about her deed. She feels no remorse, an emotion which can only result from the betrayal of one's inherent moral code, one's "honor";

Katharina has not betrayed her code. No remorse, therefore, is felt, either by the heroine or by society, which has no moral code to violate. Katharina's concept of "honor" is obviously an unfashionable anachronism. This upside-down world in which morality becomes a stigma is recognizably the world in which we all might find ourselves trapped.

The innate morality of Katharina serves as a standard by which the rest of the representatives of society are judged. Her insistence on precision and correctness far exceeds that of the policemen who question her. The Police Commissioner casually invades her privacy by wiretapping with no moral or legal hesitation; he even publicly praises the *News* for collecting and publishing information which the police could not legally obtain.

The press, as exemplified by the *News* and its star reporter, Tötges, is a sensational exploiter of half-truths and fabrications, and cares only for its own profits. Even Tötges' murder and funeral are used as an occasion to extol a "victim of the profession" who has, ironically, victimized Katharina, her mother, the Blornas, and, potentially, Else. Only the economically powerful Sträubleder, who tried to force his attentions on Katharina, and who has the political contacts to control the paper, escapes—by turning attention on his friends, the Blornas. Katharina's murder of the reporter, of course, can only have symbolic value: he is immediately replaced. The paper's sensationalistic exploitation will continue because the public will pay for such stories.

This novel, then, becomes not

simply a "new twist" in the murder mystery genre, but an indictment of the "lost honor" of modern society. The crimes of Katharina and Götten are clearly less than those of their "civilization." Götten steals from an already corrupt system—the Army—with the collaboration of some of its admired, well-known leaders; Katharina lies to protect the man she loves and kills to avenge her honor. The true indictment is brought against the establishment itself. The narrator, almost hysterically, remarks at one point that no one is excluded: the Church, which takes no moral stands; the lawyers; the "industrialists who are professors or politicians on the side"; the Crime Commissioner; and the system of justice which does not worry about the moral and psychological effects of wiretapping, even on the men who are paid to eavesdrop. Even the rejects of society, the prisoners, will reject Katharina for the same reason society sent her to jail: her moral incorruptibility. The narrator clearly has a hard time attempting to bring the order of a well-constructed novel to bear on a world which no longer has the sense of order and cohesiveness which comes from shared moral values. Furthermore, Böll indirectly suggests that most modern art, like the *News,* panders to the worst of human nature. The indications of deterioration and collapse in the lawyer Blorna at the end likewise seem to apply, not primarily to him, but to his society, which at best lacks any concern for morality, and at worst persecutes the true moralists, be they housekeepers like Katharina or artists.

The full ironic significance of the setting of the novel, the Christian festival of Carnival, is seen only in retrospect. The traditional spiritual meaning of the festival, in which man both celebrates the joys of the world and the flesh and prepares to bid them farewell for Lent, can only be recognized in the attitudes of Katharina and Götten. In contrast, society (as epitomized in the Carnival "officials," the town's leading businessmen) worries about the "sacrilege" of the murder because it might damage business profits—the only reason Carnival has been restored and promoted.

At one point in the novel, a character questions whether the *News,* the most obvious villain of the novel, operates as it does because of the structure of society. The answer is yes. Blame lies with society's lack of morality: the whole establishment, in one way or another, commits "acts of violence" against the individual's sense of privacy, decency, and morality, acts which are accepted as normal or even commendable procedures. *The Lost Honor of Katharina Blum* may exaggerate the problem, but exaggeration is an effective traditional tool used by morally indignant masters of social satire such as Jonathan Swift. As the narrator comments after one brief eruption of violence settled by an artist, "From this occurrence plus the preceding acts of violence it should be possible to deduce that Art still has a social function." Böll's novel becomes a case in point, analyzing as it does the causes and effects of acts of violence in our civilization.

Ann E. Reynolds

LOVERS & AGNOSTICS

Author: Kelly Cherry (1940-   )
Publisher: Red Clay Books (Charlotte, N.C.) 74 pp. $3.00 (paperback)
Type of work: Poetry

The first collection of poems by a remarkably promising and exciting young writer

Kelly Cherry's first novel, *Sick and Full of Burning* (1974) was praised for its wit, its intricate structure, and its humor. This favorable comment appeared in fashionable places, such as the *Chicago Tribune* and the *Atlantic Monthly.* This book of poems, on its own terms, is every bit as good as the novel, but it is with wry resignation that one imagines how it would strike the fashionable reviewers.

Lovers & Agnostics is almost fiercely unfashionable in its display of technical and thematic ambition. As Fred Chappell says in a brief and somewhat feisty Foreword to the collection:

> Ms Kelly Cherry . . . has purposely written a poetry of intellection (not an "intellectual poetry," which is a different kind of thing and often a rip-off), and by this means has widened, if not obliterated, the boundaries of her sympathies; she has gained the freedom of the observer, having quite seen through the easy pose of the false confessor. She has abjured notions in order to attain to ideas.

Cherry has also attained remarkable feats of characterization, of both men and women, and the creation of a more extended world than poetry usually contains, in a long sequence called "Benjamin John." In scope and technical accomplishment, this is a splendid collection. Even its few flaws are noteworthy, as being the consequences of considerable risks.

The collection is arranged in four sections, the second and third being sequences. The first section, "Among the Mighty Dead," opens with a chilling soliloquy, "The Bride of Quietness," spoken by a woman who has become her husband's creation; when she departs in various ways from the classical outlines in which he has imprisoned her, he departs from her. However,

> He always found poetic justic
> Amusing, and he knows I wait my turn.
> The artist dies; but what he wrought
>   will last
> Forever, when I cradle his cold ashes
>   in this urn.

The most ambitious poem in this first section is "In Memory of Elaine Shaffer," a flutist who died in 1973. There are small lapses in this poem which are evaded by the shorter "Song for Sigmund Freud," or "Advice to a Friend Who Paints," but this elegy is still an achievement of much greater magnitude. Its first stanza states its theme:

> *They lie—all those who so smartly insist*
> *That any correlation can exist*
> *Between meaning and music. There is*
>   *none.*
> *Only a point at which the audience*
> *For both stands and reveals itself as one.*

The poem moves through five sections, whose varying prosodies and lengths make them suggestive of the movements in a musical composition; but for the reasons quoted above, the parallel is not labored, not insisted upon. And, while the poem's major theme is the nonexistent correlation between meaning and music, its subject is, of course, the poet's world as it appears now that Elaine Shaffer has been removed from it.

The first section, after the italicized first stanza, proceeds to establish the personal dialectic between the poet and the musician; the second is a brief list of those great women, like Sappho, Elizabeth, and Curie, who "survive/ In the unconscious"; now "another of our sex, forever freed,/ Wakes from life to this lament of the unliberated." By this time the reader is aware that he is in the presence of an elegy composed along surprisingly classical lines. In an aesthetically satisfying transition from Section II to III, a lament in rhymed tercets, the customary questions are posed: Why the musician instead of the poet? What was the nature of her uniqueness? Where is she now? These questions are put in personal and distinctive ways: tradition serves the poem, rather than the other way around. The fourth section returns to the major theme, regret over the inadequacy of poetry to express the poet's present ideas and emotions. The strong final section contains a brief digression on the plight of the poet, cosseted in a tame college, and a tentative consolation in the motion of opposites toward harmony. The concluding lines are themselves a splendid harmony of the poem's thematic ambition and its emotional pressure:

> O Elaine, Elaine,

> In that progression toward the plane
>   of spirit
> You and I, however unalike, move
> Hand in hand, the poet and musician,
> Behind the curtain's formal bow, and
>   know
> That when it closes for the final time
> Our audience has always been the same
> Demanding dream, the shadowy critic
> Whose fearful standard fathers short-
>   lived sisters
> In sound, related through our haunting
>   chorus:
> The silence in the wings that waits for us,

> *The silence in the wings that waits for us.*

If the poem is not flawless, it is because the poet has tried something that few have the nerve or the knowledge to attempt. In the third section, the lament, for example, there is a use of the musician's last name which strikes an odd note, as in Wordsworth's address to the "Spade! with which Wilkinson hath tilled his lands." Even so, this is a remarkable poem, worth keeping around for a long time, just as we keep, say, "Kubla Khan" complete with its "fast thick pants" or the Intimations Ode, complete with its "six years' Darling of a pigmy size." It takes less nerve to mention this poem in the same paragraph with Coleridge and Wordsworth than it did for the poet to achieve it in the first place.

The usual custom in arranging the poems in a collection decrees that things shall not go steadily downhill after a point one third of the way through the book. That rare reader who goes straight through this collection will therefore wonder how he will fare following "In Memory of Elaine Shaffer." It turns out that the author of the next section, "Benjamin John," could have written the elegy with relative ease. This sequence is one of the rarest achievements in recent American poetry.

The sequence concerns the life of an academic; it begins in his youth, and takes him through graduate school, marriage, a career, and on toward death, though it stops just short of reporting that inevitability. The tone of the sequence as a whole is splendidly ambiguous, as individual poems range from compassionate portraiture to satirical cartooning.

Benjamin John emerges as one of those men for whom almost everything is a burden, especially personal attachments and responsibilities. He is continually hounded by the everyday, by the attractiveness of his female students, and by occasional visions of the Green Queen, a shadowy figure who may be a woman he might once have been able to win, and whose departure into realms of the unattainable he is not quite prepared to acknowledge. It would be unfair to quote from the sequence; it must suffice to say that it never falls below the expectations aroused by the first part of the book, and when it exceeds them, as it often does, it achieves magnificent flights of intense characterization. It is the work of a highly accomplished poetic technician who is also at home with fiction; it has the novelist's breadth and depth of empathy.

"A Lyric Cycle" of eleven short poems makes up the third part of this collection. It is notable for the chiseled, smooth precision of its language; lyrical in the classic sense of the word, the poems have been set to music for soprano solo by the Soviet composer Imants Kalnins. Though the poems recount and respond to various moments, painful and otherwise, in a love affair, they have been purified of background, like certain kinds of Oriental paintings, so that the moments and feelings that are delineated hang suspended, ringing like tapped crystal, as in "Circe," the concluding poem of the cycle:

> "But as the fading sun clips you from
>   my sight,
> I will remember you.
>
> "When you have gone,
> the sun
> like a silent song
> will burn up the far side of night."

The book concludes with the title section, which contains nine poems more nearly miscellaneous in theme and manner than those assembled in the earlier sections. It is here that Cherry revels most explicitly in her debt to classical literature; there are translations from Catullus, remarkable for their understanding of the originals, and for the boldness with which they avoid literalness in order to convey that understanding. A witty monologue in deft stanzas jostles with more "subjectivist" visions in more open forms. But the voice is always there, always true to itself. Many books are greeted with excessive praise, as if only shouting could be heard above the rumbling of the inexhaustible presses; but when the shouting dies down, it is safe to predict that this book's voice will still be audible. It is a remarkable example of rare devotion to craft, rare integrity of purpose.

Henry Taylor

THE MAZE

Author: Eileen Simpson
Publisher: Simon and Schuster (New York). 250 pp. $7.95
Type of work: Novel
Time: The 1950's
Locale: Italy, England, and Massachusetts

A double exploration into the nature of genius and the qualities that compose a marriage, and into the demands which both make upon the individual personality

Principal characters:
BENJAMIN BOLD, an American poet
ROXANA (ROSY), his wife
RODNEY MUNSON, Benjamin's old friend
MARGARET MUNSON, his wife
THEO ADDIS, a writer and lecturer, Rosy's possible lover
TULLIO FANCELLI, a friend of Benjamin and well-known Italian novelist
ANDREW MALLORY, Benjamin's friend and fellow poet

The Maze is a novel about survival, about the struggle of the individual to survive in the face of psychological and moral disasters, and about the equally fierce struggle of talent, or genius, to survive in a world that refuses to yield to its demands. The clash between these forces creates much of the drama in this vivid and subtle portrayal of a disintegrating marriage. Benjamin Bold is forty, an American poet who has waited twenty years for fame. Having at last completed the long poem that he expects will make his reputation, Bold seeks to recuperate from the creative effort by traveling to Italy with his wife. In Rome, they encounter other Americans, mostly academics and writers, who tend to grate upon one another's egos. It soon becomes obvious that Bold is a suicidal drunk who cannot resist any opportunity to make scenes or to offend those who might help him. The presence of his wife makes him behave even worse. Gradually, she tries to make her way through the maze that Bold has imposed upon her life. Much of the story deals with her efforts to survive as a person while attempting to hold together her marriage. Finally, realizing that he wants to be rid of her, she leaves him, only to find that he expects her to return. Bold is unchanged at the end of the novel, and one feels that he will never change, but his wife, the long-suffering Rosy, has learned to recognize just what kind of people they are, and courageously has taken the first steps toward an independent and viable life.

The Maze takes place almost entirely inside Rosy's consciousness. The character of Bold is fascinating, with his collection of contradictions and eccentricities, but he is also exasperating. There is nothing sympathetic about him. One believes in his genius, but cannot respect his behavior. The author has achieved the difficult feat of creating a person who is both real and unpleasant, dynamic and self-alienating. Benjamin Bold is as selfish as he is talented, and would willingly sacrifice every other human being in the world to his poetry. It is a measure of Eileen Simpson's skill that the reader does not become too disgusted with Bold's antics, as seen from his wife's point of view, to continue the book. Actually, Bold provides much of the life in the book, for Rosy is as weak as he is strong. She clearly cannot define herself except in terms of a man, but we do not know why she is this way. As the central consciousness in the novel, Rosy might have been probed more deeply. The reader craves to understand better *why* she endured her husband as long as she did.

Although at times the book seems rather like a case history, and is filled with unnecessary and empty chattering by crowds of minor characters, the author has a sharp eye for the complexity of people's emotional lives. This, perhaps, is the real strength of the book. Simpson is the former wife of the late poet John Berryman; she knows of what she writes and never oversimplifies. A clinical psychiatrist, Simpson made a study of creativity in poets, a study which served as her thesis for a graduate degree in psychology at New York University. The reader feels this authority on every page. The immediacy of some of the scenes is almost unbearable. Yet, she avoids "big" scenes or melodramatic situations, preferring to rely upon the telling gesture and precise dialogue.

Creativity always has fascinated both writers and readers. How do genuine talents function? How are the towering works of music and art and literature created? What are the torments that drive these great artistic geniuses? The author has addressed herself to these questions and has succeeded in producing a vivid and compelling portrait of such a genius. Perhaps one could make too much of the similarities between Benjamin Bold and John Berryman, yet one cannot forget the fact that Simpson's portrait inevitably owes much to her intimate knowledge of that poet. Berryman and Bold were both of the generation that matured in the Depression and began to produce during the World War II years. Both were educated first at American universities, after which Berryman studied at Oxford, Bold at Cambridge. Both taught at various American universities and won many awards and fellowships. And both wrote experimental poetry, poetry which strove to make clear, direct statements with sharply-honed imagery. As Berryman said of his own poetry, Bold believed that poetry should have "guts." And both men were poets of integrity, poets who stood by their work and dared to let their work stand against the best poetry of the past. By the end of the book, the reader has glimpsed, as if by flashes of lightning, the creative process and the inevitable pains that follow such intense efforts. It is a hazardous existence, for both the poet and those close to him. One is both grateful that anyone is willing to endure such an existence in order to create the art that illuminates life for the rest of humanity, and alarmed by the torments endured by the poet and those around him.

Subsidiary characters represent other types of creative artists, from the most successful to the not-so-successful. Tullio Fancelli, a friend of Bold and a well-known Italian novelist, typifies the "successful" writer who has achieved both critical recognition and economic rewards. But he has sacrificed something for his success, or, perhaps, merely lost something as he gained it, for the other characters all feel that he was more "interesting" when he was young and struggling. The author explores with sensitivity the dangers of success versus the agony of failure. Andrew Mallory and Theo Addis are different kinds of writers, satisfied with limited success and recognition, neither struggling with the terrible pressures of genius. Both are willing to compromise, to settle for the "good life" and a reasonable portion of happiness. But, whatever else Benjamin Bold is capable of, he cannot compromise with his poetry. It is his religion.

A minor theme, gradually developed in the novel, is that of the human need for some kind of religion. Rosy is a lapsed Catholic. She finds, as she tears herself away from Benjamin, that she needs the consolation of her Church. But Bold's religion is art, creation, his own genius. The symbolism of the novel, from Hadrian's Villa and the temples of ancient Rome to the medieval and Renaissance churches, suggests that man's needs for art and religion are one. Without either, we have hopelessness and death. It is significant that the novel begins with Bold waking up from a nightmare, part of the suffering that he experiences after the completion of his great poem. He cannot find peace except in creation. The process itself is hellish, yet to *not* be creating is worse agony.

Another metaphor developed for the process of artistic creation is that of giving birth to a child. Bold never wanted an actual child. Perhaps he

was afraid of a rival for his wife's affection, but more than that he saw his works of art as his children. He felt that the creation of a poem was the same as the growth in the womb and the birth of an actual baby. He even believed that he suffered a postpartum depression such as mothers sometimes experience. He is both the child and the parent, demanding that Rosy both mother him and help him to give birth to his poetry. At the same time, he insists that she worship at the altar of his genius and worship *him,* as the creator, and his poetry, the "holy" child to which he has given birth. The symbols and metaphors in the book are richly and cunningly developed; they are both psychologically and morally compelling.

But it is the maze which is the ultimate and central metaphor in the novel. Rosy sees her life as a maze such as those found in Italian gardens, a maze full of false clues, cul-de-sacs, and mislabeled paths. She tries to plan her escape, to outsmart her jailer, but, as panic engulfs her, she finds herself frantically racing up and down the endless paths. The maze is Benjamin Bold, his genius, his erratic life style, his temperament, his selfishness, and his love. Finally, the maze is their marriage together, the bloody scenes of their life, and the false starts that they continue to make together. The only way to escape the maze is to escape Benjamin, the one decision most painful for her to make.

The maze metaphor is subtly developed as Rosy travels around Italy and Europe. She flees from an outraged, drunken Benjamin and becomes lost in Rome; wandering through the dangerous, dark streets of the Eternal City, she confronts her essential problem, and realizes that she has let herself be led into this emotional and physical trap which is her marriage. And on the ancient island of Ponza, a place which for centuries served as a prison, she also ponders her life and the future of her marriage. Other men offer her options, but she rejects them as false escapes. If she does find the way out it must be alone, for nobody can save her but herself. The individual must stand, finally, separate from everyone else. Benjamin Bold, as a poet and a man, must function in self-imposed isolation, and Rosy, as a woman, as a human being, must find her own unique salvation. No one, Simpson implies, can save anyone else, but, perhaps, we can win a little time for ourselves.

Bruce D. Reeves

THE MEDITERRANEAN
and the Mediterranean World in the Age of Philip II

Author: Fernand Braudel (1902-   )
Translated from the French by Siân Reynolds
Publisher: Harper & Row Publishers (New York). Illustrated. 2 vols. 1,375 pp.
$35.00
Type of work: History
Time: Second half of the sixteenth century
Locale: Mediterranean Sea and the countries surrounding it

An encyclopedic panorama of the Mediterranean world, its people, its problems, and its civilizations

Principal personages:
> PHILIP II OF HABSBURG, King of Spain, 1556-1598
> DON JOHN OF AUSTRIA, illegitimate half-brother of Philip II and commander of the fleet of the Holy League in the Battle of Lepanto

Fernand Braudel, the distinguished French historian, brought out the first edition of *The Mediterranean and the Mediterranean World in the Age of Philip II* in 1949. The second revised edition of his massive, erudite study appeared in 1966 and formed the basis, with further revisions, of the excellent English translation which was published in 1972-1973. The revisions in both subsequent editions were mainly designed to take into account fresh knowledge and new approaches to historical problems and thereby strengthen the objective of this enormous monograph, namely that of presenting a complete, dynamic description of the entire Mediterranean world in the age of Philip II of Spain. Braudel, however, as the title of his book might otherwise suggest, does not confine himself solely to the period of Philip II; on the contrary, to attain his objective of understanding the Mediterranean world in depth, he investigates the historical antecedents of his subject back to ancient times. In pursuing his objective, Braudel divides his study into three parts, each virtually a book unto itself. First, he undertakes an investigation of the impact of the environment and geography of the Mediterranean world on the human condition in the sixteenth century; then he examines social structures of the time, including the nature of societies, civilizations, economic systems, empires, and forms of war. Finally, he provides a traditional political history of Mediterranean Europe during the epoch of Philip II. Braudel states that the book's three parts constitute a dissection of history into various planes—the division of historical time into geographical time, social time, and individual time.

In analyzing the geographical and social foundations of Mediterranean man, Braudel is attempting, in his own words, "to encompass the history of the Mediterranean in its complex totality." He accomplishes this enormous task of writing total history through exhaustive research in numerous archives and by drawing upon the writings of specialists in disciplines related to history, including, among others, anthropology, geography, botany, and geology. The resulting synthesis in Parts I and II is by far the most valuable contribution of the book, as it provides the reader with a veritable mine of information on a wide range of diverse, yet related, topics. By the very vastness of its scope, Braudel's synthesis fulfills his conception of history as one involving all facets of man's environment and development, not just the political and diplomatic events of his past.

Braudel seeks in Part I, "The Role of the Environment," to define the interrelationship between the physical and human geography during that "brief moment of Mediterranean life, between 1550 and 1600." In discussing the mountains, plateaus, and plains that make up the peninsulas of the Mediterranean world, or in describing its islands, coastal areas, and climate, Braudel makes geography come alive by showing how, over the centuries, these various elements of the environment have influenced the tone and level of civilization. He uses the comparative method, drawing analogies between the same types of geographic entities in various parts of the Mediterranean basin, and demonstrating how similar developments are discernible in each. The result is the emergence of a historical pattern.

For example, in his discourse on the nature of the mountains which encircle the area, the author observes that civilization in the mountainous regions is never very stable. This instability is particularly evident in the shallow attitudes which the mountaineers have held in the past toward the established religion of the neighboring plain. He demonstrates that because the relatively isolated Christian mountaineers in such diverse places as the Caucasus, the Balkans, and Crete were only slightly influenced by Christianity, they converted *en masse* to the advancing tide, in various centuries, of Islam. Because of their location and their method of conversion, these mountain people were no more confirmed in their new faith than they had been in their old one. Hence, according to Braudel, a separate religious geography seems to emerge for the mountain world, which constantly had to be conquered and reconquered. Numerous minor facts, he observes, which are encountered in traditional history take on new meaning in this light. Seminal ideas such as this (subject, to be sure, to argument and controversy among historians) characterize the entire book.

Braudel concludes his analysis of the Mediterranean environment with a chapter on cities and the communications between them. Here he devotes his attention exclusively to human geography and demonstrates that it was only through human ingenuity, and the land and sea routes thereby developed, that the unity of the Mediterranean was created. This unity was not a political one, but more significantly, a permanent unified human construction slowly imposed on geographical space by cities and their various forms of communications. The main intention of the author throughout Part I is to explore, using the concept of geographical space, the nature of the permanent, slow-moving or recurrent features of Mediterranean life.

In Part II, "Collective Destinies and General Trends," Braudel deals with social history and is obliged, he observes, to meet two contradictory purposes. First, he has to be concerned with social structures, including economic systems, states, societies, civilizations, and forms of war; that is, those mechanisms which more or less withstand the march of time. Secondly, but simultaneously, he must address himself to the development of these structures. In order to discover the collective destiny of the sixteenth century Mediterranean, therefore, Braudel must combine what he refers to as structure and conjuncture, the permanent and ephemeral sides of an institution—in his words, "the slow-moving and the fast." True to his twofold purpose, Braudel analyzes, for example, the origin and nature of the Spanish and Turkish empires and the process of their respective declines by 1600. He also discusses the character of the traditional classes of society, the nobility, the bourgeoisie, and the poor, and observes that between 1550 and 1600 a gradual polarization of rich and poor took place which resulted in crisis in the next century.

In analyzing the economic systems, Braudel acknowledges the great impact which the New World had on Europe. He devotes considerable space to the question of the impact which gold and silver from the Spanish Indies had on the inflationary crises of the period. Citing leading authorities on both sides of the argument, he explains that prices had begun to rise in Europe before Columbus sailed to America, in part because of the devaluations of money in various countries.

The concluding section of the book, "Events, Politics and People," is traditional history, in which the author evaluates major political currents and events and describes the deeds and exploits of individual men. Despite his conviction that he must include in his book a traditional history of his subject, the author confesses that he is by temperament a "structuralist" little tempted by historical events, and is convinced that what freedom the individual in history possesses is limited by a destiny which he has had little hand in shaping.

The central individual in Braudel's survey of the later sixteenth century is Philip II, King of Spain from 1556 to 1598. Major attention is focused on the problems of the Spanish and Turkish empires and on the great clash between the two in the Battle of Lepanto in 1571. Braudel offers a vivid description of the role in this naval engagement of the commander of the fleet of the Holy League (Spain Venice, and the Papacy), Don John of Austria, the illegitimate half-brother of Philip II. Most historians have dismissed the significance of the Christian victory at Lepanto because the allied fleet did not pursue the Turks, who managed by the following year to rebuild completely their shattered navy. Braudel, however, regards the victory as the end of a period of genuine inferiority complex on the part of Christendom and as a halt to further Turkish advances. At the close of Part III, the author reflects on the death of Philip II, a man of narrow vision, Braudel avers, who probably never had a clear concept of the Mediterranean and its significance; geography had not been part of his education. These are all sufficient reasons, according to the author, why Philip's death was not a crucial event in the history of the region. True to his concept of history, Braudel asserts that the life and death of Philip II offer good reasons for reflecting upon the distance separating biographical history from the history of structure, and especially from the history of geographical areas.

Fernand Braudel's brilliant study of the Mediterranean world is towering in its scope and sweep. It provides an excellent example of the effort of one historian to write what he calls "total history," a construct based on the interdisciplinary and comparative methods. The end product is a monumental synthesis in which the author, by harmonizing the three levels of human geography, social groups, and individual exploits, conveys to his readers a philosophy of history which emphasizes the importance of structure. Although at times Braudel's explanations of the mechanics of his philosophy of history are less than lucid, his study offers a rich harvest of ideas for all readers, whether specialist or nonspecialist. Numerous charts and illustrations, and a massive critical bibliography of more than sixty pages, are admirable additions to this authoritative and distinguished work.

Edward P. Keleher

MEETING AT POTSDAM

Author: Charles L. Mee, Jr. (1938-   )
Publisher: M. Evans & Company (New York). Illustrated. 370 pp. $10.95
Type of work: History
Time: July and August, 1945
Locale: Potsdam, Germany

A study of the Potsdam Conference and of the personalities and national aims of the Big Three leaders

Principal personages:
HARRY TRUMAN, thirty-third President of the United States, 1945-1952
JOSEPH STALIN, Soviet Dictator, 1924-1953
SIR WINSTON CHURCHILL, Prime Minister of Great Britain, 1940-1945; 1951-1955

In his book *Meeting at Potsdam,* Charles L. Mee, Jr., for many years the editor of *Horizon* Magazine, presents a readable—if highly debatable—account of the last major conference of the Big Three Allies held during World War II. Mee's thesis is that the Big Three leaders, Harry Truman, Joseph Stalin, and Winston Churchill, each used the Potsdam Conference to increase the power of their countries and of themselves. Perceiving that they could enhance their quest for power more certainly in a world of discord than in one of peace, Mee contends that they deliberately set out to quarrel. The result of their quarrel was, by the end of the conference, not the dawning of peace but rather the outbreak of the Cold War. In part, Mee arrives at these conclusions by relying heavily and selectively on anecdotal material contained, as he observes in his Prologue, "in the notes of the informal chats, in the recollections of dinner parties, in the jokes and the laughter" of the Big Three leaders. This approach, combined with the absence of any substantial reflections on the

Yalta Conference held in February, 1945, leaves the reader with a book on the Potsdam Conference which is a pleasure to read but which fails to establish a proper historical context in which to understand the attitudes of the Big Three leaders prior to their last wartime meeting.

The first three chapters of *Meeting at Potsdam* are devoted respectively to Truman, Churchill, and Stalin and their careers and aspirations, with brief portrayals of the advisers and statesmen who surrounded them. Writing in a breezy style, Mee sorts through a wide collection of anecdotes in an effort to find some sinister purpose in the minds of the two Western leaders. Truman thus comes off as a poker-playing politician, a product of the Pendergast machine, who confidently arrived in Potsdam intent on building the "American Century" based on the recent American victory in Europe and the possession of the atomic bomb. Citing the date of July 12, the author dramatically observes that while the bomb's plutonium core was being transported to the testing grounds of

Alamogordo, New Mexico, high spirits prevailed among Truman and his party as they sailed for Europe; this mood contrasted sharply with the gloom in Tokyo where, on the same day, Emperor Hirohito expressed his anxious desire to end the war as soon as possible.

In contrast to his description of Truman as a vigorous and confident leader of a powerful nation, Mee depicts Churchill as being just as exhausted as the country he represented. Both he and Great Britain had passed their zenith, Mee remarks, though neither yet realized it. In a subsequent passage, however, the author contradicts this point by attributing to Churchill a strategy at Potsdam that was necessarily based on a clear realization of his country's exhausted condition. Churchill's strategy, according to Mee, consisted of exaggerating the Russian threat and exacerbating the difference between Russia and America so that he could grab the leadership over a Western European bloc. The author attempts to strengthen his criticism of Churchill and his grand design by offering a few random quotations from Machiavelli, comparing the Prime Minister with the Prince, and by expressing shock over Churchill's willingness to use captured German troops to help block any further advance of the Red Army. He ignores the fact that the Western Allies made similar use of German troops against the Bolsheviks for some months after World War I. The historical evidence simply does not support Mee's view that Churchill deliberately sought to disrupt relations between the United States and the Soviet Union.

Mee has little image-breaking to do where Stalin is concerned; relying heavily on Adam Ulam's recent massive biography on the Soviet dictator, he flatly regards him as "one of the supremely evil men of history." The author, therefore, devotes more attention to what he regards as Stalin's solid grasp of military and political realities and to his skill as a negotiator. When analyzing Stalin's conduct of Soviet foreign policy, however, both at this point and throughout the book, Mee strangely failed to consult Ulam's equally important study, *Expansion and Coexistence*. Nevertheless, he presents a much better portrait of Stalin than of Truman and Churchill. The Soviet dictator is shown testing the Americans before and during the Potsdam Conference to see whether on such questions as Russia's demand for a friendly Polish government, they were naïve, determined ideological crusaders for freedom, or possessed of some ulterior motives. In order to understand America's true position on the fate of Eastern Europe, Stalin saw fit to raise the desirability of encouraging the Spanish people to overthrow Franco's fascist dictatorship. Furthermore, as Mee points out, Stalin deliberately made demands for any number of things which were of no real interest to him. By dropping these sham demands, he hoped to gain concessions from his Western counterparts on those subjects which involved Russia's security in Eastern Europe and in East Asia.

With these estimations of the Big Three leaders in hand, the author devotes most of the remaining chapters of his book to day-by-day summaries of the Potsdam Conference, which ran from July 17 to August 2, 1945. He also discusses one of the more interesting subjects relating to the Potsdam Conference and the days immediately following its conclusion: President Truman's decision to drop the atomic bomb on Japan. On July 21, Truman received a full report from Washington that the atomic bomb test at Alamogordo had been a complete success. Mee observes that an earlier plan among the President and his advisers about using the bomb to intimidate the Russians in Europe could now be tested, since Truman possessed the atomic power to back up his word. Hence, during the next several days of the Potsdam Conference, Truman attempted to negotiate forcefully with Stalin on such issues as Poland's frontiers and German reparations. Stalin, who as yet knew nothing about the bomb, did not allow himself to be pinned down by Truman on any of these questions. When at the close of the conference session of July 24, Truman finally informed Stalin of America's possession of the atomic bomb, the Soviet leader showed no special interest. Hence, according to Mee, Truman was unable to intimidate Stalin, whether he knew of the bomb's existence or not, short of actually dropping it on the Russians.

Mee's assessment of the failure of the atomic bomb to intimidate the Russians is correct up to this point, but he then proceeds to the theory that President Truman, still persisting in his efforts to intimidate the Russians while obviously not willing to drop the bomb on them, decided instead to drop it on Japan. Mee contends that the dropping of the bomb was not a military necessity, as Japan would have surrendered any-

way. Stalin, in Mee's view, held to this position in August, 1945, and hence was most impressed when the United States used its new weapon to obliterate Hiroshima and Nagasaki. Although ultimately the dropping of the bomb on Japan may not have been necessary, Truman's primary motive in using it was to end the war as soon as possible—not, as Mee states, to impress or intimidate Stalin. In fact, Stalin, during the initial Cold War period, 1945-1947, as surveyed by Mee in the epilogue to his book, did not allow America's fleeting monopoly of atomic weapons to intimidate him, as he proceeded to violate the Potsdam accord and tighten his grip on Eastern Europe. *Meeting at Potsdam* is an absorbing excursion into popular history which provides the reader with a view of the Potsdam Conference that is better described as solid entertainment, in the best sense of that word, than as solid historical analysis and interpretation. Many of Mee's assertions on such matters as the postwar policies of the Big Three leaders and America's aims in dropping the atomic bomb on Japan can be subjected to considerable criticism, as can his statement that the Big Three deliberately used the Potsdam Conference to launch the Cold War. He fails to realize that the Big Three needed one another less in July, 1945, than at the time of the Yalta Conference, when they were still fighting against Germany. As so often happens in history, the worst thing that can happen to a wartime alliance is the final defeat of its common foe. The collapse of Hitler's Reich produced immediate misunderstandings between Russia and the Western powers as to how the Big Three were to manage postwar Europe. These misunderstandings are the proper point of departure for an examination of what happened in the Potsdam Conference.

Despite these serious shortcomings, the student of history who wants to savor the atmosphere of a major wartime conference can profit from this book. Its value is further enhanced by two sections of photographs and two appendices that provide the texts of the Potsdam Proclamation, in which the United States, Great Britain, and the Republic of China called upon Japan to surrender unconditionally; and the Potsdam Declaration, in which the decisions reached by the Big Three powers at the conference were set forth. Finally, the book contains a useful bibliography, although one wishes that the author had also consulted both Adam Ulam's aforementioned study, *Expansion and Coexistence,* and Diane Clemen's *Yalta,* for the sake of providing a more judicious treatment of the background of the Potsdam Conference.

Edward P. Keleher

MEMOIRS AND OPINIONS: 1926-1974

Author: Allen Tate (1899-   )
Publisher: The Swallow Press (Chicago). 225 pp. $8.95
Type of work: Essays, speeches, memoirs
Time: Mid-twentieth century
Locale: The American South, Paris

A collection of essays, speeches, and memoirs which are equally divided between recollections of life with good friends and opinions of the state of literature in America

Allen Tate is a man of letters, an elder statesman of American literature, a link with controversies of the past, and a commentator on the contemporary literary scene who can speak from a perspective of long experience that few can match. In a long and distinguished career as a poet and critic, he has received most of the honors which America can bestow on its men of literature. Whatever he says or writes is therefore always of great importance; he commands our attention and respect as only those who have lived so long and have participated in so much have a right to expect. In recent years, Tate has acknowledged his position at the end of his career, at least implicitly, by engaging in projects of summing up, projects which bring together his past achievements and indicate those things which he wishes to be remembered for. The most notable of these is his recent *Essays of Four Decades* (1968), a compilation of those works of literary criticism which he feels are worthy of preservation. If the present work is a more relaxed volume, a collection of more occasional and informal pieces, it too has its rightful place in the summation of a career. In it, we get a glimpse of Tate in a reflective, remembering mood, commenting on Ernest Hemingway, Gertrude Stein,

Robert Frost, John Crowe Ransom, T. S. Eliot, and other founders, with Tate, of a distinctively modern American literature. We are asked to recall the early and exciting years of this century—the people and the events which made American literature not just the writing of a new, isolated, and provincial nation but a major literature of the world. We are also asked to remember the literature of the American past which made that mature literature possible, and to reflect on the outcome of all the hopes and dreams of that time, as they have been realized or shattered in the intervening years. To read this volume is to spend a relaxed and pleasant evening in the presence of a rare creature in our age—a great writer who is also a gentleman. If these essays do not always challenge us, if occasionally some of the controversies reviewed seem dated, they serve always to remind us of the heritage of contemporary American literary life in all its richness and diversity. For that we must be grateful to Allen Tate.

Tate's involvement in modern American literature has always been from the perspective of his Southern past. A member of the Fugitive group at Vanderbilt University from its earliest days, and later a participant in the agrarian movement and contributor to its manifesto *I'll Take My Stand,* Tate shows in this volume that the concerns of those days are still living issues for him. He reprints here his memoirs of the Fugitives ("*The Fugitive,* 1922-1925: A Personal Recollection Twenty Years After"), his tribute to John Crowe Ransom, and his essay attacking the humanism of Irving Babbitt, Norman Foerster, and Paul Elmer More ("Humanism and Naturalism"). Present in all these is a deep sense of regret at the urbanization and industrialization of the South, its remaking in the image of the conquering North, and its acceptance of the values and ways of thinking which support the abandonment of an agrarian society. Tate has opposed all these things with remarkable consistency; one can only imagine the profound regret he must feel that those processes he opposed so long ago have gone so much further than even he and his fellow agrarians could have understood or predicted in the 1920's and 1930's. Yet his more recent writing is remarkably without bitterness; the only trace of it in these pages is in his hint of annoyance with William Faulkner that Faulkner never joined with other Southern writers in a united front. An admirer of Faulkner, Tate complains that he pretended to be a farmer, and this "was not a friend of anybody who conceivably could have been his peer" ("William Faulkner: 1897-1962").

A number of the essays in this volume are reminiscences of Tate's days in Paris during the late 1920's, the time of the "Lost Generation" expatriates, when Gertrude Stein's salon was the center of life for Americans in Paris. In the light of recent celebration of the importance of the circle of Americans around Stein in the formation of modern American literature, Tate's perspective is strikingly refreshing. If Hemingway learned to write there, if American modernism was born there, Tate seems strangely untouched by it all. He remembers that he never got any of Alice B. Toklas' American cake, "not even much education"; although he admits his provinciality by wondering how Miss Stein could be a great lady without being a lady first, and is perhaps more revealing than he might intend in his confession that he spent most of his time in Paris writing a biography of Jefferson Davis, the President of the Confederacy. Tate's response to the other Americans in Paris implies a set of values which are distinctively Southern; it suggests strongly the role of the South in the United States as a unique subculture, a distinct province, as Tate describes it at one point, with its own sense of the nature of ladies and gentlemen, its own deeply ingrained view of the order of things. If the Southerner in his native clime is comfortable in his values because the culture of the region supports him in holding them, when he confronts the realities of modern life outside the South he appears as a man apart, able, as Tate does here, to see things in ways different from most of those involved.

The response of Tate and many of his fellow agrarians to the coming of industrialism in the South was to create a world of value in art, especially in poetry. In this way, if not politically, Tate and other agrarians such as John Crowe Ransom, Robert Penn Warren, and Cleanth Brooks have reshaped American thought in significant ways. What they created was a way of thinking and talking about literature, especially about poetry, which has come to be called the New Criticism. Based on a close reading of the diction, images, and ambiguities of poetic language, the New Criticism has enriched our experience of poetry in a radical way. All contemporary criticism of literature is either modeled on its approach or is a reaction against it. Tate's essays in criticism in this volume remind us once again that the New Criticism is best practiced, and best understood, by those who founded it. Essential to this approach to poetry is a sensitivity to language, to all its nuances and shadings of meaning, which Tate masterfully displays here in his readings of Robert Frost ("Robert Frost as Metaphysical Poet") and Edgar Allan Poe ("The Poetry of Edgar Allan Poe"). Also significant in this regard are Tate's memories of other founders of the New Criticism, especially John Crowe Ransom, and of that contributor to the movement, T. S. Eliot ("Homage to T. S. Eliot"). Tate, the Southerner, and Eliot, the expatriot Midwesterner, shared a sense of unease with the mainstream of twentieth century American life; both men sought in tradition and in authoritarian society and religion a sense of order and stability to serve as an antidote for the rootlessness and restlessness of much of American society. Tate's tribute to Eliot is one of the most moving pieces in this volume. His sensitivity to the private Eliot, his sense of the gulf between the public figure and the essential man, attest to the two men's deep sympathy for each other. Tate's sense of "Tom" Eliot

the man, as distinct from T. S. Eliot the public poet, anticipates, as well, recent trends in the discussion of Eliot's work.

The essays which begin and end *Memoirs and Opinions* take us from Tate's boyhood in Kentucky and Virginia to his old age, as poet laureate of the South, a resident of Sewanee, Tennessee. The first essay, entitled "A Lost Traveler's Dream," is an affectionate reminiscence of childhood and young adulthood. Largely anecdotal, it surveys Tate's discovery of his birthplace in Kentucky, years after his mother told him he was born in Virginia. Such an incident is typical; Tate's family was restless and traveled widely in search of a place in which his mother would feel comfortable—they never lived in one place more than three years. This search for a place becomes for Tate a search for identity; when he is taken to visit an ancient former slave who tells him he resembles his grandpa, he gets clues to that identity in a sense of a past. The past becomes, first, a Southern past; later it is to become a literary past. This second sense of the past, and with it, a sense of identity, is fully in the foreground of the concluding essay, "A Sequence of Stanzas Compiled and Read to a Group of Friends on My Seventy-Fifth Birthday." Tate's text in this piece is a quotation from Walter Savage Landor, in which the older poet on *his* seventy-fifth birthday proclaims his readiness for death in an appeal to nature and to art. Tate says that since 1850 man has done violence to nature; therefore, nature is not open to appeal. All that is left is art; in this mood Tate quotes from a few of his own poems before turning to ones by Edwin Muir and George Seferis. Muir makes the claim that Tate would affirm; "Love gathers all." Seferis sets the tone for what is to come; "And it is now time for us to say the few words/ we have to say/ Because tomorrow our soul sets sail." Secure in his poetic voice, secure in the faith that poetry speaks the words which can be heard and believed, Tate accepts the life that has been his and the life that is yet to be his. With this, he accepts his identity as poet, as one who says the few words that can be believed. No one can deny him his success in that role.

John N. Wall, Jr.

THE MEMOIRS OF A SURVIVOR

Author: Doris Lessing (1919-   )
Publisher: Alfred A. Knopf (New York). 213 pp. $6.95
Type of work: Novel
Time: The future
Locale: A large city

A dark, futuristic fantasy-fable about three people's struggles to survive in the nightmarish setting of an urban center which has reverted to anarchy and barbarism

Principal characters:
> THE NARRATOR, an elderly, genteel woman
> EMILY, the child mysteriously left to her guardianship
> HUGO, Emily's devoted beast
> GERALD, Emily's lover and leader of a commune of children

Memoirs of a Survivor is about the last gasp of a failed civilization. The narrator, an elderly woman, describes the scene from her window; what happens there on the pavement, in her block of flats and around the neighborhood, shows in microcosm a worldwide reversion to barbarism. The narrator herself is genteel, well off, and solitary. Her tone is calm, expository, as she describes the events of "the protracted period of unease and tension before the end." The state of things was such, she says, that normalcy was abnormal; which inversion lends plausibility to the two axes of the story: her guardianship of the girl Emily, and her adventures "beyond the wall."

Emily's arrival is unexpected and unexplained; the little girl appears in her flat, accompanied by a man who says simply, "She's your responsibility," and departs. She brings with her only her clothes and her strange animal Hugo. A pretty, healthy twelve-year-old, she foils the narrator's attempts at friendliness with a bright protective shell of cleverness and politeness. At first she is content to stay indoors with her beast and to

view the increasingly anarchic life of the street from the safety of a window. But her body, forced into hothouse bloom by the exigencies of the times, propels her out to mingle with the tribes of young people forming up to migrate into the still-unravished northwest. Her protectress fears that she will depart with one of these bands, but she chooses to stay with her animal, who must remain hidden to keep from being eaten.

Emily attaches herself to the young chieftain Gerald, leader of a band of children. She and Gerald set up housekeeping in an abandoned building and organize the children into a commune, employing considerable ingenuity in gathering and growing food, procuring clean water and other essentials, and defending their encampment. Though spending most of her time looking after her household, Emily still remains true to Hugo and her guardian, spending some hours at the flat each day.

The emergence of the "kids from the Underground" ends this idyl. A gang of very young children emerges from the subway tunnels, where they have been living on rats, and terrorize the district. Gerald persuades his group to take them in, but the kids, utterly wild, cannot grasp the idea of communal responsibility; they snatch food from the mouths of others, spread filth everywhere, tread down the garden, and generally bite the hands that feed them. The commune disbands, Emily returns home, and Gerald, obsessed by a sense of responsibility, stays with the kids from the Underground in hopes of taming and saving them.

By this time the neighborhood is virtually deserted; migrating tribes no longer form up in the vacant lots, the street markets and peddlers have vanished, the air becomes daily more foul. Emily and her protectress live alone with Hugo, waiting for the end. In the flat above lives Gerald, a prisoner of his terrible little charges. One night the kids murder a passerby, haul him upstairs, and eat him; Gerald, unstrung, wanders out into the snow and is rescued by Emily. After that, the four of them huddle together in the dark and cold, waiting.

This outward reality has its correlative "beyond the wall." Just before Emily's arrival, the narrator finds her living room wall becoming transparent, permeable; one day she actually walks through it to find herself in a set of rooms, long unused, which someone, possibly herself, is about to refurbish. She senses "a promise, which did not leave me, no matter how difficult things later became, both in my own life and in these hidden rooms." The rooms behind the wall seem to her to be her true home; the advent of Emily brings her reluctantly back to the actual world. Soon afterward she realizes

that there is a connection between the scenes behind the wall and her life with Emily; further, that these scenes are of two kinds: "personal" and "impersonal." The "personal" experiences have a characteristic atmosphere of tension, of imprisonment and constraint; in them the narrator recognizes Emily as an infant and child, her mother and father, her nurse, her younger brother. In the "impersonal" realm, a feeling of lightness and possibility prevails; though she seldom sees the same rooms twice, and though there are always problems to be solved and work to be done, she feels the near presence and approbation, and later the counsel and guidance, of a mysterious female personage.

The personal scenes reveal the tenor of Emily's childhood. The disliked and disparaged first child of an energetic and self-confident woman, she was made to bear the brunt of her mother's rebellion against maternity. Her infancy had been ruled by the clock, by custom, and by the iron strictures of her parents' characters, her mother's vivid self-absorption backed by her father's guilty neutrality. Her efforts to claim her parents' love time after time met with rebuff, so that the need to prove herself lovable and useful had grown into a passion. Thus the uncritical love of the beast Hugo and the need of Gerald and the commune children touch the deep springs of her character. And not only of Emily's character: in one episode in which a little girl is found playing with her own feces and given a tongue-lashing and a scalding bath, the narrator comes to realize that the child, whose miserable, abandoned weeping penetrates the wall, is both Emily and the hearty, self-sufficient woman who is her mother.

The impersonal realm is small at first, consisting of a finite set of rooms, but gradually expands into a kind of dream-labyrinth. The narrator sees rooms in all stages of disrepair and neglect, sumptuous rooms in which all the furnishings are slightly shopworn, empty rooms ready for repainting, rooms with broken walls and grass growing through the floor; the state of things behind the wall becomes more ruinous as real life outside the flat deteriorates. In each room she notes what needs to be done, sometimes overwhelmed by the work before her, sometimes actually accomplishing it, but always accepting without question her responsibility to cope, and always with a sense of the invisible female presence. "Very strong was the feeling that I did as I was bid and as I must; that I was being taken, was being led, was being shown, was held always in the hollow of a great hand which enclosed my life." Above all, even when things are at their most disordered in the rooms behind the wall, she feels that choice is possible, that one might repair some, or all, or throw everything out and start again. In the personal rooms, on the contrary, the smallest things, the ticks of the clock, have been elevated into law.

As time passes, the wall seems to thin, so that the narrator feels moods and urgencies from beyond it streaming through into real life. She senses a ripening, a coming to terms. Denned up with the two young people and the faithful beast, in the cold and dark at the end of the world, she waits, calm. One morning the wall opens, the hungered-for Presence beckons, and the four walk through, transfigured, into the future.

A key to this dreamlike and enigmatic climax is the set of virtues clustered under the heading of responsibility. Characters and groups stand or fall by whether or not they possess a sense of responsibility: the narrator puts aside her explorations behind the wall to accept guardianship of Emily; Gerald and Emily hold the commune together by accepting responsibility for the well-being of all. Conversely, the tribes of youths seem to have relinquished individual responsibility; the kids from the Underground seem never to have learned it. It is her sense of responsibility for the upkeep of the rooms, her desire to comfort and nurture the neglected child, that the narrator feels is most approved by the Presence behind the wall. Emily stays with Hugo because "she could not leave him without harm to herself." About the kids from the Underground, Gerald feels that "to give them up was to abandon . . . the best part of himself." Responsibility, in short, is the saving virtue, the key to the future.

But what is the future? To what place of peace and rest is this history related? Two powerful images suggest an answer. The first occurs as a scene behind the wall: a room in which a dozen people stand gazing down at a patterned carpet. The pattern is empty of color, without force; from time to time, someone applies a bit of cloth to it which fits exactly, causing that part of the carpet to come alive, at which the other people express relief and quiet pleasure. The narrator enters the room; she too extracts a piece from a jumble of rags, fits it into place, and then moves on. Unable to find this room later, she nonetheless retains a sense that the activity there continues, that its importance is enormous, not only to those engaged in it but to everyone. The second image occurs twice, and is frequently referred to: the egg as a metaphor for potential, hatching as a breaking down of constraints and imprisoning certainties. When the narrator first becomes aware of sounds from beyond the wall she puts her hand on it and feels it pulsing like an egg about to hatch. A wall that she scrubs down and paints finely reminds her of "a cleaned-out eggshell." At one point she sees Emily and her parents admiring a gigantic egg on a wide green lawn; at the end she sees the egg, blackened and pitted, suddenly open to reveal the life-metaphor, the room of the unfinished carpet. Then that too fades, leaving only the sought-for She, the apotheosis of love and care, leading onward "as the last walls dissolved."

Jan Kennedy Foster

MERCIER AND CAMIER

Author: Samuel Beckett (1906-   )
Translated from the original French by the author
Publisher: Grove Press (New York). 123 pp. $6.95
Type of work: Novel
Time: The present
Locale: A vaguely Irish city, village, and countryside

   A novel about the pain, meaninglessness, and absurdity of life

   Principal characters:
      MERCIER, a man who leaves his wife and children behind
      CAMIER, a man who leaves his job as private investigator behind

Mercier and Camier is a rarity in the field of publishing: a book that the author did *not* want published. In 1947, Samuel Beckett withdrew it from his Parisian publisher, and for twenty-four years has refused to permit its publication, claiming that it was only a working draft, an experiment in new fictional technique. In 1970, his French publishers finally convinced Beckett that he should publish an authoritative version; three years later, the author's own English translation was finally completed. The slender volume is an important and valuable addition to the Beckett canon for two reasons: it marks the shift in Beckett's writing from English to French, and it introduces the vagabond vaudevillian couple, a device which became extremely successful in later prose and dramatic work. In addition, Beckett scholars will find recurrent themes and techniques in this novel that are found in all of his major works: *Malloy, Malone Dies, The Unnamable, Waiting for Godot,* and *Endgame.* It is, however, important to remember that Beckett has never considered this novel a finished, polished literary work.

   The essence of the work defies reduction and over-simplification in either plot or theme, but its basic vision of the human condition is constant. Life is presented as a journey or as waiting. The narrator of *Mercier and Camier* makes it clear in the first paragraph that this journey will not be the heroic and successful Grail Quest of a medieval knight, nor even the journey of an adventurer such as Gulliver or Robinson Crusoe; he details all the dangers and sufferings that the two protagonists will *not* have to meet. In addition, their goal is obscure: the Grail has vanished, is no longer remembered; rituals as well as heroes have been reduced to insignificance. Only the traditional wasteland of the quest remains, in the form of labyrinths and mazes of cities, empty fields, bogs, and ruins. Man as heroic Knight Errant, as adventurer-explorer, has here given way to man as nonheroic, unpretentious tramp-wanderer, stripped not only of glory, but of most of his humanity. Mercier and Camier, like other Beckett "heroes," stumble along as pathetic, almost transparent nonbeings; their journey is predestined to failure. The reader realizes that they will not progress, but will instead pursue their certain circular path until it is interrupted finally by insanity, suicide, or anguishing despair and *ennui.* This disintegrated condition of man and of his quest underlies the majority of Beckett's major work.

As Mercier and Camier proceed on their intermittent, often delayed journey toward their unknown goal, the reader encounters more of the familiar Beckett themes. The two main characters find themselves progressively alienated from society, God, nature, and even from the basic necessities of life—possessions, clothes, food, sex—and finally from each other. Their alienation from society is evident as Mercier abandons his wife and family, blaming himself for participating in his children's conception, and Camier destroys all that connects him with his job in society. Most dramatically, they seal their separation from society by brutally beating a policeman to death. Their alienation from God and nature is equally clear. Early in the novel, Mercier curses God; nature itself is hostile to them, as the almost continual rain, wind, and darkness disheartens them, making their journey more difficult. When they do leave the city for the countryside, they find only fields and hedges that all seem the same, or the desolation of bogs and ruins, landscapes with nothing to offer man except a place to die.

Typically, Beckett reduces the necessities of his heroes to the bare minimum. Mercier and Camier have only a few essentials: a rucksack, an umbrella, a bicycle, and a raincoat; before leaving the city, they lose all but the latter, which they abandon as useless. Later, in a vague hope that their lost possessions might be important, they return to the city only to discover them useless or irrevocably lost. Functions such as eating and sex are also stripped to the minimum: food becomes an occasional snack, while sex is reduced to the level of the mechanical copulation of the dogs in the first scene.

In the midst of this alienation, Mercier and Camier still have the consolation of each other's friendship, although, like Didi and Gogo, it is a blend of love and recoil. Because of a failure of communication at first, they almost never get together. When they separate for an afternoon, Camier realizes that he basically dreads Mercier's return and the burden of friendship. As they leave on their last journey, their isolation from each other is emphasized as each one walks on the far side of the road from the other. Only when physical and mental strength vanish and touching is necessary for survival do they go arm in arm. But a final breakdown in communication occurs the next morning, and, without speaking, with Chaplinesque courtesy, each bids farewell to the other, as they go their way in total alienation. Their quest to escape loneliness, meaninglessness, and darkness, has been in vain.

The total meaninglessness and pain and absurdity of life is stated many times. "One does what one can, but one can do nothing. Only squirm and wriggle, to end up in the evening where you were in the morning." Suicide seems, at first, a desirable solution; accidental death, even more appealing. However, Mercier later states that they might as well accept "this preposterous penalty and placidly await the executioner." Beckett's nonheroes face the existentialist position, but they refuse to impose meaning on it, realizing that to do so would only be to impose a known fiction upon chaos.

Technically, *Mercier and Camier* is an interesting experiment. Beckett here works out the dialogue form which is used so successfully in *Waiting for Godot,* using puns, rhythm, *non sequiturs,* and vaudeville routines between the heroes to create warmth, humor, and humanity. Traditional elements of the novel—character, setting, clock time, causal plot—all disintegrate as this story moves on. Beckett also establishes the device of resurrecting "heroes" from other works, as in the case of the appearance of Watt in the concluding scenes. Experimentally most interesting is Beckett's use of the narrator to underscore themes of the journey. The narrator fluctuates between an objective yet sympathetic view of his main characters, and a stance of ironic detachment. Likewise, Beckett's use of plot structure and setting follows a similar course. Structurally, the interspersing of short summaries of the action after every two chapters serves to mock that "action," while the many fragmented references only serve to emphasize

the triviality of what has occurred. Just as time in the heroes' lives is wasted, so repetitious and irrelevant incidents in the plot accumulate.

In addition, Beckett creates a sense of fragmentation by having the narrator alienate the reader from characters such as the policeman, and even Mercier and Camier, and dropping constant reminders that the heroes' world is artificial rather than real. This occurs most forcefully in the conversation between Mercier and Camier in which they declare that it would take two fat volumes apiece to recount their lives. Beckett's narrator thus ironically undercuts his own tale, which recounts *both* their adventures in a padded 123 pages. Neither characters nor narrator know where they are headed; Beckett refuses to control or guide them as an omniscient author, to consider them as real human beings. Their predicament is thus parallel to the situation, as the author sees it, of man in this world: that of a lost creature deprived of his belief in an all-knowing God who orders and makes meaningful his life and universe.

Ann E. Reynolds

THE MESSAGE IN THE BOTTLE

Author: Walker Percy (1916-   )
Publisher: Farrar, Straus and Giroux (New York). 352 pp. $8.95
Type of work: Essays
  "An attempt to sketch the beginnings of a theory of man for a new age" based on his language-making capacities

Walker Percy, author of three fine and important novels (*The Moviegoer,* 1961; *The Last Gentleman,* 1966; *Love in the Ruins,* 1971), has compiled a deeply serious collection of personal essays with an apparently flip title: *The Message in the Bottle: How Queer Man Is, How Queer Language Is, and What One Has to Do with the Other.* But the title contains the substance of the book.

Percy begins by talking about the "queerness" of man, especially modern man, and the fact that, despite the mass of data available, there is no coherent theory to explain that queerness. The first five pages of the book are devoted to a series of provocative questions which culminates with this query:

> What does a man do when he finds himself living after an age has ended and he can no longer understand himself because the theories of man of the former age no longer work and the theories of the new age are not yet known, for not even the name of the new age is known, and so everything is upside down, people feeling bad when they should feel good, good when they should feel bad?

Although hardly a modest collection, Percy does not claim to answer all these questions. He does, however, posit a theory which he likens to "the sort of crude guess a visitor from Mars might make if he landed on earth and spent a year observing man and the beasts." His theory has surprising unity and coherence considering that the book is actually a gathering of essays written over a twenty-year span and previously printed in such wide-ranging publications as the *Sewanee Review, Psychiatry, The New Scholasticism,* and *Philosophy and Phenomenological Research.* Ideally, *The Message in the Bottle* should be reviewed by a committee made up of a literary critic, existentialist philosopher, M.D., ethnologist, behaviorist, Jungian analyst, semiologist, psycholinguist, and theologian, so diverse are the points of view of its essays.

Actually, it is appropriate that the book be reviewed by an amateur, since Percy emphatically claims that label for himself without apology or irony. Taking Webster's first definition of an amateur as "a person who does something for the pleasure of it," the label fits. Percy's self-designation also implies an assumption about "experts" that runs through all of the essays: "language is too important to be left to the linguisticians," the mind to the psychiatrists, religion to the theologians, and so on. All such "professionals" are partisans, advocates of parochial views with built-in prejudices, inconsistencies, and blind spots. Morevoer, one of the reasons for contemporary man's dilemma is that he has conceded these vital areas to the professionals and accepted their dogmatic judgments on faith.

The "amateur" has the fresh view and disinterested posture that is necessary if a new synthesis is to be found; that is the rationale behind Percy's identification of himself as a "Martian." "One must be a Martian or a survivor poking among the ruins to see how extremely odd the people were who lived there."

But lest the title of the book and use of terms like "amateur" and "Martian" suggest a casualness or superficiality in these essays, let the reader be warned: *The Message in the Bottle* is an extremely difficult, sometimes abstract, sometimes technical, frequently abstruse set of essays that get more difficult as the book goes along. Amateur or not, Percy has read deeply, widely, and thoroughly in the literature of all the disciplines he treats, and he spares the reader not at all. He meets the experts in their own territories with their own weapons and battles them at least even; the dilettante will be lost a good deal of the time. Percy himself has no illusions about the general appeal of his rhetoric:

> Most readers will not want to read all chapters. It is hard, for example, to imagine anyone at all at the present time who would want to read the last. Only after writing it did it occur to me that it had, for the moment at least, no readership whatever.

So why bother? Because Percy has asked the most fundamental questions, asserted himself against the most important dogmas of his time, and suggested approaches to these problems in most of his essays that can be pondered to great benefit by any sensitive, intelligent person willing to make the effort. The more technical and foreboding essays need not put off the willing reader, since Percy's message is stated with precision and density in the first two-thirds of the book.

In the first essay, "The Delta Factor," Percy singles out language as the distinctive human trait upon which to build his theory—but not language as it is usually thought of and studied. Of all human activities, Percy believes, the use of language is the least understood and most misrepresented, despite all the volumes written on the subject. To the author, language is neither a static, objective entity to be described (the linguistic theorists) nor a psycho-physiological process to be tested (the behaviorists); it is a distinctively human act and its importance lies in that fact. "So the book is not about language but about the creatures who use it and what happens when they do."

Since Percy's fascination with language as act leads him to a new philosophical vision, he proposes this approach to the reader: "Instead of starting out with such large vexed subjects as soul, mind, ideas, consciousness, why not begin with language, which no one denies, and see how far it takes us toward the rest?" Where it ultimately takes us is to a theory of language which does not actually *explain* the phenomenon, but which suggests that it is an attribute which confirms man's identity as a unique creature in a God-centered universe. To understand the development of this view it is necessary to look at Percy's philosophical and religious underpinnings.

Two unusual facets of Percy's personality—unusual for a contemporary American novelist, at least—have shaped his thinking: he is a believing Catholic and a trained scientist (an M.D.). It greatly oversimplifies Percy's view of language to say that he considers it a divine gift, although that implication is central to the essays. His scientific training has given him, on the one hand, a hard-headed empiricism, but on the other, a solid awareness of the limits of science; he sees inflated claims for science as a central factor in man's present confusion and loss of meaning. As a scientist he wants an objective, empirically valid explanation for the phenomenon of language; as a Christian he expects that theory to confirm the uniqueness of man and his divine connections.

His theory provides such a confirmation by resolving the intellectual paradoxes evident in man's current view of himself and the bizarre contradictions between his beliefs and his actions. In "The Delta Factor" Percy points out the incompatability between the scientific notion of man as "an organism in an environment . . . endowed genetically like other organisms with needs and drives, who through evolution has developed strategies for learning and surviving," and the religious view that he is "somehow endowed with certain other unique properties which he does not share with other organisms—with certain inalienable rights, reason, freedom, and an intrinsic dignity." The result of this the author describes with the popular catch-all phrase "alienation," although he gives the term a very personal definition in the course of his essays. "A theory of man must account for the alienation

of man," he concludes. "A theory of organisms in environments cannot account for it, for in fact organisms in environments are not alienated."

Percy's answer, which he labels the "Delta Factor" in this essay, came to him almost like a religious revelation. He recounts the time when, reading about Helen Keller's first symbolic use of language, he realized suddenly that her experience was a microcosm of the dawning of human intelligence. One morning in 1887, as Miss Sullivan poured water into one of Helen's hands and wrote the word on the other, the girl suddenly made the connection between the two, and began to name everything in her environment.

> . . . . Eight-year-old Helen made her breakthrough from the good responding animal which behaviorists study so successfully to the strange name-giving and sentence-uttering creature who begins by naming shoes and ships and sealing wax, and later tells jokes, curses, reads the paper, writes *La sua volontade e nostra pace,* or becomes a Hegel and composes an entire system of philosophy.

This naming process, man's capacity to symbolize, this mysterious ability to make connections, Percy insists cannot be explained behavioristically or linguistically or in any other way: the "Delta Factor" is a unique, spontaneous capacity that accounts both for man's special place in the world and for his feelings of alienation from it.

In "The Loss of the Creature," Percy shows how modern society, particularly through education, has contributed to this alienation by telling the individual what a thing ought to be like and what his proper response to it should be, thus depriving him of the authentic experience ("the thing is lost through its packaging"). Scientific theory then disposes of the object by turning it into a "specimen" rather than an autonomous, particular thing. He describes various literary approaches to alienation in "The Man on the Train," but ultimately suggests that the problem is not aesthetic, scientific, or cultural; it is religious. And in the Christian view of man, the condition of alienation is the essential human situation.

But orthodox religious belief has dissipated, he concedes; its "vocabulary is worn out," he laments in "Notes for a Novel About the End of the World" (written three years prior to *Love in the Ruins*). The vague possibility of a rejuvenation through language is sketched brilliantly in "The Message in the Bottle," the title essay; and in "The Mystery of Language," a deceptively short and mild introduction to the dense, technical discussion of lan-guage that makes up the latter part of the book, Percy returns to his central theme.

These last essays, bearing such foreboding titles as "Culture: The Antinomy of the Scientific Method" and "Symbol as Hermeneutic in Existentialism," are actually extended technical footnotes which define and elaborate on the assumptions and analyses of the central essays. Readers with the interest and expertise will find them fascinating and/or irritating. But the substance of Percy's message—with all of its religious connotations—is found in the first essay, "The Delta Factor," and expanded in "The Message in the Bottle." In the last essays Percy is the psychologist-semiologist-existentialist-linguist gadfly challenging the experts; in the earlier essays he brings to bear all of his formidable skills both as a thinker and also as a novelist in order to present a most compelling and provocative discussion of modern man's condition.

Keith Neilson

MINAMATA

Authors: W. Eugene Smith (1918-   ) and Aileen M. Smith
Publisher: Holt, Rinehart and Winston (New York). 192 pp. $20.00
Type of work: Photographic journalism
Time: 1956 to the present
Locale: Japan and Canada

A report, through pictures and words, of the devastating effects industrial pollution has had on the life and people of Minamata, Japan

Principal personages:
    W. EUGENE SMITH and
    AILEEN M. SMITH, journalists personally involved in the tragedy
        of Chisso-Minamata Disease
    KENICHI SHIMADA, President of Chisso Corporation
    TERUO KAWAMOTO, leader of the victims
    DR. HAJIME HOSOKAWA, Chisso physician who discovered the
        cause of Chisso-Minamata Disease and failed to treat it
    SHINOBU SAKAMOTO, retarded victim of the disease

For centuries Minamata had been a rural fishing and farming area on the isolated southern Japanese island of Kyushu. Little change had ever come to this area until 1907 when Chisso Corporation built a chemical factory on a bluff overlooking Minamata Bay. By 1925 the Bay was foamy, clouded with industrial waste products, and local fishing had seriously deteriorated. Chisso began paying token hush money to the more vocal protesting fishermen. In 1932 Chisso's Minamata plant began producing acetaldehyde, a synthetic substance used in making plastics, drugs, perfumes, and photographic chemicals. Pollution and boom times continued for Chisso and Minamata even through World War II. In the early 1950's Chisso turned their now outmoded Minamata plant into an almost total production of acetaldehyde, even more important now because of the huge postwar demand for plastics. Fishing continued to erode, but employment in the area was high. Minamata's population had reached fifty thousand.

In April, 1956, a five-year-old girl entered the pediatrics ward of Chisso's Minamata factory hospital. She could not walk; her speech was incoherent; she was delirious, severely disoriented. Doctors puzzled at the lack of either high fever or injury, their surprise increasing a day later when the child's two-year-old sister entered the hospital with these same symptoms of profound damage to the central nervous system. The mother of these two girls revealed that a neighbor child also had the same symptoms. A team of hospital investigators dispatched to this family's locale immediately found two more children and one adult with the same symptoms. Within the next month the number of people similarly afflicted increased steadily. Perhaps it was mere coincidence that virtually all cats had disappeared, the team noted, many dying in violent "suicides" or a "dance of death."

By the end of 1956, Dr. Hajimé Hosokawa of Chisso Company Hospital knew he had an epidemic on his hands, but he also had discovered that the disease was not contagious. He realized that the outbreak of this mysterious disease was related to the fish diet of people in Minamata, and this, in turn, threw suspicion on his employers who had been dumping chemicals into Minamata Bay for generations. Under no legal indictment but under considerable public pressure, in 1958 Chisso temporarily shifted their waste spill-off to a delta on the other side of town. The dumpage now passed near a district called Hachiman whose people, in a few months, began developing symptoms of the sickness. By now, as Dr. Hosokawa knew, outside scientific investigations were pointing to organic mercury as the causative agent, the mercury so necessary as a catalyst to produce the profitable Chisso acetaldehyde. In October, 1959, Dr. Hosokawa proved Chisso's guilt to Chisso's management. He injected acetaldehyde effluent directly into "cat number 400," and all could observe the animal's disorientation, shrieking, and final convulsion. The numbers of people suffering from the disease continued to increase steadily. Some died, but most lived on as their minds grew dim, their muscles atrophied, and their bones became cripplingly arthritic. Families prayed for and cared for their victims. No one recovered.

What soon came to be known as Chisso-Minamata Disease had devastating effects upon its victims. Symptoms began with a numbness in the extremities, tremors, difficulty in fine motor coordination (writing, holding chopsticks), increasing inability to speak or walk, and eventually paralysis and deformation. Pathological tests revealed cellular deterioration of the cerebellum, lesions throughout the cerebral cortex, and unregenerative eroding of peripheral nerve fibers. In the early 1960's a congenital strain of the disease was established. The poisonous mercury had become organic (absorbable in human tissue) by being "methylated" in the acetaldehyde process. The sludge which poisoned people and cats was methyl-mercury chloride, a chemical capable of passing through a mother's placenta or into her breast milk. Thus, an apparently healthy woman could become a carrier of Chisso-Minamata Disease. The congenital victims from birth demonstrated physiological symptoms associated with cerebral palsy. In addition to the C. P. symptoms, severe mental retardation was always present. With medical and pharmaceutical treatment virtually useless, rehabilitative programs on an individual basis became mandatory.

By late 1959, the Chisso Corporation realized that they were responsible for the world's first widespread methyl-mercury poisoning caused by man-made environmental pollution. Chisso's response to this appalling, possibly cataclysmic, fact was contradictory. President Kenichi Shimada was openly sympathetic toward the victims, visiting their homes for prayer and consultation, keeping an open door policy for journalists, researchers, and angered victims and their families. In December of 1959 he installed a cyclator, a treatment center to purify waste water. He negotiated a contract of *mimai* (consolation), a form of payment to the victims. He joined the government in establishing special rehabilitation services, especially for the children.

These actions represented Chisso's recognition of a moral responsibility, but they showed little legal or financial culpability, which the victims of Minamata and their champions came to demand. President Shimada worked with the government to prevent further research into the origins of the disease. When the cyclator proved ineffective in containing methyl-mercury chloride, no new attempts were made to prevent pollution which continued spewing into Minamata Bay. The Fisherman's Union, angered at the virtual disappearance of their trade, stormed the factory, but settled for meager payments and no cleanup. For a time, this seemed, if not enough compensation, all anyone would ever receive. Even today, according to the Smiths, most Minamata citizens side with Chisso, regarding the company as a victim of history which not only greatly raised the area's standard of living but provided assistance to the five percent of the population it had hideously, although inadvertently, maimed.

Minamata, however, was not a self-contained tragedy. In 1965 a similar outbreak of mercury poisoning occurred in another part of Japan, the prefecture of Niigata. These victims took their poisoner, Showa Denko Chemical Company, to court and won compensation in five figures for each appellant. Minamata took heed. Two groups formed: the trial group (pre-1959 patients) and the explosive "direct negotiations" group, headed by new victim Teruo Kawamoto, a remarkably effective organizer who believed in head-on confrontation with the Chisso management. Joined by the Smiths and numerous others, Kawamoto's group put relentless pressure on Chisso and governmental agencies for action. Meetings and counter-meetings, charges and counter-charges, sit-ins and demonstrations were the order of the day for years. Kawamoto refused to give up, despite violence occurring on several occasions. Chisso installed iron bars at the entrance of their Tokyo offices. In the Goi incident, many victims and supporters were brutally beaten, including Eugene Smith, who was permanently disabled. Kimito Iwamoto slashed his wrists on a negotiation table in front of President Shimada. The victims' persistence, the wrist slashing, and Dr. Hosokawa's incriminating death-bed testimony resulted in a judgment by Japan's Central Pollution Board in April, 1973. $68,000 would be awarded to "heavy" cases and $60,000 awarded to "lighter" cases. By January, 1975, Chisso had paid indemnities totaling more than eighty million dollars.

This story is indeed a terrifying and moving one, and no one should be better able to render it than the Smiths. W. Eugene Smith is one of the most respected and courageous photojournalists alive. He suffered severe shrapnel wounds in Okinawa for his insistence on following American infantrymen into battle to record their lives in photographs. His "The Walk to Paradise Garden" became the famous conclusion to the Family of Man exhibit at the Museum of Modern Art. For *Life* magazine he created a series of monumental photographic essays, including the much-reprinted studies of a Spanish village and of Albert Schweitzer. He has received three Guggenheim Fellowships and a prestigious award from the National Endowment of the Arts. His photoessays have led to the building of a nursing clinic and to the rebuilding of what was, to all intents and purposes, no better than a concentration camp. Aileen Smith has often been the indispensable partner in her husband's creative work, but never more so than with *Minamata*. Born in Tokyo, Mrs. Smith speaks and writes fluent Japanese. She made many textual notes from which the book was written, and took about one-fourth of the published photographs. Their collaboration contains a good deal of patient, careful research and compassionate, personal involvement.

Almost without exception, the photographs are outstanding. Posed, gimmick shots or cheap melodramatic close-ups are avoided in favor of vérité scenes of places and real people in action. The Smiths portray in very able fashion a tragic story's unfolding, and the often captionless prints bear close study. Subtle themes emerge from these exclusively black and white photographs—the smiles of courage, not self-pity, or the motionless bodies seated or prone, for example. The clasped, manicured but tense hands of President Shimada are juxtaposed with the stained, gnarled, and horny fingers of the victims. This is no documentary scrapbook of a disaster. Rather, the Smiths use photojournalism to create a detailed and sensitive moral statement in *Minamata*.

The book interrelates two distinct aspects of the Chisso-Minamata tragedy. First is the public aspect, an in-depth treatment of the origins and causes of the poisoning and an account of the subsequent legal battles and their outcome. Second is the private aspect, a series of personal and family accounts of what the victims did, how they felt, how they coped, and how they looked. The longest and perhaps most representative photojournalistic essay portrays Shinobu, a congenital victim. The photographs are penetrating, often exquisite, examples of a powerful understatement that captures in facial expression, body language, and activity, the character of a young woman who has accepted, even triumphed, over what she must endure. Aileen Smith writes of being powerfully affected:

> When I first met Shinobu she was fifteen. She moved with difficulty and could not even add four plus five, but she is so beautifully lyrical, with an intuitive humor. Strangely, I feel a soft comfort when she is present.

This tone of sacrality or hallowed awe toward the victims betrays the central weakness of this book: the text is at odds with the photographs. In the Prologue, W. Eugene Smith's first words are: "This is not an objective book." True enough. While guilt and sympathy pervade the text, silently inviting comparison with such other devastations as Hiroshima and Nagasaki, one wonders what the book's goals are intended to be. With persistence the victims received more money, but $68,000 is hardly compensation for such a tragedy. The photographs indicate that the victims see themselves as neither celebrities nor pariahs, but ordinary people who could use some special rehabilitation services rather than any special rescue from a hideous oppressor. The financial awards seem more a curse than a blessing to many. Chisso Corporation is clearly the villain, but the eighty million dollars in retribution has not sent them spinning into bankruptcy, and they continue to manufacture acetaldehyde and pollute the Bay, although the government has stopped all fishing there.

Through a sense of fighting the good fight, the Smiths move from Minamata to a location in Canada with potential for a similar tragedy. The message of impending worldwide disaster from industrial mercury poisoning would have been more powerful with more examples, which do exist. The disease itself remains perplexing, the situation still "un-clear," according to Dr. Masazumi Harada, who wrote an informative medical analysis for the Appendix in *Minamata*. The poisoning should have most affected those who ate the most fish, but while the Smiths' text implies this, the medical report holds no such simple answer. Thus, while the prose cries out for order, responsibility, and justice, the photographs and the facts portray the actions of an amoral, hostile fate, the true heroism being demonstrated by families who worked together, day after day, year after year, in the care and service of their stricken loved ones.

Patrick Morrow

MONEY: WHENCE IT CAME, WHERE IT WENT

Author: John Kenneth Galbraith (1908-   )
Publisher: Houghton Mifflin Company (Boston). 324 pp. $10.00
Type of work: Economic history
Time: Antiquity to the present, with a concentration on the period since 1600
Locale: Europe and the United States

An analytical survey of the history of money, banking, and financial systems and the impact which they have had on the modern world

John Kenneth Galbraith has had a long and distinguished career both as a scholar and as a public servant. For many years Paul M. Warburg Professor of Economics at Harvard University, Galbraith is a past president of the American Economic Association and a former Ambassador to India; during World War II he served as price controller in the Office of Price Administration. As the result of his vast experience in government and academe, he has written several major books, the latest of which is *Money: Whence It Came, Where It Went.*

Although this book deals with the history of money, it is primarily concerned, as Galbraith points out, with the lessons of history. "Its purpose," he writes, "is didactic and expository, less in relation to the past than to the present." Galbraith, accordingly, does not explain the nature of money by studying the logic of past and present institutions; on the contrary, he uses the evolutionary approach in an effort to explain how these institutions came to be the way they are. In keeping with this approach, Galbraith is highly selective in the subjects which he covers to illustrate the historical evolution of money as a medium of exchange. Concentrating mainly on the period since 1600, the author devotes several chapters to such topics as the development of paper money, the several panics in nineteenth century America, the Federal Reserve System, and Keynesian economics. Galbraith writes his book with the conviction that there is nothing about money which a person of reasonable intelligence cannot understand. He decries the fact that much of the discussion about money "involves a heavy overlay of priestly incantation," some of which is deliberate. Since money is equally important to those who have it and those who do not, both groups, Galbraith asserts, should have a concern for understanding the subject and should proceed with full confidence that they can do so. Galbraith's book is intended to strengthen this confidence, and to a major extent it succeeds.

Chronologically, Galbraith's book is roughly divisible into four sections. In the first, the author examines the historical foundations of a monied economy; that is, coinage, banks, and paper money, from ancient times through the American and French Revolutions. He then moves to an analysis of money and banking in nineteenth century America. In the third section, he devotes more than half of the book to monetary and economic problems in twentieth century Europe and America. He closes his study with a chapter on prospects for the future of money management. Within this loose chronological framework, however, Galbraith frequently develops comparisons between similar developments in different eras—for example, the importance of paper money in the success of the American, French, and Russian Revolutions. Hence, despite the vastness of his subject, the author manages to weave effectively his major topical interests into a smooth, meaningful synthesis.

In examining the historical foundations of a monied economy, Galbraith observes that for all practical purposes, throughout most of time, money has been more or less a precious metal. The earliest known division of gold and silver into coins of predetermined weight is attributed by the Greek historian Herodotus to the kings of Lydia, about the latter part of the eighth century B.C. Coinage spread throughout the Mediterranean world, and in ancient and medieval times, Galbraith writes, the coins of different realms converged at the major trading cities. The tendency on the part of tradesmen to circulate adulterated or otherwise debased coins while retaining the good ones inspired Sir Thomas Gresham's enduring observation in 1558 that bad money always drives out good. To deal with his problem as well as with the great influx of precious metals from Spanish America, the Dutch in 1609 founded the Bank of Amsterdam, an institution which Galbraith describes as the first notable public bank. Another important central bank, the Bank of England, was founded in 1694, and by the middle of the following century stood as the guardian of the money supply as well

as the financial concerns of the British government. Galbraith describes how during this same period several American colonies authorized their own banking institutions and inaugurated the modern use in the West of paper money in lieu of hard coin to pay off their debts. Parliament, fearing these monetary experiments, terminated them by the middle of the eighteenth century. Once the American Revolution was under way, however, the Continental Congress and several of the states authorized note issues. It was by these notes, Galbraith observes, that the American Revolution was financed. He goes on to show how, in similar fashion, the French and the Russians financed their respective revolutions through the use of paper money.

Galbraith's penetrating analysis of money and banking in nineteenth century America is of particular interest as it shows how the new nation coped—and as often failed to cope —with major monetary problems. These problems included the struggle between the proponents of a central Bank of the United States and those who supported state banks, the proliferation of a multiplicity of state bank notes during the middle third of the century, the free-silver issue, and the various panics which occurred at approximately twenty-year intervals between 1819 and 1907.

The panic of 1907 inspired the establishment in 1913 of the Federal Reserve System, toward which the author levels considerable criticism. Designed to remedy defects in the inelastic National Banking System which had existed since the Civil War, the Federal Reserve System, in Galbraith's opinion, created more problems than it solved. Interestingly, he points out that in the twenty years before the founding of the system there were 1,748 suspensions, while in the twenty years after it ended the anarchy of unreliable private banking, there were 15,502 failures. Galbraith also holds Federal Reserve policy in the 1920's responsible for much of the severity of the Great Depression which began in 1929.

In dealing with monetary and economic problems in Europe and America after 1914, Galbraith is primarily concerned with the shattering impact of the two world wars and the Great Depression on the fiscal stability of countries large and small. His chapter "Ultimate Inflation" is especially valuable as it explains the nature of the great inflationary spiral which occurred after World War I. The most significant result historically of the German inflation was that it left the German people with a grave fear that it would recur. Observing that in the history of money the strongest action is generally taken against inflation when it is least needed, Galbraith regards the action of the German government in 1931 of reducing wages and increasing taxes as being a contributing factor in the rise to power of Adolf Hitler two years later. Subsequently, Hitler's unsuccessful war left his country and Europe in the throes of economic and fiscal collapse. One of the major steps in restoring order to international monetary arrangements was the establishment at the Bretton Woods Conference in July, 1944, of the International Monetary Fund and a companion organization, the International Bank for Reconstruction and Development. The prime mover, writes

Galbraith, in the Bretton Woods design was John Maynard Keynes, the foremost British economic and financial expert, for whom the author reserves considerable praise throughout his book.

Galbraith, in assessing the thirty years following the end of World War II, observes that the good years of economic management in the United States came to an end in the late 1960's with the escalation of the Vietnam War. Wartime spending and resulting demand sent prices upward. "With American failure," notes the author, "came world failure," for in all major industrialized countries from the late 1960's on, prices soared upward because of increased demand and higher wage claims. The inflationary spiral thus unleashed remains a problem in the middle 1970's. Looking to the future in the last chapter of *Money: Whence It Came, Where It Went,* Galbraith expresses the hope that the caretakers of the American economy will more realistically accommodate themselves to problems that exist at a given moment of time instead of falling back on the useless expedient of trying to make better economic forecasts. Only through such vigorous leadership, in Galbraith's view, can America hope to solve its pressing economic and fiscal problems.

Galbraith's book is a thoroughly absorbing introduction to many of the economic currents which have helped to shape the history of the modern West. Writing in his usual contentious and witty style, the author enlivens a subject that tends to be dull and boring. Galbraith excels in putting across the lesson to his reader that down through the ages, the so-called experts who have largely determined monetary actions have rarely known what they were doing. If he is at times overly opinionated and ideological in dealing with such complex subjects as Keynesian fiscal theory, the author accomplishes his stated objective of providing the non-specialist with an overview of a subject generally regarded by most people as beyond their comprehension. The general reader will thus come away from this book with a greater understanding of those economic and financial institutions which so vitally influence his own daily life.

Edward P. Keleher

A MONTH OF SUNDAYS

Author: John Updike (1932-   )
Publisher: Alfred A. Knopf (New York). 228 pp. $6.95
Type of work: Novel
Time: The present
Locale: A resort in the American desert

A first-person account of a clergyman's encounter with his mid-life crisis and the American sexual revolution

Principal characters:

> THE REVEREND THOMAS MARSHFIELD, a forty-one-year-old clergyman
> JANE MARSHFIELD, his wife
> NED BORK, his curate
> ALICIA CRICK, his first mistress and organist of his church, who is also having an affair with his neighbor
> FRANKIE HARLOW, his second mistress
> MS. PRYNNE, the manager of the resort

Christians have been going to the desert to escape the temptations of life in the world since the earliest days of the Christian era. The Reverend Thomas Marshfield's sojourn of one month in the desert is therefore in the mainstream of Christian tradition, differing only in the fact that it is an enforced vacation, a retreat ordered by his bishop "as the alternative to the frolicsome rite of defrocking," as Marshfield puts it. Updike has had his fun with American sexual myths before, in *Couples,* and with the Episcopal priesthood, in *Rabbit, Run.* Here, he puts his interest in the American pursuit of salvation through adultery together with his concern for the state of the clergy; the result is a novel both delightfully funny and remarkably moving. Updike has the layman's fascination with the ordained ministry; happy on the one hand to point out its problems, he is also eager to show us how well he could do if he could change sides of the pulpit. Updike has for a long time been devoted to a Barthian concept of the Word; *A Month of Sundays* begins to acknowledge the value of the Word-made-flesh, of a more sacramental view of the relationship between God and man.

The novel consists of Marshfield's reflections during his thirty-one days of retreat at a motel in the desert. As part of the retreat, he is required to write during the morning hours each day; the afternoons are devoted to golf, tennis, swimming, and the like, while the evenings are spent at poker and drinking with the other clergy who have been sent by their ecclesiastical superiors because they, too, for various reasons, are having trouble living as clergy in the modern world. Thus, the book contains thirty-one chapters, divided into four sections by the four sermons Marshfield writes on the Sundays of the month, with a fifth and final section taking him from the last Sunday to the day of leavetaking. The contents of Marshfield's chapters include a retelling of his life, especially the events which led up to his temporary, but forced, exile, and his reflections on the significance of his stay in the desert.

The figure of the lascivious clergyman has been with us always, or at least since Chaucer's Friar. Appropriately, Updike's Marshfield finds his life filled with allusions to that other great American tale of the adulterous clergyman, Hawthorne's *The Scarlet Letter.* It is inevitable that his wife's maiden name was Chillingworth, and that the woman who runs the retreat is named Ms. Prynne. Isolated against his will for acts he considers only expressions of his human nature, and without Bible or other reading matter more serious than detective stories, Marshfield is left with only the ironies of his situation and with words themselves. As a result, his productions are filled with wit, with wordplay, and with an increasingly moving sense of the need all men share to know and be known, to love and be loved. Updike has always built his novels on the clichés of popular psychology: *Couples* explored the claims put forward for the "post-pill paradise," while *Rabbit Redux* examined the black-white encounter, the cult of youth, and the impact of the moon landings. In *A Month of Sundays,* he takes up the male mid-life crisis, but as in all his works it is the essential humanity of his erring characters which for the reader transcends their all-too-obvious failings and makes them forgivable in the profoundest Christian sense.

Because the four sermons Marshfield writes divide the book into convenient sections, as well as mark his progress toward a new understanding of himself, they provide a convenient perspective from which to look at the book as a whole. The first sermon comes on day six of Marshfield's enforced exile; in it he combines Christ's forgiveness of the woman taken in adultery with his strictness on divorce to argue that while marriage is a given, adultery is inevitable and should be rejoiced in as a sign of paradise in the hell of earthly union. This sermon follows a series of essays in which Marshfield describes the beginnings of his affair with Alicia Crick (inevitably, in the punny world of this novel, the organist of Marshfield's church). We learn that he grew up with an asexual clergyman-father, and that his affair came as a great release for him, a confrontation with his "sexual demon," a rediscovery of childlike play, an affirmation of his worth in the eyes of another human being. He gives us a striking image of himself as half white, half black—a good side, accepted by God, and a bad side, consisting of most of his humanity, unloved by the God he preached. Seen from this angle, his affair reclaims a small, but important, bit of the bad side by enabling him to find good in it and love it. In this context, his sermon affirming adultery is an affirmation of the divine acceptance of the humanness of his creation. He ends with an image of Christ as the divine fool, dancing in the light of the eternal sun, giving variety and life to a monochromatic and deadly dull universe.

But that is not the whole picture, and the rest of the novel fills in the balance of the story. The second sermon, on the thirteenth day of his exile, ends on a much more depressing note. Its subject is Christ's miracles, which Marshfield sees as signs of Christ's faith, a faith which comes as judgment to us who cannot muster it. Christ again appears as the fool, the Charlie Chaplin figure, who acts for some and not for others, in a seemingly capricious way. That all our problems are not solved through divine intervention makes us angry, yet Christ goes on, showing that the purpose of His miracles is demonstration, not alleviation. We pray for miracles, and yet none come; we lack the faith that moves mountains. Marshfield's conclusion is that we are damned; he curses his congregation and bids them rot in their faithlessness.

The source of this despair is the preceding week's reflections, which take Marshfield through his courtship of his wife, the daughter of his seminary ethics professor, and the increasingly dull years of their marriage, to his attempts to legitimize his affair with Alicia by encouraging his wife to have an affair with Bork, his curate. We learn of his conflicts with Bork, who is a young man involved in ministry to the drug culture, and who, worst of all, is a student of Tillich and liberal theology. To make matters worse, Marshfield is beginning to consider an affair with Frankie Harlow, the wife of a parishioner. And, more than that, while Alicia is putting on the pressure for him to break with his wife, she has also begun an affair with Bork, who lives next door to Marshfield. Her car parked in Marshfield's driveway while she visits the curate is a frequent source of angry frustration. The week's ruminations end with an account of Alicia's coming to Jane, the wronged wife, and telling the whole story of the affair. The resulting con-

versations between Marshfield and his wife amount to the first real communication they have had in a long time, yet the result is Marshfield's sense of being bound tighter than ever to the marriage he is coming to hate.

The sermon of day twenty is more hopeful; its subject is the potential for life which lurks at the heart of the desert and in the heart of the driest and most unfaithful of men. The week's reflections have taken us through his attempts at having an affair with Frankie Harlow (never consummated, since with her he is impotent), his reflections on the children he is trying to rear, and perhaps more important his visits to his senile father. The elder Reverend Marshfield has, in his senility, recovered some of his sexuality; all he can talk about are his war experiences with the women of France. What is coming clearer is the increasing complexity of Marshfield's situation, and its increasing ludicrousness. The affair with Alicia leads to the affair with Frankie, which leads to a series of casual liaisons with women he meets in counseling situations. A crash is coming; when Alicia finally tells all to the vestry, exile is inevitable. Yet, the confessions bring self-acceptance, as the despair of sermon two turns into the hope of sermon three: "We *are* found in a desert place. We *are* in God's palm. We *are* the apple of His eye. Let us be grateful *here,* and here rejoice."

Throughout his writings, Marshfield has become aware that someone, probably Ms. Prynne, is reading them. In the last week's reflections, the here-and-now of his situation becomes increasingly important. He is aware of those fellow exiles, and finds himself trying to minister to them. Especially important is his attempt to bring one man to see that his maintaining an empty church is not a sign of failure, since the purpose of the Christian community is witness, not conversion. The final sermon is a proclamation of his faith that the irrational Gospel of resurrection is man's only hope, and that the continued proclamation of that Gospel is a sign of God's presence and reliability.

A quick affair with Ms. Prynne concludes the book. Confession and reflection have brought Marshfield to a sense of his forgiveness, his acceptance, by his God. It is a complete acceptance, not qualified by the dichotomy he described at the beginning. As a result, he is ready to return to his responsibilities and his duties, to the ambiguities of his life. His acceptance by Ms. Prynne becomes a sign of divine acceptance. In this process, Marshfield's confession becomes a unique one; not all need to follow the same path toward the divine love.

John N. Wall, Jr.

PASSAGE TO ARARAT

Author: Michael J. Arlen (1930-   )
Publisher: Farrar, Straus and Giroux (New York). 293 pp. $8.95
Type of work: Memoir and social history
Time: The present
Locale: New York City; France; Fresno, California; Soviet Armenia

An American of Armenian background discovers his heritage and in the process confronts hidden truths about himself and his father

Principal personages:
>   MICHAEL J. ARLEN, the author, a journalist seeking to understand his cultural past
>   MRS. ARLEN, his wife
>   SARKIS, their official guide in Soviet Armenia
>   MICHAEL ARLEN, the author's deceased father, a sophisticated English novelist of the 1920's
>   WILLIAM SAROYAN, American novelist and playwright

The search for identity, for self, is the great modern myth, perhaps the underlying force of modern culture itself. After two world wars, the West has little faith in nationalism or myths of historical community; this lack of faith only intensifies the difficulty of self-discovery. A world without social or political coherence does not provide a fruitful context or model for the integrated self. Michael J. Arlen's poignant search for his Armenian heritage dramatizes the universal modern dilemma of alienation.

Although the tragedy of modern Armenian history constitutes a unique heritage, Arlen makes clear that his people's suffering, a fact he must finally face in all its horror as the undeniable truth of his psychic and truth of his psychic and spiritual past, is the general burden of our time, "a Lear among centuries" as Arlen aptly puts it. In probing his people's past, Arlen only makes clearer to all of his readers the painful necessity of restoring a sense of the very past we think we can do

without. In Arlen's case, the veils that must be lifted, the vast distances in time and space that must be crossed, the painful memories that must be resurrected all make for an epic journey.

As a child, Arlen was prevented from acquiring any true sense of his Armenian heritage by his father's determined and nearly categorical rejection of his own past. The younger Arlen shared with Stephen Dedalus, Joyce's archetypal modern hero, the search for a spiritual father; but his search is thwarted by the father's refusal to know himself. Michael Arlen was a sophisticated novelist of Edwardian manners, who succeeded in suppressing nearly all signs of his Armenian background. He dressed and behaved like the quintessential Englishman. Armenian was never spoken at home, although his wife was also American and Greek. In boarding school in France, young Arlen thought he was English and was surprised to discover that his teachers and classmates considered his father an "Armenian writer." If it were not for an uncle or two, and his father's occasionally taking the family to an Armenian restaurant on the east side of New York, young Arlen would hardly have had reason to believe there was any particular connection between things Armenian and his father. When his father died, his mother, who had in private called her husband by his Armenian name Dikran, held the funeral in a Greek Orthodox church rather than an Armenian one, because "All his life, he wanted to be free of the Armenians," she said at the time.

The father's refusal to give his son a sense of their cultural heritage forced the author to deal with two mysteries at the same time: his father's identity and his people's past. The confluence of the two lent an intensely personal and strongly psychological dimension to the son's quest; he had to explore both the darkest corners of his own memory as well as his people's history. *Passage to Ararat* becomes an exploration of dreams that are even stranger and more compelling than the distant plateau of Soviet Armenia where Arlen and his Presbyterian, American wife go in search of his cultural past. Just before flying to Armenia, Arlen has a dream that he "had dreamed many times in his youth," ever since his father had died some twenty years before. In it, father and son are driving down a sunlit road in France. They follow a turn marked "TO THE AIRPORT." The father walks toward "a large blue plane" and beckons his son to follow. The son runs to join his father in the plane, but "all is darkness. *Black*. I have never seen such empty darkness as in that dream airplane I peer into, and then, somehow, I am

standing on the grass again, the wind is blowing, and the blue plane is gone."

When Arlen and his wife land at Erevan, the capital of Soviet Armenia, he is astonished at suddenly being entirely surrounded, in a matter-of-fact way, by Armenians. "The sky was a faded blue," he writes, but the reader and Arlen both know he has landed where the father in his dream had taken the "blue plane." The son has literally taken the journey his father could make only through sublimation (his novels), detachment, repression, and isolation. The son must now feel openly what the father had never allowed himself to feel and had tried to protect his son from feeling: the full impact of being an Armenian.

The son's "progress" is painfully cautious. The official guide, Sarkis, an Armenian who spent his youth working for an English businessman in Cairo, wants to express his respect for Arlen's famous author-father: "I'm sure he was a wonderful man. Armenian men make wonderful fathers." It is just the sort of thing to put Arlen on edge, and his sensitive wife perceives his discomfort. Sarkis insists that the first site they must visit is the Monument to Armenian Martyrs. Custom requires that a small flower be dropped in a flaming bowl. Arlen freezes. He manages to drop the flower Sarkis has put in his hand only after Mrs. Arlen whispers a desperate "Please. . . ."

"Think of the Armenians who died," says Sarkis, and Arlen obeys his Virgilian guide by beginning a long period of concentrated reading and reflection. We learn, as he reads, of the prominent role Armenians played in the Crusades as supporters of the various Western Crusader kings. Armenian devotion to Christianity earned a lasting enmity from the world of Islam. Arlen "hears" the anguish of the religious scribes of the fourteenth and fifteenth centuries as they describe the suffering of their people at the hands of Turkish, Mongol, and Arab invaders. As Arlen becomes more sensitized to the tragic history of the Armenian people, he becomes increasingly self-conscious of his own "coolness and detachment." He recognizes the same icy defensiveness in the portrait of an eighteenth century Armenian merchant in the local museum at Erevan. Suddenly he grasps the defining element which he, the portrait, and his own father all share—the state of being crazed: "Not 'crazy' in the colloquial sense . . . or even . . . certifiably mad. But crazy: crazed, that deep thing—deep where the deap-sea souls of human beings twist and turn."

Now steeled to the spiritual truth of his condition, Arlen achieves a cathartic temper. He begins to face his personal and cultural heritage with feelings of release and illumination. The subtle support he receives from his wife shows her awareness that health and serenity are the rewards this difficult journey offers.

For Arlen to understand his "crazed" state, he must understand the Turks, the people who subjected the Armenians to their greatest suffering. During a literary evening at Sarkis' home, a young high school teacher named Arshil quietly says, "Do you know what I think was worst about the trouble with the Turks? It was that the Turks and Armenians were brothers." These words provide a vital clue to the essence of the Armenian trauma: How could a people who had been close neighbors turn against you with such barbarity? How could they bludgeon and torture your men, rape and mutilate your women, bayonet your children? How could they try to wipe you out completely, as if you had no right to life, no right to be human like them?

Arlen reviews the history of the Ottoman Empire and the marginal existence of Armenians within its borders. Always thought of as outsiders, even though they had lived in what became Turkey long before the Ottomans had conquered the area, the Armenians were distrusted and constrained in their movements. Among the few opportunities open to them were moneylending and banking, professions not exactly calculated to promote good will. The Armenians became the perfect scapegoat, and their fate was similar to that of the Jews in Europe. Pitilessly persecuted by the Sultan, the Armenians suffered even more at the hands of the revolutionary forces that overthrew the Sultanate. These fiercely nationalistic revolutionaries resented the Armenians turning to Europe for guarantees of safety and political reform. With irrational fury the liberated Turks slaughtered the Armenians on a scale and with a cruelty comparable to that seen in Hitler's Germany. Twentieth century genocide began in Turkey.

The fate of their people largely ignored by the rest of the world, men like Arlen's father slipped into acute depression. Having been "hated unto death" left a mark of collective guilt and self-hatred. Now, having confronted the past, the younger Arlen rises above his father's condition. He relaxes into an acceptance of his heritage. The young Soviet Armenians, despite the strictures of Communism, seem to have the power "to set their fathers free." Arlen closes by celebrating Armenian survival itself: the miracle of an ancient people, unprotected by nationhood or property, somehow preserving its uniqueness by a dedication to things both simpler and grander than political assertion. Before leaving for Armenia, Arlen went to Fresno to visit William Saroyan, and left with a strengthened impression of the Armenian folk ethic. But the mountain of Ararat that sheltered Noah's ark is finally a nobler landmark for the Armenian soul than the cemetery of Fresno. Like Noah's family, the Armenians have survived the flood of history and continue to embody the humanity in us all—the only thing worth saving.

Peter A. Brier

PASSIONS AND OTHER STORIES

Author: Isaac Bashevis Singer (1904-   )
Publisher: Farrar, Straus and Giroux (New York). 312 pp. $8.95
Type of work: Short stories

A seventh collection of short tales, humorous and philosophical, drawn from the unique tradition and experiences of the Yiddish-speaking Jews of Eastern Europe and the Hasidic sect

Singer's writings are all autobiographical to a greater or lesser degree; that is, he writes either out of his own experience or out of those of his people, the Yiddish-speaking Jews of Poland. In fifteen of these stories the author appears either as the protagonist or as the one to whom the story is told; two others take the form of topical disquisitions by a trio of village sages. At least half are about the Hasidim, and almost all reflect the mystical and apocalyptic character of Hasidic orthodoxy.

The Hasidic sect was founded in Poland around 1750 in reaction to the formalism and ritual laxity of Jewish worship of that time. The Hasidim, the "pious ones," live by a strict rule in daily expectation of the Messiah. They are ascetic, reclusive, studious, sorrowing yet full of hope. Hasidic scholarship traditionally takes the form of exegeses of sacred texts, of parables, and of enigmatic and hieratic utterances similar to the impenetrable utterances of a Zen master. The present collection of stories owes much to this tradition.

Another element in the background of the stories is the Holocaust of World War II and all that it meant for the Jews of Poland. The whole collection is elegiac in tone, as recalling times and faces that are past; the mention of a date throws a doomed light on the events of some

stories, lends a dreadful poignance to the humor in others.

Last, there is the tradition of storytelling, a means of transmitting history, affirming kinship, and asserting values, as well as of passing the long winter night. Certain individuals and situations are depicted with wonder and delight at the infinite permutations of human character.

Six of the stories have the instructional quality of parable, though the texts they illustrate are not necessarily sacred. In "Errors," three elders one-up each other with anecdotes about a perfectionist who fell into a rage because a prince mispronounced his name; about a scribe who deliberately made mistakes in holy writings in order to bring about the end of the world; and about a yeshiva student who, chidden for an error, takes his teacher at his word and learns to be a master cobbler as well as a renowned scholar, thus benefiting both bodies and souls. Moral: "There are spheres where all errors are transformed into truth." In "The Yearning Heifer" an impoverished writer takes a room on a farm. The farm wife yearns for the city, a neighbor woman wants to have her poems appreciated, the farmer's daughter craves love, the writer craves his girl friend at home; he comes to understand that all yearning is part of a cosmic yearning for oneness with God. "Sam

Palka and David Vishkover" is a parable about the dilemma of American Jewry: a rich man whose home life is miserable falls in love with a poor immigrant girl. Posing as a poor man, he begins a liaison with her that outlasts his own marriage; but, entangled in his lie, he can neither bring her into his plush worldly environment nor join her in poverty and orthodoxy. "A Tutor in the Village" is a story so sparely written that it is difficult to summarize. In it, a worldly young man goes to a remote village to tutor a merchant's children. Appalled by the discomfort and isolation, he resolves to leave at once; unable to sleep, he comes upon a scene which seems to sum up the history of his race:

> Reb Naphtalie sat at the table in a cotton robe with a skullcap on his head, murmuring into a volume of the Mishnah. . . . I felt both sorrow and joy. The world is asleep, but a Jew sits in this distant hamlet studying the Torah in the middle of the night.

In "Three Encounters," a citified writer meets a lovely girl in his home village and exhorts her to renounce her planned marriage for the lights of Warsaw. The next time he sees her, in Warsaw, she is pregnant and abandoned. Years later they meet again in America; she has converted and married a Catholic. She begs the writer to take her away, marry her, and help her become a Jew again; she blames him for what has befallen her and, indeed, he blames himself. Both despondently contemplate the irretrievable. In the title story the same trio of elders offers three examples of passion: a peddler who so longs to see the Holy Land that he walks there; an ignorant man who so longs for learning that he memorizes the Torah in a single year; and Rabbi Mendel, whose zeal is such that he fasts six days a week and recites the Yom Kippur service daily until he dies.

Some stories are expositions of character. In "The New Year Party," a rich man whose affairs and extravagances are legendary goes to a party given by several writers, protégés of his. He gets drunk, and disparages the talents and impugns the motives of all present, including those of Harry, his lifelong friend and factotum. Two years later he dies, leaving Harry nothing. Harry nonetheless buys him a headstone for friendship's sake, and though illiterate, reveals a spiritual profundity by his choice of inscription. "A Pair" is the tale of two poets, he a mad Hasid and she an assimilated Polish Jew, survivors of the Holocaust. He claims to have found an acrostic in the book of Genesis that explains the history of the world; she proclaims him the world's greatest lover and second-greatest poet (after herself). At his death she assumes his identity and rails against the Americanized Hasidim who come to claim his body. In "The Fatalist" a friend tells the writer about a young man who professes himself a fatalist. He falls in love with a sharp-tongued girl named Heyele and tells her they are fated to marry. She dares him to test his belief by lying down in front of a train. To her horror he accepts the challenge, on condition that she marry him if he survives. The train stops just short of him. He and Heyele marry.

"Would he do it again?" asks the writer, and the friend answers, "Not for Heyele."

"Moishele" is a portrait of a man orphaned as much by the loss of his religion as by his parents' death. Childlike in stature and in outlook, Moishele adores his unfeeling wife and agonizes with her over the break-up of her friendship with a painter. Guilt tortures him, the guilt of a child whose parents divorce; helplessly, he engineers the reconciliation that will make him a cuckold.

The remaining stories are spirit-tales, some of them ingenuous, others extremely sophisticated. Of the former sort, "The Sorcerer" is the proto-type, a tale told by Aunt Yentel on a Sabbath afternoon; in it, a crazy squire makes for himself a demon lover. Later, tired of her, he takes a gipsy mistress, but the demon kills her and the squire is sent to prison for the murder. Sometimes, it is said, his cell resounds with wanton female laughter. In the more complicated "Sabbath in Portugal," the writer is befriended in Lisbon by a publisher, Miguel de Albeira, who takes him to his home for dinner; the writer is surprised and impressed by the old-fashioned manners of the wife and children. De Albeira questions him closely about his Jewishness, then shows him a manuscript written by an ancestor which indicates that the Albeiras are Marranos, the descendants of Jews who converted under the Inquisition while keeping their faith in secret, cherishers of a birthright centuries old. As night falls, the writer sees in Senhora de Albeira's face the face of his first love whom the Nazis killed, hears the dead voice

in her voice. It comes to him that the spirits of those who died remain, animating the consciousness of all Jews, even those whose racial identity is no more than an atavistic tremor in the blood.

Strangest of all is "The Witch," set in Warsaw in the 1930's. Mark Meitels, a handsome, highly disciplined high school mathematics teacher, an assimilated Jew, stolidly endures marriage to a perfect, icy doll of a woman. Suddenly, she falls ill and dies. The teacher mourns his inability to give point to her life or to believe in the continuation of her soul in some other sphere. At the same time, he is haunted by thoughts of Bella, the stupidest and ugliest of his students, a girl who despite his best efforts would never graduate. As if summoned, Bella one night appears at his door and declares her love for him. She tells him that she killed his wife with a wish. Revolted, but queerly elated, Mark holds a knife to her throat; she neither flinches nor pleads. The totality of her surrender rouses him and they fall upon each other with animal frenzy. Helplessly, he agrees to leave Warsaw, to go abroad with her, to marry her; reconnected with the springs of life, he feels the stirrings of a spiritual awakening.

The single unifying theme of these stories is the effort of a people to grapple with the terms of existence and to make sense of their history. It is the intention of the author to glorify this struggle, to commemorate it and those engaged in it. "In literature, as in our dreams, death does not exist."

Jan Kennedy Foster

POEMS
Selected and New, 1950-1974

Author: Adrienne Rich (1929-   )
Publisher: W. W. Norton and Company (New York). 256 pp. $8.50
Type of work: Poetry

A record of the process of growing into awareness charted by a woman who uses her own pain to establish links with humanity

More than any other American poet, Adrienne Rich has uncovered the pain, rage, and joys of being a woman. Her poetry for the past twenty years has been dedicated to a series of awakenings, to "diving into the wreck" of broken dreams. This collection is above all not a summation of Rich's work but rather an edited perspective of her growth; as she writes in her Foreword, "I think of this book . . . as the graph of a process still going on." Rich is concerned with cycles, the unending frustration of men and women attempting to communicate and often destroying each other in the process. In "Ghazals: Homage to Ghalib 7/14/68:ii" she writes: "For us the work undoes itself over and over:/the grass grows back, the dust collects, the scar breaks open." Later on in the same poem dated "8/8/68:ii" she continues:

I'm speaking to you as a woman to a man:
When your blood flows I want to hold you in my arms.

How did we get caught fighting this forest fire,
we, who were only looking for a still place in the woods?

This book presents the fire and the search, the anger and the agony of a poet uncovering herself to reach others.

Becoming conscious of her sex and recognizing the particular set of personal experiences we associate with womanhood was a gradual process for Rich, and one which offers a clue to understanding her work. The early books, *A Change of World* and *The Diamond Cutters,* begin with portraits of dead-ended relationships which locked the poet into a futile pattern. These early poems are formal and controlled; the carefully constructed lines move rhythmically and are mostly rhymed, while the content of the poems points to a controlled disappointment and anger which is subtly woven into the fabric of a woman's relationships. In poems such as "Aunt Jennifer's Tigers," "Afterward," "An Unsaid Word," and "Mathilde in Normandy," the women perform domestic chores while waiting on or for their men. "Aunt Jennifer's fingers fluttering through her wool" are weighed down by "Uncle's wedding band"; the woman in "Afterward" stands "At last believing and resigned" to a kind of deadness; while the ladies of Normandy abandoned by their soldier-lover-husbands try to continue their stitchery and find that "anxiety there too/Played havoc with the skein, and the knots came. . . ." Such careful poetry is like the tapestry, laid out by a woman locked into scenes prepared for her life by outside forces.

This same kind of approach occurs in the selections from *The Diamond Cutters.* The poet uses real scenery instead of stitched ones as the primary imagistic vehicle, but still conveys a sense of superficiality, of tasks done routinely and of lives deadened by formality. "Those clarities detached us, gave us form,/Made us like architecture" ("The Tourist and the Town"). The poems begin in summer when the speaker is vacationing in Italy "Summer was another country, where the birds/Woke us at dawn among the dripping leaves" ("Holiday"), but move gradually (in "Autumn Equinox") into the autumn years of a life which has been built around a marriage guidebook mentality:

Now we are old like Nature; patient,
    staid,
Unhurried from the year's wellworn
    routine,
. . . We have become
As unselfconscious as a pair of trees,
Not questioning but living.

In the last selection, "The Perennial Answer," this routine ends with the death of a husband in March, a time when the memories of a cold winter and an unrewarding life are fresh and when the prospects for a different kind of spring awakening are imminent.

With *Snapshots of a Daughter-in-Law,* published in 1963, Rich gradually begins to change her poetic and political posture. This book includes poems written from 1955-1963 which express more openly the anger that

seethed in the tight stitches of the earlier tapestry-like poems. Fewer of these poems rhyme; the lines become more prosaic; the images move out of the parlor. In fact, the predominant image for this group of poems is one of movement out of a house or through a door or window, as seen in these lines from "Prospective Immigrants Please Note":

Either you will
go through this door
or you will not go through.
        •   •   •
The door itself
makes no promises.
It is only a door.

The title poem "Snapshots of a Daughter-in-Law" is important, therefore, because it literally launches the poet out of conventional roles into uncertain but promising possibilities. The poem begins in the kitchen of a once beautiful and fresh Southern belle whose mind "moldering like wedding cake,/heavy with useless experience . . . looks out/past the raked gardens to the sloppy sky." Clearly, openly, yet with dignity, Rich allows this frustrated woman to come alive and to take her place with other women like Emily Dickinson and Mary Wollstonecraft. "A thinking woman sleeps with monsters" writes the poet, who no longer keeps those tiger/monsters safely woven and framed. Beginning to realize that tradition and her acceptance of that tradition has kept her locked inside, she stands "Poised, trembling and unsatisfied, before/an unlocked door." Near the end of the poem, the poet seems to join the Southern belle: the pronouns and adjectives change to "we" and "our" instead of "you" and "her." Also, there is a simultaneous opening out and release accompanied by a closing of ranks:

> . . . all that we might have been,
> all that we were—fire, tears,
> wit, taste, martyred ambition—
> stirs like the memory of refused adultery
> the drained and flagging bosom of our
>   middle years.

And with the final image in "The Roofwalker," of a helicopter taking to the sky holding a precious cargo of hope and much baggage of disillusion, Rich launches herself as a poet of female sensibility:

> A life I didn't choose
> chose me: even
> my tools are the wrong ones
> for what I have to do.

Again, the title poem from the next work, *Necessities of Life,* focuses on the movement in the poet's awareness. "Piece by piece I seem/to re-enter the world," writes Rich, as she poetically retraces the steps by which that entry will be effected. She sees that she has so identified herself with others that she has lost any sense of her own identity, and gradually has withdrawn from the world. Her re-entry now is tentative. "I have invitations," she claims; and like the helicopter in "Snapshots of a Daughter-in-Law" the imagery suggests this hopefulness as it moves upward and out along a road where houses "stand waiting/like old women knitting, breathless/to tell their tales." The insight or truth which begins to be expressed in these poems is found in the repetition of images, the cycles which continue and the inevitable pain which these cycles can produce. In poems like "The Corpse-Plant," "The Trees," "Like This Together," and "Autumn Sequence," we meet again the use of natural imagery to convey inevitability and the use of open space to suggest risk or possibility. The wedding band or ring, another familiar image, has become a gold earring, but still remains a burden, and the snapshot or scenic perspective has changed into a blurry negative. Despite the "invitations," it is hard to enter this new world and it is painful, too, as the poet describes in "The Corpse-Plant":

> Lying under that battering light
> the first few hours of summer
> I felt scraped clean, washed down
>
> to ignorance.

The poet, growing wiser, begins to acknowledge her own limitations as she recounts her slow entry into an uncertain world.

In the last three books Rich has published, *Leaflets, The Will to Change,* and *Diving into the Wreck,* her poems continue to focus on the difficult matter of human communication. The 1960's and early 1970's, when these books were published, were times of change, of war, of upheaval; in "In the Evening," Rich poignantly captures these tensions by writing about the breakdown of sexual relationships and the questioning of traditional social patterns:

> We stand in the porch,
> two archaic figures: a woman and a man.
>
> The old masters, the old sources,
> haven't a clue what we're about,
> shivering here in the half-dark 'sixties.

People cannot rely on old ways of being with one another; yet for the time being these ways are all that are available in their lives. This condition of struggle, this swinging back and forth, reaching and withdrawing, prevents consummation and relief. Even the titles of the poems in *Leaflets* underscore the tension out of which the poet writes: "Abnegation," "Implosions," "On Edges," and "Nightbreak." Finally, the explosion of anger in the title poem "Leaflets" ironically provides the release for communication—if only momentarily—in the contact between poet and reader:

> I want to hand you this
> leaflet streaming with rain and tears
>
> .   .   .
>
> I want this to reach you
> who told me once that poetry is nothing
> sacred . . . .

The poems in *The Will to Change* continue the trend towards prose statements. The language is spare, less imagistic; the continual references to history, as in "The Burning of Paper Instead of Children" sound more cynical: "What happens between us/has happened for centuries . . . ." In "Blue Ghazals" Rich writes that *"The moment when a feeling enters the body*/is political," and the poet's job is to record, to feel that moment and thereby to make political statements. "I tear up answers/I once gave," states Rich in "Letters: March 1969" because even recent history cannot supply new answers: "the moment of change is the only poem."

With *Diving into the Wreck,* which was a co-winner of the 1974 National Book Award for Poetry, Rich works clearly and confidently in her role as a political poet. The titles point to her overt commitment to feminism: "Trying to Talk with a Man," "The Phenomenology of Anger," "Rape," "For a Sister." There are also a number of dialogue poems, such as "Waking in the Dark," which deal with pairs of men and women, trying to reach each other but remaining apart because of abiding and perhaps unresolvable conflicts.

Although Rich returns with relentless tenacity to the topic of frustrating sexual relationships, searching beyond the easy answers to a clearer understanding of her predicament as a poet and as a woman, her poems continue to make similar statements; namely, that we are caught in times and conditions which divide us and destroy some of our capacity for loving, and that in the end "this way of grief/ is shared, unnecessary/ and political."

Faith Gabelnick

POWER SHIFT

Author: Kirkpatrick Sale (1937-   )
Publisher: Random House (New York). 362 pp. $12.95
Type of work: Contemporary history
Time: 1945-1975
Locale: The United States

    A theoretical analysis of the rise of the "Southern Rim" and its challenge to the "Eastern Establishment"

    Kirkpatrick Sale is one of the most highly regarded of the "new journalists," that fiery breed who have expanded the "who, what, where, when, and why" role into social history. Perhaps epitomized by Tom Wolfe (*The Electric Kool-Aid Acid Test, Radical Chic and Mau-Mauing the Flak-Catchers*), and Hunter Thompson (*Fear and Loathing on the Campaign Trail*), the new journalists aim to give factual reporting a sense of consciousness and conscience. They are often at their best doing features on significant new developments, and at their worst when their prose becomes slick and self-indulgent. Sale's particular strength is in his argumentation rather than his prose, in his ability to synthesize material and present a generalized panoramic picture that accounts for numerous diverse, but possibly related, phenomena.

    Typical of the new journalists' writing, Sale's work is grounded in history. He asks and attempts to answer the difficult question of how contemporary situations relate to the long view of history. Sale's two earlier books, *SDS: A History of the Students for a Democratic Society* and *The Land and People of Ghana,* were both well-researched, carefully crafted studies. *Power Shift* is considerably more ambitious and speculative than these previous works. Sale has turned to nothing less than an explanation for the how and why of America's vast changes since World War II. At the least his analysis is provocative, a large-scale conceptualization of what many people have suspected but not very clearly articulated.

    Sales argues that in the last thirty years a significant power shift has taken place in America. This shift has nothing to do with Democrats and Republicans, management and labor, urban and rural, or young and old. Rather, it is the shift of wealth and power away from the "Eastern Establishment" toward the "Southern Rim." Sale's definition for both areas is quite broad. By Eastern Establishment he means not only the Northeast, but New Jersey and Pennsylvania, plus Wisconsin, Michigan, Illinois, Indiana, and Ohio. These latter states he considers the manufacturing area for the East, relatives by climate and heritage. The Southern Rim is roughly what Kevin Phillips called the "Sun Belt" in *The Emerging Republican Majority,* a work from which Sale draws much information and many conclusions. Sale's Southern Rim is the United States south of the Thirty-seventh Parallel which includes North Carolina, Tennessee, Arkansas, Oklahoma, New Mexico, Arizona and all states South. In addition, the Southern Rim includes southern Nevada and central and southern California, plus San Francisco. Much of the shift involves population, Sale notes. Since World War II thirty million people have moved from the older, colder sections of the North to the younger and sunnier South and Southwest. This dramatic increase in population has brought a correspondingly dramatic increase in power for the Southern Rim.

"If the Southern Rim were an independent nation," writes Sale, "it would have a gross national product bigger than any foreign country in the world except the Soviet Union . . . ." This economic power is built on "six pillars," Sale explains, and these are: agribusiness, defense, advanced technology, oil and natural gas production, real estate and construction, and tourism and leisure. With a barrage of convincing statistics, Sale shows that the Southern Rim, not the Corn Belt, is the great agricultural area of the United States. "Southern Rim farms supply almost all the cotton, fruit, nuts, sugar, and rice produced in this country, and two-thirds of its tobacco and poultry products. California is the leading grower of fruits and vegetables, with Florida second. . . ." The Southern Rim also produces much beef (Texas) and the majority of processed food. The enormous new industries of technologically advanced defense, aerospace, and oil are also centered in the Southern Rim.

Here, the mid-century real estate boom has been almost as spectacular as the oil boom. Such formerly small towns as Albuquerque, New Mexico, Birmingham, Alabama, and Fort Lauderdale, Florida, have grown into nationally prominent cities. A formerly pastoral orchard, Orange County, California, has become a densely packed metropolitan area covering hundreds of square miles. Multinational corporations such as ITT and Republic Steel have relocated in the Rim, where overall growth steadily continues. These "new migrants" seem well enough off financially to spend more on recreation and leisure than on any item except food. To satisfy their needs, there are giant "theme parks," such as Disneyland and Disney World, at each end of the Rim. Entertainment, airlines, motel chains, and sports have all relocated and dramatically prospered in the Southern Rim.

The political aspects of the Southern Rim are even more fascinating than the area's economic power and geographical cohesion. With chilling documentation for his theories, Sale accounts for a prolonged involvement with the Vietnamese Civil War on the basis of protecting Southeast Asia's offshore oil for future Southern Rim exploitation, thereby also expanding the area's defense contracts. Sale's conception of the Southern Rim's "new morality" (expediency and profit is all) would seem to account for the vast number of financial frauds perpetrated in this area, including the multi-million dollar failure of the United States National Bank in San Diego and the land and condominium swindles in Florida. Sale believes this "new morality" is grounded in rightism, racism, and repression. The idea is do whatever you can to obtain the most money and power while making sure racial minorities appear to be criminals, not victims, and while making sure all your illegal dealings are carefully covered up. The author moves Richard M. Nixon to the foreground as the epitome of corrupt Southern Rim leadership.

Analyzing Nixon's fall from empire, Sale takes an unexpected position. He sees the resignation as a form of poetic justice, a successful Yankee counterattack. Nixon is damned for illegal governmental activities; he is also accused of turning the Presidency into a monarchy and of being the pawn of organized crime, which, as Sale argues, has moved to the Southern Rim like practically everything else. Nixon's brash imperiousness managed to direct the Eastern-based press and judiciary system from a state of alienated horror into stern and swift legal action. Sale feels "the cowboy conquest" has abated only for the moment with Easterner Gerald Ford in the White House.

Sale's theory accounts for so much that has happened in America since World War II that it should be the explanation that *does* make everything perfectly clear. But the theory collapses under the weight of its own evidence. The crucial, all-pervading problem with *Power Shift* is that Sale's schemata allows no contradictions, which turns his journalistic social history into a dogmatic tale of the good guys versus the bad guys. Immediately one may quarrel with his geographic redistricting of the United States. Why are not Maryland and certainly Washington, D.C., part of the Eastern establishment? Why are not Kentucky and Virginia Southern states? What about Seattle, Portland, Minneapolis-St. Paul, and St. Louis? Millions of people live there, too, as do others in the Farm Belt. These areas have also changed, but their contribution to contemporary America is ignored. San Francisco and Los Angeles seem almost antithetical cities coexisting in the same state by historical and geographical accident; yet, Sale places them both in the Southern Rim. This geographical oversimplification is a key to further distortions, many of which damage his case against the Southern Rim.

While often convincing in his detailed attacks against Southern Rim economic and ecological exploitation, Sale lapses into oversimplification with the South, substituting the familiar media-based metaphors for this area instead of providing some original insights. George Wallace is portrayed as "a racist, a demagogue, a crude, vindictive, power-hungry bigot." With such language Sale's argument becomes self-serving, almost the rhetoric of violence which is supposed to be a Southern Rim fault. No mention is made of Wallace's significant achievements in raising the standard and quality of life in Alabama, or that racial violence has been a recent problem not in Montgomery or Tuscaloosa, but in Boston and Detroit. Sale blithely dismisses political corruption in Maryland and New Jersey, but asserts that "the Rim's development seems to give it a greater propensity for this affliction and a more brazen disregard for its improprieties." A Sale saint in the political pantheon is Adlai Stevenson, and a Sale demon is Alabama Senator John Sparkman. No mention is made that Stevenson-Sparkman was the Democratic ticket in 1952. A Southern law-oriented liberal such as Estes Kefauver is regarded as a misplaced Yankee. Atlanta, as progressive and liberal as any American city its size, is dismissed by silence. One defense plant, however large, does not Mississippi a California make. Once again, Sale falls into caricature instead of recognizing complexity and contradiction.

The most serious shortcoming with *Power Shift* is its view of the political process. Sale certainly documents corruption and profiteering in the Southern Rim, but his whitewash of the Eastern establishment's political motives is unconvincing. He calls the counterattack against Nixon "not a *thing* but a *process,* not a plan but an eventuality." The word "eventuality" suggests a kind of divine sanc-

tion, raising the possibility that Nixon may have been chased out of office by a latter-day Yankee witchhunt. Sale would like to circumvent messy, nepotistic political power with legislation by morality. Unfortunately, the relationship between law and the public good is as complicated and subject to corruption as is political power for the public good. Even Sale has to admit that Gerald Ford, the Eastern standard bearer, granted Nixon an "unconstitutional pardon."

Power Shift is provocative, but the value of its theory diminishes in the light of too many easy answers. Still, there is something to be said for the believability in spirit of this book's message.

Patrick Morrow

THE PROBLEM OF SLAVERY IN THE AGE OF REVOLUTION
1770-1823

Author: David Brion Davis (1927-   )
Publisher: Cornell University Press (New York). 576 pp. $17.50
Type of work: History
Time: 1770-1823

An analysis of the historical contexts and consequences of the changing view of black slavery in the period from the American Revolution to the end of the Latin American wars of independence

This volume is a sequel to David Brion Davis' *The Problem of Slavery in Western Culture,* a study which examined the cultural, moral, and intellectual background of the struggles over Negro slavery in the eighteenth and nineteenth centuries. The former volume also sought to explain the change in moral perception which eventually led people in European as well as American culture to view slavery as a moral evil, rather than as a traditional, accepted institution. The present study, in the author's own words, "extends the inquiry both in time and in the nature of the questions asked."

Present-day Americans are inclined to think of Negro slavery as an institution peculiar to the American South. Their ignorance both of history in the rest of the Western Hemisphere and of the importance in our own history of the Civil War have seemingly distorted for later generations the truth that slavery was found throughout the hemisphere in the eighteenth century. Abolition of the slave trade and the emancipation of Negro slaves were problems that involved many European nations, as well as their colonial possessions in the New World. In this study Davis clearly demonstrates the international nature of the problem, although he probes more deeply into antislavery activity in Britain and the United States than elsewhere.

Davis has organized his study carefully. In his first three chapters he delineates the setting for the antislavery controversy between 1770 and 1823, emphasizing broad cultural, political, and economic aspects. After reviewing philosophic and cultural elements that undermined centuries-old justifications, he examines the institution of slavery itself, identifying those strengths and weaknesses which made universal emancipation a realistic possibility. He probes both the consequences of challenging this long-accepted institution, and the ways in which questions of sovereignty, jurisdiction, and political representation are bound up with slavery, in Britain and France, as well as in America. Chapters Four and Five explore the social circumstances which either helped or hindered growth of antislavery thought. Davis examines specifically the effect of the Enlightenment and evangelical revival on the American South, and the activities of groups such as the Quakers, who openly opposed slavery.

The core of Davis' book is contained in Chapters Six through Nine, in which he keeps before the reader the realization that the antislavery movement was seen, during the half century which witnessed the upheavals of the French Revolution as well as the wars of independence in North and South America, as dangerous doctrine. To eliminate slavery by discrediting the justifications for it was to risk endangering the justifications for other widely accepted forms of domination and subordination which were considered both useful and desirable. The final two chapters of the study examine the specific implications of the antislavery movement for law and religion. The era of revolution brought new views of mankind, views which caused conflict between different laws. The same era also introduced religious conflict over interpretation of the Bible, between different orthodoxies on one hand, and between orthodoxy and disbelief on the other.

The significance of Davis' book lies in his careful treatment of a complex network of attitudes, and he shows that attitudes toward abolishing the slave trade and ending Negro slavery were not the same in all parts of the slave-owning world. He points out that prevailing birth rates and death rates among slaves had an effect on attitudes toward the slave trade. In the islands of the Caribbean, for example, slaves were in relatively constant demand because their natural reproduction rate did not keep up with their death rate; whereas in North America—particularly in Virginia—natural reproduction increased the number of slaves. It seems no accident, then, that in Virginia, abolitionist sentiment came into being earlier than in other slaveholding areas. Another interesting factor involved the wide-reaching effect of

the slave rebellions in the West Indies on other portions of the slaveholding world. Fear of slave rebellion has plagued slave owners throughout human history, and the slave rebellions, especially in San Domingo, appeared to justify those fears. The atrocities committed by the slaves were given wide dissemination, with the result that serious attempts were made to prevent the sale of slaves from the West Indies in the United States. Even the transporting of slaves to this country by fugitive whites was discouraged, lest their rebellious spirit infect slaves in the American South. Davis also includes an analysis of the attitudes and actions of Thomas Jefferson, who was a Virginia slave owner, as well as one of the architects of the American governmental system. Despite much urging, Jefferson did not say a great deal about slavery, although he believed that slaves in some future generation ought to be emancipated, with the children prepared, as wards of the government, for useful lives as freemen. He also believed that those emancipated slaves should be deported. While such a view may seem callous two centuries later, it was held by many people in both the North and South, as well as in Europe; the slaveholders in the South shared their concern for rights of property and their racism with people all over the world. Rather than be overly harsh on Thomas Jefferson as some writers have been in recent years, one must, the author argues, view Jefferson as a national leader burdened by conflicting fears, roles, and responsibilities. When Jefferson saw that slavery put justice and self-preservation in conflict, the preservation of his universe became more important to him than justice.

The Society of Friends, or Quakers, played an important role in the antislavery movement, during the period from 1770 to 1823 as well as later, in the United States as well as in Britain, where Quakerism originated. The organization developed an effective abolitionist campaign which was coordinated through constant communication and visitation; the Quakers' lives of travel and correspondence provided a natural avenue for antislavery sentiment.

In his Preface, Davis claims to offer no messages of relevance to present problems; as a professional historian he wishes to understand the past, not offer solutions to past or present problems of a social or moral nature. Specifically, he has not tried to interpret the abolitionists either as men cast in a heroic mold or as misfits in society. He writes that he has consciously underplayed the question of race, for his work has led him to believe that, so far as slavery was concerned, racist arguments often were only an excuse for motives difficult or impossible to verbalize. He even suggests that both the abolitionists and their opponents unconsciously collaborated to accept race as an ultimate "reality," a collaboration which obscured more fundamental issues.

In his Epilogue, however, Davis offers a view which he obviously intends to be taken seriously, when he discusses Hegel's *Phenomenology*. The author suggests that Hegel, in his genius, has shown us that as a model, slavery offers a set of meanings that apply to every form of physical and psychological domination; and Davis reminds us of Hegel's warning that man's emancipation, physical or spiritual, must come from those who have endured and overcome some form of slavery.

Gordon W. Clarke

RAGTIME

Author: E. L. Doctorow (1931-   )
Publisher: Random House (New York). 271 pp. $8.95; paperback $2.25
Type of work: Novel
Time: 1902-1917
Locale: Primarily New York City and New Rochelle, New York

A vivid, panoramic view of American life in the years between the turn of the century and World War I, focused on the fate of three families, and including brief appearances by several historical figures

Principal characters:
> FATHER, a manufacturer of American flags, buntings, and fireworks
> MOTHER, his wife, later married to Tateh
> LITTLE BOY, their son
> MOTHER'S YOUNGER BROTHER, a sensitive young man, an inventor, revolutionary, and Evelyn's lover
> EVELYN NESBIT THAW, a famous beauty and the central figure in the notorious Thaw-White murder scandal
> HARRY HOUDINI, the famous magician and escape artist
> TATEH, a Jewish immigrant, initially a silhouette artist, later a film maker
> LITTLE GIRL, his daughter
> EMMA GOLDMAN, the famous radical agitator and feminist theorist
> COALHOUSE WALKER, JR., black jazz pianist and violent insurrectionist
> SARAH, the Family's young black maid and mother of Coalhouse Walker III
> COALHOUSE WALKER III, the illegitimate son of Coalhouse and Sarah
> J. PIERPONT MORGAN, the multimillionaire financier

At the very least, E. L. Doctorow's *Ragtime* is a marvelous *tour de force*: a vivid, exciting story told with great skill, precision, and economy that evokes the mood and atmosphere of a vital historical period. The characters are sharply defined against a colorful background of the sights, sounds, smells, and events of America's last "innocent" time, the "ragtime" era stretching from the asendancy of Teddy Roosevelt to the beginning of World War I. The narrative is adroitly developed by interweaving and juxtaposing the stories of three families— that of a successful upper middle-class flag manufacturer, that of a Jewish immigrant silhouette artist, and that of a Negro jazz pianist—with and against the larger happenings of the period and the careers of various celebrities of the time.

The secret of the book's success lies in its language, which is precise, active, always controlled, frequently witty and ironical, occasionally intense, and sometimes beautiful; the rhythm of the writing is carefully and deftly modulated and punctuated to suggest a prose equivalent of the music that gives the novel its title. The style is factual and impersonal, almost journalistic, yet very visual and highly charged; it offers distance without detachment and involvement without subjectivity. Doctorow is able to present succinctly the larger movements of the period without losing the intimacy needed to focus on the personal conflicts that dominate the book. In short, the surface of the novel is absolutely dazzling—but, when one looks beneath that surface, nagging qualms emerge that somewhat mute the huzzahs.

Although about a specific epoch, *Ragtime* is not a conventional historical novel—or, perhaps it is a radically new use of the genre. Real historical figures are not merely atmospheric decorations, but are integral, individualized (if exaggerated, perhaps caricatured) personages who interact with the book's main characters, operating both realistically and symbolically. Some of the famous figures—Sigmund Freud, Henry Ford, Admiral Peary, Booker T. Washington, Harry K. Thaw, and Stanford White—have little more than walk-on parts, but a number of others— Evelyn Nesbit, Harry Houdini, Emma Goldman, and J. Pierpont Morgan— are vital not only to the book's atmosphere, but to its actions and themes as well. Doctorow deliberately and without apology blurs the lines between historical fact, logical conjecture, and artistic license: "If you ask whether some things in the book 'really happened,' " he has stated, "I can only say, 'they have now.' "

Hence, Evelyn Nesbit, a turn-of-the-century sex symbol and *femme fatale* in socialite Harry K. Thaw's murder of architect Stanford White, meets radical agitator Emma Goldman and has a massage; Harry Houdini has a mystical precognition of Archduke Ferdinand's assassination; Henry Ford and J. Pierpont Morgan meet secretly for lunch and trade other worldly visions; and Sigmund Freud leaves America disgusted by the bad food and paucity of public toilets. But, despite the importance given these historical characterizations, the core of the book remains centered in the fictional creations.

The three families represent three major socioeconomic units: the white middle class, the new immigrant, and the black. The interrelations of these three groups provide not only the novel's narrative thrust, but also its thematic implications. The characters can be seen both as individuals and as representative types. With one exception, the fictional characterizations are given only titles that fix their familial and social roles, and Doctorow's impersonal point of view keeps us from delving very deeply into their separate motivations or psychological processes. And yet, because of the sharp rendering of specific, revealing details from their everyday lives, as well as the intensely dramatic confrontations between them, they are quite convincing as particular human beings. Our identification with them may not be deep and complex, but it is certainly immediate and vivid.

The primary family is made up of a Father, Mother, Little Boy, and Mother's Younger Brother. Father is stiff, conventional, and moralistic in his attitudes toward others, but pragmatic in terms of himself, physically courageous, and generally baffled by the directions his world seems to be taking. Mother is intelligent, compassionate, inhibited, vaguely dissatisfied, and generally resigned to her role, although, on occasion, stubbornly rebellious. Mother's Younger Brother, when we first meet him, is "a lonely, withdrawn young man with blond mustaches . . . thought to be having difficulty finding himself." The Little Boy is no more than a background figure, although he is the most likely candidate for the narrator of the story. All three adults undergo varying degrees of change and development, ranging from the Father's modest insights, to Mother's growth into an autonomous human being, to Younger Brother's extreme and violent metamorphosis into a radical.

The second family, consisting of Tateh (Yiddish for Dad), Mameh, and the Little Girl, is very nearly destroyed by the pressures of economic degradation and racial discrimination. Tateh, a ghetto silhouette artist and would-be socialist agitator, is old and defeated at thirty-two. In order to feed them, his wife "offered herself and he has now driven her from his home and mourns her as we mourn the dead." Poverty forces Tateh and his daughter to flee from New York City to the textile mills in Lawrence, Massachusetts, where he is immediately swept into a violent strike, beaten, broken, and dehumanized. But, in one of the book's major ironies, Tateh almost accidentally realizes the American Dream overnight. To relieve boredom and please his daughter, Tateh makes a book of silhouettes that are animated when the pages are flipped. He impulsively takes his "movie book" to a novelty company; it is purchased; they are

saved. He then drops from the novel to reappear with a new identity near its conclusion.

The third grouping never quite becomes a real family. It is brought into the novel when Mother finds a black baby neatly wrapped and left in the garden. After locating the infant's mother, a young girl named Sarah, Mother takes the two of them into her household. Sarah is soon contacted by the child's father, a jazz pianist named Coalhouse Walker, Jr.

Coalhouse is the only fictional character in the book with a name rather than just a title—and even his name is derived from literary and historical antecedents. He is named after the hero of Heinrich von Kleist's *Michael Kohlhaas,* and his progression from supremely proper Negro gentleman to violent black revolutionary is, in many ways, an updating of the nineteenth century Kliest tale (which was, in turn, based on an actual historical event). His naming is just one of the signs of Coalhouse's primacy in the book. It is his reaction to the cruel, racially inspired desecration of his automobile that provokes the book's major conflict.

Passing in front of a volunteer fire station, Coalhouse is boxed in and his brand new Model T Ford is damaged. It is further mutilated when he goes for help, and he reacts with righteous indignation. His agitation so alarms his fiancée (he has postponed the wedding until he receives justice), that she attempts to present his case directly and emphatically to Vice-President James Sherman. Her gestures are misconstrued and she is shot as a potential assassin.

Sarah's death provokes Coalhouse to armed revenge. He recruits a gang of disenchanted Harlem youths, and they set out to kill as many of the firemen as they can find, burning firehouses as they go along. The "insurrection" intensifies until the six blacks—plus Mother's Younger Brother turned revolutionary complete with blackface—occupy the J. P. Morgan Library, a storehouse of priceless art treasures, and threaten to blow it up unless their demands —that the car be restored and the fire chief turned over to them—are promptly met. After Booker T. Washington fails, Father becomes the intermediary in working out the violent finale of the tragicomic ritual.

The embarrassment of having a would-be revolution originate in his own household stimulates Father to take the family to Atlantic City. There they meet the "Baron Askenazy"—who turns out to be Tateh, now a successful film maker. After Father goes down on the *Lusitania,* Mother marries Tateh, and their three children—"his daughter with dark hair, his towheaded stepson and his legal responsibility, the schwartze child . . . a society of ragamuffins, like all of us"—become the inspiration for his last and greatest cinematic triumph, the "Our Gang" comedies.

But the success of *Ragtime* lies not just in the way the author has re-created a bygone era, but also in the manner he relates it to our own. In Doctorow's view, this pre-World War I period of innocence and tranquility was neither innocent nor tranquil; its innocence was self-deception and its tranquility a façade. Doctorow has isolated and dramatized those aspects of the 1902-1917 period which he feels have become

central to contemporary experience.

Two broad concerns emerge from the book: old-fashioned class struggle, and, for want of a better term, the "theatricalization" of American life. The historical figures Doctorow chooses to dramatize are either products of a class struggle duality— radical activist Emma Goldman, tycoons J. P. Morgan and Henry Ford, "Uncle Tom" Booker T. Washington—or relate to show business in a very contemporary manner—Harry Houdini, who is tormented by the essential triviality and pointlessness of his success, and Evelyn Nesbit, "whose testimony created the first sex goddess in American history . . . inspiration for the concept of the movie star system and model for every sex goddess from Theda Bara to Marilyn Monroe." Cheap thrills and sensationalized sex—the two staples of the modern American popular imagination were predicted and embodied in these two early prototypes.

The same thing is true of the non-historical personages. Father is the typical WASP businessman; Mother, the ignored and exploited housewife; Mother's Younger Brother, the sensitive young man driven by conscience, guilt, and passion to violent revolution; and Coalhouse Walker, the degraded black provoked to justified, if unfortunate, violence. Tateh, on the other hand, is the theatrical genius, the lucky individual whose odd but special talents fit into the new theatricalization of America in which the human essence becomes the visual image, and appearance not only obscures, but actually replaces, reality.

It is in these contemporary implications of the book that it is, perhaps, most vulnerable to serious criticism. For all of the brilliance evident in the book, its action finally polarizes into a rather simplistic, perhaps clichéd, "good guys—bad guys" dichotomy. All of the virtue present in the book can be found in its downtrodden characters—women, radicals, blacks, immigrants—while its folly, vice, and cruelty are affixed to representatives of the white WASP middle and upper class business cliques.

Thus, Emma Goldman seems contemporary because she *is* contemporary—a late 1960's radical feminist; Coalhouse Walker's insurrection has a decided post-Watts flavor, and his "debate" with Booker T. Washington echoes the integration versus black nationalism, nonviolent versus violent rhetorical postures of that decade; Mother's growth of awareness and Younger Brother's violent radicalization are typical of behavior patterns found in the life, and more often in the literature, of our times. On the other side, J. P. Morgan and Henry Ford are extreme caricatures of the robber baron, and, further down the economic ladder, Father exhibits all of the narrowness and inhibitions of his sex, race, and social class—although in his case a likable human being keeps threatening to break through in spite of the author's intentions.

Yet, even as a class struggle document *Ragtime* is impure. The narrative detachment and sustained irony of Doctorow's presentation denies the reader the emotional involvement necessary for a polemical novel. The nostalgic mood works against the political vision. It is possible that much of the book's enormous popularity can be traced back to the fact that Doctorow first gives his reader a "fashionable" political view, culled from the antiwar/civil rights/women's liberation rhetoric of the late 1960's, and then insulates him or her from the most disturbing implications of that view through nostalgia and irony. Therefore, his irony is actually a form of sophisticated sentimentality.

But such doubts about the depth, meanings, and ultimate importance of *Ragtime* cannot obscure its obvious immediacy, impact, and beauty. It is certainly one of the most brilliantly written novels of recent vintage and one of the relatively few stimulating and provocative political novels in our literature.

Keith Neilson

THE REALMS OF GOLD

Author: Margaret Drabble (1939-   )
Publisher: Alfred A. Knopf (New York). 354 pp. $8.95
Type of work: Novel
Time: The present
Locale: England, Europe, Africa

A realistic portrayal of a woman archaeologist's return from personal and professional isolation to her family roots and to her estranged lover

> *Principal characters:*
> FRANCES OLLERENSHAW WINGATE, a noted archaeologist and
>   lecturer
> KAREL SCHMIDT, her lover, a professor of history in London,
>   from whom she has been separated
> DAVID OLLERENSHAW, her cousin, a geologist
> JANET OLLERENSHAW BIRD, her cousin, unhappily married to a
>   chemist
> HUGH OLLERENSHAW, Frances's brother
> STEPHEN, Hugh's son

The Realms of Gold is Margaret Drabble's seventh novel in her literary career of twelve years, in addition to which she has published a lengthy scholarly biography of Arnold Bennett, a prolific English novelist of the Edwardian period, whose art is related to her own. In some respects this novel is a departure from her earlier style, but aspects of it—the portions involving Janet Bird and describing life in the Midlands town of Tockley—are closely linked to her earlier characters and themes. While her last novel, *The Needle's Eye* (1972), was highly praised, critics have received *The Realms of Gold* with a somewhat more mixed judgment, in part because of her experimentation with narrative techniques. The locale of the novel stretches from England across the Continent and on to Central Africa, and the story jumps from character to character, often quite abruptly, as the narrator, acting rather like a stage manager, turns from one plot line to another.

Yet the novel does give the impression of closeknit unity, most obviously in the tight web of relationships binding the characters together. Indeed, aside from Karel Schmidt, they all belong to one family: the Ollerenshaws, who seem to be affected with a virtual family curse, the "Midlands sickness," which finds tragic expression in various ways in each of their lives. The central figure, Frances Ollerenshaw Wingate, is first encountered in a mood of black depression. She is a notably successful woman, an archaeologist who has discovered the lost Saharan trading city of Tizouk, and is called upon to lecture and attend conferences all over Europe. Though she is divorced, she has four satisfying and independent children, whom she loves sincerely although her work constantly calls her away, and leads her to a life of lonely hotel rooms and the solace of alcohol. She is a woman who has attained success and independence, even from her lover, Karel; yet she is not happy, and the novel traces her return to her own roots, to her family, to her lover, and to her search for a sense of self. In this novel the professions of the characters are revealing, almost symbolic, and one might define Frances' quest as an excavation into the sands of her own memory. Her archaeological quest for the realms of gold is a kind of pursuit of a utopian dream, of a land which she knows never existed except in the imagination. In the real world of her family and of her own divided consciousness, one speaks not of victory, but of survival.

Drabble does not, however, imagine that frustrations and isolation are limited to the independent woman. Frances' cousin, Janet, is even more isolated in the confinement of a loveless marriage, and within her narrow horizons suffers endless anxieties over domestic trivia, such as what to serve for dinner. Her husband is a plastics chemist, and her whole life is cluttered with the plastic litter of our modern age. A fifty-page section in the middle of the book follows Janet through an afternoon of planning a dinner party, creating almost a short story within the larger work, a slow-moving examination of Janet's preoccupation with the only content her life has. She, too, eroded by trivia, is nonetheless also a survivor, and her life is not without its small pleasures.

The Ollerenshaws come from a Midlands agricultural family, and Frances' lover, Karel, is a historian who specializes in agrarian life of the eighteenth century. His presence is felt throughout the novel, although he appears only late. He is a Czech *émigré,* the sole survivor of his family, which perished in the Nazi concentration camps. That he shares with Frances an intellectual concern with the past and with the earth reinforces the recurring motif of the novel. It is both comic and meaningful when he and Frances make love in the mud of a trench, uniting not only with each other but with the earth which is the object of their quests. This same quest manifests itself in David, her brother, who is a geologist. Yet David's geology relegates man to his most elemental natural context, while Frances labors to extract the remains of man from the rocks and sand which obliterate the traces of the past.

Opposed to these survivors are the other members of the Ollerenshaw family. It is the death by starvation of great Aunt Connie that serves as the catalyst which brings the characters together, and the final catastrophe is the death of Stephen, who simply goes off into the woods with his infant daughter, having reached the conclusion that it is better to be dead than alive. He has thought life through to the final absurdity and acts upon his conclusion. It is perhaps the strong links of the main characters to the empirical facts of the earth that give them a means of resisting the self-destructive urge that seems to affect the family. Even Janet, whose life is comparatively empty, can focus on the minute objects around her and take satisfaction from her minor victories. In the spectrum of the Ollerenshaw family we find a whole world of responses to the basic insufficiency which is shared by all, the universality of which is pointed up by Frances' research into the distant and romanticized past, the "realms of gold" of legend, which reveal themselves to contain the same human failures and vulnerability as our own times. All is "toil and subsistence, cruelty and dullness," and life is structured for the modern family, as for the ancient tribe, around the universal human experiences and rituals of living and dying. At its deepest, this novel does go beyond its characters to speak of civilization itself, and the continuum of joinings and separations that link the lovers is seen as an instance of the same forces that span families separated in space, and generations proceeding through time.

Drabble has developed her novelistic style from her beginnings with the first-person style centering around a single female character—the type represented here by Janet, oppressed and relegated to a kind of half-life by her subordination to her husband. In later works, Drabble moved to the third-person style and broadened her approach to include a variety of focal characters. In the present work, we find multiple focal points, and the shifting between them is managed by a strong narrator, who intrudes freely, at times seeming to be omniscient in the manner of a Victorian narrator, but then at times professing to be quite baffled by the developments of the plot. The author's voice provides a unifying factor in the work, turning from one scene to another, commenting freely, addressing the reader, and even demanding of him a measure of cooperation and creativity. It is a typical trait of this narrator to offer several possible motivations or explanations for an act or event, and leave the matter undecided. Rather than strong exposition,

the reader finds a style which requires him to join in the search, to become a bit of an archaeologist or historian himself, and to involve himself in the progress of the novel.

Thus the narrative style is complementary to the theme of the novel, and, in fact, the telling of the story in some respects overshadows the plot itself. The tone is frequently essayistic, holding the reader by intellectual fascination in spite of certain weak stretches in the plot. Because of this tendency toward discursiveness, the novel moves rather slowly and does not strongly engage the reader's emotions. Indeed, the love interest of the plot is strangely devoid of passion, and the narrative voice is more interesting than most of the characters. The structure of the novel, with its shifts among several centers of focus, also tends to absorb the reader's attention, as does the machinery of the plot. One occasionally has the feeling that events are being manipulated for the sake of the plot, as is the case of the postcard bearing a message of reconciliation, which is delayed by a postal strike and thus postpones the denouement of the novel. The narrative tone reinforces this feeling, and develops a current of irony which counterbalances the basic seriousness of the novel and the often depressing events and situations. When Karel's wife conveniently removes herself as an obstacle between the lovers by becoming a lesbian, the effect verges on the comic, and when Drabble comments on this development with "invent a more suitable ending if you can," the reader, who has been drawn into the creation of the novel, must find himself amused at being included in the joke. Yet, in spite of this self-conscious and ironic tone, the novel does leave one in a basically thoughtful mood. Like Brecht's alienation effect, the distance between narrator and story provides a space in which the reader can exercise his own intellect and apprehend for himself the meaning of what he is being told.

Stephen C. Schaber

RESIGNATION IN PROTEST

Authors: Edward Weisband (1939-   ) and Thomas M. Franck (1931-   )
Publisher: The Viking Press (New York). 236 pp. $10.00
Type of work: Political theory and history
Time: Twentieth century
Locale: Washington and Westminster

   Historical comparison of the protocol of political resignation in the United States and Great Britain at the cabinet level

   Principal personages:
      WEBSTER DAVIS, Assistant Secretary of the Interior under William McKinley
      WILLIAM JENNINGS BRYAN, Secretary of State under Woodrow Wilson
      HAROLD L. ICKES, Secretary of the Interior under Harry S Truman
      ELLIOT L. RICHARDSON, Attorney General under Richard M. Nixon
      SIR JOHN SIMON, Home Secretary under Herbert Asquith
      LORD ROBERT CECIL, Under Secretary of the Foreign Office under Lloyd George
      ANTHONY EDEN, Foreign Secretary under Prime Minister Neville Chamberlain

Edward Weisband and Thomas M. Franck have collaborated in the past few years on several interesting projects dealing with modern political phenomena. One such work is a revealing study of the importance of political language—its phrasing, tone, and connotations—in world diplomacy, entitled *Word Politics: Verbal Strategy Among the Superpowers* (1971). They have also edited an anthology of essays by political leaders and journalists from all over the world centering on the problems resulting from the interaction of government and media, entitled *Secrecy and Foreign Policy* (1974).

This latest joint venture bears the subtitle "Political and Ethical Choices Between Loyalty to Team and Loyalty to Conscience in American Public Life." The authors' careful research into the historical events surrounding the resignations they document, not to mention the simple facts of the resignations themselves, lend overwhelming support to their contention that in the United States, advisers to the Chief Executive stress team loyalty over conscience; indeed, they seem to consider loyalty to the President more important than loyalty to the nation. In the shadow of Watergate this is an important revelation and suggests that the situation in Nixon's cabinet and among his advisers was only an extreme example of an established practice endemic to the people clustered around the President.

Weisband and Franck's findings derive dramatic emphasis from the context provided by their comparison of American and British patterns of resignation. In Britain, resignations of protest are common; the resigning official "goes public" without endangering his career, which is less likely in America. Anyone publicly deserting the President's team is rarely picked by any future administration for another position. In Britain, on the other hand, an open resignation of conscience with declarations to Parliament and the press often aids a man in his political career. His probity with the people is established. When a new government is elected, he will not be passed by simply because he deserted the previous Prime Minister.

Although the comparison is instructive, it must be noted that the American Presidency is a time-locked affair. For at least four years, a President and his cabinet are committed to the difficult task of governing a giant nation with some cohesion and direction. In Britain the tenure of office for a Prime Minister and his government is not prescribed, and governments theoretically can rise or fall in congruence with the issues and positions they champion. In such a situation the public is encouraged to know the difficulties and tensions *within* a government so that it can vote intelligently to restore order in an impromptu election. Public resignations can serve this purpose. In the United States, for better or worse, a President and his cabinet are expected to muddle through for at least one term; the public withholds its right to change the government until the four years are up. This encourages the cabinet to present a united front. And indeed, the American public, with its pragmatic bias, usually wants its cabinet to be industrious, to get things done. In all probability, the American voter is less anxious than the British voter when it comes to the individual cabi-

net member's conscience and view of government policy; he is more concerned with the cabinet member's ability to serve the Chief. Although the American President gets four years no matter what he does (excepting an impeachment situation), the law does not permit him more than four years without an election; the British Prime Minister can lose power in a year or less—or keep it for a lifetime.

Despite their glossing over the inherent differences between the two systems, Weisband and Franck make an effective case for the importance of correcting the American fascination with blind team loyalty. Granting that "efficiency and order" are important values, they are no more important than what our authors call "ethical autonomy, the willingness to assert one's own principled judgment, even if that entails violating rules, values, or perceptions of the organization, peer group, or team." The reluctance to speak out publicly has grown with the years: 21.7 percent of the "prime" resigners between 1930 and 1939, the decade of the Great Depression, took their grievances to the public. 10.7 percent did so during the war years; 5.1 percent in the decade of postwar affluence, 1950-1959; 6.3 percent in the era of the Vietnam war, 1960-1969. It is clear that "ethical autonomy" has decreased in direct proportion to the growth of the power of the executive branch. But the reasons for this "organization ethic" lie deep in the American consciousness; they cannot be attributed exclusively to increased presidential power. Weisband and Franck themselves cite the work of sociologists such as David Riesman

(*The Lonely Crowd*) and William H. Whyte (*The Organization Man*).

If the American religion of conformity provides some explanation for the reluctance of resigners to make public declarations (and instead to offer bland excuses such as poor health or family pressures), the British love of eccentricity and traditions of political individualism may explain why resigners usually make an excessively clean breast of things. Of the seventy-eight "prime resigners" in Britain between 1900 and 1970, forty-two, more than half, left office in a declaration of protest against a government policy. In the United States only 8.7 percent in the prime resigner group went "public."

Weisband and Franck leave little doubt that they find the American trend disturbing. They note that, sadly, there are very few examples in American political history similar to the one set by William Jennings Bryan, who resigned from his post as Secretary of State in Woodrow Wilson's cabinet because Bryan's pacifism made the President's war policy unacceptable. "Top federal executives" around the President should be men with a proven capacity for "ethical autonomy." A good secretary of defense must be as clear about his principles, cherished beliefs, and political convictions as he is knowledgeable in military affairs. It is also important for a President's advisers to have political clout, to speak from a base stronger than a cabinet position. Unfortunately, a President's cabinet is almost always composed of men who owe their immediate power solely to the President who chose them. In contrast, in Britain the members of a minister's cabinet are politicians in their own right, having been elected to Parliament, and they have public followings of their own to give them leverage with the Prime Minister.

American cabinets tend to defer to the President, and cabinet meetings are usually perfunctory and colorless affairs because the President often makes important decisions in private consultations with individual cabinet members. Because most cabinet members in Britain are also members of Parliament, they feel directly responsible to their constituents for what the cabinet does as a whole. Hence the cabinet functions as a unit, with all of its members and not only the Prime Minister responsible to the public for its decisions. In such circumstances resignation is a way of calling attention to a government in crisis. A trivial resignation is *de rigueur* in America but inexcusable in Britain.

Since so many of the President's advisers come from the business world, the business ethic has a strong influence on cabinet behavior. The business ethic does not encourage "going public." Discreet service to the chief executive (corporation head) is a must. Dissent is tolerated, but it must be "modulated and respectful of hierarchy." Once a policy decision is made, all must unite behind its implementation. In Britain, businessmen and lawyers also serve as cabinet members, but once in government service they subscribe to the ethics and protocol of a new and distinct career: elective politics.

The growth of democracy in England has always been in direct alignment with the extension of the franchise. To be elected means to represent the spirit of political evolution itself, and it should come as no surprise that through the years the elective process in Britain has developed a code and manner entirely its own and commensurate with its ideological and social importance. The British cabinet does not provide a respite from the electorate and is therefore no stranger to confrontation. Cabinet members do not risk their careers, as is often the case in America, by dissenting from government policy. Indeed, they often strengthen their careers by defecting from the cabinet and championing the campaign against a controversial policy. Appeasement of Hitler was rejected by Eden and Churchill in exactly this way, and both men knew that "the British system could accommodate their period of dissent and facilitate their eventual return to office."

The prohibition on public protest resignations in America leads inevitably, according to Weisband and Franck, to "countersystem" measures for the airing of dissent. They argue persuasively that the American cabinet's insistence on adhering to the rules of a secret club or fraternity make unavoidable unorthodox challenges to its power: "A system which encourages McNamara's silent resignation and prohibits going public in the Anthony Eden style makes it inevitable that the countersystem will invent a Daniel Ellsberg."

To encourage "ethical autonomy" at cabinet level in the United States, cabinets should be composed of men who are or have been elected to Congress. In making this recommendation, our authors concede that the Constitution would have to be amended to require the President to draw his cabinet from among elected members of Congress. The difficulties of constitutional reform could be avoided by the presidential nominee's naming his key cabinet choices early in the campaign. But finally, no constitutional change can alter a society's view of appropriate political behavior. So long as Americans hate "tattling" more than they love social responsibility, Weisband and Franck do not believe that the pattern and tone of political resignation in this country will change.

Peter A. Brier

SAMUEL JOHNSON: A BIOGRAPHY

Author: John Wain (1925-   )
Publisher: The Viking Press (New York). 388 pp. $12.50
Type of work: Biography
Time: 1709-1784
Locale: England, chiefly London

The life of England's foremost man of letters in the eighteenth century, especially concerned with his struggles to overcome poverty and disease in order to achieve a place for himself in the literary society of London

Principal personages:
SAMUEL JOHNSON, English poet, critic, editor, and dictionary writer
MICHAEL JOHNSON, his father
SARAH JOHNSON, his mother
ELIZABETH JOHNSON, his wife
JAMES BOSWELL, Johnson's friend and traveling companion, whose memoir is the most important single source of information about him
DAVID GARRICK, important English theatrical producer and friend of Johnson
HESTER THRALE, close friend of Johnson in his later years

Samuel Johnson is a major literary figure better known and more important for what he was than for what he wrote. Clearly the outstanding writer of his age, Johnson produced no single important work of imaginative literature. A tragedy, *Irene,* which nobody remembers, a few satires, a minor work of prose fiction entitled *Rasselas,* the fiction in the *Idler* papers, and a few occasional poems, comprise the work of a lifetime. More important, of course, are his scholarly and critical writings—the Dictionary, the edition of Shakespeare, the *Lives of the English Poets,* the *Rambler* papers—but these are known more by the specialist than by the general reading public. It is, however, Johnson the man—the man of letters, the storyteller, the man of conversation, especially as given to us by James Boswell in his famous biography, who is the impor-

tant Johnson, the famous and well-remembered Johnson. A man of copious reading, mostly self-taught, Johnson in conversation was the voice of his age, summarizing its best and sharply criticizing its worst features.

It is to the occasional and fragmentary state of Samuel Johnson's reputation that John Wain addresses himself in this biography. Wain, a novelist and poet as well as a long-time student of Johnson and Professor of Poetry at Oxford University, sets out from the premise that Johnson has not yet been accorded his rightful reputation. Wain believes that Johnson for the most part is thought of as a "stupid old reactionary," rather than as the fine, humane man of deep compassion for the unfortunate of the race. Wain's goal, therefore, is to present a picture of Johnson "as he actually was instead of as he is thought of." He blames for the distorted picture of Johnson both Boswell's romantic Toryism and Johnsonian scholars' tendency to write to each other rather than to a larger public.

Wain, therefore, has written a popular biography which contains no fresh research. As he admits in a concluding acknowledgment, he is heavily dependent on the work of exactly those scholars whom he chastises at the beginning of the book for not making Johnson better known. Only time will tell how well Wain succeeds in bringing Johnson to the attention of the larger public. What he has achieved is the writing of a highly readable popular biography which presents most, if not all, of the information on Johnson's life which will interest a nonscholarly public. One might fault Wain for not acknowledging his sources more directly; without footnotes, the work conceals differences of scholarly opinion and hides its dependencies from all but those familiar with the works from which it derives its information. One cannot fault the author for his own love of his subject; the work's most moving moments are Wain's own descriptions of the importance Johnson's writings have held for him over the years.

The major emphasis in Wain's treatment of Johnson's life is on the Great Cham's struggles to rise from the disadvantages of his boyhood. The son of a poor bookseller, Johnson began life with a number of strikes against him. A physically unattractive man, Johnson was recognized as a genius from early in his career. Unfortunately, because of his family's precarious financial situation, his education was not the best; this

situation he made up for by copious reading among his father's books. Forced to leave Oxford after only one year, he turned, unsuccessfully, to schoolteaching, and, finally, to writing for hire for the *Gentleman's Magazine*. This step led him to move from Litchfield, his birthplace, to London, which was to be his home for the rest of his life.

Johnson married a widow some years his senior. While this brought him temporary happiness, it also brought greater pressure to find a way to support himself and his family. After a time of writing the published versions of Parliamentary debates, as well as other paid writing assignments, he hit upon the possibility of preparing an edition of Shakespeare. When this plan was frustrated by a publisher's refusal to give up its claim to the publication rights for Shakespeare, Johnson turned to another scheme, the preparation of a dictionary of the English language. When a number of wealthy Englishmen pledged support for this undertaking, Johnson finally was able to move himself and his family above the poverty level.

Happiness proved a fleeting thing, however; Wain's version of Johnson shows us a man increasingly trapped in a marriage to an aging woman, yet bound by religious scruples from searching for companionship elsewhere. Even her death did not release him; Johnson never remarried, a failure Wain attributes to a combination of Johnson's guilt feelings over neglecting his first wife and of a lack of many suitable women to choose from. The pattern of Johnson's life, in Wain's view, is the move from physical poverty to emotional poverty, from disease to disease, from loneliness to loneliness.

The companionship of James Boswell and of Hester Thrale became the only bright spots in Johnson's later years. The issue of Johnson's sexuality is of major concern to Wain; careful to show that any argument for sexual union between Hester and Johnson is erroneous, he traces the movement of Johnson's sexual appetite (which he assures us over and over was enormous) from frustration to frustration, ending in unrealized masochistic fantasies. What one trained in such matters might do with the facts of Johnson's birth to a woman of forty, with whom he always had a strained relationship, his marriage to an older woman, and his long relationship, never sexually consummated, with a younger woman, is a point of some speculation. Such argument must await another biographer; Wain simply brings the issue up and leaves it hanging. His concern is to remind us of the agony of Johnson's life; marriage and related failures only added to the already heavy burden of physical unattractiveness, childhood disease, poverty, and the increasing agonies of advancing age. In Wain's view, Johnson's life is the stuff of tragedy —a sequence of hardships, broken only occasionally by moments of success, stretching from the emotional and physical poverty of his childhood to the great loneliness and illness of his old age.

What one misses from this account of Johnson's life is any real sense of the relationship between the content of Johnson's work and the life that produced it. As W. J. Bate has taught us, the sum of Johnson's work is the fulfillment of English neoclassicism. Free in his writings of the excesses of those who would apply the tenets of neoclassic literary theory so strictly that they would consider Shakespeare a bad playwright because he did not observe the unities of time, space, and action, Johnson enunciated a view of life and of art which stressed balance, order, degree, and proportion in their best sense, as the touchstones for what is true and good in human achievement. Johnson's conversation at its best reflects a similar concern for the avoidance of excess, of extremes, of the odd and the unusual, and for the affirmation of the sound, the general, the well-balanced. Surely in the light of Johnson's difficult life, there is something to be said for the significance of such a vision. Surely we might ask what the links between his values and his experiences might be. Yet, for the most part, Wain avoids such considerations. On the matter of Johnson's writings, he argues basically that their glory is in the fact that he got them done in the face of his erratic work habits and the distractions of poverty, loneliness, and disease. Wain is eloquent on the meaning of the writings, especially the *Lives of the English Poets,* for him, but he rarely has much to say about what these efforts, which clearly cost Johnson a great deal to produce, could tell us about Johnson the man.

In summary, Wain's biography fulfills a need, perhaps an urgent one, for a popular record of the life of Samuel Johnson. It is readable, if perhaps occasionally overwritten, and accurate so far as it goes. We should always be thankful for what we have, but it is also not inappropriate to wonder what we might have had if Wain had been less interested in making up for what he feels scholars have not done and more interested in using all the evidence for the fullest possible portrait of a man who is clearly an important influence in Wain's own life.

John N. Wall, Jr.

SEASCAPE

Author: Edward Albee (1928-   )
Publisher: Atheneum Publishers (New York). 135 pp. $7.95
Type of work: Drama
Time: The present
Locale: A beach

An imaginative drama in which a human couple and a lizard couple discuss the meaning of their lives and the problems of their relationships

> Principal characters:
> CHARLIE and
> NANCY, an affluent, middle-aged, married couple taking their
> vacation at the beach
> LESLIE and
> SARAH, a happily mated pair of sea lizards

Edward Albee's earlier plays have offered a negative view of contemporary life: *Zoo Story* (1959) pictured purposeless existence; *The American Dream* (1960) satirized failing family values; and *Who's Afraid of Virginia Woolf?* (1962) presented a grim portrait of marriage. Refreshingly, *Seascape* is positive in its whimsical approach to growing old, to the meaning of life in general, and to the purpose of life in particular. Still using his absurdist free-flow of conversation (actually, as always, carefully and economically structured as topics pass by again and again, each time acquiring new meaning until an epiphany is reached), Albee here matches an aging human couple, Charlie and Nancy, with a similar pair of sea lizards.

Charlie and Nancy are on vacation at a beach. As most of the first act passes, we learn that they are well-off and fancy-free, having already reared their family. But they are different from each other; Nancy is impulsive and wants to enjoy life, while Charlie seems worn out by life and wants to do nothing. Early in the play the viewer realizes the basic di-

chotomy between the two approaches to life. Charlie's recollection of his childhood game of sitting on the bottom of the sea symbolically suggests his retreat from life, his withdrawal from its problems into that dark, murky world from which life first emerged. But Nancy's suggestion that they spend their days following the sun from beach to beach clearly paints the opposite, "do not go gentle into that good night" approach. Nancy even urges Charlie to try his old game again to "reconfirm"; but she shows her irritation with him when, as he reminds her of what a good provider he has been, she exclaims, "Well, we'll wrap you in the flag when you're done, and do taps."

The dilemma being presented in the first act, then, seems to be rather trite: to grow old with dignity or to grow old and still be active. Another familiar idea appears to be part of Albee's theme. From time to time jet planes fly over the beach, and each time one crosses, Charlie and Nancy fall into this litany: "Such noise they make"; "They'll crash into the dunes one day. I don't know what good they do," indicating a disgust with our machine age. But as the pair of sea lizards, Leslie and Sarah, appear near the end of Act One, things become more complicated, and the rather worn out ideas begin to take on new meaning as Charlie and Nancy are compared with their sea-world counterparts.

The females are rather alike, bright and inquisitive; and so are the males, cautious and protective. A great number of humorous parallels arise as the couples explain their life styles. Sex is, of course, the dominant topic. They agree that they have one thing in common—they "couple"; but Nancy is amazed that Sarah has laid eggs right and left, and Sarah is completely surprised that Nancy has cared for her young for eighteen years, rather than letting them "just float away." Although one may suspect for a time that Albee is suggesting the innate superiority of women as the two alert creatures talk, while their mates glower and fail to comprehend, this is not really the point.

Albee has presented the great disappointments of life—growing old and a seemingly purposeless existence —but these are merely the preparations for his affirmation of what Bernard Shaw called the "life force." The difference between man and beast becomes clear when Nancy tries to make Sarah understand about emotions such as love or loss. The lizards do not have emotions. When another jet flies over, terrifying the lizard couple, Charlie now proudly explains that the airplane is a machine. Man has invented machines that can do anything; man has even concocted a machine that will go under the water. Here the metaphysical nature of the play begins to become apparent.

Even though life as we know it has its drawbacks, its wastes (such as Charlie's and Nancy's old age), it is preferable because it is a part of the necessary evolution. Evolution has not stopped, but is a continual process; maybe some day everything will be better. Perhaps the play becomes somewhat heavy-handed at this point, when Charlie, proud that he has no tail, that he has mutated, explains Descartes' theory to Leslie, who is still happy with his enormous tail. But the play does end with a dedication to the life force, or, as Nancy had earlier stated, a "reconfirmation."

When Leslie and Sarah decide that it is time to return to the sea, the human couple invites them to remain and become advanced creatures who use tools, create art, and become aware of mortality. But Leslie and Sarah do not understand mortality; so, to explain the concept, Charlie asks Sarah how she would feel if Leslie went away and she knew that he was never coming back. When Sarah finally understands the question, she sobs. The life force is at work; she has begun to acquire emotions, and Charlie and Nancy have found a purpose: "We could help you. . . . Take you by the hand." The play ends with the word "begin," as the lizards decide to remain and become a part of civilization. Paradoxically, Albee's play at its beginning prepares the audience for a hackneyed invective against "this modern world in which we live," only to pull the rug out from under them at the end by affirming the process of which we are all a part.

Seascape brought Edward Albee his second Pulitzer Prize. While the play is whimsical and delightful in its free-wheeling dialogue, it is at the same time a carefully structured and thought-provoking work. In a way, it is a throwback to the turn-of-the-century "Drama of Ideas" and to Bernard Shaw, who made Darwinism a dynamic creative concept in *Man and Superman*. Yet it brings thought amidst smiles and laughter: a considerable accomplishment.

Harry A. Hargrave

A SEASON IN HELL

Author: Percy Knauth (1914-   )
Publisher: Harper & Row Publishers (New York). 111 pp. $6.95
Type of work: Limited autobiography
Time: 1939-1957
Locale: New York; New Haven, Connecticut; Berlin; Paris; Ankara, Turkey

A harrowing account of a man's nearly complete victory over depression, by a courageous writer who confesses the deepest hurts of his lifetime in order to assist other victims of mental illness

> Principal personages:
> PERCY KNAUTH, author, editor, former National Mental Health Chairman
> BEHRI, his wife
> A FRENCHWOMAN, his first wife, who deserted him after thirteen years of marriage
> DR. MYRNA WEISSMAN, epidemiologist at the Psychiatric Division of the Yale-New Haven Medical Center
> DR. DE LA VERGNE, the physician who prescribed anti-depressant medication to Knauth

Several years ago, after a fitful night of despondency and wakefulness, Percy Knauth, then fifty-seven years old, reached over to his bedside table for a bottle of sleeping pills. He had decided to swallow the contents of the bottle at one gulp. Following months of suffering the terrors of depression, he no longer felt that he could continue a life which had once seemed secure and reasonably content. During the late 1930's he had served as Berlin correspondent for the *Chicago Tribune* and later for the *New York Times;* more recently, a successful free-lance writer, he contributed articles to *Time, Life,* and *Sports Illustrated* magazines; and at this fateful moment he was a staff editor for Time-Life Books, earning a handsome salary, respected in his profession for his achievements over twenty-eight years as a journalist and editor. His wife of nearly twenty years, mother of his two children, stirred by his side. She gathered into her arms his trembling form, rocked and cradled it as she would an infant, while her husband wept. For the moment he would not commit suicide. Yet his "season in hell"—the torments of depression—was to continue until, with courage, insight, and proper medical assistance, he was at last able to cast off the most terrible of his demons and, with restored sanity, resume his normal life.

Like Arthur Rimbaud's brilliant *Une Saison en Enfer* (1873), Knauth's autobiographical fragment is charged with illumination into the dark corners of the soul. Whereas Rimbaud's adventures in gratuitous wickedness often seem designed to startle the bourgeoisie, Knauth's experiences with madness are by no means exhibitionistic. His suffering is real. The message of Knauth's book is that "acute clinical depression," the most widespread mental illness, can be controlled, if not wholly cured, by proper pharmaceuticals. So on one level his book, published with the approval of the Mental Health Association, offers to the afflicted new hope for recovery. The author, who served as National Mental Health Chairman in 1975, is an apt writer to publicize for a general audience the advanced research in psychotropic drugs intended to facilitate recovery from depression. A lucid stylist, Knauth has the special ability to make technical scientific information clear and available to the common reader.

On another level, however, *A Season in Hell* is an authentic human document, a powerful, sometimes painfully candid revelation of a person in torment. Searching for a key to his mental illness, Knauth probes with austere courage the roots of his affliction. Detective-like, he investigates every clue from the past that might yield an answer: his once-happy marriage to a French girl, shattered after thirteen years by the pain of a traumatic divorce; his subsequent remarriage to a sensitive American woman; his attempts to shore up, through a routine of hard work, a life already critically flawed by secret griefs. For months, in spite of his earnest, even desperate efforts, he failed to discover the hidden source of his depression. Because he once underwent a classical although incomplete Freudian psychoanalysis, he understands all the external signals of madness. But he cannot reach internally, to the core of his special case. Ironically, his knowledge of psychology profits him little, except to further his sense of hopelessness. With the skill of a master storyteller, Knauth plays upon the reader's emotions, so that the protagonist's fearful struggle becomes his own.

Gradually, by slow degrees of self-discovery, the author ventures upon most of the solutions to his problem. But he saves until nearly the end of his book his most dramatic insight—a plausible psychological explanation for the causes of his depression. Until that point, he experiences with remarkable fortitude all the agonies of madness. He moves from bewilderment to resentment to rage, finally to despair. As Knauth describes his descent into hell, he makes clear to the reader the waste, in terms of human resources, that results from mental illness. His mind is plagued by the devils of self-doubt, confusion, inarticulate anger, and sloth. To be sure, he is able to maintain his job as editor of a Time-Life series of books, is even capable of performing his duties with competence. But all the time his self-image is that of a madman.

Knauth's cure, never complete but very nearly satisfactory, began in 1970 at the Depression Research Unit at New Haven, Connecticut. Posing at first as a journalist interested in the treatment of depression, he came to understand that modern chemical treatments of the illness had been showing excellent results for most patients. From his conversation with several physicians and researchers, particularly Dr. Myrna Weissman, he learned that anti-depressant drugs could alter, in remarkable ways, the reactions typical in cases of exogenous and endogenous depressions. Knauth declared himself a victim of the mental illness, directly began taking the prescribed anti-depressant pills, and continued the medication two and half years, up to the date of the publication of his book. As he makes clear to the reader, he will surely continue to take the pills the rest of his life. Once, when he neglected to take his treatment for a brief while, he suffered immediate harmful results. From the depressed person's standpoint, Knauth says, medication is as important to the control of his illness as insulin is necessary to a diabetic. For both sufferers the maladies are rarely "cured"; they are merely controlled.

Some months after he had started his treatment with psychotropic medicine, Knauth experienced a particularly vivid and frightening dream. He recalled a time during the spring of 1947, when he was driving on the autobahn near Brauschweig in West Germany. His vehicle, fallen into a mud hole, had to be pushed back to the highway toward Berlin. Suddenly the memory of Berlin started in the author a train of association of past events. In 1939, a foreign correspondent in that city, he had been passionately in love with a Frenchwoman, who was a fugitive living under the protection of the American embassy. Their love affair, at first mutual, was intensified by the dangers of the war, for it seemed to thrive on the excitement of the moment. After the war, thirteen years from the time of their first meeting in Berlin and their later marriage, Knauth was stunned when his wife left him for another man. Always he had concealed from his mind the tragic significance of her departure. Now, as he returned in memory to the early days of happiness, he slowly came to understand that his love had never been securely founded. The terrors of wartime, rather than an enduring affection, had brought the two aliens together as frightened lovers in a foreign land. In retrospect, Knauth realized that, although his passion had been sincere, he had been youthfully idealistic and innocent at the time. Hence he need not have blamed himself for the collapse of the marriage. Yet all these years, his subconscious feeling of inner defeat had worsened, inevitably resulting in his depression. The flaw in his mental sufficiency, once understood, was now capable of a measure of control. Although the author could not change the defeats from his past life to success, he could come to terms with himself.

The great value of *A Season in Hell* is that it restores to the reader, whether quite sane or depressed, a measure of the sense of dignity that Knauth rightfully claims for all people. Other, more extended scientific books could, presumably, cover the same technical grounds on mental health. But Knauth gives to his study a human dimension that is precious; he speaks as one who has suffered and endured. An artist, he makes the hell of depression seem both terrible and, from a visionary insight, strangely beautiful. Like Rimbaud, he illuminates moments of intensity: his hallucinatory visions of the healers Hippocrates and Paracelsus; his memories of anguish; his memories of brief, bitter passion. More than a limited view of depression, Knauth's engaging book is a memorial to the courage of the human spirit.

Leslie B. Mittleman

SELECTED LETTERS OF JAMES JOYCE

Author: James Joyce (1882-1941)
Edited, with an Introduction and notes, by Richard Ellmann
Publisher: The Viking Press (New York). 440 pp. $18.95; paperback $5.95
Type of work: Letters

Drawn largely from the three-volume collection already published, but including important additions of previously excised passages and ten revealing new letters

James Joyce likes to cast himself in the role of artistic hero. His youthful letter to Henrik Ibsen (March, 1901) hails the Norwegian not as a social realist, but as one who, with "absolute indifference to public canons of art, friends and shibboleths . . . walked in the light of inward heroism." As far as the nineteen-year-old Joyce was concerned, there had been a laying on of hands, and he accepted the verdict of the future: "your willful resolution to wrest the secret from life gave me heart," and "as one of the youthful generation for whom you have spoken I give you greeting." As one might expect, Joyce's letters as a group provide us with a somewhat different picture; they suggest the image of a human vessel filled to the brim with human nonsense. The nonsense, of course, was justified by *Dubliners, Portrait of the Artist as a Young Man, Ulysses,* and *Finnegans Wake.* It was, in fact, necessary to Joyce. But one should not, as some reviewers have, perceive the nonsense as something else —as in itself heroic.

The warning is particularly pertinent in connection with certain passages printed for the first time in *The Selected Letters of James Joyce.* The selection is, of course, drawn almost entirely from the three large volumes already in print, and Richard Ellmann has done an extraordinarily sensitive and sensible job in making his selection. He has also included ten new letters and, in a number of cases, has replaced passages that he had been forced to excise in earlier publication. Some of these, already famous, are likely to become classics of their kind—the notorious "dirty" passages that appear in letters to Nora Barnacle, the girl who agreed to run away with Joyce when, in 1904, he left Ireland for an uncertain future on the Continent.

All Joyceans know the story. In 1909 Joyce returned to Dublin for a visit, leaving Nora in Trieste. Maliciously, he was told that, back in 1904, Nora had two-timed him, and that, on the days when she was not with Joyce, she was seeing someone else. Joyce was crushed. He fired off an all-is-over-between-us missive, filled less with jealous rage than with enormous reservoirs of self-pity: "O, Nora, I am unhappy. I am crying for my poor unhappy love." He went into ecstasies of self-torture: Was his son really his? Had Nora given his rival the same favors she had given Joyce: "Did you place your hand on him as you did on me in the dark . . . ?" Convinced by another friend that he had been misled and Nora slandered, Joyce turned around and began to abase himself: "My sweet noble Nora, I ask you to forgive me for my contemptible conduct but they maddened me. . . ." Within a few days, Joyce was outlining his fantasies: "When I go to bed at night . . . . I see you in a hundred poses, grotesque, shameful, virginal, languorous. Give yourself to me, dearest, all, all when we meet." A bit later: "Tonight I have an idea madder than usual. I feel I would like to be flogged by you. I would like to see your eyes blazing with anger."

Joyce returned to Trieste, but in little over a month was back in Dublin as advance man for a cinema company. This time his letters did more than outline his fantasies. Employing all the appropriate four-letter words, Joyce, in great detail, describes intercourse in various positions and with various costumes. The letters incorporate fetishism, fellatio, analism, flagellation; more than once they link the sexual and the excretory organs. And yet these letters contain also passages of tenderness and adoration as Joyce attempts to define precisely what Nora's love has meant to him. Joyce was perfectly aware of the fact that he was approaching her in two different ways: "One moment I see you like a virgin or madonna the next moment I see you shameless, insolent, half naked and obscene!" As far as Joyce was concerned, he was expressing the elements of his nature as he felt called upon to do: "My love for you allows me to pray to the spirit of eternal beauty and tenderness mirrored in your eyes or to fling you down under me and. . . ." Ellmann accepts this version, insisting that the correspondence "commands respect for its intensity and candour, and for its fulfillment of Joyce's avowed determination to express his whole mind."

But there may be another, less noble, less heroic explanation of what can, after all, be seen as an effort to punish both Nora and himself. In 1902, Joyce went to Paris, ostensibly to study medicine. He was in constant need of money and his family did what they could. In March, 1903, he wrote to his mother:

> I cannot cash your order today. . . . My next meal therefore will be at 11 a.m. tomorrow (Monday): my last meal was 7 p.m. last (Saturday) night. So I have another fast of 40 hours— No, not a fast, for I have eaten a pennyworth of dry bread. My second last meal was 20 hours before my last. 20 and 40 = 60—Two meals in 60 hours is not bad, I think. As my lenten regulations have made me somewhat weak I shall go up to my room and sit there till it is time to go to bed.

There are other letters in a similar vein. Joyce knew full well what his family was doing in its effort to support him: "I hope the carpet that was sold is not one of the new purchases that you are selling to feed me." He offered to return the money but immediately launched into further complaints. There can be little doubt that Joyce needed to punish his mother and that he also needed to feel guilty about it. When his mother died, he saw her as a victim and listed his own "cynical frankness of conduct" as one of the forces that destroyed her. Clearly we are dealing with a mental set that may be taken back to infancy.

To that same set we may attribute Joyce's famous willingness to see conspiracy and rejection everywhere. He had, he told Nora, a "contemptuous suspicious nature." In fact, as Ell-mann points out, he seems to have courted betrayal, making constant and increasingly inordinate demands upon family and friends. One of the constant themes in Joyce's letters is money, his lack of it, and his assumption that others would supply it. To leave for the Continent in 1904 he borrowed from everyone in sight. Having discovered that there was no job waiting for him in Zurich, he asked his brother Stanislaus to "go about the highways of the city but not to any of my touched friends and make up £1 before Saturday. . . ." Settled in Pola, he assumes that Stanislaus will be delighted to pay a printing bill he left behind him. Later, having enticed Stanislaus to Trieste and having himself gone to Rome to take a job in a bank, Joyce calls for money, not now and then, but month after month: "If you cannot do something at once to help me over this month I do not see how I can live." One week later: "I expect you will be able to raise something for me today." These letters are, in fact, remarkably similar in tone to the letters Joyce wrote home in 1902 and 1903. But his demands were not always financial. He demanded trust, loyalty, understanding. A failure anywhere was proof of betrayal and rejection. Apparently Stanislaus did have a breaking point, though the immediate cause of the dispute is unknown: in 1911, Joyce wrote a very stiff note to his brother telling him that he intends to "clear out" and leave to Stanislaus and the two Joyce sisters who had joined them "the city discovered by my courage (and Nora's) seven years ago, wither you and they came in obedience to my summons, from your ignorant and famine-stricken and treacherous country." The break was smoothed over. Joyce did not leave Trieste.

Obviously Joyce was far more than a psychopath. Among other things, he was often aware that much of his behavior was extreme, many of his postures foolish—or at least he could put them in perspective. The evidence is to be found on every page of *Ulysses* and *Finnegans Wake,* and the selected letters provide an excellent introduction to this multi-sided genius. On the way to Paris in 1902, Joyce saw himself as "arrayed against the powers of the world." Back in Dublin and wooing Nora Barnacle, he wrote a series of letters explaining himself, for he felt that she must understand him fully: "My mind rejects the whole present social order and Christianity—home, the recognized virtues, classes of life, and religious doctrines." Waiting for her one night, "It seemed to me that I was fighting a battle with every religious and social force in Ireland for you. . . ." Once on the Continent, Joyce wrote regularly to Stanislaus, and that body of correspondence is one of the most interesting in the volume, for it relates the progress both of his reading and his writing. Embedded in this series are letters recounting Joyce's luckless experience with publishers. Grant Richards, having contracted for *Dubliners,* then refused. In the course of his wrangle with Richards, Joyce wrote his famous letter outlining his goal: "My intention was to write a chapter of the moral history of my country and I chose Dublin for the scene because that city seemed to me the centre of paralysis." The Richards episode was, of course, only the first in a long series.

In 1915, after writing the first chapter of *Ulysses* and after moving to Trieste to avoid being swamped by World War I, Joyce made a number of new friends and contacts. Money began to flow both from funds and from benefactors. Others began to make his cause their own and saw to the publication of *A Portrait of the Artist As a Young Man* and *Dubliners*. *Ulysses* was serialized as Joyce produced it. There are letters to Ezra Pound, who had busied himself in Joyce's behalf; to Harriet Shaw Weaver, who sent money and eventually sought to establish a permanent trust for Joyce; to Frank Budgen, an English artist and writer with whom Joyce discussed *Ulysses* and who wrote what is still one of the more readable introductions to that work. Ellmann is careful to include letters to Weaver and Budgen that contain explanations of some of the more difficult episodes in *Ulysses,* explanations that have become the common currency of Joyce scholarship. He includes also letters to the Swiss woman Martha Fleischmann, with whom Joyce carried on a comic-opera affair, addressing feverish rhapsodies to her before he even knew her name:

> I had a fever yesterday evening, waiting for a sign from you. But why do you not want to write even one word to me—your name? And why do you always close your shutters? I want to see you. I do not know what you think of me.

There is some disagreement over whether the affair ever got beyond the looking-writing-talking stage, but it was, in any case, concluded when Martha entered an asylum and her lover, Rudolf Hitpold, angrily warned Joyce off.

During most of his later years, Joyce lived in Paris, where he found friends and admirers eager to help. Even so demanding an individual as Joyce had to be gratified: "By the way," he wrote to Budgen, "is it not extraordinary the way I enter a city barefoot and end up in a luxurious flat. Still, I am tired of it." The bomb that was *Ulysses* went off satisfactorily, but *Finnegans Wake* tended to fizzle, and many who had ardently admired the earlier book were baffled by the latter. A large number of letters went to his benefactress, Harriet Weaver, who, if she could not come to terms with *Finnegans Wake,* at least made an earnest effort; Joyce, in turn, attempted to explain matters to her. Of five new letters to Miss Weaver, four contain glosses of episodes in the work. Since, unlike others, Miss Weaver remained sympathetic to Joyce, his letters to her provide a fine running commentary on this portion of his life, a commentary that is, if anything, clearer for having been lifted out of the context of the larger volumes.

At the end of his life, Joyce, like so many in Europe, was on the move again, leaving Paris and then France to the Nazi conquerors, and dying, finally, in Zurich.

Max Halperen

SELF-PORTRAIT IN A CONVEX MIRROR

Author: John Ashbery (1927-   )
Publisher: The Viking Press (New York). 83 pp. $5.95
Type of work: Poetry

A Pulitzer Prize-winning collection of reflective poetry by one of America's most challenging and important writers

John Ashbery's first commercially published book of poems, *Some Trees,* appeared in 1956 as Volume 52 in the Yale Series of Younger Poets. Since then, he has published six other major volumes of poetry, all of which have been enthusiastically received by a relatively small audience consisting largely of other *avant-garde* poets and artists. His latest book, *Self-Portrait in a Convex Mirror,* is, however, the first to bring him wide recognition among the general poetry audience, winning for him three of the country's most respected book awards (the National Book Critics Circle Award, the National Book Award, and the Pulitzer Prize), and making him, at least briefly, the most widely read and discussed "serious" poet alive in America.

The current popularity of Ashbery's poetry seems more likely to be due to changing tastes among readers than to any particular recent development in his own work, although it is true that *Self-Portrait in a Convex Mirror* contains some of the most "accessible" poetry this difficult poet has so far produced. His last book, *Three Poems,* for example, consisted of three audaciously long and dense prose meditations, weaving in and out of such enormous questions as the construction of identity, the validity of subjective knowledge, and the perception of time. But though the form of the poems in *Self-Portrait in a Convex Mirror* may make them more

immediately readable than *Three Poems,* and though their diction may be for the most part more relaxed (and thus less intimidating), the same concerns continue to resonate through the core of Ashbery's new poems. More importantly, the same aesthetic stance serves as point of departure for the latest poems as for the earliest ones, and it is a stance that sets him apart from most of his contemporaries of comparable stature; namely, that it is the process of thought and not its objects that ultimately matters in poetry.

It is this underlying principle that makes Ashbery's work difficult for readers accustomed to most other American poetry; unlike, for example, Robert Frost, or Sylvia Plath, or Robert Lowell, Ashbery consistently refuses to present clear, central subject matter in his poetry. He chooses, rather, to produce poems which, commenting relentlessly upon themselves, take as their subject a state of mind conducive to the making of poetry. Because it does not appear to be "about" anything in particular in the world external to it, many readers have found Ashbery's poetry obscure and hermetic. Hermetic it may be—an Ashbery poem seems to take on meaning only when it is accepted as a whole, surrendered to rather than attacked—but to call it obscure is like calling music obscure because it does not present any paraphrasable information. In this respect, John Ashbery is clearly the poetic descendant of Paul Valéry and Wallace Stevens, rather than, for example, Ezra Pound or William Carlos Williams.

Ashbery's preoccupation with time and the changes wrought by time stands as a corollary to his conception of the poem as process. The poems in this volume, continually drawing attention to their own movement by reason of their shifting subjects and moods, also concentrate upon the passage of time and the processes associated with it: the cycle of the year and of the individual day, the shared past of our cultural heritage, and, above all, the progress of the individual human being from childhood to adulthood, a progress in which memory comes to be equated with identity. "Grand Galop," for example, begins, "All things seem mention of themselves/ And the names which stem from them branch out to other referents." In its context, this is not only a statement of the power of language to organize reality; it is also a statement of the function of memory in the individual's perception of the world around him, of the fact that we can understand things only as we relate them to other things we have known before. As if to prove this point, the poem moves into a recollection of school lunch menus, which classifies the days of the week according to them: "And today is Monday. Today's lunch is: Spanish omelet, lettuce and tomato salad,/ Jello, milk and cookies." The occasional childishness of diction in this poem ("Puaagh. Vomit. Puaaaaagh. More vomit.") reflects the ability of the present to recall childhood, the fact

that the present seems real only as it becomes past. At its conclusion, "Grand Galop" contrasts the security of past experience, which selective memory makes almost automatically comprehensible, with the confusion of unordered experiences which constitutes the present:

> How long ago high school graduation
>   seems
> Yet it cannot have been so very long:
> One has traveled such a short
>   distance. . . .
> But now we are at Cape Fear and the
>   overland trail
> Is impassable, and a dense curtain of
>   mist hangs over the sea.

Such a contrast, in terms of comprehensibility, may be drawn between present and future as well as between present and past; as another poem in the book has it, "Tomorrow is easy, but today is uncharted."

Like "Grand Galop," most of the other poems in *Self-Portrait in a Convex Mirror* build toward an ending that laments the irrecoverability of the past while bringing the reader back into his own present moment, outside the poem. The poem itself is seen as past experience as it nears its end, and this ability of poetry to serve as both past experience (memory) and present experience (in the act of reading or writing) is seen as an essential part of the importance of poetry in providing meaning, as at the end of "Scheherazade": "And the man who makes the same mistake twice is exonerated." The closing lines of many of the poems in the collection refer to a move from past to present time, as, for instance, "Ode to Bill" (" . . . we must, we must be moving on.") or "A Man of Words" ("Just time to reread this/And the past slips through your fingers, wishing you were there"). Unlike Shakespeare's sonnets, for example, which frequently end with a declaration that they are "monuments in verse" commemorating a person or experience, these poems declare in their closure that they are themselves experiences which take place in time, events rather than things. There is, therefore, no need for the speaker in the poems to get everything down on paper at once: "Someday I'll explain. Not today though" ("Ode to Bill").

Perhaps the most striking departures in Ashbery's latest book are the moments when he allows himself an outpouring of sentiment unlike any seen in his work before. This is not to say that his previous work has not had a strong emotional quality, but he has rarely before been as direct in talking about love as at the end of "No Way of Knowing":

> Why must you go? Why can't you
> Spend the night, here in my bed, with
>   my arms wrapped tightly around you?
> Surely that would solve everything by
>   supplying
> A theory of knowledge on a scale with
>   the gigantic
> Bits and pieces of knowledge we have
>   retained:
> An LP record of all your favorite
>   friendships,
> Of letters from the front? Too
> Fantastic to make sense? But it made
>   the chimes ring.
> If you listen you can hear them ringing
>   still:
> A mood, a Stimmung, adding up to a
>   sense of what they really were,
> All along, through the chain of
>   lengthening days.

Here the implied statement is that feeling is more important as an organizing principle in constructing a knowledge of one's life (and of the world) than is any information one might possess. But the self-conscious simplicity of these lines brings to the poem not only a strong lyrical quality, but a carefully balanced irony. "No Way of Knowing" stresses feeling over intellect, while parodying the idea of doing so at the same time—as, quite clearly, does "Poem in Three Parts": "Feelings are important./Mostly I think of feelings . . . ."

The book's long title poem is a meditation upon Parmigianino's famous self-portrait. Ashbery, himself an art critic (he was for several years an editor of *Art News*), considers the reactions of critics to Parmigianino's painting within the poem, bringing in a scholarly, detached tone normally associated more with essays than with poetry. But in the progress of the discourse it becomes clear that the author is contemplating not so much the painting, but the ways in which art is perceived and responded to: critical analysis, personal associations, private symbolism, and so on. In short, Ashbery presents this poem, certainly one of his finest, as an inspection of himself triggered by an identification with a painter contemplating his own image, radically distorted in a convex mirror. The reader, too, comes directly into this system, in that he stands in the same relationship to Ashbery's poem as Ashbery does to Parmigianino's painting. There is, then, perhaps a warning as much as an invitation to enter the world of the poem in Ashbery's comment on Parmigianino's precision in reproducing his mirror image: ". . . you could be fooled for a moment/Before you realize the reflection/Isn't yours."

"Self-Portrait in a Convex Mirror" is a bewildering, but absorbing, maze of mirrors, of dialectically argued propositions about the nature of art and memory, of carefully constructed ambiguities. If it is somewhat confusing to the reader new to Ashbery's work, it is because, as we have noted before, Ashbery is a poet who concentrates more upon the process of the poem than on delivering to the reader any immediately comprehensible statements about the world. Given their focus upon the dynamics of thought, it is not surprising that the poems in *Self-Portrait in a Convex Mirror* encourage the reader to move back into the world when the poem is over, to keep finding new objects of thought, new poems in the world. Perhaps a statement Ashbery makes about Parmigianino's self-portrait is the most important thing we can learn from his own poetry:

> I think it is trying to say it is today
> And we must get out of it even as the
>   public
> Is pushing through the museum now so
>   as to
> Be out by closing time. You can't live
>   there.

Bernard Welt

SHOGUN

Author: James Clavell (1924-   )
Publisher: Atheneum Publishers (New York). 803 pp. $12.50
Type of work: Novel
Time: 1600
Locale: Japan

A shipwrecked English mariner finds himself drawn into a power struggle for control of feudal Japan

Principal characters:

JOHN BLACKTHORNE, Pilot-Major of a Dutch trading fleet
who is shipwrecked in Japan
YOSHI TORANAGA, Lord of the Kwanto
YOSHI NAGA, Toranaga's son
TODA HIRO-MATSU, Commander in chief of Toranaga's armies
TODA BUNTARO, Hiro-matsu's son
TODA MARIKO, Buntaro's wife and interpreter to Toranaga
FUJIKO, Hiro-matsu's granddaughter
KASIGI YABU, Lord of Izu
KASIGI OMI, Yabu's nephew
ISHIDO KAZUNARI, Lord of Osaka
SAIGAWA ZATAKAI, Lord of Shinano
GYOKO, a Mama-san and Tea House manager
KIKU, a courtesan
FATHER MARTIN ALVITO, a member of the Society of Jesus, and
an interpreter
VASCO RODRIGUEZ, Pilot of the Portuguese fleet

The writer of historical fiction possesses a signal advantage over other novelists in that plausibility is enhanced by the very nature of his material. After all, the localities his readers visit really existed and the events they experience either occurred or are within the limits of probability; the people they encounter had prototypes who actually lived. Suspension of disbelief is almost automatic.

At the same time that it presents fewer initial obstacles to reader acceptance, the historical novel imposes truly formidable challenges upon its author. A vanished world must be painstakingly researched in all its infinite variety and then re-created with as much authenticity and completeness as the limitations of a book permit. Landscapes, architecture, institutions, thought patterns, attitudes, and traditions must be resurrected and infused with life. The history of which they were a part must be chronicled accurately, and, if liberties are taken, they cannot do violence to the major thrust of that history. Added to these essential ingredients are those required of all fiction: perceptive and skillful characterization, appropriate plotting, and a logical, well-paced narrative. Ideally, the reader should be able to experience this re-created world as though it were a separate reality that can be entered at will, inhabited by people who are real and complex individuals. And, when the book is finished and laid aside, it should leave behind a conviction that its writer's vision is true.

The interweaving of fact and fancy necessary to accomplish these ends or an approximation of them, and to keep the story moving through masses of detail, requires unusual literary skill. The finished product is inevitably lengthy and, if successful, is an eloquent testimonial to the storyteller's art. *Shogun* is an ambitious and generally effective attempt to produce a historical novel in the classic mold. It is primarily a tale of adventure. John Blackthorne, Pilot-Major of five Dutch galleons, brings the only surviving vessel of his command to a haven in Japanese waters during the spring of 1600. To all intents and purposes shipwrecked, he finds himself the captive of a totally alien culture in which great beauty and elaborate ceremony coexist with ferocity and violence, where sudden death is never more than a word away from anyone.

To make matters worse, Blackthorne discovers that the Spanish and Portuguese have been well-established in Japan for over forty years; their political wing, composed principally of Jesuits, is constantly intriguing for power, subverting and converting Japanese in high places to promote colonial expansion. They hold positions of influence and act as interpreters. To them Blackthorne is not only an enemy but a potential competitor, and they misrepresent him to the Japanese—who look upon him as even more barbaric than all other foreigners. Imprisoned for a time, Blackthorne is fortunate enough to attract the favorable notice of Yoshi Toranaga, President of the Council of Regents, who is engaged in a life-or-death power struggle for a position as Shogun, the supreme dictator of all Japan. Blackthorne is able to consolidate his own position by saving Toranaga's life on more than one occasion. Toranaga is not motivated by gratitude, but he appreciates the Englishman's forthrightness and ingenuity and sees where he may be useful. Blackthorne becomes widely known as Anjin-san, or "The Pilot."

Communication becomes easier when Toranaga assigns Mariko, an interpreter he can trust, to teach Blackthorne Japanese. Mariko's husband is Buntaro, the son of Toranaga's most trusted general. Inevitably Blackthorne progresses rapidly in his knowledge of Japanese civilization, and inevitably he and Mariko become lovers—a course of action far more perilous than in his own society, for Buntaro possesses all the fierce pride, keen sense of honor, and hair-trigger temper characteristic of a samurai warrior. Blackthorne accepts the risks, human nature being what it is; but he can never face death with the equanimity and even enthusiasm of the Japanese, who believe they will be born again in forty days, probably into better circumstances.

In the meantime, Toranaga matches wits with his enemies, his competitors, and his subordinates, surrounded by intrigues of bewildering complexity. When the battle is finally joined, it transpires that this beleaguered statesman who has appeared to vacillate and weaken in order to gain time, has in reality outguessed everyone and will indeed emerge the victor. Toranaga is decisive and entirely ruthless, as conquerors must be when only ruthlessness will serve. He does not hesitate to sacrifice pawns, and when his strategies have run their course, Blackthorne's newfound happiness and security are destroyed. Although Blackthorne is unaware of its extent, Toranaga's protection continues; and although Blackthorne still cherishes a dream of returning to England, it is clear that Toranaga will never let him go. The old warrior, recognizing that Blackthorne is the one person close to his office who will never conspire against it, entertains a certain regard for him and realizes that there is no other human being on earth he can call a friend.

Shogun is a fast-paced and absorbing tale, replete with action, but it is most noteworthy for its vivid portrait of feudal Japan during that country's transition from a chaos of warring provinces to a consolidated, centralized state. This portrait is probably as complete and perceptive as any that could be painted by one who is heir to a different heritage, and it is often splendid. There are moments of sensitivity and beauty, as in the tea ceremony performed by Buntaro and Mariko, or in this haunting evocation of the contemplative mood: "Ueki-ya had told him that a garden must be settled around its rocks, that without them a garden is empty, merely a place of growing. . . . One of the rocks was jagged and ordinary but Ueki-ya had planted it so that if you looked at it long and hard near sunset, the reddish glow glinting off the veins and crystals buried within, you could see a whole range of mountains with lingering valleys and deep lakes and, far off, a greening horizon, night gathering there. . . ."

The reader remains an outsider, just as Blackthorne does, but he nonetheless gains a deeper understanding of the seventeenth century Japanese world than outsiders would normally acquire.

The narrative is not without its ironies, amusing and otherwise. We may instinctively identify with Blackthorne because the glories of Elizabethan England are a shared heritage; but after we are confronted with the normal Elizabethan eating, drinking, and bathing habits, we are reluctantly forced to side with the Japanese and pronounce him a barbarian. The inability of two highly dissimilar cultures to comprehend each other fully is explored with sympathy and humor. It is to the author's credit that Blackthorne, although partially enlightened and as a consequence shocked and repelled by his surviving shipmates, remains true to his origins and a source of continuing fascination to the Japanese. The irony of Mariko's relationship with Blackthorne is essentially tragic, and is handled with appropriate sensitivity. A samurai who is also a convert to Catholicism, her already divided loyalties are compounded when she falls in love with one who is both a barbarian and a heretic. Blackthorne never acquires fully her ability to compartmentalize anxieties and maintain a state of serenity, but in time he does learn to accept burdens patiently as a part of his destiny.

Toranaga, the dominant force in the novel, is powerfully drawn. A master of intrigue and strategy, he makes it his business to know everything about the people he deals with, to avail himself of their strengths and exploit their weaknesses, to manipulate them and to think only in terms of practical usefulness.

Blessed with a sense of humor he never allows to interfere with hard realities, endowed with incredible patience and the ability to take decisive action at precisely the right moment, he is admirably equipped to shape a nation's destiny. Like other great tyrants, he is a curious blend of the admirable and the terrible, and is, most of all, a supremely practical man.

Shogun is not without certain flaws. Most regrettable of these, perhaps, is the author's decision to provide fictitious names for those characters with historical prototypes. Comparisons with actual history are made unnecessarily confusing, although it must be admitted that the actual names are far less impressive than those which have been supplied. It is also unfortunate that the author has not seen fit to render a common expression of polite apology in some other form than the stereotyped phrase "so sorry"; a further jarring note occurs when he occasionally employs modern slang instead of closer approximations to the speech of the time. Inevitably, anachronisms and errors have crept into the fabric, particularly in the nautical scenes.

It is interesting to note in closing that Will Adams, the prototype of Blackthorne, continued as adviser to the shogunate until his death in 1620, outliving by four years the great Shogun Tokagawa Ieyatsu, upon whom the character of Toranaga is based. Adams was popular with the Japanese, and they erected a monument in memory of him. Spanish-Portuguese influence, and indeed all foreign influence, endured in Japan for no more than a century all told; by 1640 all the barbarians had been expelled and the outside world sealed off, this time for two hundred years.

John W. Evans

SIGNALS FROM THE SAFETY COFFIN

Author: John Engels (1931-   )
Publisher: University of Pittsburgh Press (Pittsburgh, Pa.). 67 pp. $6.95;
  paperback $2.95
Type of work: Poetry

A second collection of poems, gathered over seven years, by a young poet with a carefully structured vision

In his second book of poems, *Signals from the Safety Coffin,* John Engels seems to have stripped his poems to the barest essentials to proclaim his solemn theme: that the unity of life and death is overshadowed by man's consistent failure to find a comfortable mode to deal with death. His first book, *The Homer Mitchell Place,* dealt with death in a similar fashion; however, in the second book Engels seems to have refined the theme to a form that uses stark passages and empty settings to justify his concerns.

Signals from the Safety Coffin is divided into three sections: "Signals from the Safety Coffin," "An Angler's Vade Mecum," and "Exorcisms." A fisherman by hobby, Engels' long poem "An Angler's Vade Mecum" departs from the rest of the book and focuses more clearly on his form of art, while the other two sections sustain his themes of life and death. The twenty-nine poems are divided in such a way as to offer periodic breaks in the stark landscape of Engels' singular vision. The first section includes thirteen poems unconnected except by the author's pervasive fascination with death; their innocuous titles often belie their depth and power. The second section consists of the long poem, "An Angler's Vade Mecum," in which the poet links his views of death and art with the rites of fishing through the eyes of an angler. The poem, divided into six sections, departs from the stark mood of the previous section and employs a richer narrative voice throughout. The third section opens with the only formal piece in the book, "Sestina: My Dead in the First Snow." Following the sestina are four poems which act as a transition between the narrative of the middle section or the formality of the sestina, and the shorter, starker nature of the final seven poems.

In "Moonwalk," from the first section, Engels describes Neil Armstrong's ghost-like dance on the moon and the contrast of the astronaut's shadows against the bleak, foreboding landscape of the lunar surface. On the barren surface of the moon, man is once again confronted with the singular vision of death. This time Armstrong has a reason for not looking back and confronting his vision in the black shadows of space: if he does, the sun's unshielded glare will blind him. Engels sees a dual symbolism in this blinding, the black vacuum of space signals one thought.

> . . . man is
> on the moon. Behind him
> runs horizontally the
> black cast of the freezing
>
> shadow where the walker
> must not look . . .

the sky is the memory
of no light
it is the first time
I have wanted to walk

here myself. I
can see the black deep
of the center drawing near,
and the man-shaped night remaining
    total.

The walker, despite his resolution, looks back, and the act of seeing, whether in memory or in fact, crystallizes his own image of death. Engels shows that man shapes his own picture of death through those innermost frames of consicousness which make up his individual mind. Other poems in the first section continue the bleak descriptions of stripped landscapes, bones, and death. In "Hawk," the speaker finds the decomposed body of a hawk grotesquely hanging, its skull pierced, from a fence wire with the body of a dead snake protruding from its beak. As the speaker confronts the dead bird, eyes transfixed, he explains how

. . . I read blindly
names in bones, not seeing as
my eyes see. I can read
your name and others, I

have names the spine will not accept.
I see this hunting bird is dead, that
is the first name. And blind,
that is the next.

Engels once commented that "God may as well be Malevolent as benevolent." However, both "Moonwalk" and "Hawk" seem to refute that notion, since both the voice in "Hawk" and the walker in "Moonwalk" seem capable of shaping their own vision and steering their own destiny.

The absurdity of "Signals from the Safety Coffin" differs dramatically from the tone of the other poems in the first section. In this piece, inventor Count Karnicki, who once heard the cries of a prematurely buried Polish girl, is interred in a coffin set to sound alarms if its occupant should somehow come back to life. And, of course, he does, amid "alarm bells ringing, the red flag waving/a beacon flashing. . . ." When summoned to the grave by Karnicki's signals, however, the narrator of the poem refuses to hear the signals and makes no attempt to save the Count. *"Why should I?"*

He seems as entombed on earth as Karnicki is entombed in his coffin. "The sky encloses me," he states, as he defies his bizarre situation:

. . . You have awakened
and call out for help: I answer that

whatever the dark volumes of the graves
from which the dead man whispers up
    his breathing tube
and flashes his lights, in which the dead

tree speaks, the moon a soft explosion
in high mists, as I lie down to sleep
my silence is greater.

The absurd notion of the safety coffin quickly dissolves into the horrifying realization that man is never far from death.

From this ironic statement the book moves to "An Angler's Vade Mecum," a poem rich in language, written in the form of a vade mecum, or type of guidebook, which describes an angler's quest and his tools. The angler describes the type of salmon he is hunting, its habitat, and how to catch it. Some of the angler's possessions are described including his most prized, a *papier mâché* salmon:

> As a
> sportsman and angler the exact
> reproduction of natural objects
> appeals very much
> to me.

Then the angler acquires a new rod, snappy and lightweight, a model ahead of its time: "and if with this rod I cannot / handle any fish as I please, / I know it is not the fault / of the rod. . . ." As the poem progresses, images of sport fishing gradually take on added meaning until the poet is ready to state his beliefs concerning the art of poetry.

This transitional piece moves the reader into the third section, which begins with "Sestina: My Dead in the First Snow." Although the sestina is rich in style and language, Engels quickly moves back to the stark landscape of the dead, where an empty house shivers and rattles with memories. There is movement through the seasons, but the transition is too slow for the characters in the poem and it is not heeded:

> The lions too will die of the fire.
>   Remember we are followed
> Through all our rooms; through the
>   spaces of our fields,

The sun turns on us, window to window.
It is taking a long time.

The formality of the sestina yields to the foreboding tone of "O All the Dead of Ponderous Design!," *"Terribilis est locus iste,"* "The House of the Dead," and "Nothing Relents." These four exorcisms continue the richness of the sestina without its formality, yet move back toward the spare style of the first section.

In "The Fish Dream," for example, Engels describes Bikini Island, site of A-bomb testing. He evokes an almost mythic mood as he describes the mutant fish, a product of the test: ". . . fish with six-/inch needle teeth creeps out on fins like weed / stems over the red-hot deck. . . ." This horrifying mythic dream rekindles Engels' dread for the unknown vision of death, a death that manifests itself in countless ways which man refuses to see.

Engels has said that while writing this book, dirges and requiems flowed constantly through his head. Monotonous and somber beats are certainly evident in the work; yet the spark of life, never fully kindled in the poems, is never really missed either. The only order in this poet's world is the order of death: a dark vision, yet one which enriches the spirit of his work.

Paul M. Deblinger

SLAMMER

Author: Ben Greer
Publisher: Atheneum Publishers (New York). 298 pp. $8.95
Type of work: Novel
Time: The present
Locale: A state penitentiary in South Carolina

A dramatic slice of life in a contemporary prison, at once objective and deeply shocking, which explores the relationships of confined and dehumanized men

> *Principal characters:*
> AARON WALSH, a young guard
> WARDEN CATES, the new warden
> FATHER BREEN, the old priest
> FATHER MICHAEL WHITE, Breen's new assistant
> DANIEL CHILDS, a new, young, white prisoner
> JAMES MOULTRIE, a new black prisoner and former civil rights organizer
> LYMAN DONALDSON (SPOONS), a black prisoner, friend of Moultrie
> RHINER, an experienced and ambitious guard
> SHEBRAR, a Black Muslim prisoner and underground leader of the convicts
> JOHN DARCY, an old black prisoner and murderer, known as the Angel of Death
> MONTANA RED, the prisoner who acts as secret pimp for the convicts

With economy of action and precision of style, Ben Greer lays open in this novel an entire subculture. Although crowded with many characters, the novel presents with clarity and vividness the tormented and often violent lives of the sequestered men of the prison system, both guards and guarded. The characters are sharply delineated, and pulsate with a life rare in recent works of fiction. Unlike many more pretentious contemporary novelists, Greer has chosen to create art from the stuff of realism, in the tradition of the greatest Western novelists, from Dickens and Tolstoy to Faulkner and Fitzgerald, rather than to write obscurely for a minute, academic audience. *Slammer* is a novel which is accessible to readers on a variety of levels —as a suspense, action thriller, as a psychological and sociological study, and as a symbolic parable of the human condition. It has justly been called the best first novel to come out of the South since James Dickey's *Deliverance,* with which it bears a certain resemblance in tone and attitude.

Although he became a prison guard to write the book, Greer avoids the predictability of documentary fiction by filtering the facts through his artistic consciousness, as any first-rate writer must. Technically, the novel is nearly perfect; Greer knew what he could achieve and attempted that much and no more. Such discretion and moderation in a first novel is as rare as the intelligence and warmth which also distinguish this book; one of Greer's strongest virtues is his honesty and lack of intellectual pretense.

In the slammer, or prison, each character is matched with his natural antagonist (sometimes himself), and the truth about each man is revealed through the resulting battle. Perversity, greed, generosity, and love all struggle for domination within the prison walls, but none wins over the others permanently. The stabilization born of violence can only be temporary. For these inmates there can be no forgiveness or salvation, only endurance. With authenticity and intensity, Greer exposes the darker regions of human nature. Perhaps a certain sentimentality intrudes into the representation of the characters' feelings, and the storyline is predictable; but these aspects of the novel arise inevitably from its subject matter, rather than from any lapses of imagination or style. The grotesque characters are real and heartrending, even if, ultimately, they fail to stir the deepest levels of our imaginations and emotions.

Although the parallel must not be taken too strongly, it is possible to say that Greer has created in his prison setting a society in miniature, heightened and reduced to essentials. The pains of ordinary life, the boredom and violence, as well as the love and loyalty, are exaggerated behind the prison walls. Men seek to prove themselves, as they do in any society; they search for affection and friendship, striving to make the best of their situation and, one way or another, to survive. Even the young guard Walsh does not feel that he has proved himself until, during a prison fight, he rescues another guard; only

then does he belong. Superstitions and fears are also exaggerated in prison; this is why the death of the old black beekeeper takes on such importance for the men. Each society must establish its own moral level, and so it is in this prison; the darker corridors of the human mind and soul are explored, but also the tender and vulnerable aspects of the human heart. The men in *Slammer* are men like any other men, but forced to exist in inhuman conditions.

Perhaps the most interesting contest in this novel of conflicts is that between the two Catholic priests. Twenty-five years a priest, once ambitious, now fifty years old and almost beyond hope for any kind of personal fulfillment, Father Breen nevertheless tries to bring what comfort he can to the men in his spiritual charge. He is a realist, tough, with the body of an athlete and the temperament (as Father White tells him) of a cop. Father Breen is capable of hearing a man's confession and giving him absolution while they are working together with a welding torch on a car in the prison garage. Whenever Breen is upset or depressed, he works out in the gym or lifts weights in the exercise yard or runs on the track. He tries to escape his powerful, often uncontrollable, emotions through physical exertion. The new priest, sent to Breen from the Church authorities, is young and idealistic, intelligent but not wise. It is inevitable that the conflict between White and Breen must build to a confrontation; when it does, it is in the boxing ring. Their physical battle shocks the prisoners and guard who observe it, but it gives them a new respect for each other.

The symbolism of death broods over the novel, enriching it with ironies and half-hidden meanings. Moultrie, the black revolutionary, is as drawn to Darcy, known as the Angel of Death, as he is to death itself. Moultrie's father was a mortician, and he recalls that his father often smelled of death. He can sense the presence of death, and actually becomes aware before anyone else that another prisoner has just died. The Angel of Death is, along with Rose, the old retired male prostitute, one of the two most original and profoundly conceived characters in the novel. The reader is as impressed as Moultrie when the Angel of Death illustrates his technique with an ice pick in a pair of oranges. It is fitting that the Angel of Death suffers from a vile form of cancer which causes him to exude a foul odor. Out of jealousy, Moultrie hires John Darcy to commit a murder; but when he orders Darcy to kill Father Breen, the murder ricochets and he himself becomes the victim.

The earth is the final prison, and night is its ever-ready assistant. The night and the clay of the river bottom and the red earth all enrich the novel with their imagery. A careful, complete description of a man going to the electric chair heightens awareness of the inevitability of death for the men. Even if they are not condemned to death, the endless sleep is waiting for them, as it waits for all men. They, too, will end up beneath the red dust of the South Carolina soil, while the rivers meander toward the ocean and the trains in the distance send out their lonely sounds. Like a shadow, death in its various forms moves through the prison, gliding across the silent walls, bringing fear to each beating heart.

Another equally important theme which dominates the novel is the loss of innocence. Two of the characters, both new to the prison, reflect their innocence in their names: Childs, the young, blond-haired convict, and White, the priest just out of the seminary. Childs makes friends with a starving puppy and sneaks it into his cell. Naïve and simple, he finds it difficult to cope with the highly ritualized, brutal life of the prison. His fear of the other men leads him to move in with Montana Red, not realizing that Red is the prison pimp; soon, however, he is working for Montana Red to pay off his debt to him. His loss of innocence is symbolized by the rhinestone earring which he begins wearing and by his murder of the puppy. Harper, the desperate, worn-out male whore with only shreds of self-respect left, provides Childs with an example of what he can look forward to becoming. The only alternative open to the boy seems to be the more grand but equally pathetic retirement of Rose, the most famous and most loved male prostitute in the history of the prison. Rose tells Childs that, whatever happens to him, he must belong only to himself.

A precarious balance exists in the prison; the unnatural, strained life within the walls is safe only as long as it is founded upon an unassailable routine. But once the balance is broken, once events get out of hand, chaos is the result. The novel illustrates such a loss of balance and the violence which follows. No one individual is to blame; each man contributes in his way to the breakdown, and each suffers as a consequence. The prison, like the world, is a complicated place, and each man is a part of the whole, whether or not he is willing to admit it. *Slammer* drives home this old, but always profound and necessary, truth. At times the novel is reminiscent of Poe or Melville or Genet, but in the end, Ben Greer has created his own vision, as rich and moving as it is fierce and genuine.

Bruce D. Reeves

SNEAKY PEOPLE

Author: Thomas Berger (1924-   )
Publisher: Simon and Schuster (New York). 315 pp. $8.95
Type of work: Novel
Time: The 1930's
Locale: The American Midwest

A nostalgic re-creation of small-town America during the decade of the Sheffield cigarettes and Bonnie and Clyde

Principal characters:

BUDDY SANDIFER, owner of a used car lot who wants to murder his wife
RALPH, his fifteen-year-old son, a typical adolescent
LEO, his eccentric employee who lives with his mother and obnoxious parrot
LAVERNE, his voluptuous mistress
CLARENCE, his janitor and murder weapon

Literary critics and reviewers agree on Thomas Berger's continuing importance as a "major comic writer" whose early novels, *Crazy in Berlin* and *Reinhart in Love,* dealt with the alienated postwar hero. *Little Big Man* has been called the greatest novel ever written about the American West, "a large-scale parody and serious appraisal of . . . its myths and actuality." Mottram calls *Killing Time* (1967) "a masterly dramatization of the confusions between law and criminality, normality and madness," and *Vital Parts* (1970) "a shrewd caricature of the American as competitive individualist." *Sneaky People* may be, as D. Keith Mano concludes, "a convincing imitation of the thirties . . . but in essence this book is simply an exuberant and crudely humorous entertainment, distinguished from the rest of the drugstore rack by its professional finish and its zestful language." R. W. Williams agrees with this assessment: "Reading this novel is a bit like dining at a three-star restaurant having a bad night with the chef."

To begin with, Berger's oral style is inconsistent. At its worst, it resembles Fariña, disjointed instead of nonchalant, cute instead of witty: "Ralph let some Coke exhaust its effervescence on his palate." At its best, it approaches the honest, deeply humorous realism of Twain (to whom Berger has been too often compared) and even the direct and surprising innocence of Salinger. Leo imagines writing to the sweet young girls whose pictures he admires in the weekly rotogravure section:

Dear Miss Wilhelm: Under separate cover please find my contribution to your worthy efforts in behalf of charity. You are a fine, upstanding young person. I trust you do not smoke though, and you get your cigarette foil from father, uncle, etc., and other adults. A Friend

The thought of Thelma opening the package with a little chirp of pleasure, and cupping his silver ball in her slender white hands on which the nails were all chewed, was very erotic to Leo.

But Berger does not sustain the humor with the cohesive satirical vision which breathes evenly through the prose of West's *Miss Lonelyhearts* or Heller's *Something Happened*. Instead, he lapses into a pseudo-literary language based not on character but on the kind of extraneous assumed complicity with the reader more characteristic of Wodehouse or Thorne Smith: "Buddy's sense of elapsed time had been deranged by the wine. He had expected a longer journey. Still, he did not return to the dread of yore."

Perhaps the novel is most successful in evoking the mood of the 1930's, and in fashioning characters who, even though too typically, correspond to that mood. Berger capitalizes, on the one hand, on the gangsterly casualness of *Bonnie and Clyde* and *The Sting*: "Leo of course knew nothing of his plan to have Naomi killed. It was not the sort of thing you could reveal even to its beneficiary." On the other hand, he incorporates the nostalgia of *American Graffiti* and *The Last Picture Show*: "Elmira's, the local hangout. Outside it looked as if all the booths were filled with people eating potato chips and drinking Cokes, a combination that cost a dime." But Berger-style nostalgia is not worth a book in itself, much less a film, because it lacks both the rhythm of pure entertainment and the persistent melody of a central satirical theme.

The key to the apparent theme is supposed to be in the title, but the people of Berger's little town are not well defined enough as substantial human beings to make their "sneakiness" more than pathetic and melodramatic. "A lot of nuts live in this town," Ralph says, but even before we see them all we know that these people are no better or worse than the petty denizens of *Peyton Place*. Motivation is equally unconvincing. Buddy plans to kill his wife, Naomi, because of what might be, in a stronger portrayal, profound existential *ennui* and anti-feminist repulsion: "You work hard to give a woman everything she wants, and what you get back is shit. . . . She don't fix her hair anymore. Hell, she don't even wash it regular. . . ." She doesn't clean the sink, ". . . so it don't drain; it's full of dirty hair and green grease! Makes you want to puke!"

Maybe so, but to kill? His male chauvinist attitude of outraged domesticity becomes even less convincing when, almost whimsically, he finally decides that he loves Naomi after all and does not want her dead. Meanwhile, the plot has been set in motion and Buddy can do nothing to stop the course of crime; Berger stops it for him, by having a surprise ending for each of the characters. The premise seems to be that funny things happen to sneaky people, but Vonnegut does a much better job with that premise, making the things that happen as profoundly funny as the people to whom they happen are realistically superficial. Berger's people waver between psychological realism and Hollywood stereotypes, and the things that happen to them are as predictably unpredictable as reruns.

Nonetheless, during the hectic three days of the story we meet several characters who nearly overcome their stereotypical nature by achieving the level of caricatures. Buddy Sandifer, with a "soft spot in his heart for inept men," is the tough-speaking, woman-enslaving softie whose view of life is as smugly self-satisfied as it is pathetically glib. His attitude toward his mistress, Laverne, is an example of his distorted egocentrism: ". . . her day was a blur of candy, movie mags, and radio serials. Unlike Naomi, she had no mind whatever." It does not matter that Buddy is not around when we discover how wrong he is about Laverne because we know the revelation would not have changed him. Laverne herself —whose whole name is "Laverne Linda Lorraine, a song in itself"—is an unlikely combination of the profane and the sacred only if the reader is ignorant of the historical occupation of vestal virgins. Buddy loves to apprehend her "in the act of bleaching her hair with cotton balls dipped in a saucer of peroxide or washing her step-ins," or to sneak in on her when she's wearing his favorite costume: "a short frilly pink apron over black-lace step-ins and brassiere, long-gartered silk stockings and platform shoes." Dorothy Parker has already expressed the appropriate female response to Buddy's simplistic assessment of Laverne as "a big blonde, a real armful." The caricature comes close to human insight when we recognize that, underneath her complicity in the subordination of all women by all men, Laverne, in rare moments of lucid reflection, regards men with a mixture of gentle pity and disinterested disdain:

> Having so much time on her hands, Laverne thought about the entire male race and believed she would have a lot more respect for them if they stayed permanently hard and did not after such a temporary friction spill and go limp.

In another of the misfired ironies of the novel, Buddy's fifteen-year-old son Ralph, a mild-mannered Portnoy whom Berger portrays with swift if not exactly deft strokes, plays his little part in the saga of growing up sneaky by stumbling through the litter of Berger's plot into the arms of Laverne who, in a scene nearly equal to that in *The Last Picture Show,* forgets her newly found religious vocation long enough to introduce young Ralph to manhood. "I just couldn't help it," she says to him; but after all, religion has many altars, and Laverne is only too glad to serve when and where she can.

The town philosopher-fool, and its most poignantly unremarkable eccentric, is Leo, who, within the framework of his strange triangular relationship with his hypochondriac mother and their intolerable parrot Boy, comes closest to presenting the reader with a satirical mirror he can reflect in and on. Leo, for all his unextraordinary foibles, is lovable: he "always had a ready suggestion. He saw life for other people as a collection of immediate problems for which simple solutions were available." Like Joseph Heller's hero in *Something Happened* (Bob Slocum), Leo is an updated Babbitt, "frightened by sudden changes of policy in any area." When he disappoints his tyrant pet by running the vacuum sweeper the wrong way around the cage—in a scene which, in retrospect, remarkably resembles the close of Benjy's section of *The Sound and the Fury*—Leo is much more upset by Boy's belligerence than he is by his mother's death-rattle. The vacuum's whine, the bird's shrieks, and the dying old woman's choking all combine to dismantle the simple mind of Leo, whose only sneaky habit was to adore, from afar, "the earnest good will of young girls" pictured in the weekly newspaper. Even the consequences of Leo's insanity are milder than they are satirically irritating. He shoots the bird—the single act of poetic justice in this unlikely novel that doesn't seem contrived.

Kenneth John Atchity

A SORROW BEYOND DREAMS
A Life Story

Author: Peter Handke (1942-   )
Translated from the German by Ralph Manheim
Publisher: Farrar, Straus and Giroux (New York). 70 pp. $5.95
Type of work: Biographical reminiscence
Time: 1920-1971
Locale: Austria and Germany

Peter Handke tells the story of his mother's life in an attempt to understand the meaning of that life and the reasons behind her suicide

Principal personages:
> PETER HANDKE, the narrator, a playwright and novelist
> THE MOTHER, who committed suicide at fifty-one
> THE LOVER, Peter's real father
> THE HUSBAND, a weak-willed, ineffectual man

Since 1966, novelist-playwright Peter Handke has been one of Germany's most exciting, provocative, and controversial artists. With his first plays (or "Speaking Pieces" as he labeled them), *Offending the Audience* (1966) and *Kaspar* (1968), he disrupted current theatrical practices even more drastically than the Absurdists of the previous decade; subsequent "plays"—*"My Foot, My Tutor* (1971), *The Ride Across Lake Constance* (1971), *They Are Dying Out* (1973)—have for better or worse, extended, elaborated, and developed Handke's resolutely "anti-theatrical" theater. His novels, *The Hornets* (1966), *The Peddlar* (1967), *The Goalie's Anxiety at the Penalty Kick* (1972), and *Short Letter, Long Farewell* (1974) are perhaps not quite so radical, but they, too, have stimulated vociferous debate among the critics. And his personal polemics—his direct assault on the critics of his works, his angry denunciations of contemporary political and artistic institutions, his impassioned defense of his own theories,

and his sometimes frenetic behavior (especially between 1966 and 1968) have established him as a controversial artistic "personality" in the best and worst connotations of that word.

But *A Sorrow Beyond Dreams* is not experimental, at least as the word is applied to the above-mentioned works. It seems to be more of a personal experiment, an attempt by a sensitive writer to understand, primarily for himself, the meaning of a crucial event in his own life:

> My mother has been dead for almost seven weeks; I had better get to work before the need to write about her, which I felt so strongly at her funeral, dies away and I fall back into the dull speechlessness with which I reacted to the news of her suicide.

Handke begins the memoir with the most mundane, impersonal of citations, a newspaper filler: "In the village of A. (G. township), a housewife, aged 51, committed suicide on Friday night by taking an overdose of sleeping pills." This formality is, of course, a mask, an attempt to put some emotional distance between himself and his subject matter. Handke's own stated posture of "objectivity" notwithstanding, he understands his subjective involvement and the aesthetic problems it raises. A minor theme of the slim volume is the near impossibility of turning such material into an artistic product without succumbing to either self-indulgent emotionalism or statistical detachment.

Midway through his narrative, Handke pauses to digress at length on this creative impasse. On the one hand he fears that a narrow concentration on his mother's particular plight may not "be of interest to anyone but myself"; on the other hand, overly generalizing the material results in "a literary ritual in which an individual life ceases to be anything more than a pretext." To resolve this tension Handke postulates a new approach; he will begin "with the already available formulations, the linguistic deposit of man's social experience." He presents this new procedure in a neat formula:

> Accordingly, I compare, sentence by sentence, the stock of formulas applicable to the biography of a woman with my mother's particular life; the actual work of writing follows from the agreements and contradictions between them.

But on the very next page he admits that his new methodology has collapsed. "She refuses to be isolated and remains unfathomable; my sentences crash in the darkness and lie scattered on the paper." Life again defeats art. In the end all Handke can do is give hints of the horror that lies behind his mother's experience:

> This story . . . is really about the nameless, about speechless moments of terror . . . moments when the mind boggles with horror, states of fear so brief that speech always comes too late; about dream happenings so gruesome that the mind perceives them physically as worms . . . it is a record of states, not a well-rounded story with an anticipated, hence comforting, end.

The biographical approach is a pose destined to fail from the start, but it is the only literary mode available to him. Handke has tricked us with his theorizing, as he does in his plays and novels, but this trick forces us not to an acknowledgment of the artificiality of art, but of the uncapturable horror of real life. In an ironically Brechtian touch (ironical because Brecht has been one of his primary rhetorical targets), Handke uses the unreality of art to remind us of the distance between art and life, and so sensitizes us to respond more directly to life itself.

Both as a unique person and as a type, his mother followed an obvious and painful course in her life. She was born into a peasant household in a fairly remote Austrian village. In that time and place the "fortune tellers at our church fairs took a serious interest only in the palms of the young men; a girl's future was a joke." Handke describes life in the village for a woman as one of:

> No possibilities, it was all settled in advance: a bit of flirtation, a few giggles, brief bewilderment, then the alien, resigned look of a woman starting to keep house again, the first chil-

dren, a bit of togetherness after the kitchen work, from the start not listened to, and, in turn listening less and less, inner monologues, trouble with her legs, varicose veins, mute except for mumbling in her sleep, cancer of the womb, and finally, with death, destiny fulfilled. The girls in our town used to play a game based on the stations in a woman's life: Tired/Exhausted/Sick/Dying/Dead.

Thus, *A Sorrow Beyond Dreams* is not the story of a single act of suicide, but of a lifetime of gradual atrophy punctuated by occasional gestures of self-assertion that only emphasized the helplessness of the situation. At first she was crushed by simple raw poverty, then by poverty of the spirit.

As a young girl his mother had been cursed with a lively intelligence and a vivid imagination. She ran away to pursue the only career available to a girl of her sort, at a cooking school in the city. There she was caught up in the excitement and sense of national possibility stimulated by the rise of Hitler (Handke touches on Nazism, but only as it affected his mother's development or nondevelopment). In the atmosphere of the pending war, which upset social relationships and moral proprieties, his mother took a lover, a married bank clerk and petty party functionary, who fathered Peter. But, even in the city during a time of social chaos, the peasant ethic prevailed. In order to give Peter a name, his mother married a soldier she found repulsive, but willing. The war forced them back to her home, where her previous experiences and flirtations with independence were only a burden.

Her basic situation was fixed for life. An oppressive environment deadened her spirit. With no possibility of expressing her freedom, her impulses turned inward and dried out. She became sexless. She attempted the role of bourgeois housewife and even failed at that: "From my childhood: ridiculous sobs in the toilet, nose blowing, inflamed eyes. She was; she became; she became nothing."

As his mother passed into middle age, the economic conditions in the family improved and simple survival gave way to the petty comforts of the lower middle class. These modest financial gains afforded her a temporary respite. A student by this time, Peter introduced her to literature (Hamsun, Dostoevski, Faulkner) and she became excited: "It's making me young again," she said. She began to go out a little, to assert herself by "drinking coffee in the tavern" and socializing; she even ventured to assert political positions out loud.

But, like all of the feeble rebellions in her life, these self-expressive acts ultimately turned into cruel jokes, reminders of the distance between her situation and any real self-fulfillment. Fixed in her stagnant, petty environment, his mother became progressively alienated and frustrated. She developed severe headaches, became disorganized and disoriented, feared insanity. Given the comforting diagnosis "nervous breakdown," her condition apparently improved and she reorganized her life, but the desperation deepened. In the end, "mere existence became a torture to her."

Handke describes the suicide itself in meticulous, almost impersonal detail, punctuated only by his final interjection:

> She sent the child to bed; the tele-

vision was still playing. She had been to the hairdresser's the day before and had had her nails done. She turned off the television, went to her bedroom, and hung up her brown two-piece dress in the wardrobe. She took all the sleeping pills and all her antidepression pills. . . . At the end of her letter to me, which otherwise contained only instructions for her funeral, she wrote that she was perfectly calm, glad at last to be falling asleep in peace. But I'm sure that wasn't true.

The author concludes his reminiscence with an account of his own reactions to her suicide. His initial response was almost euphoric; "throughout the flight I was beside myself with pride that she had committed suicide." Hurrah for self-assertion! But the physical fact of her death and funeral upset him; at the grave site his composure dissolved:

Standing beside it, I looked up at the motionless trees: for the first time it seemed to me that nature was really merciless. So these were the facts! . . . I felt mocked and helpless. All at once, in my impotent rage, I felt the need of writing something about my mother.

The writing, however, does not work; the essay ends on a note of indecision and frustration: "It is not true that writing has helped me. In my weeks of preoccupation with the story, the story has not ceased to preoccupy me." Fragments of memory and details from the mundane world about him are, finally, the only reality that he can capture, and finally he gives up: "Someday I shall write about all this in greater detail."

The final irony of this fascinating memoir is that Peter Handke, arch anti-realist, enemy of descriptive writing, foe of gratuitous emotion, has written a most touching biographical lament about his mother and has demonstrated the central validity of realism—that a precise, concrete, sensitive rendering of a unique human being's existence attains universality through the very fact of its particularity. Although Handke talks about the artistic incompatibility of the individual and the type, he has, in fact, fused the two perfectly. His mother is both a special person and a universal type—the individual of intelligence, sensitivity, and imagination who is progressively isolated and destroyed by an environment that offers no possibility for self-realization. Questions remain: whether or not he has succeeded in communicating the horror beneath the story is problematical, and whether or not he finally managed to exorcize his personal demons is unresolved. But, conclusive or not, the power and beauty of this remarkable biographical reminiscence is undeniable.

Keith Neilson

SPECIAL ENVOY TO CHURCHILL AND STALIN, 1941-1946

Authors: W. Averell Harriman (1891-   ) and Elie Abel (1920-   )
Publisher: Random House (New York). 595 pp. $15.00
Type of work: Historical memoir
Time: 1941-1946
Locale: Washington, London, Moscow

An account of Harriman's experiences as Roosevelt's personal emissary to Churchill and Stalin and as United States ambassador to the Soviet Union

> Principal personages:
> W. Averell Harriman, American business leader and diplomat
> Franklin D. Roosevelt, President of the United States
> Winston Churchill, British Prime Minister
> Joseph Stalin, Russian leader
> Harry Hopkins, adviser to F.D.R.
> V. Molotov, Russian Foreign Minister
> John R. Deane, head of military mission to the Soviet Union

W. Averell Harriman belongs to the power elite in the United States. The inheritor of a great railroad fortune, Harriman has spent much of his life in the company of the world's movers and shakers. This well-written book describes his activities as Roosevelt's personal emissary to Winston Churchill and Joseph Stalin—F.D.R. gave him the unofficial title of "Defense Expediter"—and later, from 1943 to 1946, his service as American ambassador to the Soviet Union. Co-authors Harriman and journalist Elie Abel write in the third person, but as Harriman notes, "the analysis and the judgments expressed conform to my own." The authors rely heavily on Harriman's own papers for documentation and provide us with a participant's view of the actions and decisions, large and small, which helped shape the conduct of World War II and of the Cold War which followed it.

Special Envoy to Churchill and Stalin, 1941-1946 should appeal to two sizable audiences. The first is composed of those interested in the game of international power, or what is called "diplomatic history" in academic circles. The second and probably larger group is made up of those fascinated not by the game itself but rather by the players, historical giants named Stalin, Churchill, and Roosevelt, who seem to move armies, governments, indeed whole nations across the playing board like so many chess pieces.

For this second audience, the authors offer an abundance of sharp and shrewd character assessments. Harriman is not adverse to using his moment as historian to settle scores with old political antagonists such as Harold Ickes. Secretary of State Cordell Hull is portrayed as "forceful, stubborn, difficult to handle"; one ssuspects that he was perceived by both Harriman and F.D.R. more as an obstacle to be overcome than as a fellow statesman. A real villain is Secretary of State James Byrnes, whose chief crime seems to have been his unwillingness to lean on Harriman's expertise. Hell hath no fury like a power broker scorned.

The book is not without its heroes, however. Harry Hopkins emerges as a dedicated public servant, racked by ill health but still in harness, whose intelligence and candor won the respect and admiration of both Churchill and Stalin. Sometimes even bit players wander across the stage and impress. One example is Harold Stassen, observed by Harriman at the San Francisco conference which established the United Nations, before his promising political career strangely degenerated into a bad joke.

Concerning the historical giants of his acquaintance, the author is perceptive but often baffled by the enigma of greatness. About Roosevelt, who probably more than any other American politician of this century deserves the accolade "humanitarian," Harriman recalls: "He always enjoyed other people's discomfort. I think it is fair to say that it never bothered him very much when other people were unhappy." If F.D.R. was paradoxical, Joseph Stalin was ultimately unfathomable. Better informed than Roosevelt, more realistic than even Churchill, the Russian dictator was "in some ways the most effective of the war leaders." Yet he was also, as Harriman knew, a cruel tyrant capable of monstrous crimes. In the end, Harriman finds himself completely unable to understand "the most inscrutable and contradictory character I have known."

Regarding the historical issues that swirled around him, Harriman tells us little that is really new. His story of the onset of the Cold War is a familiar one. He admits to sharing at first F.D.R.'s hope that the United States could get along with Stalin, by sheer force of good inten-

tion if need be. But such optimism was quickly dispelled. The inability—the unwillingness, in Russian eyes—of the Western allies to launch an invasion across the English Channel until 1944 poisoned relations with the Soviet Union almost immediately.

As the war progressed, such basic disagreements were compounded by a host of petty differences. Stalin's suspicion of foreign influence ran so deep that at one point he refused to allow the British to station air units in northern Russia to protect the allied convoys making the dangerous Murmansk run, a decision which forced the temporary suspension of such shipping. In response to such difficulties, both Roosevelt and Harriman became increasingly wary of Soviet intentions.

It was, however, the Polish question rather than the constant stream of minor irritations which finally broke apart the Grand Alliance, and which extinguished Harriman's hopes for Soviet-American cooperation. At the time of the abortive uprising of the Polish Home Army against the Germans in Warsaw in 1944, he cabled Roosevelt, "I am for the first time since coming to Moscow gravely concerned by the attitude of the Soviet Government." The ultimate responsibility for the Cold War, he insists, belongs to Russia.

Still, some nagging questions remain. Throughout the book Harriman is pictured as the supreme realist. During the 1930's he risked the wrath of his more conservative business colleagues by attempting to establish good relations with Roosevelt's New Deal. Harriman was always one to accommodate his goals and behavior to the reality of the moment.

Why then, one must ask, was Poland such a sticking point for Harriman personally and for United States policy as well? An important key to the Cold War was the unwillingness of American leaders to allow the Soviets their own sphere of influence in Eastern Europe. Precisely how was America's national interest served by this refusal? Was the motivation economic? Or, as Harriman implies, were we driven by a devotion to freedom and democracy? His is surely a curious argument for a hardheaded realist to make. As Latin Americans have long testified, freedom and democracy are abstractions which the United States has proven it can forego in a pinch. Unfortunately, the Polish puzzle remains unsolved.

One also wishes that the authors had provided a fuller discussion of the totality of American policy in these crucial years. While Soviet actions in Eastern Europe are described in detail, the reader is spared a recitation of American maneuvers designed to minimize Communist influence in those conquered territories under Western control, such as Italy and Japan. As a result, Soviet policy is often viewed out of context. Given Harriman's position in Moscow, perhaps it is natural that America's global policies are accorded little scrutiny. But a bird's-eye view can easily warp one's perception of large-scale events. It is worth noting that both General Marshall and Secretary of War Stimson feared that the rough treatment accorded Harriman almost daily by the Soviets had soured the ambassador. In short, Harriman was more on the receiving than on the giving end of things. This is not necessarily the best vantage point for Olympian judgments. Critics of America's Cold War policies will not be convinced by Harriman's case.

Yet, there is no escaping the evidence mustered by the authors that the Russians were incredibly difficult allies. One must ponder the terrible suspiciousness manifested by the Soviets during the war and wonder whether any combination of policies short of complete acquiescence in Russian expansionism could have avoided a falling out after the defeat of the common enemy, Nazi Germany. In very important ways, Roosevelt, Truman, Churchill, and Stalin thus appear to be more the prisoners of history than its masters.

For those not given to such weighty considerations, this book can be recommended simply as interesting reading. The exercise of power fascinates and the authors give us a close-up view. Power was the *leitmotif* of Harriman's career, and it is clear that he had an aptitude for seeking it out. *Special Envoy to Churchill and Stalin, 1941-1946* begins with Harriman importuning Harry Hopkins to take him along on Hopkins' first diplomatic mission to London in early 1941. It is altogether fitting that the book ends five years later with President Truman calling Harriman, who was in London, long distance to ask him to return to the United States to serve as Secretary of Commerce. Our protagonist turned to his luncheon companion and asked whether he should take the job. "Absolutely," Winston Churchill replied. "The center of power is in Washington." Harriman started packing almost at once. The scent was in the air.

Robert M. Collins

THE SURFACE OF EARTH

Author: Reynolds Price (1933-   )
Publisher: Atheneum Publishers (New York). 491 pp. $10.95
Type of work: Novel
Time: May 1903 - June 1944
Locale: Rural North Carolina and Virginia

A moving, detailed chronicle of two Southern families during the first half of the twentieth century

Principal characters:

> BEDFORD KENDAL, a North Carolinian patriarch
> RENA KENDAL, his youngest daughter
> KENNERLY KENDAL, his son
> EVA KENDAL, his oldest daughter
> FORREST MAYFIELD, a rural schoolteacher, Eva's husband
> ROBINSON MAYFIELD, JR., their son
> HATTIE SHORTER, Forrest's older sister
> ROBINSON MAYFIELD, SR., Forrest's father
> MARGARET JANE (POLLY) DREWRY, housekeeper-companion to Robinson, Sr., and later, to Forrest
> GRAINGER WALKER, a black personal servant to Forrest, Robinson, Jr., and Hutch
> RACHEL HUTCHINS MAYFIELD, Robinson, Jr.'s, wife and mother of Hutch
> RAVEN HUTCHINS (HUTCH) MAYFIELD, son of Rachel and Robinson, Jr.
> MINNIE THARRINGTON, a longtime friend and confidante of Robinson, Jr.
> ALICE MATTHEWS, Rachel's girlhood friend and counselor to Hutch

For better or worse—both, actually—*The Surface of Earth* is a solid, old-fashioned, Southern novel. It is "solid" because of the slow, meticulously detailed chronology in which each character and incident is carefully and organically integrated into the larger scheme to create not only a story, but a vision of a particular time, place, and social organism. It is "old-fashioned" because the characters are strongly motivated and sharply individuated, yet, at the same time, clearly identified as products of their environment; because the author eschews modern stylistic devices in favor of a relentlessly classical, almost archaic, manner; and because his concerns—romantic love, personal honor, family traditions and obligations, guilt and self-sacrifice, self-indulgence and moderation—are rare in contemporary fiction. It is "Southern" because these concerns are developed in a context of values which seem related to that region, particularly to its views of women and its preoccupation with racial mixture, and because the Southern rhetorical tradition—especially the work of William Faulkner and Thomas Wolfe—dominates the narrative presentation.

The Surface of Earth traces the experiences and relations between two families, the North Carolina Kendals and the Virginia Mayfields, by focusing on three male products of the two clans: Forrest Mayfield; his son, Robinson, Jr.; and his grandson, Hutch. Price emphasizes this focus by dividing his novel into three relatively short time spans that pinpoint the critical events in the life of each of the Mayfield men. A short title fixes the place of each segment in the book's thematic development. Part One, "Absolute Pleasures," covers the years from May 1903 to February 1905, and focuses on Forrest; Part Two, "The Heart in Dreams," covers from May 1921 to July 1929, and focuses on Robinson, Jr.; and Part Three, "Partial Amends," deals with the days of June 5-14, 1944, and focuses on Hutch. The gaps in between are filled in by lengthy stories (every major character and many minor ones tell their life stories), letters, interior ruminations, narrative expositions, and easily explainable dream sequences; very little is left out.

Like Faulkner, Reynolds Price views the major events in a story not only as vital causal factors, but also as archetypal patterns of behavior. They not only set off practical consequences in the immediate future, but also point backward to earlier events and project forward to like situations in the more or less distant future. Hence, the sins of the fathers are vented on the sons and daughters not so much because of any direct cause-and-effect sequence, but because the same needs, impulses and drives keep determining the same kinds of acts, mistakes, and results.

The crucial event of the novel is the elopement of sixteen-year-old Eva Kendal, an intense, intelligent high school senior, with Forrest Mayfield, her thirty-two-year-old Latin teacher. Her apparently impulsive rejection of family disrupts the Kendals and provokes her mother to a suicide that seems more spiteful than despairing. After the traumatic birth of her son, Robinson Jr., a year later (Price gives childbirth its worst press since the finale of *A Farewell to Arms*), she is drawn back to the Kendal homestead for a visit that lengthens into a lifetime. Thus, Eva's "desertion," first of family and then of husband, establishes the basic action of the book.

Eva's need to flee her home for love and her discovery that the forces pulling her back are too strong provide the focal point for the book's emotional tensions and moral ambiguities. When Forrest asks her to come back home, she responds "I am home. . . . Wherever you or I might happen to camp, *home* is here. I'm as sorry as you." Price seriously questions fellow North Carolinian Thomas Wolfe's dictum that "you can't go home again"; he wonders if it is even possible to leave. Or, as Eva writes her son on the eve of his marriage to Rachel Hutchins: *"Give much thought to two things—your family history (mine and your father's; every day I breathe I believe more strongly that your home is your fate, all laid down and waiting) and your own long future with the few little scraps of freedom you possess."*

Although he never states it openly, Forrest Mayfield accepts Eva's judgment and reconciles himself—perhaps too easily—to losing her and his son. In reaction he begins a quest of his own. Having deserted his son, he sets out to find his father, Robinson, Sr., who had likewise left wife and child behind. Thus, if the women in the novel are bound to home and family so tightly that they cannot escape, the men are cut loose from theirs, and must cast about fitfully and painfully to find that sense of security and meaning they have abandoned.

Old Robinson Sr., turned out of the house by Forrest's mother for "niggering" (sex with available black girls), sets up a substitute second home with the help of Polly Drewry, a similarly alienated young lady. He also takes in a young black boy, Grainger Walters, as a kind of half-son, half-servant (Grainger is actually the result of that "niggering," the son of a man fathered by Robinson, Sr.). Robinson, Jr., flounders through most of his youth, aimless except for his brief marriage to Rachel Hutchins, who gives him a son and dies in the process, and, in his middle age, settles into the role of amiable, undirected drunk. He, too, seeks and finds the lost father and establishes a "good relationship" with him—probably too late to repair the psychic damage. And he, too, deserts his son; Rob's wanderings and general inability to hold a steady job have resulted in young Hutch being reared by the same women—Eva, her sister Rena, Sylvie the maid—who reared the father.

In the last section of the novel it is Hutch's turn to seek his identity in his lineage. Although only fourteen, he forces Rob to an acknowledgment of failure as a father and returns to his deceased mother's home. There, joined by a repentant father, he will attempt to establish a new home and a personal identity. The novel ends with a feeling of muted hope and ambiguous reconciliation.

Thus, *The Surface of Earth* is a novel about love and hate between blood relations, their need for one another and their need to escape the familial bonds; it enumerates and analyzes the factors that hold together and those that pull apart—love, hate, tradition, habit, guilt, fear, general weakness, unselfish devotion, selfish possessiveness, self-deception, and existential anguish. And it focuses, finally, on the necessity of coming to terms with these contradictory needs and impulses in order to make sense out of life.

Toward the end of the book Hutch quotes Grainger as saying: "some people leave you and some people stay . . . you should know which and lean on the stayers." The characters in the novel can be roughly divided into those two types. The "leavers," who provide most of the book's narrative thrust, are those who seek self-realization by trying to make the world conform to their own dreams. The stayers, who give the volume its ethical center, are those who accept their situations, attempt to make the most of them, and freely serve those who need them.

Thus Eva begins as a leaver, and her flight rends the delicate fabric of the Kendal family, provoking her mother to suicide and her other kin to lengthy bitterness. But after her return she establishes herself as a "stayer"; her long ministrations to her father and her role as mother to both her son and grandson certifies her moral stature. Conversely, Forrest is guilty of a breach of faith by his clandestine courting of her however innocently he views it. This dooms the relationship from the beginning, a fact that he tacitly admits in giving her up so easily. In the search for his father, he is helped first by his older sister, Hattie Shorter, and then by his father's companion-housekeeper, Polly Drewry, who, after Robinson Sr.'s death, accepts a like role with him. Through them he achieves, finally, a kind of partial happiness based on an understanding of himself and his role as teacher to disadvantaged Southern blacks. In short, Forrest, too, becomes a "stayer."

Both Robinson, Jr., and Rachel Hutchins are leavers and dreamers and this dooms them both, he to aimless drunkenness and she to an early death in childbirth. As Alice Matthews, Rachel's girlhood friend, tells Hutch:

> "They thought they had *rights.*"
> "To what?"
> "Their wishes. Their wishes fulfilled."
> "What's wrong about that?" Hutch said.
> "Very little—provided people know that wishes are dreams, stories people tell themselves; that wishes aren't orders which the world will obey. Rob and Rachel didn't know that one simple fact. Rob may have changed since. Rachel never did, I know; never could have, however many years she got."

Life gives no such rights, as every character must learn for him or her own self. Forrest apparently realizes it at the end. Robinson, Jr., who becomes the novel's central figure, learns it the hard way. Young Hutch knows it almost from the beginning, as evidenced by this exchange between father and son late in the book:

> "People get what they need if they stand still and watch till the earth sends it up, most people I've known— Mother, Forrest, Rachel. What they need, not want."

Hutch said, "I knew that."
"How?"
"It's happened to me."

What makes this possible is the network of relationships that supports, corrects, and guides the "leaver" back to his origins and to himself. And the cement that holds these relationships together is *love*. As Rob, in the midst of his gropings, tells his longtime female friend, Min Tharrington:

> "I knew there was something called love in the world. Most children do; it is God's main gift, once He's given blood and breath. It may be His last if you don't take it and work it. I *knew* as I say not from hearing folks praise it or do it in my sight but from parts of my heart that had always been with me. A loving heart."

But love is a complex and ambiguous emotion to Price. It is the antithesis of the romantic "dreams" of young Eva, Robinson, Jr., and Rachel; it is above all realistic. Love involves service, personal abnegation, and an acceptance of the imperfection of the individual coupled with an acknowledgment of obligations necessitated by blood ties, tradition, or even simple affection. Most of the exemplars of this virtue are female—single white ladies like Rena, Hattie, Polly, and Min, or stoic black servants like Sylvie, Della, and Flora—although a black man, Grainger Walters, best illustrates the type.

Thus, Reynolds Price works out a complex and profound moral vision in *The Surface of Earth*. But many readers may be unable to accept his essentially passive view of obligation, love, and familial commitment, and he pays a stiff price for his meticulousness and high purpose. The novel is overwritten and the action frequently flags; many of the lengthy descriptions, letters, and dream sequences seem unnecessary or, at best, too long; the declamations tend to escalate into baroque rhetoric that blurs the characters' particularity; and Price's fine dramatic sense is often lost in the sheer verbal weight of the narration.

So *The Surface of Earth* is not a novel for everyone. It makes considerable demands upon the reader in terms of patience and sensitivity, and it probably requires a basic sympathy toward the author's moral posture. But for the reader who has grown impatient with the fragmentary or grotesque surfaces, the amorphic, sometimes nonexistent, characters, and the ethical ambiguity, even amorality, of much contemporary fiction, *The Surface of Earth* offers a powerful return to the certainty, stability, and moral vision of the traditional novel at its best.

Keith Neilson

THE SURVIVAL OF THE BARK CANOE

Author: John McPhee (1931-   )
Publisher: Farrar, Straus and Giroux (New York). 114 pp. $7.95
Type of work: Contemporary history
Time: Since 1965
Locale: New England

A report on how a young American has kept alive the ancient art of building birchbark canoes

Principal personages:
HENRI VAILLANCOURT, canoe builder
JOHN MCPHEE, the author, a canoe enthusiast
RICK AND MIKE BLANCHETTE, Vaillancourt's friends
WARREN ELMER, the author's friend

The Survival of the Bark Canoe is an unusual book. Its subject matter is unique, its form uncommon. The basic subject matter is a branch of marine architecture, for much of the book relates how a birchbark canoe is constructed. But the book involves much more; within the frame story (which originally appeared as a series of articles in *The New Yorker,* for which the author is a staff writer), John McPhee presents considerably more material. The frame story, which tells of his meeting with Henri Vaillancourt and a subsequent journey by canoe on the waters in the Maine woods in two birchbark canoes built by Vaillancourt, also presents the author with the opportunity to relate the biography of the young canoe-builder, commentary on the design of canoes, advice on the use and care of bark canoes, and some details of the history of the bark canoe and its use in North America. In addition, there is an appendix containing sketches and models of bark canoes by Edwin Tappan Adney, who was a key figure in keeping alive knowledge of the art of building bark canoes.

The central figure of the book, then, is Henri Armand Vaillancourt, a descendant of French-Canadians, who lives and works in his native town, Greenville, New Hampshire. A young man of twenty-six at the time the book was written, he is one of a handful of builders of bark canoes, working with almost the same tools which were used by centuries of Indian practitioners of the art. Vaillancourt began building his first canoe by trial and error, when a boy of fifteen. His first efforts were fruitless, until a cousin sent him an old copy of *Sports Afield,* the popular sporting magazine, which contained an article on how Indians had built their canoes. But Vaillancourt's education as a canoe builder began when he bought a copy, about 1966, of *The Bark Canoes and Skin Boats of North America,* a publication of the U.S. Government Printing Office, written by Howard I. Chapelle of the Smithsonian Institution, and published in 1964. But Chapelle based what he wrote about bark canoes on the research notes, sketches, and models of Edwin Tappan Adney, who had spent the last six decades of his life, from

1888 to 1950, in research on the bark canoe. So, although indirectly, Adney, who died in the same year as Henri Vaillancourt was born, became the young man's teacher.

In the ten years between 1965 and 1975 Henri Vaillancourt built more than thirty bark canoes, each a work of craftsmanship and a labor of love, built to order for buyers, but delivered from his hands only with reluctance. His buyers paid eight hundred dollars and more for a canoe, depending on the size, for Vaillancourt has built canoes ranging from twenty-pound hunting canoes to a thirty-six foot fur-trading canoe capable of carrying four tons of cargo. The buyers are canoe lovers, hunters, and even universities (who use the canoes bought by the institution for instructional purposes). All the canoes have been built at Vaillancourt's parents' home, where he lives and works. Such work as can be done in winter is accomplished in a nine-by-fourteen-foot room in an old tar-papered shed; the real construction, done in warmer weather, goes on in the adjoining yard, in the centuries-old way.

Vaillancourt's tools guarantee quality in his construction, but they are simple hand tools—a froe, an axe, an awl, and a knife. His knives, which are the finishing instrument, are of a somewhat unusual crooked design, purchased by mail from the Hudson Bay Company, who have sold them for well over a century. The materials for the canoes are the same as the Indians used, searched out in the woods by the builder. The basic material is birchbark, taken in a roll from a standing tree. The roll of bark, pieced out amidships, where the canoe is broadest of beam, is given its form by a handcut framework of cedar thwarts, gunwales, ribs, and stems, the whole fastened together with split tree roots and careful, hand-carved joinery. The only nonnative material Vaillancourt uses (because he insists it is better) is tar for seams and patching, instead of pitch from trees. Strength for the bark covering comes from thin cedar planks fitted between the covering and the ribs. One great advantage to this construction, as the frame story twice demonstrates during the canoe trip in the Maine woods, is that repairs can be made from materials at hand in the wilderness.

Native builders of small boats all over the world have evolved enduring designs, through centuries of building and use, and the American Indian of the Eastern woodlands was no exception. The bark canoe, contrary to popular opinion, is a sturdy craft that will serve its owner well for a decade or more. Its strength, durability, and seaworthiness are remarkable, as McPhee's account of a canoe journey demonstrates. Rocks, logs, even submerged tree stumps are less likely to damage a bark canoe than one constructed of such materials as canvas, metal, or fiber glass. Explorers, hunters, trappers, traders, and settlers adopted the bark canoe when they found it in North America: its advantages for travel were immediately obvious to users of heavy wooden boats propelled by oars. Indeed, travel by canoe, because of laborious portages, was possible over long distances where heavier craft could not be taken. Further, the bark canoe enabled men to travel easily in the centuries before railroads and highways and cars, using the waterways nature provided through the wooded wilderness of eastern North America. Later generations have forgotten, indeed they have never known, how important streams, rivers, lakes, and seacoasts once were to travel, although even a superficial study of maps will reveal how in the era before the railroads and highways, cities and towns grew up beside the waterways. As McPhee points out, the bark canoe was probably necessary for the evolution of exploration, fur trade, and settlement in Canada and the northeastern United States, where the materials—birch and cedar—were naturally available.

The frame also reminds the reader of another New Englander and one of his books: Henry David Thoreau and his *The Maine Woods,* published posthumously in 1864. The canoe trip which the author Henri Vaillancourt and three friends take in Maine covers many of the same waterways, through the same forest wilderness, which Thoreau traveled with his Indian guide in the 1850's. The twentieth century travelers, having read Thoreau's book, look for moose as he did, see some of the same sites he describes, still unchanged, and talk about Thoreau as a thinker, traveler, and wilderness lover. Of the five modern-day travelers, perhaps John McPhee, the author, is the most Thoreauvian. His interests, choice of material, organization, and style in *The Survival of the Bark Canoe* all carry echoes of Thoreau.

Gordon W. Clarke

TERMS OF ENDEARMENT

Author: Larry McMurtry (1936-   )
Publisher: Simon and Schuster (New York). 410 pp. $9.95
Type of work: Novel
Time: 1962-1975
Locale: Houston, Texas

A realistic novel set in Texas, generally comic but sometimes poignant, with a gallery of sharply drawn, memorable characters

Principal characters:

AURORA GREENWAY, a middle-aged widow with a penchant for attracting suitors
EMMA, her daughter
GENERAL HECTOR SCOTT, the favorite among Aurora's suitors
VERNON DALHART, an oil millionaire, another suitor
TREVOR WAUGH, Aurora's former lover and perennial suitor
ALBERTO, retired Italian opera singer, another suitor
EDWARD JOHNSON, a bank officer, another suitor
ROSIE DUNLUP, Aurora's longtime maid, mother of seven children
ROYCE DUNLUP, Rosie's husband

With the publication of his sixth novel, Larry McMurtry extends his reputation as a social realist concerned with Texas and the American Southwest. Along with three other significant contemporary Texans— Walter Prescott Webb, Roy Bedicheck, and J. Frank Dobie—McMurtry takes as his subject the changing societal and moral codes of his native state. Although his first two novels, *Horseman, Pass By* and *Leaving Cheyenne,* are more strictly regionalist—treating in modern terms the myth of the cowboy-rancher— his recent fiction, still centered generally in Texas, ranges beyond this specific locale. *The Last Picture Show* (1966), a scathing satire on social injustice and moral corruption in Thalia, Texas, indicts as well the whole cultural desert of Smalltown America. Never before has McMurtry satirized moral decadence with such broad strokes, nor indeed with such wild comic burlesque. His last three novels, *Moving On* (1970), *All My Friends Are Going to Be Strangers* (1972), and *Terms of Endearment* (1975), are funny-sad stories, realistic studies of Americans who mostly just happen to be Texans.

McMurtry's special strength has always been characterization. In *Terms of Endearment,* he creates fully detailed, exuberant personalities who are so charged with the spontaneity of life that they seem to burst from the pages of the book. Chief among them is the formidable Aurora Greenway, a strong-willed, garrulous, humorous, shrewd, entirely independent widow who, during the course of the novel, comes to terms of endearment with her daughter, Emma, together with a string of unlikely suitors. On the level of social comedy, her story travesties the familiar modern theme of mating. Aurora, a middle-aged veteran of romance, quite overpowers her aging boy-friends, unequal combatants in the wars of sex and love. With her sharp tongue, her sensible but fixed view-points about nearly every subject, and her posture of rigorous moral superiority, she reduces her lovers to the condition of miserable suppliants. In the mating struggle, she is supreme victor. Like Shaw's dominating Woman, controller of the Life Force, Aurora controls the passions of her male friends, at times mothering them with tender solicitude, at other times banishing them from her presence like naughty children. Aurora, the Great Mother, is a comic-ironical version of Philip Wylie's American "Mom," half-despot, half-Madonna. She is both a castrating lover and a divine mother. An original type in fiction, she is as real, as fully fleshed, as life itself.

Aurora's chief suitors are Edward Johnson, vice-president of the tidiest bank in River Oaks; Alberto, a washed-out Italian tenor; General Hector Scott, returned from the great wars but engaged now in his final erotic struggles; Trevor Waugh, Aurora's ancient lover, whose major claim to her heart is his finely tailored clothing; and Vernon Dalhart, the oil millionaire and sex novice, who for the first time in his meager life falls in love—with the widow. Strange to say, Aurora's attractions are devas-tating to men. She is far from a beauty, being overweight and over-powering. Yet she has backbone, a rare integrity, and a surprising gen-erosity of spirit that softens her con-tours. The reader comes to under-stand how her suitors, all of them de-ficient in some regard, cling to her for strength. Poor Edward Johnson lacks Aurora's wit and intelligence; Alberto, a shadow of his former self, lacks the "nerve of failure"; General Scott, her most nearly successful lover, lacks refinement; Trevor lacks resolve; and Vernon lacks experience. By the time Aurora sweeps from the scene, still flowing with vitality, she has reduced most of her boyfriends to putty. But the fault is not hers; though superior to her lovers, she must settle for an inferior specimen of the opposite sex. For a woman of Aurora's fine but admittedly difficult temperament, the problem is to dis-cover the proper terms of endearment —the right formula for mating.

Her greatest problem, however, is not how to pick an acceptable boy-friend; it is how to resolve her con-flicts with her daughter. Like most of McMurtry's novels, this book deals with the significant theme of the re-conciliation of generations. From his earliest novels, *Horseman, Pass By* (titled *Hud* in the movie version) and *Leaving Cheyenne,* McMurtry has established as a plot complication the struggle between parents and chil-dren. Aurora, like Homer Bannon or Adam Fry, is a strong, domineering parent figure. To bequeath to her daughter the values she has nurtured, she must contend with the mores of a different generation, one out of sym-pathy with her rigorous, somewhat eccentric code. Aurora, after all, is not a native Texan. A New Englander whose roots are in the Puritan ethic, she has a background of enterprise and culture. Her prized possessions, inherited from her mother, Amelia Starrett, are two valuable oil paint-ings, the less-admired by Paul Klee and the other—her favorite, which hangs on her bedroom wall—a small but superb Renoir. To Aurora, the paintings represent her buried life. A romantic, she loves beauty, grace, and perfection. Another side of her character, also derived from her Boston and New Haven inheritance, is an iron will. She has only contempt for the lackadaisical existence of most Texans. Although secure in her transplanted Houston surroundings, she is nevertheless restless. She believes that her daughter, like most of her suitors, is too passive, too lethargic. Aurora wishes to master fate; Emma seems resigned to it.

At the beginning of the book, the antagonism between mother and daughter centers around this conflict in temperament. Married to a phlegmatic English professor at a small Texas college, Emma—dumpy, slatternly, and pregnant—at twenty-two is already in the doldrums. She is bored with her husband Thomas (or Flap, as he is called), who is slow at everything except sex, for which his responses are much too spasmodic to provide her any satisfaction. By Aurora's standards, she is living in squalor, psychological as well as physical. Yet she lacks the fortitude to change her condition. Miserable, she fantasizes secret lovers who might carry her away from herself. She dreams mostly about Danny Deck (the narrator-hero of *All My Friends Are Going to Be Strangers*), a successful novelist, even while she squabbles with Flap over his pedantry. Seemingly unlike her energetic mother, Emma chafes at her existence and—because she is also a romantic—develops slowly, during the course of the novel, a spirit as independent as Aurora's. By the end of the book, mother and daughter are reconciled,

and the generations come together in unity.

As an artist, McMurtry details the process of this reconciliation by gradual and finely observed stages. He allows the reader to discern how Emma changes, especially in the second section of the novel, from a neurotic, baffled housewife to a woman of passion, courage, and some small measure of achievement. Only because Emma's life is cut short by cancer is her achievement limited. But by that time, fourteen years after we are introduced to the characters, Emma has given birth to three children, has come to dominate her weak husband, and has—with discretion—enjoyed experiences with several lovers. Informed that she must soon die of her malignancy, she responds to her doctor without childish hysterics or petulance, as she might have shown years earlier, but with a mature acceptance of the inevitable. Above all, she grows closer in temperament to her mother, deriving from Aurora the strength, the moral resolve she now needs. In a touching scene, Aurora passes on to Emma, in her hospital room, Amelia Starrett's painting of Renoir. The gift is not simply a sentimental gesture. For her courage and grace, Emma has proved worthy of the painting. Just as Aurora had earned the rights to her mother's inheritance, so Emma—through her growth of moral experience—has earned the same rights from her mother. The terms of endearment that pass from one generation to another, McMurtry seems to say, must similarly be worked out, negotiated, as a result of the hard job of living.

To be sure, McMurtry is too much

an ironist simply to moralize these sentiments. His irony is applied from within, from the structure of the novel, not externally as a gloss. His sentences bristle with wit. Whole scenes are riotously funny. Yet *Terms of Endearment,* for all its spirited comedy, is more than an entertainment. Like Joyce Cary, McMurtry is an artist who merges the limits of comedy and pathos, who contrasts the themes of freedom and discipline, of vitality and apathy. Always on the side of life, he feels compassion for those who are cheated by life. Yet he believes that mere vitality, crude animal spontaneity, is not enough for civilized people. They must also live for the sake of some values, must cherish their own inherited strengths. Because of his concern for meaningful values, McMurtry is a writer whose best fiction teaches the reader how to live.

Leslie B. Mittleman

A TIME TO DIE

Author: Tom Wicker (1926-   )
Publisher: Quadrangle (New York). 342 pp. $10.00
Type of work: Report of prison riot
Time: September 8 to September 13, 1971
Locale: Attica prison, Upstate New York

An account of the Attica prison rebellion by a reporter who participated in the negotiations between prisoners and prison authorities

Principal personages:

> TOM WICKER, an observer, columnist and Associate Editor for the *New York Times*
> HERMAN BADILLO, an observer, columnist and Associate Editor of the *New York Times*
> ARTHUR O. EVE, an observer, New York Assemblyman
> ROGER CHAMPEN, ELLIOT JAMES BARKLEY, AND OTHERS, prisoner leaders
> WILLIAM QUINN, the guard killed in the uprising
> JAYBAR KENYATTA, an observer, Black Muslim leader and former Attica inmate
> JOSE PARIS, an observer, member of Young Lords Party
> VINCENT R. MANCUSI, Superintendent of Attica
> HENRY F. WILLIAMS, Captain of the New York State Police
> RUSSELL G. OSWALD, Commissioner of Correctional Services
> WALTER DUNBAR, Assistant Commissioner
> NELSON ROCKEFELLER, Governor of New York

The tragedy precipitated by the uprising at Attica prison in Upstate New York in September of 1971 lives in Tom Wicker's dramatic personal account. No doubt, it also still lives in the nightmares of those participants who survived, and in the memories of the families of those men who did not. But for most of us, it has become merely another bloody footnote in the violent history of our troubled times, another "body count" in the progression stretching from My Lai 4 and before to Munich and after. Although Wicker includes a brief examination of the general problems of crime and punishment, along with an honest self-examination of his own changing attitudes, it is his description of the events of those six days in September which most effectively carries the ominous message of his book.

As is the case with most sudden rebellions, the potential for the one at Attica had been building for a long time. Racism was rampant, not so much among the prisoners as between the prisoners and guards. The prisoners were mostly black or Puerto Rican, and the guards, with the exception of one Puerto Rican, were all white. There were the usual physical deprivations: poor food, indifferent medical treatment, occasional beatings. There were the equally usual psychological degradations: contempt from the guards and indifference from political leaders; the frequent use of solitary confinement; the housing of 2,250 men in a facility built to hold 1,600; an average pay of twenty-five cents a day; fourteen to sixteen hours of cell time a day with ten hours of absolute silence; one shower and one clean pair of socks per prisoner per week; an annual recreation budget of one dollar for each inmate; no viable job-training program. Despite the efforts of New York's progressive Commissioner of Correctional Services, Russell G. Oswald, Attica, like most prisons, remained a place for punishment, not rehabilitation.

Meanwhile, partly because of the revolt of minority groups during the 1960's and their growing pride, and partly because of a faith that, by a united front, they might be able to force some attention to their grievances, the inmates had formed a semi-government of their own. The Black Muslims, Black Panthers, and Young Lords (Puerto Ricans) had imposed a discipline to which even many of the whites willingly submitted. As Tom Wicker was later to perceive, there probably was less racism among the closely confined prisoners than within the outside society. This, in fact, was to be no small factor in the tragic outcome of the Attica affair.

On September 8, a scuffle between two prisoners led to solitary confinement for both, and to cell restriction for an irate inmate who threw a soup can at a guard. The next morning the discovery of the restricted prisoner in the mess hall caused all A-block prisoners to be sent back. The angered inmates charged the metal gate that sealed off their block.

Here occurred one of those ironic twists that often punctuate major tragedies. The gate was held by a defective bolt that gave way under the assault of bodies. Had the cracked bolt held, the rebellion would have been confined to A-block and quickly put down. Furthermore, the gate guard, William Quinn, was one of the best-liked officers, one of the few for whom the inmates had little animosity. Quinn went down under the rush, sustaining a fractured skull. He was to die two days later, the only guard or hostage killed by the inmates, and his death, along with the false rumor that he had been thrown out of a window, was another factor in the ultimate failure to prevent further violence. The rebelling prisoners seized forty-two hostages—later releasing four—and encamped themselves in D-yard.

The inmates, under the leadership of Roger Champen, who had not taken part in the uprising, but was the most respected prisoner leader among all factions and racial groups, quickly organized themselves, set up protection for their hostages, and began drawing a list of demands. They rebuffed a negotiation attempt by Superintendent Mancusi, whose removal was one of their demands.

Later that day, two outsiders acceptable to the inmates, Herman Schwartz, a professor of law from the State University of New York, and New York Assemblyman Arthur Eve, met with the rebels, along with Commissioner Oswald. The prisoners presented their demands. One of them—amnesty for staging the revolt—was to become the main issue in the negotiations, and the major factor in their eventual breakdown. The inmates also wanted a group of observers from the press and varied political persuasions to act as witnesses to the safety of the hostages, and to publicize their demands.

One of the observers requested by the prisoners was Tom Wicker, columnist and Associate Editor of the *New York Times;* Wicker's columns on the rights of prisoners had not escaped their notice. At one time or another there were to be thirty-seven observers, fourteen of them at the request of the inmates; others were invited by Commissioner Oswald. Some came of their own accord.

The observers soon became not just observers, but active participants. After a second stormy visit with the prisoners, Oswald decided that the risk of becoming a hostage himself had grown too great, and the observers were drafted for the job of carrying proposals back and forth between the prisoners and the authorities. Wicker made five risky trips into D-yard. Among other observers who made most or all of the trips, and tried their best to make a settlement without bloodshed, were Congressman Herman Badillo, Assemblyman Arthur Eve, State Senator John Dunne, and New York publisher Clarence Jones.

It soon became apparent to the observers that they had a hard, possibly hopeless task. Wicker formulated his personal goal—"nobody gets killed"—on his first visit to D-yard, but as they came out Badillo made a prophetic observation. "Funny thing, I get the feeling they liked us better in there than they do out here." Badillo was right. The authorities were in no mood for compromise, especially in regard to the key issue of amnesty. The prisoners may have been victims of their own rhetoric and a false belief in the safeguard of publicity. To the end they seemed to believe they could get a settlement.

But pressures on the harassed Oswald continued to mount, and racism, that "Berlin Wall of the mind" in Wicker's apt phrase, increased rapidly after the death of Quinn.

The final hope rested in Rockefeller, but despite pleas from Wicker, Oswald, and others, the Governor would not budge. The social and political "order of things" had to be upheld. "The harder decision," Wicker writes, "might well have been to stay the hand of society—to grasp at the straw of life rather than to send men with guns to D-yard." Rockefeller did not make that decision. By the night of September 12, the observers and most of the others knew it was about over. "It rained all night . . . . One of the men in D-yard later wrote to Russell Oswald that God must have been crying."

On the morning of September 13, state police marksmen began to assemble. The inmates, still believing they could forestall an attack, led a number of hostages into the open, holding knives at their throats.

A helicopter dropped CS gas into the yard. The police opened fire. The assault lasted just six minutes.

Four of the hostages had their throats cut: two seriously, two slightly. The two seriously injured hostages survived. The two who were only slightly cut died, felled by the bullets of their "rescuers." The final tabulation showed ten hostages and twenty-nine inmates killed, three hostages, eighty-five inmates, and one trooper wounded—all by guns in the hands of state troopers and corrections officers. The prisoners had been bluffing; the authorities were not. "The hard truth," writes Wicker, "was that the Attica brothers had had more faith in the state than the state had had in them. Both had been wrong." Said Badillo, "There's always time to die. I don't know what the rush was."

As well as being a good newsman, Tom Wicker is also a novelist, best known for *Facing the Lions* (1973), and *A Time to Die* reads like a novel. This is partly because Wicker writes in the third person, using himself as a character rather than simply a reporter; he uses the same general technique that Norman Mailer has used in some of his books of participatory journalism, but never lets his personal involvement overwhelm his professed subject as Mailer has sometimes done. We learn just enough of Wicker's background and then-current personal problems to like him and understand his own agonized part in the tragedy that he was unable to prevent. The events, which unfold with something of the sense of tragic inevitability of traditional Greek drama, along with Wicker's sensibility, make this "nonfiction novel" a classic of its type.

This book is the story of a tormented man-in-the-middle, who understands the motives of the men inside D-yard as well as those of the people outside, but can find no formula to make each group understand the other. The ongoing tragedy is that the conditions for further Atticas continue to prevail in prisons across the country.

William Boswell

TRAVESTIES

Author: Tom Stoppard (1937-   )
Publisher: Grove Press (New York). 99 pp. $6.00; paperback $1.95
Type of work: Drama
Time: World War I
Locale: Zurich, Switzerland

A Wildean play about Lenin, James Joyce, and the Dadaist Tristan Tzara, and their conflicting theories of art

Principal characters:
    HENRY CARR, a British consulate official from whose "memory" the play is drawn
    TRISTAN TZARA, the Dadaist
    JAMES JOYCE, author of *Ulysses*
    LENIN
    GWENDOLEN, Carr's younger sister, disciple of Joyce
    CECILY, a young librarian, disciple of Lenin

During World War I, James Joyce and Lenin were both living in Zurich; so was Tristan Tzara, a Dadaist poet. So far as is known, these three creators of revolution never met, but imagine if they had. Tom Stoppard, who, as author of such plays as *Jumpers* and *Rosencrantz and Guildenstern Are Dead,* has become well-known for a marvelously fertile imagination, has fastened on this idea and brought it to life in *Travesties.* He gives us events called up from the memory of the aged Henry Carr, an official in the British consulate in Zurich during the war years. Carr, an unreliable narrator if there ever was one, furnishes recollections interrupted with "time-slips"; as Stoppard notes, the play

> is under the erratic control of Old Carr's memory, which is not notably reliable, and also of his various prejudices and delusions. One result is that the story (like a toy train perhaps) occasionally jumps the rails and has to be restarted at the point where it goes wild.

Henry Carr, a real person who had come to the British consulate after being wounded in the war, once played the part of Algernon Moncrieff in a production of *The Importance of Being Earnest* put on by Joyce and an actor friend who had determined to establish a company to perform English plays. Joyce went to the consulate to obtain support for his project from the Consul General, A. Percy Bennett. There he saw Carr and afterwards recruited him to play the part of Algernon, a role which Carr performed admirably. But later the two fell out and brought suit against each other, Carr suing Joyce for the price of a pair of trousers, a pair of gloves, and a hat he had bought to furnish out his costume, and Joyce suing Carr for slander and also for the price of some tickets Carr had sold. Joyce won on two of the suits but lost on the slander. Joyce's distaste for Carr and Consul General Bennett resulted in their literary embalming as two drunken soldiers in the "Circe" episode of *Ulysses.*

In *Travesties* Carr remembers

Joyce very well but Wilde even better. In fact, the predominant tone of the play is Wilde's. Stoppard has also taken characters, plot, and a number of lines from *The Importance of Being Earnest*. The two girls are often Cecily and Gwendolen in more than name; and Carr, an intolerable dandy, is very nearly Algy. Occasionally Joyce even becomes Lady Bracknell. A manuscript by Lenin and one by Joyce are inadvertently interchanged; though no baby in a handbag is involved in the confusion, the Joyce manuscript is appropriately the childbirth sequence of *Ulysses*. Tzara, sometimes something of a Jack Worthing, arrives at the consulate to propose marriage to Gwendolen, who is Carr's sister; he has previously taken out a library card in the name of Jack Tzara because Cecily, the librarian, disapproves of Dadaists. Embarrassingly for Tzara, Carr turns up at the library pretending to be Tristan. Cecily and Gwendolen, like their originals, meet, insult each other with finesse, and then band together when they realize they have been deceived. Each insists that her suitor be not Earnest, but an earnest admirer—of Lenin in the case of Cecily and Joyce in the case of Gwendolen. Somehow, with the straightening out of the confusion about the manuscripts and who is really who, both pairs of lovers are reconciled.

Stoppard is repeating the technique of his best-known play, *Rosencrantz and Guildenstern Are Dead*: structuring his drama around another famous play, using the structure for comic and ironic effect, and moving in and out of this other play-world. Also, like *Rosencrantz and Guilden-*

stern Are Dead, Travesties has a basic seriousness, for it is concerned with theories of art against a background of war and revolution. As the first scene opens, Tzara, Joyce, and Lenin, as well as Gwendolen and Cecily, are in the library, where Tzara and Joyce are composing. Tzara's nonsensical poem, created of words on pieces of paper drawn from a hat, alternates with Joyce's dictation to his disciple Gwendolen so that Tzara's "Whispers ill oomparah!" affords a discomforting comparison to Joyce's "Hoopsa boyaboy hoopsa!" Meanwhile Lenin's writing, in which he is aided by his disciple Cecily, is interrupted when his wife enters to inform him that revolution has begun in St. Petersburg and that the Tsar will abdicate. The news (in Russian) comes to the accompaniment of incongruous Joycean phrases. Lenin rushes out, while Joyce, who is presented as a debonair Irish reciter of limericks, strolls off singing "Galway Bay." So the play's technique of comparison and contrast of the three revolutionists is established.

Lenin's excitement and, later, his complex intriguing, which results in his leaving Zurich in a sealed train for Russia, is also contrasted with Carr's nonchalant failure to understand what the revolution is all about; his idea of a social revolution is unescorted women smoking cigarettes at the opera, and he assumes that the masters of Russia have finally turned upon their impudent and greedy champagne-consuming servants. Counterpointing this view, the play offers a good deal of political history of the early days of the Russian revolution. Carr, finally brought to understand that Lenin is a person of significance, tries to spy on him at the library. He determines that Lenin must be prevented from leaving Zurich just as Lenin's train pulls out of the station.

Even more ironic than his view of revolution is the attitude of the dandified Carr, safe in the placid land of cuckoo-clocks, toward the war raging in Europe. He talks about his part in the war in terms of articles of his apparel being ruined by mud and bullets and also speaks in series of clichés alternating between the joys-of-comradeship and the stench-and-carnage of battle. Occasionally, however, he breaks through these formulas to reveal his ecstatic delight at being released by a trivial wound from blood, filth, and danger to the blessed pacifism and punctuality of Switzerland.

The relevance of art in a world of war and revolution is the great question of the play. To Joyce, the meaning of war, or of life in general, is what lives on as art; the Trojan War received its meaning and immortality through Homer, and Joyce will double this immortality through his *Ulysses*. To Tzara, art is dead, the war has been brought on by capitalist corruption, and the times call not for art but antiart—vandalism and desecration. Considerable information about Dadaism ("What did you do in the Great War, Dada?") is introduced in the form of question-and-answer dialogue imitated from *Ulysses*.

Lenin, in a section of the drama that sags woefully under the weight of revolutionary history and reactionary literary criticism, maintains that publishing must be controlled, and all art must serve the cause of the proletariat. Once in Moscow at a friend's house he was moved by a Beethoven Sonata, but he cannot afford to be stirred by a beauty which makes him want to pat heads rather than hit them.

The really dramatic moments of the play occur in scenes in which Tzara, Joyce, and Carr storm at one another in the intensity of their feelings about art, which is of far greater significance to them than war or revolution. It is supremely important to be earnest about art.

To sum up all aspects of this quicksilver play is impossible: characters sing and dance; Joyce does magic tricks; one whole scene is composed of a sequence of limericks; and Cecily and Gwendolen do a takeoff on Mr. Gallagher and Mr. Shean. Allusions, quotations, repetitions, puns, and other wordplay astonish the reader, as do the violent contrasts and switches of tone. But Stoppard is not so wild as he is Wildean; the zaniness is carefully controlled and polished. *Travesties* is a comic and intellectual *tour de force* of great interest, charm, and variety.

It must be said, however, that criticism of Stoppard's earlier dramas as being the work of a sleight-of-hand artist who disguises a lack of substance by an amazing cleverness with language applies to this play as well. No conclusions about art are reached here, and the intellectuality is facile rather than profound. Nevertheless, the reader who knows Joyce and Wilde, and even one who doesn't, will find *Travesties* thought-provoking and instructive, as well as highly entertaining.

At the end of the play Old Cecily appears to reprove Old Carr for his failure to remember that he was never Consul as he has been pretending, that he never actually knew Lenin, and that he has thoroughly mixed up times and events. "What of it?" Carr asks, and he's right. *Travesties* with John Wood acting the part of Carr was a hit in London and New York; it is less exciting when read rather than seen, but in written form, the wit, humor, and ingenuity of its magician-author can be thoroughly savored.

Mary C. Williams

TUBE OF PLENTY
The Evolution of American Television

Author: Erik Barnouw (1908-   )
Publisher: Oxford University Press (New York). Illustrated. 518 pp. $14.95
Type of work: Critical history
Time: 1876-1975

A definitive, concise critical history of the American mass media, beginning with radio but concentrating upon the evolution of television

To Erik Barnouw, the familiar television set, Everyman's "tube of plenty," is the modern cornucopia of vulgarity, issuing from its depths a vast spew of banality. Subtitled "The Evolution of American Television," his study is both a scholarly history of the mass media and a provocative critical essay on the most lively of the arts. Barnouw comes to his subject with impressive credentials. Emeritus Professor of Dramatic Arts at Columbia University, he helped found and for many years was Chairman of Columbia's Film Division. He also helped to organize, then headed, the Writers Guild of America. As writer, producer, and director, he has worked in many areas of radio broadcasting, films, and television. His three-volume *A History of Broadcasting in the United States* won the George Polk Award, the Frank Luther Mott Journalism Award, and the Bancroft Prize in American History. *Tube of Plenty* is a useful condensation and updating of this massive work. Although the original volumes treat the subject comprehensively, with more ample footnotes, bibliographies, and appendices, the present compact volume—with its succinct chronology of major events and detailed index—is for most readers quite adequate. Barnouw addresses his book to two audiences: students

of communications, who will surely use the work for many years as a sound textbook on the history of the mass media; and general readers concerned with the social-cultural impact of television upon American life.

From a historical perspective, Barnouw defines five stages in the evolutionary growth of American television. "Forebears," the first section, treats the early theories about "Hertzian waves," Marconi's discoveries with his "black box," and the innovative thinking of Reginald Fessenden, Lee de Forest, and others. The second section, "Toddler," concerns the pioneering practical demonstrations of broadcasting theory, the beginnings of RCA and NBC, the earliest commercial ventures of the new radio medium, and the important discoveries of Philo T. Farnsworth and Edwin H. Armstrong, each to expand the field of communications. "Plastic Years" deals with the early years of television, roughly from 1945 to 1953, and "Prime" continues the saga of the glorious commercial years, from 1954 to 1963, the end of the Kennedy era. A final section, "Elder," from 1964 to 1974, begins with the years of Johnson's administration and covers the historical, social, and political events of the Vietnam conflict, Watergate, and the collapse of the Nixon presidency.

By treating the evolution of the mass media—particularly of television—in terms of political rather than entertainment history, Barnouw greatly expands the social dimensions of his study. He is interested more in the ways in which the mighty industry acquires and uses its considerable powers than simply in recording the tastes, trends, and fads of broadcasting. To be sure, his book is a valuable compendium of facts about the talents of many beloved stars of the media. But Barnouw provides these data as part of his job of chronicler. His most engaged concern, quite clearly, is with the internal machinations, the hidden forces that govern television and the other media.

For example, he describes with persuasive documentation the political origins of such trade monopolies as RCA, NBC, ABC, and the subsidiary broadcasting systems. Always the business ventures have been entangled, usually at the highest levels, with public affairs. Barnouw's revelations, by now familiar to inside-dopesters of the entertainment industry but still generally unknown to the public, detail many behind-the-scenes feuds, unsavory agreements, payoffs, and betrayals. Barnouw is careful not to editorialize; the facts speak for themselves. From their business offices the managers of television are seasoned professionals, often ruthless in their strategies for dominance, always concerned foremost with the financial rewards of the industry, and only incidentally committed to artistic excellence.

The author, on the other hand, believes that television should deliver a superior artistic product. Although he understands the commercial restraints of the medium—that television programs must please an extensive popular audience and not only an elite few—he nevertheless chafes at the failures of broadcasting to perform a more significant public service. On the basis of reliable evidence, he indicts the managers of television for their timidity, lack of principle, and moral irresponsibility. As examples, he cites the reaction of the media to the so-called Communist menace of the late 1940's and early 1950's. In 1945, "Counterattack: The Newsletter of Facts on Communism" jolted the industry by warning that the performing arts had been widely infiltrated by subversives. Two years later appeared "Red Channels: The Report of Communist Influence in Radio and Television," a paperback which listed in alphabetical order the names of 151 people, all prominent in the arts, who allegedly transmitted "pro-Sovietism to the American public." One actress included in the list, Jean Muir, was promptly notified that her role in the cast of *The Aldrich Family* had been cancelled. Other talented actors, writers, and directors were blacklisted—denied employment without any attempt to investigate the accuracy of the "citations." Instead of defending those artists who were cited as subversives, the media cowered under pressure. Years later, according to Barnouw, the "blacklist gradually dropped out of the headlines but remained a felt presence."

In contrast to the generally disappointing record of television and radio executives who failed to respond with courage to political pressure, a few personalities like Edward R. Murrow and his producer, Fred

W. Friendly, fulfilled their public service with notable integrity. In 1953, Murrow reported on *See It Now* "The Case Against Milo Radulovich, A0589839," the first of several broadcasts that examined the activities of Senator Joseph McCarthy and others. From 1953 to 1955 the Murrow-McCarthy conflict boiled, the final effect being that the Wisconsin senator began to lose crucial public support. To Barnouw, the televised Army-McCarthy hearings, the 1960 Nixon-Kennedy Presidential debates, the 1962 coverage of the Cuban missile crisis, and the 1973 Watergate debates leading to a climax with the resignation of Richard Nixon in August, 1974, represent the highest achievements of television in the public service.

The failures of television, according to Barnouw, derive from a corresponding neglect of public service. He agrees with sociologists Paul F. Lazarsfeld and Robert K. Merton that "even in their evasions, mass media are political." Because the media are essentially conservative, determined not to upset comfortable conventions, they "not only continue to affirm the *status quo* but . . . fail to raise questions about the structure of society." By applying cautious formulas of proved success, the industry settles into habits of tedium that result finally in exhaustion. Barnouw shows how the great era of original television drama, from 1953 to 1955, declined, then turned to rot. But within that golden age many outstanding programs flowed from the "tube of plenty," never again to be repeated in such panoply: *Studio One, Kraft Television Theater, U.S. Steel Hour, Goodyear Television Playhouse, Philco Television Playhouse, Omnibus, Playhouse 90*— with lesser offerings such as *Robert Montgomery Presents, Revlon Theater, Medallion Theater, Motorola Playhouse, The Elgin Hour,* and *Matinee Theater.* The pattern of success, imitation, and at last self-parody has been typical for television broadcasting. As Barnouw points out, the creative forces of the media always surrender, when pressed, to the demands of the commercial. What Newton K. Minow, former chairman of the Federal Communications Commission, said in 1961 is still true today: "When television is bad, nothing is worse." He described "a vast wasteland" through which there passes an arid "procession of game shows, violence, audience participation shows, formula comedies about totally unbelievable families, blood and thunder, mayhem, violence, sadism, murder, western badmen, western good men, private eyes, gangsters, more violence, and cartoons." Only now most of the cartoon shows appear off prime time, for the kiddies on Saturday mornings.

As a historian of the media, Barnouw perhaps exaggerates—but only slightly—television's betrayal of the public trust. After all, the mass media have never negotiated a contract to elevate the common taste. The only implied contract between broadcasters and patrons is for the media to provide entertainment, or perish. Yet Barnouw is right to register his disappointment. Over the years, he says, "Television, in spite of its 'public service' and 'free speech' spots, has been a leading agent of polluters." Nevertheless, he proves what intelligent people already know. The historical service he renders in *Tube of*

Plenty is to call to mind, for people who have forgotten or never learned the whole story, the truths we need to remember. As a work of social history, the book is more valuable than just a study of the evolution of an industry; it is also a record of morals and mores, of business ethics and politics. Although too long (in spite of its abridgement from the three-volume source), too inclusive (the section on radio could have been drastically reduced), often opinionated, and at times unfocused, the book taken as a whole is a splendid contribution to the critical study of American television—and of ourselves as well.

Leslie B. Mittleman

THE TWENTIES
From Notebooks and Diaries of the Period

Author: Edmund Wilson (1895-1972)
Edited with an Introduction by Leon Edel
Publisher: Farrar, Straus and Giroux (New York). Illustrated. 577 pp. $10.00
Type of work: Notebooks and diaries
Time: The 1920's
Locale: New York, France, England, Italy, California, Louisiana, Provincetown

Posthumously published notebooks and diaries of the 1920's by one of America's foremost literary critics

When Edmund Wilson died in 1972 he left unfinished *The Twenties,* a book principally made up of entries from his notebooks and diaries of the period. The task of completing the book fell to his friend and literary executor Leon Edel. In a brief foreword, Edel explains that in accordance with Wilson's wishes he has edited *The Twenties* "with a light hand" and that he has tried to make the book "as readable as possible." Edel's excellent introductory "Portrait of Edmund Wilson" portrays first the young Wilson whom Wilson himself presented in his autobiographical memoir *A Prelude* (1967), which covers his boyhood from age thirteen, his college years, and his period of service in Europe in World War I, and which is partly drawn from his earliest notebooks. Part II of the portrait interprets the later Wilson, the discerning and brilliant critic of modern literature, in the light of Wilson's famous essay "Philoctetes: The Wound and the Bow." According to Edel, the essay's "biographical depths" reveal Wilson as symbolically kin both to Philoctetes ("the archetypal artist") and to Neoptolemus (a kind of archetypal critic"). Edel writes that Wilson's psychological wound resulted in part

from his being the only son of an apathetic father subject to periods of deep depression and of a mother physically deaf and with no intellectual interests (she did not even read her son's books). His wound "prevented him from being poet, playwright, novelist on the scale of his contemporaries," but his "gift of intellectual penetration and of sympathy made him one with the 'common humanity' of art and society, one with Neoptolemus."

Edmund Wilson began keeping a notebook in 1914 (as he mentions in *A Prelude*). He continued the practice for the rest of his life, amassing a total of more than two thousand manuscript pages in forty-one ledger-type copybooks along with other miscellaneous pages. In preparing *The Twenties* for publication he had begun to provide notes or introductory comments for individual passages or groups of passages from his notebooks and diaries so as to make the material more comprehensible, and he had written a prefatory note in which he remarked that, "The book will be more easily understood if one has read *A Prelude* first." Edel has supplied valuable additional information in notes, some of which include quotations from letters, especially those to John Peale Bishop, that throw light on Wilson's personal life and character and on his development as a writer during a crucial decade.

The 1920's were busy years for Wilson. After trying free-lance writing for various publications he became managing editor of *Vanity Fair,* a glossy, sophisticated magazine of the time, and he fell in love with Edna St. Vincent Millay, whose satiric prose sketches (signed "Nancy Boyd") and poems he published in the magazine. He was briefly managing editor of the politically liberal *The New Republic* but rejoined *Vanity Fair* after a trip to Europe. He published *The Undertaker's Garland* in collaboration with John Peale Bishop, a Princeton friend who was also a *Vanity Fair* editor. He married Mary Blair, a divorced actress, and fathered a daughter Rosalind by her. He was drama critic for *The Dial* and *The New Republic* and he published book reviews in both magazines (among them reviews of James Joyce's *Ulysses,* T. S. Eliot's *The Waste Land,* and Ernest Hemingway's *In Our Time*). He traveled to California to try (without success) to persuade Charlie Chaplin to perform in a ballet written by himself. His play *The Crime in the Whistler Room,* starring Mary Blair, was produced by the Provincetown Players. He became associate editor of *The New Republic.* He separated from Mary Blair, drank a good deal of bootleg liquor, indulged in sexual episodes or liaisons with several lower-class women, published *Discordant Encounters,* visited New Orleans, and spent a summer in Eugene O'Neill's house in Provincetown

where he began work on several essays which were to appear in *Axel's Castle* (1931), the first of his important works of literary criticism. He worked on *I Thought of Daisy,* the first of his two novels, visited California again, and rewrote his novel. He entered a sanatorium for a nervous breakdown—"I suppose I was trying to escape from the various women with whom I had got myself so badly entangled"—but left after three weeks during which he became briefly addicted to a drug, paraldehyde. He published both *Poets, Farewell!* and *I Thought of Daisy,* he divorced Mary Blair, had a final "prompt bout" on his apartment sofa with his dance-hall pick-up mistress, and made plans to marry Margaret Canby, who became his wife in 1930.

The Twenties is a melange of many ingredients: nature descriptions, word paintings of ugly urban scenes, miniature portraits, gossip, poems, popular song titles, anecdotes, jokes and quips, lists of slang or colloquial words and phrases, sexy conversations with prostitutes, descriptions (some erotic) of both middle-class and lower-class women, tentative phrasing of ideas or themes to be developed in essays, and occasional self-analysis. The volume as a whole is largely external, revealing much less of the author himself than one might expect from such an analytical critic as Wilson. More of the inner Wilson would very likely have been revealed had he been able to complete the book.

Many of the cityscape, landscape, and seascape entries read like the literary equivalent of musical exercises that a pianist might play to keep his fingers nimble. In Boston, "The doorways melt like music on the eye. Delicious silver-knobbed doorways on Beacon Street—by Bulfinch—with wide fanlights as clear as crystal and flanked by clear white-curtained panes. . . ." At Provincetown, "The calm vista of the harbor eternally fluttered over by gulls and bounded with its yellow rim of sand that seems to lock the town in as in a world of its own. . . ." Wilson is impressed as a painter might be by color combinations on the California seashore:

> The sea scrolling silver on the kelp-mottled beach—or the silver mirrors of the ebb, and, beyond, the deep wonderful blue and the brownleaf of the kelp, and, beyond, the brown blue-washed mountains answering to the blue brown-streaked sea—or at late afternoon with a purple carpet of loam, and, beyond it, blues and purples of the sea.

In his varied roles as journalist, editor, critic, novelist, poet, and playwright, Wilson met many men and women who were prominent in the world of journalism and the arts in the 1920's, and he jotted down his impressions or opinions of them. He typed Frank Crowninshield, the editor of *Vanity Fair,* as "the born courtier who lacks an appropriate court." Condé Nast, the publisher of the magazine, he thought "the glossiest bounder I have ever seen." Wilson was sometimes invited to join the Round Table group at the Algonquin Hotel that included Alexander Woollcott, Heywood Broun, Robert Benchley, Dorothy Parker, and others, but he cared little for them. Their jokes and games he thought "rather tiresome." Dorothy Parker's wit he

could appreciate but he was suspicious of her flattery and her backbiting and he objected to her "cruel and disgusting jokes." He regretted that Dorothy's clowning friend Benchley was wasting a talent that might have been turned to serious satire, instead of which he went to Hollywood, continued his clowning in several movies, and died of cirrhosis of the liver.

Wilson had known Scott Fitzgerald at Princeton where both had written for the *Nassau Lit.,* which Wilson edited. Their friendship continued in the 1920's (and to the end of Fitzgerald's life) and when Wilson was in Paris in 1921 he wrote Fitzgerald a letter (from which Leon Edel quotes) confessing a feeling of cultural superiority "in comparison to most of the rest of the intellectual and artistic life of the country." He believed the United States was "actually beginning to express herself in something like an idiom of her own. But, believe me, she has a long way to go." Another novelist with whom Wilson was to have a long-lasting friendship was John Dos Passos, whom he met in 1922. In a note, he recalls reading, years before, Dos Passos' *Manhattan Transfer* (1925), and he remarks that "Dos Passos was, so far as I knew, the first American novelist to make the people of our generation talk as they actually did." He was afterward to object, however, to Dos Passos' conservatism in his later books.

Women appear often in *The Twenties,* and the entries in which he writes about them or quotes from his conversations with them are among the most intimately revealing of Wilson himself. In a plaintive note in the section entitled "After the War," he confides: "I soon got over my shyness with women, but I was a victim of many of the hazards of sex—from which I might have been saved by previous experience: abortions, gonorrhea, entanglements, a broken heart." He leaves the reader wondering about the abortions, but he specifies (though not by her real name) the young woman who gave him the disease. She was to appear later as Anna in the story "The Princess with the Golden Hair" in *Memoirs of Hecate County* (1946). The erotic parts of the story are only slightly toned down from the Anna passages in *The Twenties* concerning the sordid affair with a young woman he picked up at a dance hall.

A number of notebook or diary entries relate to Edna Millay, who broke his heart. Both he and his friend John Bishop fell in love with her when she was writing for *Vanity Fair,* but she left them and went off to Europe. Wilson followed shortly after and, from France, wrote Bishop about his meeting her:

> She can no longer intoxicate me with her beauty or throw bombs into my soul; when I looked at her, it was like staring into the crater of an extinct volcano . . . it made me sad . . . that I had loved her so much and now did not love her any longer. . . . I would not love her again for anything; I can think of few more terrible calamities; but I felt that, impossible and imperfect as she is, some glamour and high passion had gone out of life when my love for her died.

Rita in *I Thought of Daisy* (1929) is modeled on Edna Millay, and in the long Epilogue to *The Shores of Light* (1952) Wilson not only tells of the love affair but also contrasts the lovely red-haired woman he had loved with the physically ravaged and spiritually subdued poetess who died alone in 1950 on the staircase of her country home.

The last entry in *The Twenties* is dated January, 1930. It summarizes a meeting between Wilson and Mary Blair in her apartment following a morning in a court where they were getting a divorce. The scene is like one from a TV serial. Mary is crying and intoxicated. She raves a while, calms down, they eat supper, and when he leaves, she gives him a look which, he writes, tells him "I could count on her, she counted on me." They did remain friends afterward and we are left waiting for the next volume drawn from Wilson's notebooks and diaries. What we have had is so appetizing that we hope Edel will satisfy our hunger for more.

Henderson Kincheloe

TYRANTS DESTROYED AND OTHER STORIES

Author: Vladimir Nabokov (1899-   )
Translated from the Russian by Dmitri Nabokov in collaboration with the author
Publisher: McGraw-Hill Book Company (New York). 238 pp. $8.95
Type of work: Short stories
Time: 1924-1959
Locale: Russia, Berlin, the French Riviera, the Baltic Sea resort, Paris, and Ithaca, New York

A collection of thirteen short stories focusing on émigré *life in Europe and on the philosophical questions of the nature of life, death, reality, and appearance*

Tyrants Destroyed and Other Stories is the most recent publication of Vladimir Nabokov, a writer recognized for his work in two languages. These short stories (with the exception of the final one) were all written in Russian, Nabokov's native tongue. They appear here translated by the author's son, Dmitri, in collaboration with the author. Each story is introduced by the author in a short paragraph reviewing the story's publication history and providing what other information he considers pertinent. All but the final story were written during the period of 1924-1939; the last story was written in 1951 in Ithaca, New York.

Nabokov, perhaps the greatest stylist of the twentieth century, is well known on the basis of such works as *Bend Sinister, The Real Life of Sebastian Knight, Invitation to a Beheading, The Gift, Lolita, Pale Fire,* and *Ada;* a prolific writer, he is the author of twenty-nine books including novels, translations, short stories, poems, a critical biography of Gogol, a screenplay, a drama, an autobiography, chess problems, articles, letters, and interviews. In each of these, he demonstrates a craftsmanship, a mastery of language, and an obsession with questions of form, structure, and style. He challenges critics and readers alike to follow his lead through a course littered along the way with deliberate traps. His writing is a maze of dead-ends, a mystery of false clues, an investigation hindered by tampered evidence. Nabokov's writing is almost as much of a contest as his chess; full understanding demands of the reader total attention.

Nabokov was born in Russia. He and his family, "White Russians," left Russia in 1919 to escape the ascent to power of the Bolsheviks, and the author subsequently lived in several European cities during his expatriation from Russia and before his emigration to the United States in 1939. Berlin and Paris were familiar habitats to the young writer, who gained a reputation from publishing in the numerous *émigré* periodicals of the period. The short stories in this collection concern the period of expatriation from his Russian home and the course of his literary career in those cities familiar to the Russian *émigrés;* they reveal the early development of his literary style. Whether dealing with everyday occurrences of *émigré* life or with the bitterness and impotency of the expatriate, Nabokov demonstrates his formidable knowledge of the psychological foundations of human action and motivation. In the tradition of the great Russian novelists, Nabokov is a master of detail and the commonplace.

In the first story, "Tyrants Destroyed," Nabokov captures the bitterness and hopelessness of the intellectual at odds with the imbecility of his country's despotic ruler. Blending knowledge of the ruler's adolescence into the narrator's present hatred, Nabokov presents the forerunner of his later novel, *Bend Sinister*. Written in the first-person narrative style, this story concerns the growth and nurture of hatred and a futile plan to assassinate the country's ruler. As is frequently true with Nabokov, the story's action is less important than its character and mood, and even less important than the prose itself.

The second story, "A Nursery Tale," is a fanciful and fantastic story of a young man, his desires, and his agreement with the Devil. Erwin, shy and not particularly attractive, creates an imaginary harem and bites his lower lip whenever he sees an appealing woman. At a sidewalk cafe, a middle-aged woman named Frau Monde sits at his table, informs him rather casually that she is the Devil, and offers him the real harem of his choice. He has until midnight of the next day to select all the women he pleases, so long as the total number is an odd number. The story, while rather inconsequential in content, is an excellent example of Nabokov's skill and cleverness as a writer and gives a hint of a later Nabokovian character named Humbert in the novel and screenplay *Lolita*.

"Bachmann" is a memoir related by a narrator as told to him by an acquaintance of the two central characters. Bachmann is a pianist of eccentric habits and tastes with a fond penchant for liquor and the atmosphere of small, dirty bars. He is loved by a Mme. Perov, a middle-aged woman with a limp, whom Nabokov has nicknamed "The Lame Madonna." Mme. Perov, upon seeing Bachmann at a friend's house, begins attending all of his concerts, sitting always in the center of the front row. She assists in the search for Bachmann when he goes off on one of his journeys into the poorer sections of the city. Finally, near the end of the story, her love for Bachmann is consummated after a long search in the winter rain; the narrator proposes that "this was the only happy night in Mme. Perov's life." She dies that day, and Bachmann, having been the cause of so great a sacrifice, disappears and becomes a drunken eccentric.

In "The Admiralty Spire," Nabokov adopts a variation of epistolary fiction: the story is one long letter to the author of a fictitious novel entitled *The Admiralty Spire*. Nabokov's correspondent imagines the book's author to be his former lover who is now telling every detail of their relationship, although the details of his actual love and the relationship in the fictional novel are largely different. Although this is not the direct antecedent of Nabokov's later novel, *Pale Fire,* there is nonetheless a strong similarity between the correspondent in this story and the editor in *Pale Fire,* a novel written in the form of a definitive explication of a poem. In "The Admiralty

Spire," Nabokov's correspondent is outraged by what he sees as an invasion of his privacy and a betrayal of the confidentiality of his love; again, as is true in so much of Nabokov's work, the plot is secondary to the characterizations.

"Music" is another excellent example of Nabokovian fiction. It concerns a young man and his divorced wife together for the moment in the same room listening to a piano concert. Although they never speak— indeed, there are less than ten lines of dialogue in the entire story—Nabokov creates a figurative remarriage of the two, while relating the past events of their marriage. The entire story consists of the memories and the musings of the narrator.

"Lik" concerns a Russian *émigré* actor of questionable talents and his confrontation with his past, with poverty, and with death. "Recruiting" is a short piece of characterization and description, clothed in the pretense of a novelist observing people and figuratively recruiting some of them to appear as characters in his novels—hence the title. "Terror" describes the events leading up to the central character's separation from reality, his drift towards insanity, and his salvation from this separation by death. "A Matter of Chance," a story about the ironies of coincidence, presents a Russian *émigré,* a waiter in a dining car of a European train. A cocaine addict, he is bent on suicide, certain that his wife is dead. "In Memory of L. I. Shigaev" is a character study of the narrator and his older friend, L. I. Shigaev, the growth of their friendship, and its conclusion. "Perfection" concerns a young German boy and his tutor, a Russian *émigré* of middle age, and their fateful holiday at a seaside resort.

"Vasiliy Shishkov" is, in Nabokov's words, "an innocent joke on the most famous of *émigré* critics." The story of a poet who disappears completely, leaving behind his work, its original publication followed the publication of a poem by Nabokov, signed with a new pen name in order to determine the response it would receive from this leading *émigré* critic. When the critic's review turned out to be a glowing one, Nabokov wrote "Vasiliy Shishkov," titled after the pen name used on the poem.

The final story in the collection, "The Vane Sisters," is the only story originally written in English. It presents two sisters, Cynthia and Sybil Vane, the former having once had an affair with the narrator, the latter being a student who had an affair with a professor at her school who was a friend of the narrator.

Sybil, having been rejected by her professor-lover, commits suicide, and the remainder of the story deals with sister Cynthia's attempts to communicate with her dead sister and the narrator's perception of these attempts and their cost. "The Vane Sisters" is a story about appearance, about reality and imagination. In typically Nabokovian style, the final paragraph of "The Vane Sisters" is an acrostic.

Tyrants Destroyed and Other Stories is a valuable collection for the serious scholar of Nabokovian literature. Many of these stories are the antecedents of later novels, and many of their characters appear in slightly altered form in later works. All the stories represent the proving ground for Nabokov's style and technique, while they reveal his beginnings as a consummate craftsman and stylist. Nabokov's is a prose honed to precision and a diction heightened by irony and wit, and both his language and his characterizations are matchless. *Tyrants Destroyed and Other Stories* is an enjoyable and enlightening reading experience.

J. R. Van Laan

VITAL SIGNS
New and Selected Poems

Author: David R. Slavitt (1935-   )
Publisher: Doubleday and Company (New York). 320 pp. $6.95
Type of work: Poetry
The first retrospective collection of poems by a writer of unusual depth and versatility

David R. Slavitt is probably best known as the brilliantly facile young fabricator of Henry Sutton, a popular novelist of the 1960's. Even now, it is fun to recall people's outrage when they learned that *The Exhibitionist,* for example, was the work of someone who had also written more serious fiction, and even poetry. On the one hand, people of Jacqueline Susann's ilk were irritated because someone had done easily and laughingly what they worked hard to do; on the other hand, purveyors of solemn literature were offended at this prostitution of talent. Even Tom Wolfe, who had no reason to feel either envious or superior, took a cheap shot at Slavitt's next serious novel, saying in a review that it was not as good as *The Exhibitionist.*

Meanwhile, having found a way to excuse himself from grantsmanship and literary politics, Slavitt kept on working. This is his seventeenth book; it is preceded by four Sutton novels, six Slavitt novels, and six books of poems. This selection establishes Slavitt as one of the most interesting poets in the country.

From the beginning, Slavitt's poetry has been characterized by profound wit, neoclassical attention to form, and a generous erudition which informs the reader, rather than requiring him to be esoterically informed before the poetry will be in-telligible. Slavitt is also a master of tonal variety, so that within the same poem he can make shifts of tone which most poets would find too risky. For some time it has been interesting to imagine a book of Slavitt's poems which would be large enough to require an index of first lines; now that it is here, the index is as entertaining and provoking as one could have hoped. "The long red underwear of Randolph Scott" opens a brilliant pair of sonnets called "Ride the High Country," a coming to terms with the aging of heroes in westerns such as *Shane* and *High Noon*; and here, almost making sense, are the four first lines beginning with *U*:

Uncles wiggle their ears and then
Under an opulent sun, a *louis d'or*
Unrehearsed, for the love of laughing,
   her laughter gushed
Uraemia is painful enough without
   birds . . . .

That last one is startling enough. It turns out to be the first line of "The Death of Mozart," which is based, like so many of Slavitt's poems, on an odd fact that he has turned up and turned to use:

Uraemia is painful enough without birds
chirping their heads off, warbling in
   thirds
while you're busy dying. A little quiet,
   please.

I want no canary around for my decease.
No more did he. But still, it is bother-
    some
to think that when his final hour had
    come
Mozart sent his canary away. Did the
    bird
make mistakes? sing badly what Mozart
    heard
in his mind's ear, following a score
of canary music? Or, did the bird soar
on aviary arias, a strain
so fine that he beat time with throbs
    of pain?
Or worse, did the bird's song suggest
    a measure
there was no more time for, now, so
    that the pleasure
of composing turned to the pain of
    holding a flood,
as the body held the urine in the blood?
I fear the worst, that Mozart, as you or I,
just wanted quiet, quiet in which to die,
unbroken by any sound but his own
    breath.
With the bird gone, he had quiet.
Which was death.

This little poem, first collected in *Day Sailing* (1969), exhibits several of Slavitt's distinctive strengths. Beginning in an offhand, nearly cynical tone as the odd fact is presented, the poem moves through a series of speculations, here phrased as questions, whose tone deepens toward sympathy as the questions accumulate. So the fear in the carefully chosen cliché "I fear the worst" is earned, is genuine: silence is death.

The casual, cynical tone, often mitigated by tenderness or profound meditation, appears a little more often in the hundred or so selected poems than in the nearly ninety new ones. Slavitt's most ambitious earlier poems are perhaps "Elegy for Walter Stone," from *The Carnivore* (1965)

and "Another Letter to Lord Byron," from *Day Sailing*. Both are extended, risky, shifty in tone, and finally quite moving, with the feel of permanence. The background for "Elegy for Walter Stone" is given in a headnote: "In August of 1959, I interviewed John Hall Wheelock at his home in Easthampton, N.Y., on the occasion of the publication of *Poets of Today VI*, which Mr. Wheelock edited and which included the poetry of Messrs. Gene Baro, Donald Finkel, and Walter Stone." By the time of the book's publication, Stone had committed suicide. The first section of the poem sets the scene, sketches in a few facts, and establishes Finkel as a living foil to the dead Stone; Slavitt's Finkel transcends the actual Donald Finkel to become, by contrast, all that Stone rejected. The second section speculates on the manner of Stone's death—hanging—and on his motives and final destination. The final section moves between the conversation with Wheelock and statements about death:

> All death is nature's,
> whether by germ in the blood or idea
>   in the head,
> or sudden mischance in the wasteful
>   order of things.
> Gaze fixedly at it, and the distinctions
> disappear.

It is Slavitt's custom to gaze fixedly at things, notions, and ideas, until he can summon precise ways of stating their essence, or the essence of his reaction to them. Even when the formal gamesmanship is of a very complicated sort, as it is in "Another Letter to Lord Byron," one finds wisdom in the spectacularly rhymed stanzas. The first word of the title reminds us that Auden addressed a letter from Iceland to Lord Byron; but Slavitt mentions Auden only in order to establish his own place in what might become a tradition. The poem's actual subject is contemporary literature's low seriousness, and the vacuum which Byron's "hock and soda water" might fill. After a gloomy vision of dead authors as "volumes of blank pages, buckram-bound," the poem focuses on Byron's liveliness:

> You come through whole, and live, and
>   are not merely
>   a name on the spine of your book and
>   its index card.
> The gestures you make in your poems,
>   the jokes, are clearly
>   those of a man who's trying very hard
> —and willing to pay the price, even pay
>   dearly—
>   not only not to be boring, but not to
>   be bored
> himself. Yourself. Myself. I know how
>   it is.
> It's always tough in the Quality Lit. Biz.

In the new poems, of which there are many more than enough for a full-length collection, Slavitt avoids not only boring himself or his readers, but also being deceptive. The poems are arranged in three sections; the first, "Vital Signs," contains a number of poems having to do with the ecstasies and disappointments of love and marriage. However painful some episodes might be, the poems, like the lovers in "A Parting," are "correct, restrained." The poems are the more affecting for their restraint, their refusal to specify their autobiographical origins, whatever those may be. "A Parting" is concerned with the healing of those deep wounds which we try to keep open, out of a sense of obligation to the episodes which dealt them; it ends,

> Tenderness turns to tough
> scar tissue. We lose the nerve,
> can suffer no more than we loved. It's
>   never enough,
> but it's what we deserve.

The second section, "At Home, In the World," takes advantage of the ambiguity the comma gives the phrase, and ranges with humor and tenderness from the death of a family pet to a shop in Jerusalem. Beneath many of the poems is the idea that we pay for what we get, whether we intend to or not. "Airfield Rabbits," for instance, is a grim sonnet about rabbits who invade airfields for their lush grass and high fences, only to be deafened by jet roar, so that they cannot return to the wild where owls swoop down unheard.

Finally, "Tough Characters" takes up the study of history, which has occupied Slavitt for years; the poems dwell sometimes on extravagant revenge, sometimes on the mystery of fragmentary classical writings. "Tough Characters" are, for the most part, men like Nebuchadnezzar, Hadrian, Hitler. But the title poem is about written characters—the alphabet:

> On the Sixth Day,
> late, as if in afterthought to His will,
> the Lord brought forth written
>   characters: they
> are savage, with the reek of Chaos still.

Slavitt controls them, though, as well as any poet now writing.

Henry Taylor

THE WAR AGAINST THE JEWS, 1933-1945

Author: Lucy S. Dawidowicz (1916-   )
Publisher: Holt, Rinehart and Winston (New York) 460 pp. $15.00
Type of work: History

A historical examination of the Nazi Holocaust from both the German and Jewish sides

In early 1941, as Nazi Germany prepared to attack the Soviet Union, Adolf Hitler ordered his SS chief Heinrich Himmler to draft plans for the destruction of European Jewry. The total victory of National Socialism, Hitler believed, would come in the East. With the opening of the Russian campaign, the Final Solution, the Nazi code for Jewish annihilation, moved inexorably forward. Roving "Einsatz" squads of specially trained SS troops murdered thousands of Polish and Russian Jews in the newly occupied territories—perhaps as many as two million by the end of the war; soon the rest would be rounded up and herded into cramped ghettos. Then, beginning in 1942, these same Jews, promised a better life in the East, were "resettled" to death camps where they died by the millions in gas chambers. History has never witnessed a racial war of such staggering dimensions — genocide waged with the faceless instrumentality and efficiency of a modern industrial state. Hitler's commitment to the Final Solution was as absolute as was his commitment to total military victory. In the end, the Final Solution claimed more than six million lives (about two-thirds of the European Jewish community); it completely destroyed Europe's ancient and resilient Jewish civilization.

This unparalleled human tragedy is the subject of Lucy S. Dawido-wicz's book *The War Against the Jews, 1933-1945.* Her aim is to explain how the Germans arrived at the decision to murder systematically an entire people, and why European Jewry allowed itself to be destroyed. Based on published and unpublished sources in several languages, the book adds some clarifying information about the Final Solution, but no startling new interpretations. Its major strengths lie, rather, in the broad synthesis and fresh perspective provided for the general reader. In a survey of less than five hundred pages, the author constructs a concise and coherent overview of the Final Solution which contrasts the mindless terror of the persecutor with the human suffering of the victim.

Dawidowicz, a professor of history at Yeshiva University, begins her study by reassessing the origins of Hitler's anti-Semitism. The first shadows, she believes, appeared in the small Austrian town of Linz, where the young Hitler first encountered anti-Semitism in the pages of a local newspaper. Exposure to a wide range of anti-Semitic propaganda in provincial Austria and cosmopolitan Vienna, from rabid gutter cranks to calculating urban politicians, transformed Hitler into a man obsessed with racial anti-Semitism. While the author, like earlier writers, can only speculate about this process, she does believe that the Final Solution was firmly fixed in Hitler's mind by November, 1918. In fact, she believes that from this point until 1941 Hitler simply bided his time, waiting for the opportunity to unleash his pent-up hatred against the Jews. Except for the inclusion of the Russian Bolsheviks in the ranks of the international Jewish conspiracy, his virulent anti-Semitism remained unchanged. "Racial imperialism and the fanatic plan to destroy the Jews were the dominant passions behind . . . [Hitler's] drive for power."

While there is no dispute about the importance of anti-Semitism in Hitler's ideology, there is still considerable discussion about the point at which Der Führer decided to eliminate the Jews. It is clear from Hitler's speeches and *Mein Kampf* that the Jews were to be expelled from all German-controlled territory. Whether the Nazi policies of expulsion and deportation were the calculated prelude to physical destruction remains open to debate. Supporting this line of thought leads the author into difficulties. For example, the use of code words such as "resettlement" or "evacuation" in 1941 to refer to the mass murder of the Jews does not necessarily prove, as Dawidowicz suggests, that they had the same hidden meaning when Hitler used them in the early 1920's. The author's thesis also requires her to dismiss the plan approved by Hitler in 1940 to deport all German Jews to Madagascar as inconsequential, implying that it never received serious consideration.

The complicity of the German people in the Final Solution may also be overemphasized. "The Final Solu-

tion," the author states, "grew out of a matrix formed by traditional anti-Semitism, the paranoid delusions that seized Germany after World War I, and the emergence of Hitler and the National Socialist movement." Accordingly, German society, conditioned by layers of racial, religious, political, and economic anti-Semitism that reached back to Martin Luther, embraced Hitler as a redeemer, and in so doing surrendered itself to the "mass psychosis of anti-Semitism . . . ." That an undercurrent of anti-Semitism pervaded modern German history has been well documented elsewhere. The idea that German society was attracted to Hitler almost exclusively by his virulent anti-Semitism is less certain. Indeed, it is difficult to make a judgment on this question since the role of anti-Semitism in the Weimar Republic, certainly the most critical period before Hitler, is barely mentioned. While it is undoubtedly true that an overwhelming number of Germans turned enthusiastically to Hitler both before and after 1933, and that numerous state agencies became implicated in the Final Solution, it seems extreme to imply repeatedly that the entire German populace share an equal degree of guilt for the destruction of the Jews along with Hitler and the Nazi SS. Complicity there certainly was, but if the German nation had approved such a crime, why the need for secrecy?

If questions about the origins of the Final Solution remain, there can be little disagreement with Dawidowicz's judicious and dignified treatment of the impact of Nazi persecution on Europe's Jews. In a concise yet forceful manner, she describes how the internal war against Germany's Jews opened in 1933 with terror and disenfranchisement and culminated in 1938 with economic strangulation. Without strong leadership or ideological unity, the Jewish community found it impossible to respond effectively to the diverse and sometimes uncoordinated measures of official and individual violence. By 1935, after numerous attempts to defend their diminishing rights had failed, most Jews who were able chose the one alternative encouraged by the Nazis: emigration. Before the outbreak of World War II more than 300,000 German Jews (out of a total of 500,000) had fled Germany. This internal war against Germany's Jews proved to be a dress rehearsal for the Final Solution.

With the outbreak of war in 1939, the machinery of destruction began to appear. The technical apparatus and administrative procedures were developed with cold, impersonal efficiency. Once in operation, moreover, the holocaust rapidly gained a momentum of its own, fueled by Nazi underworld enthusiasm, immune to wartime demands for manpower, and subject only to Hitler's personal command. Entrusted to Himmler and the increasingly powerful SS, this was total war against the Jews.

The assault caught European Jewry unprepared. Badly fragmented politically, bound by traditional optimism and value for human life, the Jewish community in 1941 confronted a revolutionary attack with defenses that were more suitable to pre-modern eras of persecution. The Final Solution was an experience "without historical precedent or rational meaning, and neither Jewish tradition nor

Western rationalism had equipped Europe's Jews for Nazi duplicity and ruthlessness."

Throughout the nightmare, however, European Jewry clung to its sense of humanity and civilization. Certain individuals, seduced by promises of survival, collaborated with the Nazis or exploited the less fortunate. The vast majority, however, maintained a deep commitment to tradition, whether religious or cultural. Dawidowicz is at her best in recounting the Jewish experience in the Polish ghettos; indeed, her chapters relating what people in the ghetto did to make the unbearable physical suffering bearable are the most powerful in the book. The analysis of ghetto organizations, from the hated *Judenräte* imposed by the Nazis to the many unofficial welfare committees, is useful information on a sometimes confusing topic. It also becomes clear from these pages why resistance failed. Resistance was both more widespread and earlier than some writers have thought, but it could not have altered the course of the Final Solution. Without arms, military training, Allied support, or political unity, the Jewish community did not have the means to resist, let alone the opportunity. Not until 1942, when word filtered into the ghettos about the purpose of the "resettlement" camps, did serious discussion about resistance begin, and then it was already too late—as the abortive but heroic uprising in the Warsaw ghetto in 1943 attests. By that point, however, survival no longer mattered; it was simply a matter of honor and revenge. The utter hopelessness of the Jewish situation can only heighten the sense of human tragedy that faced the European Jews during the war.

The War Against the Jews is not a history of National Socialism, nor is it a complete discussion of Nazi anti-Semitism (a summary of the European impact of the Final Solution is relegated to an appendix which recounts Jewish losses country by country). The focus is on Germany and Eastern Europe; the approach is that of the generalist who draws composite pictures, rather than of the specialist who builds exhaustive case studies. This type of organization may not satisfy all historians, but it does provide a valuable introduction to the darkest side of the Third Reich, a shocking reminder of Nazi beastiality at a time when public interest in Hitler and certain aspects of National Socialism threaten to make this era "popular."

Rennie W. Brantz

WASHINGTON JOURNAL
The Events of 1973-1974

Author: Elizabeth Drew (1935-   )
Publisher: Random House (New York). 428 pp. $12.50; paperback $4.95
   (Vintage)
Type of work: Contemporary history
Time: 1973-1974
Locale: Washington, D.C.

A journalistic analysis of the last year in office of President Richard M. Nixon and the events leading to his resignation

> *Principal personages:*
> RICHARD M. NIXON, President of the United States
> PETER W. RODINO, JR., a congressman from New Jersey,
>   Chairman of the House Judiciary Committee
> GERALD R. FORD, a congressman from Michigan, Nixon's Vice-
>   President, and finally, President of the United States
> TOM RAILSBACK, a congressman from Illinois and member of the
>   House Judiciary Committee
> JOHN M. DOAR, special counsel to the House Judiciary
>   Committee for its impeachment inquiry
> A NAMELESS EMPLOYEE OF A DEMOCRATIC SENATOR

Elizabeth Drew, Washington correspondent for the *New Yorker* magazine, kept a journal during the final year of the Watergate episode, and drew upon it for her periodic dispatches to that magazine. Now she has compiled from her journal, and those dispatches provide a valuable report on the events of that tumultuous year.

Contrary to the implication of the title, it is not a highly personal and subjective account. While there are occasional references to the weather or to a tennis game or dinner party, *Washington Journal* is largely the product of a reporter's efforts to learn about and to communicate the events of history as they unfold. Unlike many other reporters of the period, Drew was not attempting to uncover wrongdoing on the part of President Richard M. Nixon and his subordinates, nor was she seeking to be the

first to report to the public what official investigations had produced. Her goal was to portray the mood of Washington as the capital was shaken by each new development in the scandal.

Washington reporting, like most other specialties, is an art. The art of such reporting consists in sorting out the reality from the pretense. As Drew clearly explains it, "There is a quality of a nervous system about Washington, or at least, about that part of Washington which professionally concerns itself with official events." The nervous system includes politicians and their employees, reporters, lobbyists, lawyers, and government workers, all of whom talk incessantly to one another. One event triggers talk of its probable consequences, and the talk itself frequently is a factor in subsequent events. But for all the influential talk—the reports that Senator X is lacking enough money to win reelection, or that Congressman Y is considering taking a new position on an issue—much of Washington talk is, like talk elsewhere, idle chitchat.

To do his or her job, the Washington reporter trades information, rumors, analyses, and speculation with other Washingtonians, taking the pulse of the system. Then the reporter must sift through the gossip and rumors, judging which pieces are significant and serious. Drew provides, in *Washington Journal,* some excellent examples of the skilled reporter at work. With regard to the House Judiciary Committee inquiry on whether to impeach the President, for instance, she focuses upon one member of the committee, Congressman Tom Railsback of Illinois. A Republican, like Nixon, Railsback was not committed to either position in the impeachment controversy. Drew talked frequently with him during the inquiry, reporting his inclinations to believe certain claims and to discount others. Drew understood that it was the decisions made by such men and women, rather than the outspoken and unswayable attackers and defenders of the President, who would determine the outcome of the inquiry. Another of her sources is an unnamed employee of a Democratic senator. The employee, she explains, is "in the traffic patterns on Capitol Hill."

By contrast, the author does not wait at the White House or in congressional press galleries for many official announcements, but relies instead on the broadcast media and newspapers to keep her up-to-date on the news. When she meets with some of the more often quoted politicians involved with Watergate, she does her best to probe beyond the glib statements that reporters facing more imminent deadlines must take at face value. Thus her reporting does more than report numerical outcomes of votes, or speeches and press conferences. It explains why something happened as well as what happened.

Washington Journal is not replete with ponderous commentary about the politics and values of the United States. Yet the Watergate episode did call into question some of the basic instincts of Americans. Occasionally the author addresses these issues philosophically, as when she notes:

> Societies need unifying symbols, and the Presidency has been ours. We cling to the idea that the Presidency is worthy of our respect, because we want it to be. In linking his fate with the fate of the Presidency itself, Nixon is making his ordeal ours. . . . It is humiliating to see a President subjected to humiliation, whatever its origin.

Such passages give the book much of its enduring value. The events of Watergate are on record, and surely every schoolchild in the America of the year 2000 will know that Richard M. Nixon was the first President to resign under threat of impeachment, as pre-Watergate schoolchildren knew that Andrew Johnson was the first President to be impeached. But it would be well for the future citizens of America to understand also what Watergate revealed about the strengths and weaknesses of our political system.

Drew brings back to us the sense of dread that so many Americans felt late in 1973. Besides Watergate, the nation was facing an energy crisis that threatened the economy's roots. As the United States tried to recover from the Vietnam War that had divided and weakened the country, a new war in the Middle East that could involve much of the rest of the world seemed likely. While some of the threats never materialized, America's future then seemed utterly unpredictable. One of Drew's journal entries, for October 16, 1973, conveys that sense: "Just before lunchtime, the news came over the tickers that Marines were boarding an aircraft carrier headed for the Mediterranean. Nobody knows what it means." She notes similar ominous signs throughout the period, signs that in retrospect have little import.

But it was a shaken nation that was forced that year to confront the news that the President's top assistants had conducted an illegal program of domestic intelligence-gathering that had grave implications for a free country. The existence of the taped conversations with the President was known, and there was reason to believe that Nixon had at least closed his eyes to his deputies' questionable activities.

Americans felt they needed a strong leader to see them through the crises, and it was discomfiting, at best, to consider that the President, the elected leader, might have occasioned one of the crises. Indeed, many citizens who did not condone spying on the opposition political party or lying on the part of the President preferred not to think that it might have happened. Richard Nixon's political opponents had often been quicker to criticize him than other politicians' opponents, and cer-

tainly there was an element of self-serving rhetoric in the growing outcry over Watergate.

Yet Nixon was deposed, through the workings of the same political system that had brought him to power. Drew evidently was not a Nixon fan, but throughout her book she expresses the same doubts felt by many Americans about the course of events. In the end, a weary country had rid itself of a leader it mistrusted, and Drew's doubts too were close to resolution. After she had questioned, for instance, whether politicians should determine the propriety of the President's conduct, she quotes Alexander Hamilton's Federalist Paper supporting Congress' power to impeach, and then adds:

". . . The working out of political questions is what keeps our country going. The politicians are our mediators. Sometimes we don't like their decisions, but someone has to mediate."

Washington Journal is in one sense a tribute to the political system. In the Nixon era and subsequently, it became fashionable to disparage Washington as the seat of a venal and do-nothing government. Some said President Jimmy Carter was elected in 1976 because he had not previously been associated with Washington. Drew takes note of the self-serving and corrupt in Washington, but her book is primarily an account of the government's process of cleansing itself. Her heroes are those who tried to do what was best.

And, although Elizabeth Drew's book is a distinctly Washington story, it becomes clear in her telling that the power in Washington ultimately lies elsewhere; that is, throughout the United States. The Washington nervous system continues to function, with reporters and lobbyists and bureaucrats elected by no one. Yet the real power is entrusted to those elected to office, and the elected officials cannot function if they forfeit the support of those who elected them. That is the message of Watergate which *Washington Journal* so well conveys.

Nancy B. Ferris

THE WESTERN APPROACHES
Poems 1973-75

Author: Howard Nemerov (1920-   )
Publisher: University of Chicago Press (Chicago). 110 pp. $7.95
Type of work: Poetry

Seventy-one poems produced between 1973 and 1975 and divided into three parts

Howard Nemerov at fifty-six shows no signs of diminishing vigor; these new poems follow *Gnomes & Occasions* published in 1975. Nevertheless, he seems to be taking an early backward look and finding that what he defines as "the western approaches" provides beginnings as well as endings. The final poem in the book's first section, "The Backward Look," concludes with a prayer to Earth to "Hold us your voyagers safe . . . As from the heaven of technology / We take our dust and rocks and start back down." In his title poem he applies a similar reductionism to the individual:

As long as we look forward, all seems
  free,
        .   .   .
But looking back on life it is as if   ·
Our Book of Changes never let us change.

With his chances all gone, he now understands "How a long life grows ghostly toward the close / As any man dissolves in Everyman." And Everyman's story, Nemerov writes, begins "as it always did":

In a far country, once upon a time,
There lived a certain man and he had
  three sons . . .

Nemerov's preoccupation with the ultimate sameness of experience comes through particularly forcefully in his treatment of such mundane twentieth century occupations as watching television. He makes this point memorably in "Late Late Show," "Watching Football on TV," and "TV." He builds "Late Late Show" upon the conceit that movies represent the Old Law, television the New. In television, resurrection is implicit as "Eternal return unrolls itself anew." Television's illusion makes the performers' "early lives / Become our late ones," and the swiftly scanning light addresses its "advertisements for life / To us the living, while even their dead die." In "Watching Football on TV" Nemerov writes,

To old men crouched before the ikon's
  changes,
Changes become reminders, all the
  games
Are blended in one vast remembered
  game
Of similar images simultaneous
And superposed.

The crouching old men embody the notion that there is nothing new under the sun. Yet somehow, the poet's language and energy resist expressions of mere world-weariness, even in a poem like "TV," in which Nemerov plays with Berkeley's eighteenth century epistemology to characterize what we see on television as:

> . . . shopworn,
> All soiled and secondhand goods of
>   this world
> Shaken in God's wavering attention just
> An instant before we see it as out there.

"The Spy" follows "TV" and provides a thematic summary of Nemerov's book. Its opening words "Out there, out there" link directly to the final words of "TV," and its three stanzas parallel the book's divisions into "The Way," "The Ground," and "The Mind." Despite the magnitude of the place "out there beyond the air" where the "witnessing astronomers go," and despite the inaccessibility of what's "Under the feet, under the solid ground," Nemerov insists that what's "Behind the brow, a scant deep inch away," actually creates meaning: "It spies upon the true appearances of / Our sensible old world." Nemerov's ambiguities here heighten rather than obscure his meaning.

Other pieces in the book, including the two prose statements in the final section, reach backward and forward to give the collection a sense of unity and coherence. The first prose passage, "The Measure of Poetry," foreshadows in its basic imagery the poems "The Four Ages" and "Drawing Lessons." The second prose piece, "The Thought of Trees," relates even more pervasively to the whole, reminding one of Nemerov's essentially idealistic epistemology and obliging one to reexamine every allusion to a tree in the light of the claim that "Trees imagine life, and our imaginations follow as they may." Nemerov has prepared his reader for this claim many pages before; in "Late Summer," he writes of trees "overhead, / Yet out of reach of, unaffected by, / The noise of history and the newsboy's cry." Nevertheless, they

> . . . continue quietly making news,
> Enciphering in their potencies of pulp
> The matrix of much that hasn't
>   happened yet.

Unfortunately, despite these evidences of interrelatedness among the poems in *The Western Approaches,* the reader must block out a certain amount of material if he wishes to discover the "meaning-in-order" promised by the book's three-part division. A shorter book would probably have been a better book, for many aphoristic and merely clever poems obscure what is fine about this collection. Some of the poems suffer from Nemerov's tendency to draw back from personal commitment and to undercut a poem with devices apparently intended to keep them *statements of themselves without appeal to the real world*—a paraphrase of Nemerov's explanation of his preference for W. H. Auden's work over Stephen Spender's and Randall Jarrell's, reprinted in *Poetry and Fiction: Essays* (1963). John Ciardi observed a similar fault in Nemerov's *New and Selected Poems* (1960), and called it "aesthetic self-indulgence." The fault persists, or, at any rate, the poet continues to retreat into ambiguity, or irony, and to pile up largely verbal effects when he senses the danger of appealing to the real world (whatever that is). Never does he prettify the poem, but he often sterilizes it.

Nemerov's distinguished career in literature dates back to the 1940's and combines fiction and criticism with an on-going effort (in his words) to learn "what poetry is and . . . to see . . . how the art is constantly redefining itself" (Preface to *Poetry and Fiction*). Precisely because he is a man of letters in the oldest and best sense of that term and practices literature with the professional's passion, one must admire the craft of his work and seek to understand, if one may, what appear to be his lapses. His own attitude toward critical method is simply to read what the poem says and not to read what it does not say. None of the poems here is inferior, none shoddy, but those cited already and a few more constitute the major strengths of the book. The few more necessarily include "The Dependencies," "Playing the Inventions," "Drawing Lessons," and two translations, "Childhood" (from Rilke) and "The Banquet" (from Dante). In these poems there is no drawing back from the moment of judgment and discrimination, no retreat, apparent or real, into poetry-making as a ruse to conceal concern.

Finally, "Boy with Book of Knowledge" stands among the most poignant and effective of the poems, possibly because of its intensely personal nature. In some ways, it refutes the recurrent idea of all things being one. The boy with the Book of Knowledge may be Nemerov; at any rate, "Sepia portraits of the hairy great, / The presidents and poets in their beards" inspire him to be a poet. Possibly the boy discovers "poetry rare as raisins" in the "vast pudding of knowledge." But "being now / As near his death-day as his birthday then," the poet "would acknowledge all he will not know." Imagining the lighted library as "a luxury liner on what sea / Unfathomable of ignorance," Nemerov brings the poem to uneasy rest—

And poetry, as steady, still, and rare
As the lighthouses now unmanned and
  obsolete
That used to mark America's dangerous
  shores.

Leon V. Driskell

WHAT THOU LOVEST WELL, REMAINS AMERICAN

Author: Richard F. Hugo (1923-   )
Publisher: W. W. Norton and Company (New York). 71 pp. $6.95; $2.95 paperback
Type of work: Poetry

Hugo's fifth book of poems since 1961, organized in three parts, which looks back in time without sentimentality

In this fifth book of poems, Richard Hugo looks back in time yearningly, refuses to sentimentalize, to prettify, what the mind or camera recorded then. Hugo's poems demand person-to-person contact. In "Indian Girl," he knows "Stars are not in reach," and realizes that "We touch each other / by forgetting stars in taverns, and we know / the next man when we overhear his grief"; the poet comprehends and shares other people's degradation and suffering. The book confirms Hugo's importance as a poet, both through the sheer excellence of individual poems and through the larger interconnectedness of the whole. "Who holds this book holds a man," Whitman wrote a little more than a hundred years ago; now Hugo, without posturing and without self-advertisement, gives substance to Whitman's boast.

Under the heading "A Snapshot of the Auxiliary," Hugo's opening fourteen poems reveal his boyhood past; the next twenty ("Strangers") dwell upon a more recent set of experiences; and the final thirteen ("Lectures, Soliloquies, Pontifications") look to a future folded back upon the present and preoccupied with missed opportunities and ventures not tried.

Early in the book, in "The House on 15th S.W.," Hugo spells out the burden of his book and of his life.

He speaks of his "certainty of failure / mined by a tyrant for its pale perverted ore," and he recognizes that his "pride in a few poems" and his "shame / of a wasted life, no wife, no children, / cancel out." All this would seem self-pitying and merely confessional were it not for the important ways in which earlier, obviously personal, poems connect with the final poem, "The Art of Poetry." There, Hugo advises "sad Raymond," apparently his alter ego, "to search your sadness for the man." We know the man next to us in the bar when we overhear his grief, and we know ourselves when we know the extent and depth of our sadness. In *What Thou Lovest Well, Remains American,* Hugo seeks to come to grips with that sadness and to know himself and his art.

The fading photograph is among Hugo's recurrent, unifying images. In "Last Day There," old snapshots chiefly reveal studies in gray:

. . . two horses and a man, a barn
dark gray against gray light I think
    was sky
but could be eighty years of fading.

In "Iowa Déjà Vu," Hugo questions whether he came "from this, a hardware store / in photos long ago." The Iowa life he invokes contains "all the hate / that makes today tomorrow"; it is a place of "planting time and never harvest, / nothing but the bitterest picnics." These poems do not glorify a remembered America made glorious or heroic through memory.

In his opening poem, "A Snapshop of the Auxiliary," Hugo observes with something like shock that "That gray / in the photo was actually their faces." The women in the photo, circa 1934, are German, "short, squat, / with big noses, the sadness of the Dakotas / in their sullen mouths." After the speaker recalls having once been terrified by the sound of the church bells in the "drab board frame / you see in the background," he goes on to the next photograph, a shot of "our annual picnic. We are all having fun." Not for a moment does one believe that the gray women and their gray children could have fun at their picnics or anywhere else. Relentlessly, Hugo returns, in other poems, to disastrous picnics, recording "fun" which never really happened.

In "The House on 15th S.W.," Hugo begins his road-not-taken theme when he finds himself incapable of entering the dream house he has tried to escape, though now he knows that its "Light would be soft / and full, not harsh and dim remembered";

The children, if there are children inside,
would be normal, clean, not at all
the soiled freaks I had counted on.

The yet-to-be-shaped future beckons, but the canceled-out poet cannot enter.

"A Snapshot of 15th S.W." records progress, a gain earned by accepting the "pastness" of the past. The poem opens imperatively: "Burn this shot. That gray is what it is."

By the final stanza, however, the poet can say: "Don't burn it. That gray is what it was." Furthermore, the poet can now observe "Deep back, out of camera range / . . . sun pulses on fields you might still run to." Later, "Last Day There" suggests departure from 15th S.W. Hugo writes, "I'll leave believing we keep all we lose and love." Home is a place already lost, and, resignedly, Hugo says of his house: "I own this and I know it is not mine."

"Places and Ways to Live" brings the sense of displacement to its most poignant pitch, and it too evokes a snapshot: "Note the stump, a peach tree. We had to cut it down." This poem tantalizes with its not-quite-told story of loss which roots the poet in the past. He listens to radio stations "that play old tunes like nothing worthwhile's / happened since that funeral in 1949." He watches the events of his new neighborhood with detachment, but says, "I'm taking it in, deep, where I hope it will bloom." His wishes for his friends include the hope that their "favorite tree be blooming in December" and that they "never be dispossessed, forced to wander / a world the color of salt with no young music in it."

Displacement assumes more complex dimensions in the title poem, in which poet and reader return to the locale of "A Snapshot of the Auxiliary" and "House on 15th S.W." The poet home from war tries to see change as progress, but "Lawns well trimmed remind you of the train / your wife took one day forever, some far empty town, / the odd name you never recall." He blames the neighborhood for his degradation; he must live with the memory of Mrs. Jensen, "face pasted gray to the window":

You loved them well and they remain,
    still with nothing
to do, no money and no will. Loved
    them, and the gray
that was their disease you carry for
    extra food
in case you're stranded in some odd
    empty town
and need hungry lovers for friends,
    and need feel
you are welcome in the secret club
    they have formed.

What one loved well remains, though past, as a disease qualifying one for membership in the secret club of American loneliness.

The poet's sense of degradation carries over into the book's second section; the first poem in "Strangers," entitled "Goodbye, Iowa," opens, "Once more you've degraded yourself on the road." In the closing lines, despite the need to "joke back / spasms of shame from a night long ago," he crosses the state line "and the state you are entering / always treated you well." This section affirms that the individual makes his own world; twice in "Late Summer, Drummond," the poet declares "Real chance to make it: None." Still, the poem ends with gray transformed, turned "sheer silver in the rain," and with the town drunk waving goodbye "to cars that flash east / safe as cattle when their dreams revive the grass."

The first poem to treat the function of poetry in creating one's own world is "Reading at the Old Federal Courts Building, St. Paul," which opens with the poet degraded, sentenced for crimes against women. By the end of the poem, "renovation's clearly underway," for his young woman accuser now teaches high school and

didn't know me when she said she loved
    my poems,
was using them in class to demonstrate
    how
worlds are put together, one fragment
    at at time.

The poem serves as a pivot, and Hugo signals as much with the words, "renovation's clearly underway." In the same section, "Indian Girl" expresses the poet's willingness to share the degradation of others and to hear their grief; in "Cattails," the poet's sharing of a policemen's dream of girls prevents his planned suicide and allows him a moment of freedom from guilt.

Several poems in the final section move away from Hugo's personal/ subjective voice and employ dramatic speakers. The speaker in "Plans for Altering the River" perverts the river to turn turbines, and once he achieves his ends he rejects the idea of flowers, parks, salmon, and cedar. "We ask for power," he says, and, that achieved, he apparently regards the river as settled. Demands for flowers come, "Just when the water was settled and at home." With similar irony, the speaker in "Three Stops to Ten Sleep" fails to recognize that he carries with him the corruption he hoped to leave behind when he set out for the mountains. Even more to the point, "Approaching the Castle" dramatizes a quest for an El Dorado in which the explorers stop short, "intimidated somehow by the banner / saying 'Welcome,' one side / loose in wind and slapping stone." In "Starting Back," Hugo summarizes human progress in order to question its meaning; the progress amounts to little more than movement from a time when "Each thing had one name" to "our gradual discovery / of seasons, four names accounting / for the ways trees looked." Hence, it seems hopeful to hear that "Some of us are starting back, tearing down / the factories, designing on purpose / flimsy tents."

These ideas, and the chief ideas of the book, come together in "Graves in Queens" and in "The Art of Poetry." In both, Hugo speaks in his own voice rather than a character's, and in both the recurrent, unifying word is "sad." In the first poem, the poet is riding a bus toward an airport and wondering "How long will these graves go on?" At the end, "The bus and graves go on. Millions— / and the lines of stone all point our way." The recurrent phrase "a damn sad thing" relates "Graves in Queens" to "The Art of Poetry," perhaps the single finest poem in the collection.

"The Art of Poetry" does not mention poetry as such; instead, it reveals the source of poetry as knowledge of the self's sadness and the self's independence from externals. Hugo addresses sad Raymond who glares "across / the sea, hating the invisible near east and your wife's hysteria"; by the end of the poem, Hugo tells sad Raymond that "The near east isn't near / or east," and offers this final piece of advice: "Better to search your sadness for the man." Poetry, Hugo indicates, does not stem from what we are, or were; nor does it stem from what we seem. Poetry grows from sadness, our own and what we share of others'. Hugo's final poem both completes and reinterprets what came before.

Leon V. Driskell

WHO SHALL LIVE?
Health, Economics and Social Choice

Author: Victor R. Fuchs (1924-   )
Publisher: Basic Books (New York). 168 pp. $8.95
Type of work: Sociological analysis
Time: The present
Locale: The United States

A serious study of the inequalities and inadequacies of health care in the United States

"The state department of health—a sprawling bureaucracy that affects the health and pocketbook of every citizen—is in deep trouble."

"The department's prepaid health plans for the poor are a nationally publicized disaster."

Statements such as these appear in newspapers around the United States almost daily. Each state has its health care crisis; each county and city has its health care scandal. Legislatures on both the state and national levels debate about health care while millions of dollars vanish into the great abyss of medical assistance. This timely book attempts to confront and deal with these vital issues.

It is no surprise to most Americans to hear that something is wrong with the medical care system in the United States. For years, people have been complaining about the vast, impersonal, and often inefficient monster which consumes enormous amounts of money and energy without producing the desired and expected results. Bills rise and hospitals proliferate and fewer doctors every year choose to become general practitioners. America does not have, and has not had for a number of years, anything like the best medical care in the world, although it may have the most

expensive. How did this situation develop? And, more importantly, how can this grotesque, unfair system be changed for the better? The answers are both complex and surprisingly simple.

Confidence in health departments on all levels, in doctors and hospitals, in drug companies and other establishments which profit from illness, has been shattered. Superfluous layers of bureaucracy have stymied even well-intentioned efforts at reorganization of health care programs. Vast data processing systems lose the records of patients and feed back misinformation resulting in serious mistakes and even deaths. State-employed doctors moonlight, conducting private practices when they are supposed to be working for the state, and even refer state patients to their own private practices. There are inadequate controls in hospitals to prevent employees from stealing the money that mental patients entrust to them for clothing and other needs. All over the nation, inspection of state-licensed but privately owned facilities, especially nursing homes, is inadequate, allowing patient abuse and inhumane living conditions for thousands, perhaps millions of individuals. The majority of the population of this country has come to look upon health care as a gigantic lottery, a system in which the patient always loses.

The trouble with approaching this chaotic situation head-on is that the particulars, the horror stories, the petty annoyances, the corruption, can obscure the basic issues. While it is true that individuals are the reason for and the core of any medical system, perhaps this crisis is as much a crisis of philosophy as of organization. The issues are more fundamental than simply the number of doctors and hospitals rooms available or the profits of the pharmaceutical companies. The basic concern of interested citizens should be with the entire social structure in the United States, for it is the kind of people we are which determines, ultimately, the kind of health we have.

Fuchs, a Stanford medical economist, explains clearly that we must stop deceiving ourselves that our society is the best possible one in the best of all possible worlds. We must honestly and fearlessly examine the social, biological, and physical environments in which we are attempting to live; we must analyze the personal behavior patterns which we choose and which are forced upon us by a cynical and selfish society. Then, after gazing objectively at this environment, we must also understand that the medical care system inevitably reflects the social order and its guiding principles. If the society is flawed, so will the health of its citizens be flawed, and, it follows, so must be any system geared for maintaining the health of these citizens. The resources of our country have not fallen short; the problem lies in

the priorities of a world which places money above the psychological or physical health of its population.

Fuchs insists that we must decide what kind of people we are and what kind of life we want to lead. We must ask ourselves what kind of a society we want our children and grandchildren to inherit. And economics, for better or for worse, must play a large part in this self-examination. For example, why are health costs escalating while death rates stand still or even increase for some groups? Why can every individual recount horror stories of inadequate or sloppy medical care? Why are some families forced into hopeless debt because of catastrophic illness or accident? Why is the system so unfair? The author, one of less than a hundred full-time health economists in the United States, has approached these questions boldly with numerous facts to back up his arguments.

To begin with, the author proposes that a system of universal comprehensive health insurance would be the best way of making existing medical resources equally available to all. But this could be no more than a beginning. Physicians, he points out, are the key to the enormous puzzle, and not simply because their fees and incomes are too high. The major reason is that doctors control and determine most of the other medical costs, such as X-rays, laboratory tests, hospital use, and drug use. Also, the increased specialization, the fragmenting of the patient's treatment, and the increased need for super-specialized equipment for the super-specialized physicians to use, results in what Fuchs calls the "technological imperative"; this is the belief that every physician in every hospital should have at his fingertips all of the technological resources and equipment that he has been trained to use. In addition, the fact that these physicians are brainwashed into using the products of a near-monopolistic drug industry whose real competition is in persuasion, not price, results in a bizarre situation in which only the patient can lose. Finally, it must be realized that what medical insurance there is exists more for the benefit of the doctors and hospitals than the consumers or patients.

Perhaps the most drastic admission which must be made before the system can be changed is the truth that our society, as it has developed, tends to produce unhealthy citizens. The majority of the population drinks too much, overeats, smokes too much, and breathes polluted air. Men, women, and children are constantly bombarded with appeals to buy refined sugar-filled products, to consume foods riddled with cancer-causing additives, to smoke lung cancer-causing products, and to drink beverages which result in liver and other diseases and cause, on the streets and highways, thousands of violent deaths and mutilations every year. Millions of men and women breathe in toxic fumes and poisons in their places of employment, and either develop cancer or pass on to their children through their genes the tendency to cancer. The pressures of this irrational and corrupt society drive hundreds of people to murder and suicide annually, and put thousands more under psychiatric care. But how many more individuals exist bleakly, needing help which, under this system, they never will receive?

Something is definitely wrong with the priorities in this kind of a society. It is time that the choices are re-examined.

The fundamental solutions, Fuchs states, require that we change our life styles, change our dangerous personal behaviors, and come to grips with the enormous inequality in the country. The social injustices which create so much illness and suffering must be the consequences of the same economic system that distorts the medical care apparatus. As he points out, the free-enterprise, competitive price system may provide the most efficient merchandise for allocating scarce resources, but it results "in a distribution of income which is socially and morally unacceptable."

The major value of this important book lies in Fuchs's analysis of the economic factors that affect costs of hospitalization and drugs; his facts are clearly and illuminatingly presented. Although there have been many books recently dealing with the health care crisis, none has presented so many facts in such a well-organized and well-written volume which the general reader can comprehend and appreciate. The author defines unfamiliar terms as he goes along, and avoids the jargon with which so many similar books often are burdened.

Above all, Fuchs is a realist. He understands that the popular solutions, such as creating more doctors, building more hospitals, spending more money on the present system, will only make the situation worse. Rather than building up the system even more, it is imperative that it be decentralized. He recommends competition between different health plans and different groups of providers. He suggests the increased use of physicians' assistants, nurse-clinicians, and other health workers. He believes that we need fewer specialists and more primary-care physicians. He recommends a five-year freeze on all new hospital construction or expansion as an initial step toward the creation of a rational, regionalized hospital system. And he favors a sensible, preventative approach to health care. Sane living is still the best way to achieve health. No book in recent years has shown a better grasp of the social context of health and health care or offered more fundamental answers to the basic issues involved. The books which follow Fuchs's contribution to the widespread discussion on health care and public health can only build on his solid and important analysis.

Bruce D. Reeves

WILLIAM CARLOS WILLIAMS
The Knack of Survival in America

Author: Robert Coles (1929-   )
Publisher: Rutgers University Press (New Brunswick, N.J.). 185 pp. $8.50
Type of work: Literary criticism
  An analysis of the Passaic Stories and the Stecher Trilogy, the poet's major fictional work

Poet, novelist, short story writer, painter, essayist, critic, medical doctor, second-generation American, and political theorist are terms which recur again and again in any discussion of William Carlos Williams. Absence of any of these roles would have profoundly changed his work, and ultimately our respect for his insights and innovations. Robert Coles has considered them all in this fine, close reading of Williams' fiction.

Coles is the right man for the job. He says in his introduction:

> I have been thinking about some of the issues that come up in the following pages for many years, because the poor and working-class families I have worked with are not unlike the men, women, and children William Carlos Williams brings to life so dramatically and thoughtfully in the short stories and novels I choose to discuss here.

The shared experiences bring to this book a depth and understanding few could match with only social, historical, or critical knowledge.

Certainly, poets are not always the best critics of poetry, nor novelists the best critics of fiction. Likewise, doctors may be too close to medicine to be always clearest on that subject. But Coles is neither a poet nor a novelist. He is a doctor who loves literature, proving himself (twenty-four previous books, five hundred articles)

a formidable writer and one, like Williams, of great energy.

This book is the outgrowth of the Mason Gross lectures at Rutgers University in 1974. The author has chosen for discussion several stories from *Life Along the Passaic River* as well as *White Mule, The Build-Up* and *In the Money*—the Stecher Trilogy. Beginning with a brief biography and discussion of *Paterson,* Coles lays the necessary foundation for his discussion of the fiction. We are shown Williams the doctor, frustrated, overworked, angered by his practice (he would have preferred the literary life, yet continued his practice for fifty years), and awed by his patients' struggle against the odds of dehumanizing industrialization and overpopulation in Northern New Jersey. In short, we see Williams as participant, not as witness, or worse, as completely objective observer. He is one with those he writes about.

"Dignity" is a word that appears repeatedly in this first of three sections in reference to Williams' patients, who fight for dignity and some individualism amid the concrete, steel, greed, and progress that can so easily swallow them up. It describes Williams, too, battling anonymity in the literary world. "Williams was not so loyal to America that he didn't ache for Europe"; but, except for brief trips to Europe, he remained at home, stealing a few hours here and there to write, identifying himself with those who also "ached" for something better, something more. Not that Williams was "the proletarian poet and novelist who turns factory workers and yeomen farmers into larger than life heroes," but "Unlike Eliot, Williams feels a bond with his automatons, has by no means given up on them." As Coles explains:

> But what really distinguishes Williams from Eliot—and from Ezra Pound—is his unrelenting insistence on balance: he portrays sadness, desolation, evidence of decay everywhere, but he also gives us decent, kind, and honorable people, who are energetic, thoughtful, and impressive enough as human beings to warrant a good deal of attention from a man of letters who cares to witness and write down what there is to see and hear.

In an enlightening essay on Williams, "The True Contemporary," Karl Shapiro contends that "Williams is fighting for the existence of Poetry (while Eliot and Pound fought for the "uses" of poetry.)" This is easily extended to his fiction, too. Coles obviously agrees. These stories and novels are not parables, not morality plays; they are not didactic. Instead, they are "achievements not unlike those managed by others who lived along the Passaic."

It is not surprising, then, that there is so little abstraction in the work of Williams; there was little enough time for him to get the words on paper, let alone to construct poems and stories of an ephemeral or theoretical nature. His world was immediate and raw, and the wonder of everyday existence was enough to occupy his attention throughout the majority of his fiction.

Section Two takes up the Stecher Trilogy. Flossie's birth scene is discussed at length, and it is here that Williams as doctor and unconventional poet reveals himself: birth was a subject Williams knew all too well, and the scene, in its realism, reflects his familiarity with the subject. *White Mule* is a psychological novel which not only permits us to see how a child like Flossie develops, but how those around her change and affect the growth of her feelings. "Williams had no particular interest in psychiatry," Coles writes, and for Williams "to have resisted the narrow, psychological reductionism of the 1920's and 1930's is a minor but noteworthy achievement." While the novel is never heavy-handed, it is nevertheless filled with sensitive insights; as the author puts it, "whole books on child development have said less." Again and again Coles shows us Williams the doctor and Williams the poet, ranging widely within the conventional boundaries of the novel form, and occasionally breaking new ground, claiming it as his own.

Perhaps because poets often seem to make bad novelists, and vice versa, Williams has been neglected for many years as a novelist, when in his case neglect is unwarranted. If he was not so drastically innovative in his fiction as he was in his poetry, he nevertheless accomplished, through an accumulation of subtle changes, a startling break from tradition. He brought from his poetry "a way of condensing all sorts of issues into brief incidents or into a phrase or two." It was because of Williams' medical practice, his constant contact with people—their struggles, their conflicts with traditions, and the changes taking place in America—that his fiction seems so up to date decades later. He was one of the people; their struggles were his, their language became his, and their small triumphs excited and thrilled him.

In much the same way as his subject, Coles has not written down to a lay audience, but rather has approached his subject as a critic and writer, and not purely as a physician. Surely the temptation must have been there to render difficult analysis in the nomenclature of the field of study, to be precise as a mathematician, us-ing analytically exact words. But instead, the biographer employs lucid, everyday language, and does not lose energy or precision in doing so. Coles is to be applauded for his skill in relating even the most difficult and esoteric insights in a readable fashion.

Throughout the book Coles refers to his own experiences, if not to corroborate Williams' observations, then to shed more immediate light on them and to point out how unchanging the world is and how viable Williams' method was. Coles's book is an invaluable addition to the great volume of work already available on William Carlos Williams.

Harry A. Maxson

A WORD CHILD

Author: Iris Murdoch (1919-   )
Publisher: The Viking Press (New York). 390 pp. $8.95
Type of work: Novel
Time: The present
Locale: London

A fatalistic novel of endless introspection in which the hero's darkest memory repeats itself and destroys his world

Principal characters:
> HILARY BURDE, a toadish middle-aged clerk and "underground man"
> CRYSTAL, his sweet, uneducated, loving sister
> THOMASINA, his zany Scottish mistress
> CLIFFORD, Hilary's homosexual friend
> FRANK AND LAURA IMPIATT, friends from the office
> CHRISTOPHER, Hilary's lodger, a "flower-child"
> BISCUIT, a mysterious Indian girl
> LADY KITTY, the second wife of Hilary's worst enemy

Iris Murdoch may be one of those writers whose degree of importance will be assessed only many years after her works are complete. Since her first novel, *Under the Net* (1954), critical opinion has been consistently divided about the novels to follow, including *The Flight From the Enchanter, The Sandcastle, A Severed Head, The Unicorn, The Italian Girl, The Time of the Angels, Bruno's Dream, A Fairly Honourable Defeat,* and *The Sacred and Profane Love Machine. A Word Child* is one more piece in the perplexing puzzle of Murdoch's artistic purpose and development. Charles Osborne is certainly right to call her "one of the most complex and interesting of contemporary novelists," but the same defects found in her earlier works proliferate in this new one, a mixture of "perceptive realism with absurd gratuitous fantasy," as Mary Warnock writes in the *New Statesman.* A *Newsweek* review sums it up well:

Once again her plot sounds like the scenario for a B-movie melodrama . . . . The philosophizing and the action have not been integrated. Instead, the plot advances through coincidences that are often shamelessly contrived.

Although this judgment cannot be denied, somehow Murdoch makes us accept her shameless contrivances—certainly none of them are more shameless than those of Shakespeare or Fielding. She holds our attention and demands our respect because her writing is psychologically incisive and never fails to tease us into thought. David Bromwich remarks that "there are passages . . . which grip the reader as only art can, when it is competing with life on its own terms and fearing nothing." And that is the secret to Murdoch's constant intrigue—that she staunchly refuses to play any game but her own, transcending formal and stylistic categories imposed upon the genre by academic critics or journalistic reviewers. If sometimes she loses the game as a result, certainly that does not detract from her singleminded decision to play it her own way. Thus, the reader of Murdoch can expect to find a great deal of value while at the same time expecting ultimate disappointment.

A Word Child, as Stephen Wall comments, presents "an imagined world in which its author comes as near as she has yet done to reconciling, in her way, what she feels to be the demands of art with what she also senses as the beautiful recalcitrance of ordinary life." Hilary Burde, the toadish protagonist, is resigned to a life of degradation because of a single cardinal sin (his adultery with a fellow Oxford don's wife, leading to her death in a car accident with him. He holds the classical Greek attitude that a man cannot avoid his fate, cannot be counted happy until he is dead. But the tragic framework of the story moves from the Greek to the Teutonic, as the old affair with Anne is inevitably repeated in the present when Hilary conceives an insane passion for Gunthar's new wife, Lady Kitty. Just at the point when he and Gunthar have reached a personal reconciliation to overcome their mutual shame and hatred through the good offices of Kitty, circumstances whose agent turns out to be a minor character in the novel lead to Kitty's violent death at the scene of her rendezvous with Hilary —at the very moment Gunthar discovers them.

As we watch Hilary falling in love with Kitty in the process of the reconciliation, we clearly foresee the fatal parallel to the previous illicit affair. The inexplicable thing is that Hilary himself, for all his remarkable self-awareness, does not see it. His retro-

spective explanation (for he is the narrator of this dark romance) is erotic blindness: "I was dreadfully in love with the sort of black certain metaphysical love that cuts deeper than anything and thus seems its own absolute justification." Indeed, Hilary conceives of himself as being a knight in the service of his lady, relinquishing all critical faculties of his own and all warnings from his worried sister and concerned friends because his passion dominates him completely in the fashion fully delineated in Denis de Rougemont's *Love in the Western World*. All the rubrics for Hilary's character can be found in de Rougemont's description of the lover who is in love, not with his beloved, but with love itself—and ultimately, with death. Only this sinister love is strong enough to remove Hilary from his habitual state of self-disparaging, suicidal brooding:

> Being in love has its own self-certifying universality, it informs and glorifies the world with an energy which, like a drug, becomes a necessity of consciousness.

Hilary tells us at the outset of the narrative, "I liked to condition those around me." But we learn as the story of his daily routine is transformed into irregular excitement with Gunthar's return to London that his conditioning of others is merely a mechanism of self-defense. In all other ways he is an underground man (fully sharing the psychological consistency of Dostoevski's archetypal figure). Hilary's single hold on reality is the regularity of his weekly schedule: Mondays with his friend Clifford ("Human life is a scene of horror. I hope you enjoyed the cheese soufflé.); Tuesdays dining cheaply with Arthur, his sister's would-be fiancé ("an honest man devoid of malice"); Wednesdays and Saturdays given entirely to his orphan sister Crystal ("like a sweet gentle patient good animal," whom Murdoch portrays along the lines of Steinbeck's Lennie, in *Of Mice and Men*); Thursdays with Freddie and Laura Impiatt who toy with his emotions as a means of invigorating their own sputtering marriage; and Fridays with his mistress, Thomasina, who is not at all happy with her limited engagement. The novel's structure is dictated by Hilary's calendar, which leaves Sundays free to wrench the other days, one by one, once and then forever from their carefully maintained places in his life and mind.

This stifling regularity of his own behavior and that of his friends and sister explains Hilary's vulnerability to the unconscionable entrapment of Lady Kitty in her announced scheme to restore her husband's mental equilibrium, which simultaneously provides her with a bit of diversion from her own humdrum existence. Hilary feels great relief at having someone take over the business of pulling everyone's strings:

> I was paralysed with waiting, like a fly stung by a spider, only I was a cool resigned fly, almost without anxiety, so taken over was I by this sudden new power which had entered my life. I had been conscripted. I was under orders.

Hilary is made delirious and ecstatic by the vision of a new Beatrice, who so readily fills the place in his romantic heart vacated by Gunthar's first wife Anne that Hilary is the last one

to realize how trite and dangerous his infatuation with this particular woman must become. Impetuously he perpetuates the folly of his past, visiting his sins upon himself anew until he loses all hope—and all our sympathy. Despite the rationale of blind passion, Hilary's behavior ultimately does not make sense. Murdoch's premise remains unclear; her highly moralistic fable ends in unsatisfying ambiguity which is all the more disappointing because it holds our interest and nurtures our expectations until the very end.

Murdoch's style is also ambivalent and difficult to assess. She is capable of psychological nuance at times equal to that of Dante, as when the silent moments between responses are made to communicate more than the words themselves. In this book she develops a narrative switch-back technique very similar to that of Heller's *Something Happened,* and originating in the digressive-progressiveness of Sterne: "Tommy was sitting next to me with her skirt hitched up displaying those long perfect legs. (Quite unconsciously. She was, apart from Crystal. . . .) (Crystal's legs were like tree stumps.)" The parentheses allow us to observe the narrator's second and third thoughts in a most involving way. But progress toward a compelling style is frequently set back by pseudo-Melvillean declarations like, "Your exercise of free choice is a prodigious stirrer up of your reflection."

The central disappointment of this provoking and constantly stimulating novel, however, has to do with its choice of the wrong title. The narrator tells us at one point that he had originally intended to call the story he is recording, "The Inner Circle," because he spent so much time riding aimlessly on that part of the London Underground:

> In fact the whole Underground region moved me, I felt as if it were in some sense my natural home. . . . The coming and departing rattle of the trains, the drifting movement of the travellers, their arrival, their waiting, their vanishing forever presented a mesmesic and indeed symbolic fresco: so many little moments of decision, so many little finalities, the constant wrenching of texture, the constant destruction of cells which shifts and

ages the lives of men and of universes . . . . I loved the Inner Circle best . . . . I was indeed an Undergrounder.

That Murdoch herself recognized the appropriateness of this objective correlative to her hero's psychological labyrinth makes it all the more perplexing that she would reject the natural central metaphor in favor of an amorphous reference to Hilary's childhood love for words. Yet her choice also explains the final ambiguity of this novel's aesthetic integrity, another near-success held back from perfection by the author's own hand.

Kenneth John Atchity

WORKING
People Talk About What They Do All Day
and How They Feel About What They Do

Author: Studs Terkel (1912-   )
Publisher: Pantheon Books (New York). 589 pp. $10.00; paperback $2.25
Type of work: Documentary interviews
Time: 1970-1974
Locale: The United States

A generally grim, always candid report on the working lives of Americans, based upon interviews of more than one hundred and thirty persons, most of whom allow their real names to be used, and all of whom reveal the facts about their occupations as part of the documentary

Nearly everyone this side of senility has to work for a living—even Studs Terkel. Of course, his work is what most people would call play. A radio and television personality, he is a familiar figure to a great number of Chicagoans, who for a score of years and more have been entertained by his casual but insightful interview programs, by his lectures on jazz and folk music, and by his commentaries on the arts and social scene. Although he expresses "some delight" in his job as popular-cultural factotum, he recalls less happy times: three "traumatic" years at law school, followed by a long apprenticeship during the Depression learning the trades of writer and actor as a member of the Federal Writers' Project. In his troubled memories of these days he developed a conviction about the "surreal nature" of his work—indeed, of everybody's work. His book grew out of this conviction. Notwithstanding the fact that by training he is neither an economist nor a sociologist, he has been well-schooled in observing people. Like a "guerrilla" who has survived life, he sets about to discover what people, obscure or famous, really think about their jobs.

Because of his practical experience in dealing with people, he is a perfect researcher for the task. Despite his disclaimers, his knowledge of contemporary social and economic problems is quite adequate. Like his previous documentary studies, *Division Street: America* and *Hard Times: An Oral History of the Great Depression, Working* takes social history off the dusty library shelves and details for the public record the actual life stories of ordinary people.

For a documentary based upon interviews to succeed, the reporter must not only ask the right questions but, with the skill of a psychologist, he must also coax the respondent to confess secrets that he would never commonly betray. Terkel's special ability is to create a mood of relaxed geniality, of shared confidence, so that his respondents are, all quite casually, put off their guard. Sensing the author's sympathy, they speak from the heart. The tape recorder does the rest. Yet to stimulate their uninhibited confessions, Terkel must be a perceptive listener. He rarely interjects comments of his own. Instead, he allows his subjects to ramble, if necessary, until they fully reveal their ideas. With admirable tact, the author encourages the speakers to feel important. Although what they report about their jobs is rarely astonishing, their manner of expression is often eloquent. Simple, uneducated people describe their humdrum working hours with touching candor, some with language so agonized, so charged with poetic intensity, as to startle the reader. With an art that conceals itself, Terkel draws from most of his respondents a living history of the times—the true story of what it means to work, to suffer, to fail, or to achieve.

Organizing his volume into nine books (really, sections) with three prefaces, Terkel divides the interviews on the basis of professional groupings. Some of the divisions seem idiosyncratic, if not arbitrary. For example, Terkel includes under the heading "Appearance" not only a barber, two hair stylists, and a cosmetics saleswoman, but also a dentist, a hotel clerk, a bar pianist, an elevator starter, and an ex-salesman. Each worker in this category, according to the author's reasoning, is concerned with "cosmetics" of some sort, whether personal or collective. Thus a Manhattan hotel clerk, who acts as a representative of the unidentified management, keeps up the "appearances" of the place. And the dentist remarks that he carries with him his concern about cosmetics everywhere, even when he is not at his office. When he sees the movie *Fiddler on the Roof,* he notices that Topol's front teeth are "partials"; and he reminds his interviewer, as though he were speaking of a wonder, that Clark Gable for a number of years "had only one tooth here in front."

Although no one else, except perhaps another dentist, was aware of the phenomenon, Dr. Bartlett took professional notice of the actor's mouth. "When you're close to it, it's your life," he says.

And that comment is generally appropriate for most workers. Whether one labors as a grave digger, a policeman, a yacht broker, or a baseball player, the demands of his work condition his whole response to life. Because nearly every person interviewed uses his own name (the prostitute "Roberta Victor" chooses a pseudonym), the responses seem unusually candid and for that reason authentic. Although a few workers, conscious that their words are being tape-recorded by a prominent media personality, perhaps exaggerate parts of their stories, most people evidently respond with sincerity. Even those who might expect to suffer reprisals from their bosses or clients express their feelings openly, as though they owe a private obligation to conscience to tell the truth, no matter the risks.

What they report undermines the notion of an enduring Protestant work ethic that is supposed to be ingrained in the American character. With irony, Terkel quotes Richard M. Nixon's 1971 Labor Day speech: "The 'work ethic' holds that labor is good in itself; that a man or woman becomes a better person by virtue of the act of working. America's competitive spirit, the 'work ethic' of this people, is alive and well. . . ." On the contrary, the evidence of Terkel's book is that most people thoroughly despise their work. To be sure, a few souls still enjoy working and believe in the "virtue" of labor. Lincoln James, a factory mechanic in a glue factory, likes what he is doing (although he objects to the noxious odors of the rendering plant); Vincent Maher, a policeman, describes his work as "one of the most gratifying jobs in the world"; Pauline Kael, the prominent movie critic for the *New Yorker,* says that she enjoys her writing now, but in previous jobs she "used to have headaches all the time"; to Eugene Russell, a piano tuner, "every day is different" and challenging. But these affirmative responses are in the minority. Generally speaking, the satisfied workers are those who have mastered a craft (such as Donna Murray, the bookbinder, or Carl Murray Bates, the stone mason), belong to a creative profession (Arny Freeman, the actor), or perform a vital service for the community (Tom Patrick, the Brooklyn fireman). Greatly outnumbering the contented few are those who are bored, frustrated, exhausted, humiliated, nearly driven mad from their labor.

From the famous and the obscure, from those who perform menial tasks as well as the elite who are employed at glamorous occupations, the cry of dismay is nearly universal. Beryl Simpson, an airline reservationist, describes her work as "very routine, computerized." She would get sick in the morning, going to her job feeling, "Oh, my God! I've got to work." When Jill Torrance, a high fashion model, is called for an appointment, she would often "like to say I'm sick and can't make it. . . ." Her first reaction when the phone rings in the morning is "Oh, crap." Richard Mann, a fifty-three-year-old installment dealer, worries that he is not growing old gracefully. "I'm tired," he says. Another middle-aged man, Louis Hayward, a washroom attendant at the Palmer House, reports that his work has become so monotonously familiar that "it's almost a reflex action." The spot welder Phil Stallings similarly says that "repetition is such that if you were to think about the job itself, you'd slowly go out of your mind." Other workers testify to the numbing agony of their routine. Booker Page, a Manhattan cab driver, says, "Oh, I'm so tired. My bottom gets so . . . Oh, every muscle aches in my body." Dolores Dante, who has been a waitress in the same restaurant for twenty-three years, says that she feels "drained" at the end of the night. "I think a lot of waitresses become alcoholics because of that." And Maggie Holmes, formerly a domestic but now on welfare, says that "poor people's mental health is different than the rich white. Mine could come from a job or not havin' enough money for my kids. Mine is from me being poor."

Not simply the old, the half-maddened, the enervated down-and-out laborers who are marginal to society, but also bright, sophisticated, well-paid professionals complain about their working lives. The successful actor Rip Torn insists that his work is commercialized. "Actors have become shills. . . . An actor is used to sell products primarily." Terry Mason, the stewardess, recalls her demeaning training in the airline school. She has been taught "to be sexy," never to embarrass an offensive customer. "Even when they pinch us or say dirty things, we're supposed to smile at them." Another attractive woman, the script supervisor Barbara Herrick, describes the crude sexual invitations that come her way, usually at her hotel room at night, as an expected feature of her job. "Deep down, I feel demeaned," she says. Similarly, the tennis star Jean Douglas describes the underground, often degrading and furtive, sexual encounters common to athletes on tour. To protect herself, her social life is "zero." And the professional hustler, the prostitute "Roberta Victor," describes her former activities as a highly paid call girl. To perform sexual "tricks" without feeling any real emotion was her secret way of showing contempt for clients. In retrospect, she says, "I became what I did. . . . I became cold, I became hard, I became turned off, I became numb. Even when I wasn't hustling, I was a hustler." Typical of prostitutes, she believes that what she did was "not different from what ninety-nine percent of American women are taught to do." She took the money from under the lamp instead of Arpege. "What would I do with 150 bottles of Arpege a week?"

Terkel's mostly grim documentary on the working lives of Americans is extensive and searching but not fully comprehensive. The author interviews one hundred and thirty-three individuals or couples (actually more people, because other respondents, spouses or friends, also become involved in the tape-recording sessions); of the selection, most of the people are not self-employed or conspicuously wealthy. Choices are "in many instances arbitrary." Terkel notes some "deliberate omissions": clergymen, doctors, politicians, journalists, and "writers of any kind." He wants ordinary people who can articulate

their views without "self-indulgence." As a matter of fact, Terkel's bias is expressed in ways other than selection. Without controlling by deliberate means the workers' responses to his questions, his attitude nevertheless tacitly encourages them to complain. Offered the same questions by management or state-controlled researchers, most people would probably describe their work more affirmatively. Only on occasion do they discuss their wages, vacation benefits and other amenities, longtime friends and associates on the job, or performance satisfactions. Instead, most workers are driven to analyze not only the quality of their work but also of their lives. Taking stock, some perhaps for the first time, of the meaning of existence, they are generally disturbed—with good reason. Chances are that the banality of their jobs matches the tedium of their lives. Little wonder that most of the workers respond to Terkel's seemingly innocent questions with existential agony.

Comparing Terkel's survey with that of Henry Mayhew's 1850 reports for the *Morning Chronicle* upon the lives of London's laboring class, the reader is struck, indeed, by the vast improvement in contemporary working standards. Mayhew's research detailed the wretched quality of human suffering in mid-nineteenth century England. As Terkel points out, the studies of Mayhew "astonished and horrified" the English. In contrast, Terkel's book will probably neither astonish nor horrify readers of the 1970's. Most of the workers whom he interviews are people very much like ourselves, with job experiences that we can understand.

At no era in American history—or in the history of any other nation, it is safe to say—has the working man enjoyed the full fruits of his labor. And American workers of the 1970's, compared to those who struggled during the Depression years, are surely not enduring the same "hard times" that Terkel earlier described. With sentimentality the author dedicates his book to Jude Fawley, the stonemason in Thomas Hardy's powerful *Jude the Obscure*. Unlike Jude, however, his spirit broken more by a cruel society and the evil chances of fate than by his exhausting physical labors, most American workers have the personal and professional freedom to gripe about their jobs with impunity. They know that their lives, thanks in part to the interviews of Studs Terkel, are no longer obscure.

Leslie B. Mittleman

A WORLD DESTROYED
The Atomic Bomb and the Grand Alliance

Author: Martin J. Sherwin (1937-   )
Publisher: Alfred A. Knopf (New York). 315 pp. $10.00
Type of work: History
Time: 1938-1945
Locale: United States, Great Britain, Russia

  The history of the development of the atomic bomb and of the impact of this powerful new weapon on America's relationship with her principal allies during World War II

Principal personages:
> FRANKLIN D. ROOSEVELT, President of the United States
> HARRY S TRUMAN, his successor
> HENRY STIMSON, Secretary of War
> WINSTON CHURCHILL, British Prime Minister
> JOSEPH STALIN, leader of the Soviet Union
> VANNEVAR BUSH and
> JAMES B. CONANT, scientific advisers to the President
> LESLIE R. GROVES, officer in charge of the Manhattan Project
> NIELS BOHR, Danish physicist who argued for the international control of atomic energy

It went under various pseudonyms. President Franklin Roosevelt and British Prime Minister Churchill called it "tube alloys." Later in the war, it was referred to simply as "S-1." In the scrupulously neutral idiom of military technology, "it" was the "implosion type atomic fission bomb." In August, 1945, two such weapons destroyed the Japanese cities of Hiroshima and Nagasaki, ushering in a new era of scientific terror. After several decades of controversy over the development and use of the bomb, historian Martin Sherwin has provided the most carefully reasoned account to date of the dawn of the atomic age.

A World Destroyed examines two major issues which grew out of the attempt to harness the atom for military purposes during World War II. The first was whether or not actually to use such a new and terrible weapon against America's enemies. Not surprisingly, Sherwin finds that this question was never truly opened to debate. From the outset, America's policy makers and many of the scientists involved operated on the assumption that the bomb—if it could in fact be developed in time—would naturally be used to bring about victory in a total war. A scientific panel made up of Arthur Compton, Ernest Lawrence, J. Robert Oppenheimer, and Enrico Fermi reported to Secretary of War Henry Stimson that they could "propose no technical demonstration likely to bring an end to the war; we see no acceptable alternative to direct military use." True, a group of scientists at the University of Chicago's Metallurgical Laboratory headed by physicists James Franck and Leo Szilard argued in June, 1945, that an unannounced atomic attack on Japan would be inadvisable on moral as well as on political and diplomatic grounds. But such arguments went unheeded at the last moment. In the end, the real question was not whether to use the bomb, but, rather, how to use it. It was decided that two bombs would be dropped and that the most desirable targets would be important war plants closely surrounded by workers' homes. The bomb was viewed as a terror weapon, and terror required wholesale death and destruction.

What motivated this horrible decision? Was sheer racism an important factor? Sherwin wisely thinks not. Instead, he supports Stimson's own explanation. "My *chief purpose*," the Secretary subsequently wrote, "was to end the war in victory with the least possible cost in the lives of the men in the armies which I had helped to raise." The author argues, however, that there were other, less noble, secondary considerations at work as well. There was, for example, the hope that the demonstration of such a powerful new weapon would make our difficult Russian allies more tractable. And there was also the knowledge that, should the war drag on and American casualties mount, those who had foregone the use of such an expensive and potent secret weapon would surely be called to account by outraged public and congressional opinion. Given this combination of factors, it would have been astonishing indeed had the bomb not been used when it was. Still, Sherwin concludes that the use of the atomic bomb might not have been necessary to end the war. He insists, forcefully and convincingly, that in any event the second attack, which incinerated Nagasaki, was gratuitous.

While such judgments are hardly novel, even those well-versed in the controversies surrounding the dropping of the bomb will be impressed by Sherwin's temperate analysis.

The author breaks new ground in his consideration of the second major issue flowing from the development of the bomb: United States policy regarding the sharing of its secret weapon. There is general agreement that America's decision to retain monopoly control of the atomic bomb was an important factor in the coming of the Cold War. Most historians who have examined United States atomic policy accordingly have begun their studies sometime in 1945 and have focused on events in the waning days of World War II and in the immediate postwar period. Sherwin shifts the debate significantly by finding the roots of America's monopoly policy in an earlier period. In fact, the decision to exclude our Russian ally was made long before the bomb was successfully tested.

Those who, like physicist Niels Bohr, argued during the war for the international control of atomic energy never influenced American policy. Instead, Roosevelt was persuaded by Churchill to keep the bomb an Anglo-American monopoly in the hope of using it to counter Russian ambitions in Eastern Europe. In September, 1944, Roosevelt and Churchill specifically dismissed suggestions that the world be informed of the progress of the Manhattan Project, and that steps be taken to bring about international control of atomic energy. At the same time, they agreed to continue the Anglo-American atomic alliance into the postwar period. By December, 1944, Roosevelt and Stimson were talking about using the secret of the atomic bomb as a means of extracting a *quid pro quo* from the Russians. As Soviet intentions regarding the conquered territories of Europe became more suspect in 1945, American leaders came increasingly to view their secret weapon as a diplomatic lever. By the time of the Potsdam conference, atomic diplomacy was a reality.

Sherwin's findings will certainly cause readers to reassess America's wartime leadership. Roosevelt appears to have been less sanguine about the prospects for postwar cooperation with the Soviets than many have believed. Truman's use of the bomb as a diplomatic bludgeon was not a sudden departure in American policy but, rather, merely the forceful implementation of a decision made by his predecessor. Depending on one's view of the Cold War, blame and praise will be reapportioned accordingly. Those who see the United States as the villain in the piece will now divide the responsibility for American malignancy more evenly between Roosevelt and Truman. On the other hand, those who hold the Soviets responsible for the dissolution of the wartime Grand Alliance will praise F.D.R. for his prescient realism.

Although Sherwin is generally convincing on such substantive points, the implicit message of *A World Destroyed* is less compelling. The author regrets America's failure even to attempt to initiate the internationalization of its deadly new weapon; he is clearly troubled by the road not taken. One wonders, however, whether any such move towards international control would not have been

doomed to certain failure either during the war or shortly thereafter. Sherwin simply underestimates the very real differences and difficulties that led to the Cold War. Would American congressional opinion have allowed any president to surrender our apparent ace in the hole to supranational control? Should Stalin, a tyrant whose record of butchery properly places him in the same league with Adolf Hitler, really have been trusted? Could thirty years of suspicion and antagonism on both sides have been overcome? Given the security-consciousness of the Russian leadership and the totalitarian nature of Soviet society, is it reasonable to assume that a workable scheme of mutual inspection could have been implemented at any time in the 1940's? Why should we believe that the ambitious, expansionist superpowers that failed to reach an agreement on the Polish question would ever agree to forego possession of the ultimate weapon? Historians certainly have the right to engage in counterargument, but their what-might-have-been's must be realistic if they are to convince. Sherwin's road not taken appears to be little more than a pious wish; however noble, that wish fails to take into consideration the real world of nation-state insanity.

Sherwin's book does not, however, stand or fall on the validity of his untested assumptions. *A World Destroyed* is still the most thoughtful study to date of the diplomatic implications of the development of the atomic bomb. It is the first account to recognize the full significance of the policies developed during the bomb's gestation period, well before Hiroshima. Scholars will appreciate the extent of Sherwin's research and the penetrating quality of his analysis. The general audience will marvel at his felicity of style. All readers will be haunted by the words of the great Hindu epic poem which crossed the mind of Robert Oppenheimer as he witnessed the world's first atomic explosion: "I have become Death, Destroyer of worlds."

Robert M. Collins

CUMULATIVE AUTHOR INDEX

All twenty-two Masterplots Annuals—1954-1976

(Figures within parentheses indicate years; other figures indicate page numbers.)

I

III

X

XII

XV